Ku Klux Kulture

Ku Klux Kulture

America and the Klan in the 1920s

FELIX HARCOURT

The University of Chicago Press
Chicago and London

The University of Chicago Press, Chicago 60637
The University of Chicago Press, Ltd., London
© 2017 by The University of Chicago
Published 2017
Paperback edition 2019

28 27 26 25 24 23 22 21 20 19   1 2 3 4 5

ISBN-13: 978-0-226-37615-8 (cloth)
ISBN-13: 978-0-226-63793-8 (paper)
ISBN-13: 978-0-226-37629-5 (e-book)
DOI: https://doi.org/10.7208/chicago/9780226376295.001.0001

A portion of the material printed in this book appeared previously in the article
"Invisible Umpires: The Ku Klux Klan and Baseball in the 1920's," in *NINE: A Journal
of Baseball History & Culture* 23, no. 1, 2015, by Felix Harcourt and published by the
University of Nebraska Press.

Library of Congress Cataloging-in-Publication Data

Names: Harcourt, Felix, author.
Title: Ku Klux kulture : America and the Klan in the 1920s / Felix Harcourt.
Description: Chicago ; London : The University of Chicago Press, 2017. |
    Includes bibliographical references and index.
Identifiers: LCCN 2017007718 | ISBN 9780226376158 (cloth : alk. paper) |
    ISBN 9780226376295 (e-book)
Subjects: LCSH: Ku Klux Klan (1915–)—History. | United States—Ethnic relations. |
    Popular culture—United States—20th century. | Racism—United States.
Classification: LCC HS2330.K63 H37 2017 | DDC 322.4/2097309042—dc23
LC record available at https://lccn.loc.gov/2017007718

♾ This paper meets the requirements of ANSI/NISO Z39.48-1992 (Permanence
of Paper).

Contents

Ordinary Human Interests

There is really no better reason for outsiders to regard Klansfolk as strange, other-worldly creatures—incapable of ordinary human interests, including clambakes—than there is for Klansfolk to think that way about outsiders.

CHARLES MERZ, *The Independent*, February 12, 1927

On October 28, 1947, in front of a crowd of spectators that included Humphrey Bogart, Lauren Bacall, and Danny Kaye, the House Un-American Activities Committee questioned three screenwriters—Dalton Trumbo, Alvah Bessie, and Albert Maltz—about alleged Communist affiliations. While Trumbo was denied the opportunity to read a prepared statement, Maltz delivered an excoriating speech that the *New York Times* called "one of the most denunciatory ever uttered in the presence of the committee." A novelist and Oscar-nominated screenwriter of *Pride of the Marines*, as well as uncredited contributor to *Casablanca*, he sparred repeatedly with committee chair J. Parnell Thomas over his testimony. Maltz's greatest ire, however, was reserved for committee member John E. Rankin, the Democrat from Mississippi who had purportedly defended the Ku Klux Klan as "an American institution."[1]

"If it requires acceptance of the ideas of this committee to remain immune from the brand of un-Americanism," Maltz asked, "then who is ultimately safe from this committee except members of the Ku Klux Klan?" Like his fellow witnesses, the writer was cited for contempt by the committee. Maltz would be blacklisted as part of the "Hollywood Ten" and would not receive another screen credit until 1970. Nonetheless, he declared he would "not be dictated to or intimidated by men to whom the Ku Klux Klan, as a matter of committee record, is an acceptable American institution."[2]

Maltz had likely discussed this piece of political theater with the so-called Dean of the Hollywood Ten, John Howard Lawson, who had been cited by the committee the day before as the first of the "unfriendly" witnesses. J. Parnell Thomas had refused to allow the screenwriter to read a prepared statement that accused Thomas of being "a petty politician" serving forces "trying to introduce fascism." Lawson had then answered questions about his Communist Party membership with the accusation that the committee was "using the old technique used by Hitler in Germany . . . [to] invade the rights of Americans whether they be Protestants, Catholics, Jews, Democrats, Republicans, or anything else." The writer was ultimately escorted from the witness stand by six Capitol policemen.[3]

Twenty-two years earlier, Lawson had offered a similar argument about the threat of repressive forces in a play that the *Chicago Tribune* described as "wild and weird beyond the dreams of the most visionary of the radicals." It was also a play that offered a very different theatrical take on the Klan from that of Maltz's statement. Lawson's experimental 1925 "jazz symphony of modern life," *Processional*, depicted the Ku Klux Klan deeply embedded in the firmament of contemporary society—as an American institution. Indeed, the play's third act climaxed with what one theatergoer called "the Ballet of the Ku Klux Klan."[4]

Nor was Lawson the only one to present audiences of the 1920s with the spectacle of dancing Klan members. The touring stage production *The Awakening* drew audiences with a garish amalgam of mawkish melodrama (lifting the plot from *The Birth of a Nation*) and cabaret showgirls. One musical number in the show, "Daddy Swiped Our Last Clean Sheet and Joined the Ku Klux Klan," was a particular hit. Copies of the song could be purchased as sheet music, a piano roll, or a phonograph record. Cultural consumers in the 1920s could not only see the Klan on stage and hear about the organization in popular song, but also listen to the Klan on radio. They could read about the organization's exploits in newspapers—or buy the organization's own periodicals. They could watch the group battle it out on the baseball field. They could thrill to the adventures of the Klan in novels and on movie screens. *The Awakening* was seen by more than ten times as many people as bought F. Scott Fitzgerald's *The Great Gatsby* in the 1920s. Yet these Klannish cultural artifacts have been all but forgotten, along with their significance.

As the standard narrative goes, the Knights of the Ku Klux Klan were "reborn" on November 25, 1915, with a cross burning at Stone Mountain, Georgia. The architect and "Imperial Wizard" of this revival was William Joseph Simmons, a former circuit-riding preacher and professional fraternal organizer. Combining elements of the original Reconstruction-era Klan with romanticized ideas lifted from the box-office smash of the year, *The Birth of a Nation*, Simmons hoped to create the ultimate Southern fraternal organization. The lynching of local Jewish businessman Leo Frank for the murder of employee Mary Phagan, and the ensuing calls for a revived Klan to enforce a new "home rule," provided impetus for the Imperial Wizard's efforts.[5]

This second Ku Klux Klan initially met with limited success, garnering approximately two thousand members—predominantly in Georgia and Alabama—in its first five years. In June 1920, hoping to strengthen interest in the organization, Simmons hired Edward Young Clarke and Elizabeth Tyler of the Southern Publicity Association. In consultation with the Imperial Wizard, Clarke and Tyler created the Kleagle system, whereby professional recruiters (Kleagles) would collect a portion of the membership dues from every new inductee into the second Klan. Targeting influential locals, Protestant ministers, and members of fraternal organizations like the Masons, these Kleagles identified issues of concern in a community and promoted the Klan as a solution to those problems. While white supremacy remained a cornerstone of the organization's philosophy, the Klan widened its appeal by incorporating popular anti-Catholic and anti-Semitic sentiments sparked by immigration from southern and eastern Europe. Kleagles sold the organization as a staunch supporter of Prohibition laws and an enforcer of public morality.[6]

The self-proclaimed "Invisible Empire" began to expand rapidly, accompanied by a series of violent incidents involving masked Klansmen. The organization's growing popularity, though, seemed limited to the South. The September 1921 *New York World* "exposé" of the Klan changed that completely. The series sparked a congressional investigation, earned the *World* a Pulitzer Prize, and is remembered as one of the most celebrated pieces of American twentieth-century journalism. It also rocketed the Ku Klux Klan to national prominence.[7]

For three weeks, the Klan dominated the front page of a major New York daily and affiliates around the country. With the help of disillusioned ex-Kleagle Henry P. Fry, the newspaper concentrated on revealing as many of the organization's secrets as possible: listing violent crimes attributed to Klansmen; naming more than two hundred Kleagles nationwide; reprinting Klan advertisements, recruiting letters, and a questionnaire to determine the eligibility of prospective members; and divulging the contents of the Klan's "Kloran," or book of ceremonies, including the organization's oaths and rituals, the meaning of their titles and code words, and even a diagram of their secret handshake. These revelations were accompanied by sensationalistic denunciations of the "grotesque" organization.[8]

By the end of the series on September 26, the *World* was convinced that it had "given Kluxism a death blow." By hounding them for statements on the story, the paper had forced the majority of New York's officials into publicly declaring their opposition to the Klan. Little more than two weeks after the

World's exposé concluded, a congressional investigation into the Klan was called to order. The newspaper's assertion that the series had been read "by United States officials . . . from the White House down" may or may not have been the case. Whatever President Warren G. Harding's reading material, the *World* was lauded at the congressional hearings for "bringing the facts to the attention of the public." Reporter Rowland Thomas and ex-Klansman Fry offered damaging anti-Klan testimony.[9]

Far from a death blow, though, the appearance of the Klan in the *New York World* and its affiliates meant that word of the organization's rebirth was transmitted nationally far more effectively than Klan members would ever have been able to achieve themselves. Even as the newspaper coverage sparked a wave of condemnation, it also saw the beginning of a surge of support for the Invisible Empire. Some readers allegedly even attempted to join the reborn Klan using blank application forms that the *World* had reprinted. Historian David Chalmers estimated that the "priceless publicity" supplied by the *World* increased Klan membership by a million or more. Moreover, the fierce opposition of a liberal New York newspaper lent credibility to the organization, endearing the Invisible Empire to readers who had a natural antipathy to publications like the *World*. The exposé series was not solely responsible for the rise in membership that followed, but contemporary observers certainly believed the *World* played a key part in the process. Leaders of the Klan crowed that the "vicious advertisement" of the newspaper had been "so materially misjudged" that they "had made us instead of breaking us."[10]

By the end of 1921, the Invisible Empire had transcended its sectional origins to become a truly national phenomenon, from Portland, Oregon, to Portland, Maine, and all points between. With considerable strength in the Midwest, Indiana became the organization's new stronghold. Although violent attacks continued—most notoriously in the August 1922 "disappearance" of two white men in Mer Rouge, Louisiana, after a whipping by Klansmen—they became increasingly sporadic. Members of the Invisible Empire increasingly insisted the Klan was not an "anti" organization. It was, they said, simply a law-abiding and law-enforcing union of white, native-born, patriotic Protestants.[11]

In November 1922, purportedly concerned by Simmons's growing drinking problem and generally immodest behavior, a group of high-ranking Klansmen convinced the Imperial Wizard to relinquish his position. Hiram Evans, a dentist from Dallas and leader of the Klan there, became the new official head of the organization. Simmons, belatedly realizing his mistake and claiming to still hold the copyright on the organization's official doctrine, began a lengthy fight to try to reclaim control. After more than a year of factional battles that engendered considerable ill feeling, Simmons finally settled his lawsuit against Evans and the Klan in February 1924.[12]

Throughout this struggle, enrollment in the Klan continued to rise steeply. New members heavily outweighed the number of ex-Klansmen embittered by the fight for control of the organization. The creation of a number of partner auxiliaries, including the Women of the Klan and the Junior Klan, extended the reach of the Invisible Empire. Kleagles continued to exploit the organization's diverse appeal to encompass anti-Catholic campaigns against parochial schooling, populist anger at political corruption, and a wide range of moralistic concerns.[13]

After the 1924 election, however, the Klan began to wane in power. The election of Calvin Coolidge and, perhaps more significantly, the passage of the Johnson-Reed Act restricting immigration seemingly eased the concerns of many Americans. Although membership in each branch of the Invisible Empire fell at a different pace and for different reasons, it was clear by late 1924 that the Klan as a whole was in decline. This process was hastened by the arrest in April 1925 of David Curtis Stephenson, ex-Grand Dragon of Indiana and one of the key actors in the rise of the Klan in the North, for the rape and murder of Madge Oberholtzer. Although Stephenson had technically been exiled from the Invisible Empire the year before, he had retained effective power over the Klans of Indiana, and his arrest dealt considerable damage to the organization's image.[14]

While estimates vary, it seems likely that national membership in the Ku Klux Klan peaked in late 1924 and early 1925 at over four million Knights. In 1927, membership had dropped to little more than half a million, and by 1928 "no more than several hundred thousand" were thought to still belong to the organization. While the presidential candidacy of the Catholic ex-governor of New York, Al Smith, did breathe some life back into the Klan in late 1928, the election did little more than temporarily suspend the organization's rapid collapse. By the end of the decade, the Invisible Empire had all but disappeared from public view.[15]

For many years, academic consideration of the short but storied life span of the second Ku Klux Klan was directed by those who preferred to see the organization as the product of uneducated and unsophisticated Americans, most likely hoodwinked into membership by greedy hucksters. Since the 1990s, though, scholars of the Klan have made great strides in overcoming what Kathleen Blee called the assumption of marginality. An effective consensus has formed around the conception of the Klan as an important participant in the civic discourse of the 1920s. Recent work has sought to recognize both the Klan's deep roots in the white Protestant norms of the period and the controversy that surrounded the organization, reevaluating the Invisible Empire within the context of other American social and fraternal organizations.[16]

Yet the Klan has remained largely, and problematically, absent from considerations of the cultural 1920s. As Lawrence Grossberg notes, "We cannot live social reality outside of the cultural forms through which we make sense of it." If we do not integrate the cultural products by and about the Klan into wider narratives of the 1920s, we fail to appreciate both how the Invisible Empire made sense of the postwar cultural moment of emergent pluralism and how that same popular culture made sense of the Klan—and how that understanding influenced the lived social reality of the period. When we examine the Klan's cultural "ephemera" of the period, we see that the current consensus narrative of the rise and fall of the Ku Klux Klan remains somewhat insufficient.[17]

Exacerbating the issue is the fact that in the standard narrative of the second Klan, the issue of membership becomes prioritized. The question inherent in most studies of the Klan seems always to be how and why the membership of the group grew—whether it was a pyramid scheme, a clarion call to bigotry, a moment of postwar hysteria, a timely effort to capitalize on concerns over schooling and law enforcement. To a lesser extent, historians have debated the reasons for the organization's precipitous decline, from Stephenson's arrest to cultural competition to infighting among the leadership. The focus on debating this issue of organizational affiliation and disaffiliation, though, risks losing an appreciation of the Invisible Empire's wider influence and significance.

By concentrating on whether or not cultural actors in the 1930s and 1940s were Communist Party members, Michael Denning argued, historians had reached "a remarkably inadequate understanding of the depth and breadth" of the Popular Front. Scholars of the Klan in the 1920s face the same problem. Too often, the Ku Klux Klan's cultural clout is sidelined or dismissed as a Klannish kultur detached from modern mass culture. In treating its influence in this way, we risk misreading the Klan's reach and the tensions present within American culture in the 1920s.[18]

The postwar era saw the melding of a powerful social movement with the cultural apparatus of mass entertainment. As Denning points out, a core-periphery model of such an encounter—an interpretation that prioritizes the question of membership—is less than satisfactory. The politics and mechanisms of affiliation do not delimit the politics of culture. The Klan wielded broad cultural power that reached far beyond a paying membership. If we are to understand that power, the Invisible Empire must be understood not only as a social and fraternal organization, but also as a deeply rooted cultural movement.[19]

The modernist poet and Fascist sympathizer Ezra Pound declared that "any sort of understanding of civilization needs comprehension of incompatibles." Histories of the 1920s have often lacked that comprehension. As Roderick Nash has repeatedly pointed out, we have constructed enduring screen memories of the 1920s that continue to obscure and obfuscate the complex realities of the period. Even as scholars have pointed us toward more nuanced interpretations of the interwar period, away from the reliance on the language of cultural war or the exaggerated rural-urban dichotomies that marred earlier work, it is still difficult to dispel popular images of the "Roaring Twenties" and "Jazz Age." Scholars from the 1940s onward have focused on the idea that one of the reasons for the Klan's decline was competition from new cultural pursuits. Recent studies have continued to echo these arguments. What is too often missing in this equation is an understanding that Klan members and supporters were having a good time in the 1920s too—an understanding that the histories of parties and of prejudice are not parallel but intersectional.[20]

The central paradox in American history, Lawrence Levine has argued, is "a belief in progress coupled with a dread of change." That duality, Levine noted, was central to the post–World War I era. The 1920s saw the clash of the "urge towards the inevitable future" with alienation from modernity. This tension, though, was "not merely present in the antithetical reactions of different groups but *within* the responses of the same groups and individuals." Even as many Americans turned to the past in rhetoric and ideology, they met modernity in their actions and their lived reality.[21]

The fetishization of affiliation detracts from this understanding, prioritizing a Manichaean interpretation of the 1920s in which we draw a stark divide between those who were members of the Klan and those who were not. In this, scholars have echoed novelist Willa Cather, who declared that "the world broke in two in 1922 or thereabouts." Thereafter, there were only "the forward-goers" and "the backward"—or members and nonmembers. In this interpretation, we elide the internal dualities both of the Klan itself and of the wider cultural 1920s. Instead, we see the tendency to draw an artificially absolute delineation between a modern age marked by Fitzgeraldian fantasies of uproarious fun and a conservative Victorianism embodied in the Klan—"a bulwark against modernism," in the words of Kenneth T. Jackson.[22]

We cannot simply divide the 1920s into modernism and Victorianism, into Prohibitionists and bootleggers, into bohemians and puritans. We cannot understand the Jazz Age without recognizing that the pairing of modernism with prejudice was not at all incompatible. And we cannot understand these cultural tensions unless we escape our fixation on the question of membership. The Ku Klux Klan is one of the most striking examples of the duality of the 1920s, both in the Klan's ambivalent consumption of modern culture and in modern culture's ambivalent consumption of the Klan. In recognizing that ambivalence, we recognize that Klan members both struggled against and participated in an emergent pluralist mass culture—a culture that they simultaneously resisted and helped to create.

Without a doubt, cultural endeavors and leisure time took on new importance in the 1920s. In many ways, American culture was "remade" in the postwar era, forming the clearly identifiable base of our culture today. Spending on recreation in the United States increased by 300 percent over the course of the decade. The 1920s saw the emergence of a modern mass media, of bestseller lists and radio charts, tabloid journalism and jazz, film stars and sports heroes. Sound recording revolutionized the consumption of music. With wireless broadcasting came free domestic mass entertainment. By the end of the decade, nearly a third of Americans owned a radio and a record player. Three-quarters of the country went to the movies at least once a week, their habit supplied by the emergent Hollywood studio system and the narrative feature film. Poet Archibald MacLeish supposedly declared the 1920s to be "the greatest period of painting and music, literary and artistic innovation since the Renaissance."[23]

If we focus on the "great works" that MacLeish was championing, though, we obscure much of the cultural consumption of the time. Levine reminds us that it is important to differentiate between mass culture and popular culture—while much of what was popular was mass-produced by the end of the 1920s, not everything that was mass-produced was popular. At the same time, we must remember that not everything that was popular was particularly good or particularly memorable. The 1920s may have seen great cultural innovation, but the decade also saw, as Joan Shelley Rubin notes, the emergence and consolidation of an often forgettable middlebrow culture.[24]

The popularity of "popular" art, as Russel Nye argues, often lies in a consumer consensus, a common approval most easily won by reflecting the experience of the majority. Great works, significant cultural artifacts, tend to gain their power by anticipating a change in that consensus. They provide an aspirational focus, formalizing, in critic Frederick Hoffman's words, "the moral and social positions that we ultimately hope to assume ourselves." As such, these new cultural forms tend to tell us more about where the nation is going than about where it is. Popular art provides a far more accurate reflection of an era's current values and ideas—not to provide a new experience, but to validate the existing one.[25]

The "overall tendencies of the culture industries," per Denning, is "to make what sold, to build on popular taste." What sold in the 1920s, more often than not, was the Ku Klux Klan. Rather than a "bulwark against modernism," it is more profitable to consider the men and women of the Invisible Empire as thoroughly modern Americans. An ambivalent combination of accommodation and protest, they were immersed in the growing consumer culture of therapeutic self-fulfillment and in the turn-of-the-century antimodernist impulse identified by Jackson Lears. Ensuring the "bad" and forgettable are present in our conceptions of the cultural 1920s reminds us how tightly intertwined modernism, nativism, and a wider Anglo-Saxon Protestant chauvinism were—and how deeply embedded in American cultural life the Ku Klux Klan was.[26]

If we approach the Klan as *movement* rather than *organization*, we better appreciate the cultural politics and aesthetic ideology of Klannishness. The Klan organization was, at its heart, a deeply local structure. The national Klan was a fractured and federalized affair. Yet, across media, the forging of a shared self unified a far-reaching national movement. The Klan appropriated the melodies of popular songs, adopted the format of adventure novels and tabloid newspapers, anticipated the power of film and radio, and was absorbed by the world of sports. The Klan movement was more than capable of both enjoying contemporary mass popular culture and turning it to its own ends. Hoosiers concerned by an impending invasion of papists, Georgians who feared an international rising ride of color, or Illinoisans who reviled a perceived breakdown in public morality—all could unite behind the image of the idealized Klan member that appeared around the country and across media. In the creation of a consumable cultural identity, citizens of the Invisible Empire bound themselves to an imagined cultural community.

In reexamining the Invisible Empire as cultural movement, we look beyond the Klan's organizational rhetoric to consider the lived ideology of a wider Klannish community. Here, we see Klannish cultural practices as signifying practices, as the meaning given to cultural forms defined the social reality for the members of this movement. While the Ku Klux Klan as an organization may have positioned itself in opposition to "the modern," members and supporters of the Invisible Empire were very much both a part and a product of modern American society. The Klan was not competing with contemporary cultural consumption. Rather, this trend proved complementary to efforts to consolidate and promote a Klannish cultural identity that lay largely within the mainstream of American life.

Even as the Klan shored up its own group identity, that identity was also appropriated for wider popular entertainment. Scholars like Davarian Baldwin, Erin Chapman, and W. Fitzhugh Brundage have noted that the 1920s saw a growing commodification of black culture. While earlier representations of blackness in mass culture—particularly minstrelsy—had served to circumscribe and delimit black artistry and racial identity, the postwar period offered the possibility of creating "black images and institutions" less beholden to the "overwhelming force of white patriarchy." The new mass culture created openings for African Americans to "participate in the production, distribution, and purchase of their own popular representations." These carefully constructed "communities of consumption" promised an escape from the degrading marginalization of segregated cultural spaces.[27]

A similar (albeit somewhat distorted) process was at work for the men and women of the Invisible Empire as they became both audience and creator, consumer and consumed. While the commodification of black culture was initially driven by white appropriation, the initial commodification of Klannish culture was driven by the Klan movement itself. Cultural production was, whether consciously or unconsciously, an inherently propagandistic exercise by the Klan movement—a means of publicizing the organization and defining the Invisible Empire's identity, both for the organizational membership and for a broader public. The Klan consolidated and commodified a consumable cultural identity that attempted to brand the organization as an appealing and positive force for white Protestant Americanism. That identity was then not only consumed but co-opted by the broader culture.

This was most evident in the popular use of cultural signifiers like the hood and cross that had become a synecdoche of Klannish identity. Through the decade, such signifiers were used to sell everything from newspaper exposés and tell-all memoirs to pulp novels and Tin Pan Alley tunes. Even products with little to no connection to the Klan were sold on the back of the Invisible Empire's commercial draw. C. B. McDonald, in one memorable example, plastered New York with the promise "the KKK is coming"—only to later reveal that it was an advertisement for his vaudeville program, the Keith Komedy Karnival.[28]

Whether the portrayals of the organization were positive or negative, this commercial exploitation of the Klan helped root the movement in modern culture. Ironically, just as the *New York World* series had inadvertently delivered "priceless publicity," even condemnations of the Klan tended to legitimize the group. Commercial and ideological concerns—inextricably intertwined in the development of the modern consumerist economy of the 1920s—served to neuter critical portrayals of the Klan. In appropriating the Klan's image for mass entertainments, that image—and, by extension, the organization—was sanitized and normalized for a popular audience. Critics of the Invisible Empire condemned the organization's secrecy, even as books, films, songs, and plays thrilled at the organization's melodramatic masculinity, and critics hailed the inclusion of "a dash of Ku Klux Klan to give it spice." In doing so, popular entertainments propelled the imagined community of the Klannish cultural movement far beyond the paying membership of the organization.[29]

Perhaps the most famous—and certainly the most infamous—cultural and social commentator of his day, H. L. Mencken declared that journalists leave behind "a series of long tested and solidly agreeable lies." The same could be said regarding our collective memory of the Ku Klux Klan and the "Jazz Age." In misreading and marginalizing the Klan's cultural power, we limit our understanding not only of the Invisible Empire but of the wider cultural 1920s. Rereading the Klan as cultural movement allows us to better comprehend the tension between the organization's rhetoric and the lived ideology of its members, the highly visible nature of an Invisible Empire supposedly built on secrecy, and how an organization that was fundamentally fractured and federalized unified around a common aesthetic and cultural identity.[30]

Understanding the Klan as cultural movement provides us with a new lens to better appreciate the cultural tensions of the wider 1920s, and how those tensions expressed themselves, both between the "forward-goers" and the "backward" and within those groups. The wide reach of the cultural Klan, and particularly the commercial value of the Klan image, underscore how fluid and porous the boundaries between those groups really were. Cultural Klannishness was not necessarily a dominant culture, and certainly did not represent the entirety of American culture. It did, however, leave its marks on the Klan itself and on the cultural institutions of the country. We better understand the 1920s when we look not just at the story of how Americans moved into the modern age, but also at what they brought with them as they did so—including the Ku Klux Klan.

White and White and Read All Over

Remember Americans, when you read your daily paper, ask yourself if you are reading
facts or propaganda? And whose propaganda?
D A W N, February 3, 1923

Nowhere were the shifting cultural tensions at the heart of the 1920s—and
the power of the Invisible Empire—more evident than in the nation's newspapers. It is impossible to understand the cultural milieu of the postwar decade without clear recognition of the symbiotic relationship between the Ku
Klux Klan and the press. The Klan organization thrived on publicity. Without
that publicity, the ability of the Klan movement to reach a large national audience would have been stemmed significantly. The widely held belief that
coverage of the Invisible Empire could boost newspaper sales garnered the
complicity of a wide cross section of the American press in this process and
provides insight into the development of modern press culture. Yet that relationship has been little examined.

Benedict Anderson has compellingly described the importance of print
culture, and particularly the press, in the creation of "imagined communities." Within these vast unseen audiences, the average American can be confident of their place—their very averageness—purely through the act of shared
cultural consumption. As Roland Marchand and Michele Hilmes have noted,
this shared consumption allows for the mediation of common experiences,
communalizing certain aspects of everyday life and excluding or marginalizing others. The newspaper culture of the 1920s may not have created a single
community of discourse on the Ku Klux Klan, but the plurality of opinion
left the organization far from marginalized for millions of American readers.[1]

Histories of the 1920s have largely constructed a reassuring myth in which
the cherished American institution of the free press stood bravely against the
aberrant foe of Klanism. George Jean Nathan declared in 1926 that "outside of
the South . . . fully three-quarters of the more important newspapers of the
Republic have been and are, either openly or in spirit, against the Grand and

Exalted Order of Ku Kluxers." In 1939, journalist Silas Bent wrote that "in no public issue have the newspapers of this country exhibited sounder editorial sense than in regard to the Ku Klux Klan." The press of the 1920s, according to Bent, had worked "effectively and boldly for the general good." In this telling, the country's journalists administered a sound "drubbing" to the Klan, discrediting and—crucially, for an organization priding itself on representing white Protestant American manhood—"emasculating" the group. Historian Clement Moseley argued that "the attack upon the secret society by the nation's journalists of the twenties was virtually unanimous." No standard narrative of the Klan's rise and fall is complete without at least a mention of the *New York World*'s role in exposing the organization.[2]

Yet Nathan's statement is telling, and belies the generalizations offered by Bent or Moseley. First, Nathan feels obligated to make a clear geographical distinction—"Southern" newspapers were not subject to this judgment. Second, it is made clear that this applied only to the "more important" newspapers. Leaving aside the question as to how to clearly define a "more important" newspaper, Nathan clearly did not trust in his judgment applying to those newspapers judged less important. Third, Nathan is forced to admit that even among these "important" non-Southern newspapers, there was a definite distinction between those that openly opposed the Klan and those that did so only in spirit. How—if at all—was a newspaper that opposed the Klan only in spirit meant to convey that sentiment to readers?

H. L. Mencken, Nathan's editorial partner on *Smart Set* and the *American Mercury*, offered a somewhat more convincingly caustic assessment of American journalism. "What chiefly distinguishes the daily press of the United States from the press of all other countries pretending to culture is not," he argued, "its lack of truthfulness or even its lack of dignity and honor, for these deficiencies are common to newspapers everywhere." What marked the American press specifically was its "fear of ideas, its constant effort to evade the discussion of fundamentals by translating all issues into a few elemental fears." Study of the nation's newspapers in the 1920s certainly lends itself to this interpretation. The press could not stop talking about the Klan but rarely dared discuss the ideas that gave the movement its power and appeal. When such considerations did make it into print, it was far more likely as an endorsement of those ideals than a condemnation.[3]

In large part, the coverage afforded the Klan was an outgrowth of changes in the newspaper industry in the developing modern consumerist society. In 1920, roughly twenty-seven million Americans regularly read a daily newspaper. By 1930, that number had increased to nearly forty million, or almost a third of the total population. Magazine readership increased even more steeply in a period of "unprecedented growth" as cornerstones of American publishing like *Time*, *Reader's Digest*, and the *New Yorker* were founded. Sociologists Robert and Helen Lynd found in their study of "Middletown" that there was "no family . . . which did not take either a morning or evening paper or both."[4]

Yet even as the number of readers grew, the number of newspapers was in decline as the power of syndicate chains and wire services drove smaller competitors out of the marketplace. At the same time, the modern American tabloid was transforming the nature of that marketplace. Even with the decline in numbers, by the mid-1920s, the United States was home to some two thousand daily newspapers and six thousand weeklies. More than four thousand periodicals were reaching around 108 million people. Competition for readers became ever fiercer. Publications had to find a way to stand out.[5]

That search for a unique selling point meant, often, a move toward the tabloid model. Newspapers like the *New York Daily News* and *Evening Graphic* had an immediate and enduring impact on the style of the American press. Headlines heaped across the crowded newsstand increasingly vied to catch the eye, to shock or titillate or amuse. "Ballyhoo" journalism, often witty and sharp, sought to grab your attention in short bursts of scandal and melodrama. If you weren't drawn to the writing, perhaps the photographs would seize your interest, as pictures had become the prime weapon in the arsenal of newspaper competition. Sex and death and everything in between, just as it happened—or even as it might have happened, as the *Graphic* pioneered its faked "composographs."[6]

The 1920s also saw shifts in press content. Led by publications like the *New York Sun* in the late nineteenth century, the definition of news had long since expanded to encompass anything that might fit the "man bites dog" model. A survey of sixty-three leading newspapers between 1899 and 1923 shows that coverage of crime, for instance, increased 53 percent. The postwar period represented the consolidation and expansion of this trend as readers displayed a keen appetite for sensationalist news that took in everything from celebrity gossip to national tragedies and dramatic murder trials. Even as more and more newspapers filled their inside pages with recipes, "Bright Sayings from Children," humor columns, and more, their headlines feasted on grand melodrama, soap operas of the front page. One of the most heavily covered stories of the decade was the 1927 trial of Ruth Snyder and her lover for the murder of Snyder's husband. The relatively inconsequential but lurid murder case in Queens transfixed the nation. The clamor over the *Daily News* photograph of Ruth Snyder's execution, smuggled from the death chamber, solidified the tabloid model. The execution of Nicola Sacco and Bartolomeo Vanzetti the

same year barely registered in comparison. In this changing newspaper industry, reporters and editors soon found that coverage of the Klan fit neatly
into the sensationalistic new business model.[7]

The almost inexhaustible public appetite for news of the Ku Klux Klan
first revealed itself in the *New York World* exposé series of September 1921.
The organization had previously attracted little more than occasional comment, largely from Southern or African American publications. Nonetheless,
the newly appointed editor of the *World*, Herbert Bayard Swope, was convinced that a major feature, "The Whole Truth" of the Klan, would be both a
journalistic scoop and a massive draw for readers. Before the first article was
even printed, the *World* had promoted it for days in full-page advertisements
and agreed on a syndication deal with seventeen other prominent dailies, for
a total claimed circulation of almost two million.[8]

Beginning September 6, 1921, the *World* relegated all other news to a secondary concern for almost three weeks as headlines touted the "Secrets of
the Ku Klux Klan." Even the arrest of film star "Fatty" Arbuckle for murder
partway through the series—a story that dominated the tabloid press—barely
warranted a mention on the front page of the *World*. Article after article detailed the Klan's secret code words, its overheated rhetoric of bigotry, and its
links to vigilante violence. In doing so, the hyperbolic attack on "the most
dangerous secret agency of super-government that has ever developed within
the Republic" became a smash hit.[9]

Plaudits from public figures as varied as ex-governor Alfred Smith, suf-
fragist Harriot Stanton Blatch, labor leader Samuel Gompers, and Broadway
impresario Florenz Ziegfeld filled the pages of the *World*. Reprinted editorials
gave the newspaper "the thanks of the country" for the "journalistic coup."
One newspaper even went so far as to claim that "no greater public service
has ever been rendered." In Chicago, demand for the series was reportedly so
widespread that "local dealers find it impossible to fill the orders." In Detroit,
copies allegedly sold for as high as fifty cents—twenty-five times their cover
value. When the series is taken as a whole, historians have estimated that it
increased the *World*'s circulation by more than a hundred thousand readers.[10]

Whether or not this circulation boost was directly attributable to the series, the Hearst syndicate, one of the most powerful newspaper chains in the
country, certainly believed that coverage of the Klan was responsible for the
World's success. The chain's New York morning daily, the *American*, soon
joined the fray with its own series of articles on the Ku Klux Klan's "executive abuses." As Imperial Wizard William J. Simmons later testified, William
Randolph Hearst could not bear "seeing the *World* each day in big handsful
taking his circulation away." As a result, the newspaper magnate, "for cash

profits, also attacked the Klan." While the *American*'s series was less popular than the *World*'s smash hit, Hearst's engagement with the Invisible Empire at least seemingly staunched the loss of readers to the competition. The perception that coverage of the Klan could boost circulation also started a rush to ape the *World*'s success. By 1923, one pro-Klan publication noted that readers would "find more Ku Klux Klan news printed in a week in the New York and Boston papers than in" the pages of a Klan newspaper.[11]

The *World* and its syndication affiliates, and the subsequent campaign by Hearst, had seemingly proven that attacking the Klan could sell newspapers. As the ensuing surge in Klan membership demonstrated, however, these exposés had also proven that newspaper condemnation did very little to actually hurt the organization. In many ways, this coverage may have spurred the movement forward. The danger of providing publicity, even negative publicity, to a group that might otherwise have had only limited appeal was quickly evident. The unrelenting appearance of the Klan in the national press following the *World* series kept the organization in the public eye as new members kept flooding in.

Nonetheless, the desire—the necessity—of gaining an advantage over their sensationalistic competitors meant not only that the nation's newspapers failed to administer a "drubbing" to the Klan in the 1920s, but that their coverage of the organization often gave fuel to the wider movement. The primary aim for the overwhelming majority of publishers and editors was to increase sales. Even as coverage of the Klan became near-universal, the shape of that coverage was far from uniform in the competition for readers. As a Klan official noted in 1924, "The press of the nation seems to have no fixed plan of campaign." Condemnation coexisted and often comingled with fascination, endorsement, and even admiration.[12]

"Open and vehement attack," following the model established by the *World*'s exposé, was a popular choice for many newspapers whose dramatic denunciations of the Klan found an avid readership. The Boston *Advertiser*'s "seven-column screamer in seventy-two point type" on the front page was a fairly typical example. By the end of September 1921, *Literary Digest* was providing summaries of the "sudden, violent and widespread press attack on the Klan's methods" that had appeared around the country. By 1923, Frank R. Kent of the *Baltimore Sun* bemoaned the fact that "scarcely a newspaper is printed that does not daily blaze with indignation over the iniquities of the Klan." This keen interest also extended to the increasingly competitive magazine market, as the *Nation, New Republic*, and *Atlantic Monthly* called for the exposure of the Klan's "shams, sophistry, un-Americanism and evil."[13]

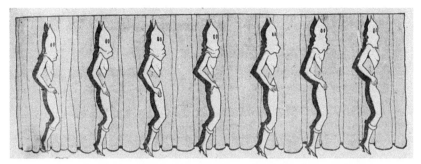

FIGURE 2.1. Detail of Jefferson Machamer cartoon. From *New York Tribune*, December 27, 1922.

Some leavened these attacks on the Klan with mockery. Humorist Don Marquis used his popular newspaper characters Archy and Mehitabel to attack the organization, from poems on the organization of the "Ku Klux Klam" to fight oysters to pieces lampooning an organization "founded on Assonance, Asininity, and Alliteration." Rollin Kirby's biting cartoons ridiculed Klansmen for the *New York World*, as did Jefferson Machamer in the *New York Tribune* (see fig. 2.1), the *Chicago Tribune's* Clare Briggs, and the *Pittsburgh Courier's* Wilbert Holloway. Satirist James J. Montague wrote a widely republished poem bemoaning the occasion that his beagle bit a Kleagle. A writer for *Collier's* claimed the Klan provided the "broad burlesque" and "delicious whimsicality" of the best newspaper comic strips. Yet this ridicule quickly proved equally ineffective at harming the growing Klan movement. As George Jean Nathan noted, the organization "could withstand ridicule to the end of its days and prosper in the midst of the thickest bombardment of custard tarts."[14]

Others saw no humor in the situation at all, and were firmly uninterested in questions of profit. The most implacable assault on the Ku Klux Klan came from the American Unity League (AUL), a coalition of predominantly Catholic and Jewish community leaders in Chicago. The AUL's weekly newspaper, *Tolerance*, was dedicated solely to exposing the Klan—one member at a time if necessary (see fig. 2.2). The first issue appeared on newsstands in Chicago on September 17, 1922, naming more than a 150 Chicagoans as Klan members. Within five months, the newspaper had printed the names of 4,000 alleged Klansmen in the Midwest and garnered a claimed circulation of 150,000.[15]

Despite this apparent success, *Tolerance* did not last long. The newspaper's editorial staff was less than meticulous in the difficult task of double-checking whether the names they printed truly were Klansmen. This tendency became ruinous with the publication of *Tolerance's* 1922 New Year's Eve issue, which

FIGURE 2.2. *Tolerance*, July 8, 1923.

named millionaire gum manufacturer William Wrigley Jr. as a member of the
Ku Klux Klan. Wrigley, declaring that the signature on his alleged application
was a "rank forgery," promptly filed a fifty-thousand-dollar lawsuit against
the AUL. Although others had sued the newspaper before for naming them,
Wrigley's suit was by far the largest. Heavily publicized, it inspired a flood of
similar, successful suits and saw the newspaper's editorial board collapse into
infighting. To add insult to injury, the aggrieved editor of *Tolerance*, Grady

Rutledge, began working with Chicago Klansmen to publish a series of stories that targeted the AUL as "intolerant fanatics."[16]

Even with the failure of *Tolerance*, condemnation of the Klan was so prevalent that during the decade five newspapers won Pulitzers for their work combating the organization. Setting the standard, the *New York World* was awarded the Pulitzer Prize for Public Service in 1922 for its initial series. A year later, the Memphis *Commercial Appeal* was awarded the Public Service prize for the work of editor Charles P. J. Mooney and cartoonist J. P. Alley. In 1928, the *Montgomery Advertiser* won the Pulitzer for Editorial Writing for denunciations of "gangsterism, floggings, and racial and religious intolerance," while the *Indianapolis Times* won the Pulitzer for Public Service for "exposing political corruption in Indiana," much of which was related to earlier Klan involvement in public affairs.[17]

The most relentless of the Pulitzer winners was the *Columbus Enquirer-Sun*, from the Klan's home state of Georgia. The newspaper had actually launched its initial attack on the organization months before the *World*'s expose, and was the only newspaper in Georgia to reprint the New York paper's series. Circulation dropped by an estimated 20 percent, and advertisers abandoned the newspaper in droves. When the series ended, more than a hundred Klansmen paraded up and down in front of the newspaper's offices in an attempt to intimidate the newsmen. Publisher Julian Harris, undeterred, stood in front of the building with his city editor and wrote down names, pretending to recognize Klansmen as they went past, until the parade disbanded. When Klan members took more direct action—including throwing sand and oil into the newspaper's presses—some of the paper's staff began carrying handguns for protection.[18]

The *Enquirer-Sun*'s greatest triumph came in 1924, when Harris forced Georgia governor Clifford Walker to admit not only that he was a Klansman but also that he had lied about his whereabouts to the press so that he could address the Second Imperial Klonvokation of the Klan. In a telling indication of public sentiment, though, not only was Walker not then impeached, he was overwhelmingly reelected later the same year. While not winning any friends in his home state, Harris attracted much praise from the press outside Georgia. When the *Enquirer-Sun* was finally awarded the Pulitzer in 1926, Mencken and the *American Mercury* noted that its articles "of a daring and unprecedented character" had made Harris's local daily "the most quoted and probably the most influential newspaper south of the Potomac."[19]

The experience of the *Enquirer-Sun* was certainly influential, but perhaps not in quite the way Mencken might have imagined. As *Tolerance* had shown, the *Enquirer-Sun* also showed that filling a newspaper with attacks on the Klan—even dedicating an entire newspaper to the task—could attract plaudits, but could lose readers. As the *World* had shown, it could also bring new attention to the Invisible Empire. In doing so, condemnation often proved an ineffective and even counterproductive tactic. A study of the Klan in Dallas found that press attacks on the Klan in that city had most likely "inadvertently enhanced the membership" of the organization. A high-ranking Klansman claimed that the press had, "more than any one agency, increased the membership" of the Klan, receiving for nothing, and "still receiving daily, advertisement that is worth millions in cold cash." Imperial Wizard Hiram Evans boasted in 1924 of the "fifty million dollars' worth of free advertising" that the newspapers had provided. Frank R. Kent of the anti-Klan *Baltimore Sun* agreed, complaining in 1923 that the Klan would already have collapsed "if not continuously stimulated by the hysteria of the press."[20]

Klan members understood that this constant and increasing coverage worked largely to their benefit. One ex-Klansman, Edgar Allen Booth, claimed that the Klan organization dealt very deliberately in provocative statements, knowing they would garner front-page headlines. If it was indeed a conscious tactic, it was a highly successful one, alienating those who disagreed with the organization's principles but garnering them valuable exposure on a regular basis. Any publicity, it seemed, was good publicity. As the Klan grew through the early 1920s, though, that publicity was increasingly positive.[21]

Part of this change was an awareness by much of the Klan leadership of the importance of good public relations. One Imperial Klan representative advised his fellow members that "the time is ripe for a closer co-operation between newspapers the country over and the Klan." Another advised members to abandon the reflexive response to "berate the daily newspapers." Instead, it made "good sense to work with rather than against them." After all, with the cooperation of the press, the Klan would "much more rapidly attain a position of dominance in the life of the nation." Thus, the supposedly Invisible Empire assiduously courted the publicity and worked to woo newspapers wherever possible.[22]

The organization could, to some extent, rely on a significant portion of the press that offered more than tacit support for the aims and ideals of the Klannish movement. The most open of these were the numerous anti-Catholic publications that predated the Klan's resurgence. Senator Tom Watson's quixotic *Columbia Sentinel* in Georgia was an early example that followed the pattern of Watson's earlier *Jeffersonian*. The old Populist was joined by the likes of Judge Gilbert O. Nations's *Protestant* in the District of Columbia, William Parker's *New Menace* in Missouri, Reverend Bob Shuler's *Shuler's Magazine* in

Los Angeles, William Lloyd Clark's *Rail Splitter* in Illinois, and Bishop Alma White's *Good Citizen* in New Jersey.

Most of these publications owed no formal allegiance to the Klan. On numerous occasions, they made their displeasure with the organization clear when they felt it had failed to live up to expectations. The *New Menace*, for example, would later turn against the Invisible Empire, claiming that the "unscrupulous bunch of scoundrels" were now in collusion with Catholics. Yet these publications became the organization's unofficial champions as part of their larger agenda of intolerance, and may have better reflected the lived ideology of the wider Klan movement than many official publications. Klan members were avid subscribers. More importantly, these publications were a valuable means of reaching nonmembers. Many Klans used them as recruiting aids. Editors like William Parker were invited to lecture on behalf of the Klan and attracted huge crowds. The King Kleagle of Tennessee described publications like the *Protestant* as "the most valuable dope" for communicating with a wider audience. Such publications allowed the Klan to reach not just members of the organization, but sympathizers with the movement.[23]

Nor was this reach limited to these kinds of specialized publications. Scores of local newspapers promoted the Klan and its goals. The oddest example of this tendency appeared in the otherwise liberal *New York Evening Post* almost a year before the *World's* series. For three months, the newspaper ran *Our Ku Klux Klan*, a cartoon strip by Alfred Ablitzer under the name "Al Zere." The strip portrayed the Klan as lovable and admirable helpers who banded together to aid others with familiar comic problems. These ranged from irascible relatives (the Klan saved a man from his mother-in-law's visit by forcing her onto a train home) to the idle rich (kidnapping a "lounge lizard" and delivering him to a factory to be put to work) to daily annoyances (abducting a noisy trumpet-playing neighbor and abandoning him on a mountaintop).[24]

Most publications were more serious in their encouragement of the Klan. The *Public Journal* in Virginia officially changed its front-page affiliation from "Independent" to "Independent and Ku Klux Klan." A front-page editorial in the Kentucky *Democrat* declared that "after careful and unbiased study," the editor was "unable to find any fault" with the principles of the organization. In Ohio, the *Noble County Leader* noted that the Klan's activities had its "endorsement and commendation," while the *Oskaloosa Independent* provided a "tardy and long-needed defense of the Klan." In Indiana, the *Kokomo Daily Tribune*, *Richmond Evening Item*, and *Franklin Evening Star* "openly gushed enthusiasm for the Klan's appearance in their communities."[25]

A number of journalists and editors were also themselves Klansmen, and duly influenced the nature of their newspaper's coverage. For several years, the managing editor of the *Atlanta Constitution* was the brother of Imperial Kleagle Edward Young Clarke, who had also worked as a reporter on the newspaper. Philip E. Fox served as managing editor of the Dallas *Daily Times-Herald*, a major city daily, until he became the Klan's national public relations director in 1923. At least one of the reporters for the *Indianapolis Star* openly admitted that he was a Klansman, while the editors of the *Arizona Gazette*, the *Daily Sentinel* in Colorado, the *Fremont Times-Indicator* in Michigan, and the *Orange County Plain Dealer* in California were all known to be members of the Klan. The editor of the *Marylander and Herald* revealed his Klan membership in particularly dramatic fashion with an editorial entitled "A Klansman I Am." These explicit endorsements of either the movement's ideals or the organization itself expanded the imagined community of Klannish support to encompass readers across the country.[26]

In the case of those whose sympathies were more pliable, the Ku Klux Klan thoroughly embraced the power of modern advertising. In the competitive marketplace of the 1920s, advertising revenue was increasingly crucial to the success of newspapers and magazines, allowing them to reduce subscription and newsstand prices to reach a far greater audience. This was particularly evident in popular magazines, which saw the pages dedicated to advertising—and the revenue gained—expand exponentially. The *Saturday Evening Post* grew so full of advertising that merchants allegedly bought the periodical in bulk as a cheap means of obtaining scrap paper. One executive summed up the trend with a claim that content no longer mattered. Magazines were simply "a device to induce people to read advertising."[27]

As more and more money went toward this end, advertising became increasingly sophisticated. Roland Marchand has noted that advertising in the twenties was a *Zerrspiegel*, a distorted mirror, which would reflect not reality as it was, but the reality that the reader wished for. No longer were these advertisements selling goods. They were selling lives, aspirations, dreams—and they were incredibly effective at doing so. The Klan was no exception. What would sell hats would also sell hates.[28]

The opening salvo in this approach even predated the *World* series. Before becoming the Klan's propagandists, Imperial Kleagle Edward Young Clarke and his partner, Elizabeth Tyler, had run a successful public relations firm. Experienced in dealing with newspapers, they perceptively recognized the benefits of national advertising, and ran copy in publications in Chicago, New York, Milwaukee, and a number of other cities. Clarke and Tyler also had the foresight to outsource much of this advertising work to add a veneer of respectability. Most was handled by the Massengale Agency of Georgia, which also represented local businesses like Coca-Cola. In a reflection of the ever-shifting cultural currents of the time, some of the work apparently also went to the influential Lord & Thomas Agency in Chicago. Lord & Thomas was not only the second largest advertising agency in the country in the 1920s; it was also headed by the influential Albert Lasker, the "father of modern advertising" and one of the few Jewish executives in the industry at the time.[29]

While some newspapers rejected the opportunity, many were tempted by Imperial Wizard Simmons's claim that the Klan had more than a hundred thousand dollars to spend on publicity. In a display of either staggering bravado or remarkable ignorance, Lord & Thomas even offered a recruiting advertisement to the *New York World* to carry on the same day the newspaper's well-publicized exposé series was set to begin. Despite such missteps, the venture was a seeming success. One publicity professional even opined that the "power of advertising" was solely responsible for the Klan's initial growth, calling it "the greatest selling campaign in recent history."[30]

Throughout the 1920s, both the national Klan and local branches used advertising liberally as a means of promotion. These advertisements were not always accepted. More often, though, newspapers were all too willing to take the Klan's business. A widely distributed two-column advertisement in 1923 shored up an imagined Klannish self-image, boasting of the virtues of members and "correcting false and malicious propaganda." Local Klaverns around the country even used the newspapers to publicly advertise their meetings, albeit often eliding the precise location.[31]

Where the carrot failed, the stick was put into play. In some cases, this meant a physical threat. Texan Klan leader H. C. McCall (soon to become a high-ranking member of the Klan's national organization) was fond of concocting baroque threats against Clifton F. Richardson of the *Houston Informer*, the second-largest African American newspaper in the state and a relentless critic of the Klan.[32] George R. Dale, editor of Indiana's *Muncie Post-Democrat*, was allegedly attacked and harassed by Klan members for years. Memorably, a severed human hand accompanied a threatening note to *Messenger* editor A. Philip Randolph.[33]

Violent incidents, however, were few and far between. The economic threat was far more powerful. Purchasing advertisements in the press had the dual benefit of disseminating the organization's message while also rendering the publication considerably less liable to antagonize its new source of income. This was reflective of a growing trend that reached far beyond those who had accepted the Klan's advertising funds. As magazines and newspapers progressively came to depend on the economic support of advertising executives, publishers and editors were increasingly conscious of the reader as a consumer. Alienating consumers meant losing much-needed advertising revenue. Any kind of controversy risked financial ruin. As the Lynds noted in their study of the newspapers in Middletown, "Independence of editorial comment happens to be in rough inverse proportion to the amount of advertising carried." To lean neutral or conservative on social issues—including the Klan—was simply playing it safe. After all, as Klan officials were careful to remind editors and publishers, there were many readers sympathetic to the Invisible Empire's ideals. The movement's reach extended far beyond the organization's membership.[34]

At the most basic level, consumers simply complained. The *South Bend Tribune* in Indiana was deluged with phone calls protesting its policy on the Klan. The Klan in Lynchburg, Virginia, adopted a resolution condemning the Associated Press for only circulating reports that ignored the organization's "constructive" efforts. The resolution was sent to local newspapers as well as the AP itself. Klan members in Carlock, Illinois, formed a committee to approach the publisher of the local newspaper about "unrespectable articles" that had been printed. The meeting was apparently a success, as the publisher assured the committee that "nothing of this nature" would appear in future.[35]

When complaints proved ineffective, the boycott rarely failed. Some were able to withstand the pressure. One of the reasons Mencken had pointed to the *Columbus Enquirer-Sun* as an example was the fact that Harris had continued his campaign against the Klan despite losing more than 20 percent of his readers. Similarly, despite the substantial loss in circulation and advertising revenue suffered by the *South Bend Tribune* after the Indiana Women's Klan launched a boycott, the paper continued to publish anti-Klan articles. Most were less hardy.[36]

Even for nonmembers, the Klan issue was serious business. One female subscriber to the *South Bend Tribune* told a circulation agent for the newspaper that she had been a consistent reader for sixteen years, but was stopping her subscription until the *Tribune* favored the Klan rather than opposing it. The *Indianapolis News* lost fifteen hundred subscribers after just one article containing "a minor misstatement of fact" was seen as unfavorable by members of the Invisible Empire. The newspaper largely ignored the Klan thereafter. A sales agent for the *Daily Oklahoman* claimed the newspaper's attacks on "a certain secret fraternal organization" had meant circulation "diminished considerably." Editors of Tennessee's *Johnson City Staff* had to "put a muzzle on the paper" when their advertisers suggested that the publisher "lay off" the Klan. When the *Dallas Morning News* reprinted the *World* series, Klan members and their allies canceled subscriptions, deluged the newspaper with letters questioning the religious affiliation of the editors, boycotted businesses that continued to advertise in it, and even threatened sales agents for the

News with bodily violence. By 1923, circulation had dropped precipitously, and cash reserves had all but disappeared, prompting the owner of the *News* to sell off one of its smaller affiliates and have editors discontinue their attacks on the Klan.[37]

The threat was clear. Overt anti-Klan sentiment could attract readers, but also lose them. At the same time, overtly pro-Klan sentiment could both draw and repel readers. As an increasingly large segment of the press had realized by 1922, however, staking out a position was not the only way to entice readers. As more and more articles appeared on Klan parades, rallies, charitable efforts, initiations, church visits, cross burnings, and more, it seemed to many that "chronicles of Klan activities" could boost circulation with or without editorial comment. A neutral approach, then, would allow publishers to have the best of both worlds—the readership that came with coverage of the Klan without the danger of having to take a side. What that meant in reality was tacit support for the Klannish movement. With story after story portraying it as an influential and popular organization, many newspapers created an image of the Klan as an accepted and even admirable part of American culture.[38]

This implicit endorsement of the Ku Klux Klan was not an unconscious, or uncontroversial, decision. The *Pittsburgh Courier*, an African American weekly, complained loudly of the "notoriety" afforded the Klan by the unceasing press fascination with the organization. Every time Klan members paraded, held an initiation, or participated in anything remotely newsworthy, they garnered "great head lines" and "liberal space" within the newspapers. Even if those newspapers opposed the Klan, the editorial policy would be "drowned in the mire on the first page." If the press continued to look only at the readership (and, by extension, the money) garnered by these "scoops" as "the criterion by which journalistic success is to be measured," the *Courier* warned, then "the end is in plain view."[39]

A survey of the press of the 1920s shows, though, that it was a relative minority that did not care "more for pocketbook than for principle." The vast majority of those that did refuse to treat the Klan's activities as news were black, Catholic, and Jewish publications. While there was no single, unified response to the Klan from members of these communities, there was a distinct trend in these newspapers and magazines to refuse to grant column inches to Klan activities. Mentions of the Klan were largely confined to the editorial page. When news articles on the Klan did appear, they were almost uniformly descriptions of its failures or reprints of denunciations.[40]

Writing in the *American Ecclesiastical Review*, an influential Catholic theological journal, Reverend Thomas M. Conroy of Fort Wayne, Indiana, noted that the "wide and intensive publicity bestowed upon the Klan" had made it "a live subject." To combat it effectively, Conroy argued, the answer was not more publicity. John B. Kennedy made a similar observation in the national Jesuit weekly *America*. It was "conceivable that there is less news interest in a group of Knights of Pythias bound for a clam bake than in a group of Ku-Klux Knights bound for a Nigger bake," but there was "no question of the relative patriotic merit" of articles on each. Leading Jewish journals like the *American Hebrew* were similarly prudent in their approach to reporting, even as Louis Marshall of the American Jewish Committee warned that the "immediate effect" of Jewish coverage of the organization would "be to increase the numbers of the Klan." A. Philip Randolph and Chandler Owen's socialist "Journal of Scientific Radicalism," *The Messenger*, simply urged its readers "not try to carry on any debating society" about the Klan. The best way to defeat the Invisible Empire would be to deny it the oxygen of publicity.[41]

Nonetheless, the far more common response by newspapers was to compete for readers by lavishing attention on the Klan. "Dignified silence," one Klansman noted, "gets a newspaper nowhere." In doing so, editors and publishers created a press landscape that reinforced Klan power and popularity. As Mencken recognized in 1924, "Whenever the Klan wins, the fact is smeared all over the front pages of the great organs of intelligence; when it loses, which is three times as often, the news gets only a few lines."[42]

Until the late 1920s, breathless accounts of triumphal parades and rallies dominated reports on the Klan. These stories were more interested in the "picturesque" (in the words of a *Washington Post* headline) nature of the organization than in violent vigilantism or any ideological issues. In 1921, the *Chicago Defender* complained that the greater part of white Southern newspapers' headline space was "taken up with the doings of the Klan." By 1922, it was clear that this tendency was not limited to the South. Front-page articles across the country reported on the "mysterious" ceremonies that attracted thousands.[43]

As the Klan grew, so did the events they staged—and the spectacle that surrounded them. The hyperbole of reporters increased accordingly. The age of the Klan was also the age of journalistic ballyhoo. In Minnesota, one newspaper called a massive initiation, complete with burning crosses and fireworks, "one of the most spectacular scenes ever witnessed in this part of the state." Alabama's *Prattsville Progress* made note of the "beautiful and interesting" character of a Klan initiation marked by "perfect order and good feeling," while a reporter present for a giant initiation ceremony in Birmingham remarked that even "the most solid anti would have admitted the ceremony was impressive."[44]

Even newspapers ostensibly opposed to the Klan fell prey to the trend. The *Dallas Morning News*, for example, had carried the *World*'s series and was known as an "implacable foe" of the organization. Nonetheless, between mid-1921 and late 1924, the newspaper averaged almost an item a day on the Klan and hailed the massive initiation held at the Texas State Fair's Klan Day as "the most colorful and unique event ever seen in the city of Dallas." This reportage was skewed even further in the Klan's favor by reporters who often simply accepted the organization's own estimates of attendance at events. Space was given not only to local Klan events but also to activity of interest from all over the country. In some rural areas, even locals traveling to Klan events became news.[45]

Nor was this tendency limited only to large-scale events like parades and initiations, even as they vied for recognition as the "largest ever" or "most spectacular." One Klansman observed that newspapers around the country were "so willing to give the Klan space that they even print stories whenever a contribution is made to a pastor by Klansmen, or whenever Klansmen take part in funeral services, or call, in a body, upon an errand of mercy." In Klan strongholds like Indiana, newspapers would publish regular front-page columns detailing upcoming Klan events and meetings. Klan officers encouraged members to approach their local newspapers about running a regular "Klan Kolumn" that would carry news of the organization and "constructive arguments for patriotic Protestant Americanism." As this broader range of Klan activities became "news," newspapers around the country not only reinforced the idea of the organization as exciting and popular; they also drew attention to the constructive and charitable social work that the Klan trumpeted as one of its most attractive qualities. "Similar activities by other fraternal organizations," one Klan member noted with satisfaction, "do not usually receive so much publicity."[46]

As members of the organization quickly recognized, the apparent hunger for Klan news meant that coverage of the movement could be manipulated. The striking unanimity in early reports of Klan initiations and parades as "weird" proceedings was no coincidence. The organization was well aware that these public events were not only for the benefit of the Klan members present. They also shaped the ways in which the Klan would be represented in the wider culture, and allowed for outreach to the wider movement—constructing the imagined community of Klannishness. As such, the Klan carefully cultivated a tantalizingly mysterious atmosphere in a tactic that predated the *World*'s exposé.

In January 1921, the "Imperial Propagation Department" of Clarke and Tyler began allowing a few short interviews with Imperial Wizard Simmons.

At the end of the month, the first "open" initiation ceremony was staged at the Alabama State Fairgrounds in Birmingham. Reporters were given a prime view of the occasion, but guards were stationed to prevent any attempt to approach closer. Nonetheless, three newspapers presented unanimously positive coverage of the initiation. With this success, the Birmingham meeting set the model for a careful balancing act of secrecy and publicity.[47]

Across the country, the prescribed pattern for initiations was the same: allow the public to draw close enough to spot the fires and ghostly figures and half hear the words of the rituals. Journalists were allowed a little closer to assure the event would appear in the newspaper, but not so close that they could see faces, recognize names, or be able to fully recount any of the secrets of the Klan. The requirement of "deepest secrecy" was apparently no bar to inviting favored reporters and photographers.[48]

Perhaps the best recounting of the experience came from Tennessee journalist L. W. Miller. The Knoxville reporter described receiving an anonymous note inviting him to "something worth seeing." Known to be friendly to the organization, Miller was allowed a particularly close view of a Klan initiation ceremony. Once the oath began to be recited, he was "led to the edge of the clearing where I joined my companions who had been on the outskirts." From there, he could "scarcely distinguish the words uttered," only catching "a few snatches"—exactly the desired effect.[49]

By controlling the access reporters had to these events, Klan members clearly hoped to control the coverage they would receive in newspapers. As in the case of Miller, those friendly to the Klan were given preferential treatment. In Houston, for example, the pro-Klan *Houston Post* was given exclusive access to Klan events, while reporters from the anti-Klan *Houston Chronicle* were denied access to the "scoop." In rural areas, prominent journalists could expect to be invited personally to events. Befitting its stature as one of the largest Klan meetings ever assembled, the "Konklave at Kokomo" featured one of the most organized attempts at controlling press coverage. Local reporters would only be allowed to attend under "special dispensation" after agreeing not to repeat the names of any speakers or participants, "other than the general officers." In order to gain admission, newspapermen would have to act as supplicants, reporting to the Klan's offices to receive a card allowing entry. Those who gave the Klan favorable attention would be rewarded with access. Those who had been insufficiently fawning would be excluded and lose the story.[50]

Nor was that the organization's only attempt at controlling its press. Part of the reason for the similar language in early reports of Klan events was Imperial Kleagle Clarke's shrewd tactic of rarely releasing typewritten or printed copy. Instead, as one historian has noted, he would send press releases "already in stereotype form for type casting from molten metal." Editors would not and could not alter the piece before publishing it. Photographers were also usually prohibited so that the Klan could control what was and was not seen of the organization. The Indiana Klans, growing particularly inventive, hired their own photographer, W. A. Swift of Muncie, who would then supply chosen newspapers with illustrations for their articles—at a price.[51]

As the Klan grew, and Hiram Evans took control from William J. Simmons, these restrictions lessened. By summer 1923, reporters still noted the "weird," "ghostly," "statuesque" nature of Klan activities, but also remarked on the Invisible Empire's increasing disinterest in a pretense of secrecy. A rally on Long Island was described by the *New York Times* as "manifestly held in the open as a dramatic gesture of strength." A year later, "the oath of the Klan and instructions to candidates were given loud and clearly" at a meeting in Boise, Idaho, "so that press representatives might hear."[52]

The Klan's leaders also reached out to publications in the hoping of trading access for favorable coverage. In a special issue of the illustrated monthly *McClure's*, journalist Max Bentley lauded the Indiana Klan as "a real factor for the betterment of municipal rule" and lavished praise on Indiana Grand Dragon D. C. Stephenson (soon to be arrested for sexual assault and murder), acclaiming him as "the outstanding man of the young generation." Both the *Chicago Daily News* and the *Los Angeles Times* printed lengthy interviews with Imperial Wizard Hiram Evans, while periodicals like the *Forum* and *Current History*, an affiliate of the *New York Times*, turned to Evans for comment on current affairs. In 1926, the *North American Review*, a prestigious literary quarterly, printed a thirty-page explanation of Klan principles from Evans. Shorter criticisms of the organization were published in the following issue, as part of a symposium to form "a nationally comprehensive estimate, pro and contra, of the Ku Klux Klan and its place among American institutions." *Time*, founded in 1923 and quickly gathering a mass following, put Imperial Wizard Hiram Evans on its cover in 1924—a few months before Sigmund Freud was similarly featured, and only one week after Pope Pius XI had appeared.[53]

After 1924, however, the novelty of the Invisible Empire seemingly began to wane for many readers—or at least for many publications. Reports on Klan events were also beginning to suffer from diminishing returns. Initiations and parades had been supplemented and then supplanted by picnics and carnivals. Seeking to stem the decline in journalistic attention, Klans competed to create news with the most lavish display of fireworks and the largest fiery cross (a record taken by the Boise, Idaho, Klan with a cross allegedly five hundred feet tall and two hundred feet across). Airplanes performed stunts, displayed electric fiery crosses, and dropped aerial bombs. Yet even as the Klan most needed the publicity to prevent an increasingly rapid fall in membership, the glut of events competing for attention diminished their news value. By 1925, as participation in the organization collapsed, and fewer and fewer sizable events were held, the torrent of press coverage slowed to a trickle, and the Klan organization was locked into a vicious circle of decline.[54]

For years, as journalist Ross Garrigus noted, many newspapers had not carried "any big expose stories." Instead, they "covered Klan rallies, and like that, but as far as getting in their inner workings, they never touched it at all." Once the organization's power began to crumble, the press seemingly rediscovered the idea that criticizing the increasingly Invisible Empire could boost circulation. Even in Georgia, as scandals and the Klan's constant infighting took its toll, the *Atlanta Constitution* (which Julian Harris had previously deemed the "Atlanta Morning Molly-Coddle" for its soft treatment of the Klan) moved to openly oppose the organization. With the risk minimized, newspapers around the country flaunted their opposition to the Klan organization. As they did so, they constructed the myth of a unified front of dedication to "drubbing" the Invisible Empire.[55]

In the construction of this myth, the complex and inconsistent relationship of antagonism and accommodation between the Klan and the nation's press was quickly, and conveniently, forgotten. Spurred by a desire to attract new readers without losing existing subscribers, newspapers around the country publicized a growing Klan. The frequently uncritical coverage of the organization's parades and picnics implicitly stripped the Klan of its controversy. Even when that controversy was foregrounded—whether for reasons of principle or profit—the effect was often to boost the Invisible Empire. At the same time, as much as they lambasted newspapers supposedly dominated by "alien" Catholic and Jewish interests, Klan members and sympathizers embraced modern advertising and public relations techniques to promote the movement to a national audience. Far from "emasculating" the Invisible Empire, the press engaged millions of Americans around the country in a daily discourse in which the Klan movement was far from marginal and the Empire far from Invisible.

3

Fiery Cross-Words

The latest literary arrival in the cause of the Klan is the *Patriot*, published at St. Louis, Mo., every week. It's a pretty husky baby, too. Eight seven-column pages chock full of Americanism and live enough for the most critical of newspaper readers to enjoy.
IMPERIAL NIGHT-HAWK, July 11, 1923

The nation's press propelled the Ku Klux Klan to the forefront of the American conversation, but with mixed assessments. For many, this was not good enough. To offer a Klannish alternative, the organization's national leadership acted to construct its own national newspaper syndicate. To do so, though, the official Klan newspaper would have to fend off dozens of local competitors established by individual Klan members and sympathizers. The press of the Invisible Empire shaped an imagined community of Klannishness, coalescing a national movement around a consumable cultural identity. At the same time, the struggle to control the delivery of that message revealed the federalized and fractured structure of the Klan organization.

Whether officially sanctioned or not, the Klan publications that were created are revealing. Klan newspapers were shaped by, and reflected, an accommodation to modern press trends—particularly in the tabloidization of news. Perhaps the clearest example of the commingling of these cultural strands was the collision of the Klan's antimodern rhetoric with the puzzle craze that gripped the emerging consumerist society. The porous boundaries of cultural division in the 1920s were on full display in the popularity of the "Fiery Cross-Word Puzzle."

From the tenure of editor Edward M. Kingsbury at the *New York Sun* in the late nineteenth and early twentieth centuries to the booming market of the 1920s, the growth of tabloid newspapers saw a changing definition of what was "news." The pioneering *Daily News* in New York, for example, sponsored (and wrote at length about) skating parties and dance competitions, offered beauty tips and lifestyle advice, sold horoscopes, and helped readers find lost pets or sell clothes. By 1926, it was the best-selling daily newspaper in the country, read by "plumbers and plasterers, secretaries and stenographers," for "entertainment, gossip, and useful information" on navigating life's hurdles. At the same time, as Donald L. Miller has noted, the newspaper was roundly criticized for pandering "in a blatant and unashamed way" to "basic instincts and vulgar tastes." It was a description that could have been, and was, equally applied to the increasingly popular Klan press.[1]

The organization's Imperial leadership dominated the Ku Klux Klan's first forays into the world of American newspapers. The *Searchlight* had been founded in Atlanta in 1919 by the nativist Junior Order of United American Mechanics (JOUAM). By 1921, the newspaper's principal stockholder was Elizabeth Tyler, head of the Klan's public relations team, while local politician and Klan organizer James O. "Joe" Wood edited the paper. The eight-page weekly proclaimed proudly that it stood for "Free Speech. Free Press. White Supremacy."[2] Similarly, in the Klannish stronghold of Indiana, an anti-Catholic publication called *Fact!* was converted in July 1922 into the *Fiery Cross*, another eight-page Klan weekly. Dedicated to maintaining "a policy of staunch 100 percent Americanism without fear or favor," the *Fiery Cross* was controlled by David C. Stephenson, the immensely powerful King Kleagle (and soon to be Grand Dragon) of Indiana, who had effective dominion over the northern Klans.[3]

In 1923, the *Fellowship Forum* of Washington, D.C., joined the ranks of semi-independent Klan publishing. The paper was the creation of George Fleming Moore, a high-ranking Southern Mason, while the funding came from local "drugstore impresario" James S. Vance. The nationally circulated twelve-page weekly had been founded in June 1921 to report on fraternal organizations across the country, but by 1923 was clearly governed by the Klan. In September of that year, at a stockholders meeting for the *Forum*'s publisher, the Independent Publishing Company, the shift was evident. Earlier directors of the company had mostly been prominent Masons. Now, Moore and Vance were joined on the board by Herschel C. McCall, Grand Dragon of Texas, the Invisible Empire's "ambassador" to Washington, D.C., and one of Imperial Wizard Evans's most trusted lieutenants.[4]

Nonetheless, the Imperial officers did not hold a monopoly on the Invisible Empire's journalistic endeavors. As members flocked to the Klan's banners through the early 1920s, the movement's press representation rapidly diversified. From the *Jayhawker American* in Oklahoma to the *Protestant Herald* in Colorado to the aptly named *Crank* in Arizona, new mouthpieces of independent Klannish sentiment appeared around the country. *Dawn: A Journal for True Patriots* materialized on Chicago newsstands in late 1922. Larger than the *Searchlight* or the *Fiery Cross* at sixteen pages, with an eye-catching front cover of a mounted Klansman holding a fiery cross aloft, *Dawn* had the feel of a magazine rather than a newspaper. By June 1923, the Chicago weekly claimed, with justification, to be "one of the strongest publications in the country supporting the Knights of the Ku Klux Klan and other all-American organizations." The Dawn Publishing Company incorporated itself with a capitalization of forty thousand dollars. In Ohio, meanwhile, there was the *Buckeye American*. In Iowa, the *Hawkeye Independent*. In Seattle, the *Watcher on the Tower*. In Dallas, the *Fiery Cross Magazine*. Some Klan dailies, like the *Pekin Daily Times* in Illinois, even began to appear. Generally run independently of any official oversight, and offering a multiplicity of voices and opinions, these publications nevertheless were strikingly effective in creating a national press culture that centered on the promotion of the Klan as an appealing and positive force for white Protestant Americanism. Even as the organization fractured and federalized in its operation, the movement united behind a common discourse of heroic Klannish identity.[5]

Not everyone appreciated this content. *Mayfield's Weekly*, a Klan publication in Texas, caused a minor firestorm in October 1921 after it claimed Mayor John F. Hylan of New York City had ordered New York police to shoot Klansmen on sight. The *New York Times* described it as "journalism of a peculiar sort." Similarly, in 1924, the paper of record complained that it would be difficult to find "a duller paper" than the *Searchlight*. It would be hard to imagine, the *New York Times* argued, a newspaper "less useful to its readers, if they want anything in the way of world or local news." The Gray Lady's estimate of utility, however, was based on a rapidly changing definition of what constituted news.[6]

The ideas presented in Klan publications were nothing new. Minus the lavish self-praise that oozed from every page, readers could have found many similar arguments in anti-Catholic and anti-Semitic periodicals like the *Railsplitter* or Henry Ford's *Dearborn Independent*. The presentation, though, was distinctly modern. While Klan members may have bemoaned the state of the mainstream media, their own publications owed much to the increasingly popular tabloid model and the growth of news magazines.

Some of the Klan publications were notable primarily for their anti-Catholic and anti-Semitic diatribes. One of the most notorious—and most popular—was the *Badger American*, a Wisconsin monthly with subscribers in fourteen states. It was set apart by the editorial cartoon that graced each issue's cover. A typical month might depict "Romanism" as a vicious-looking buzzard nestled on a pile of skulls, or show the Knights of Columbus as brutish thugs brandishing shillelaghs, guided by a papal phantasm. It was also

Our *"Little Red School House"* Edition

BADGER AMERICAN

"For the Protection and Perpetuation of American Institutions and Liberties"

| Vol. 2, No. 5 | Price: 10 cents per copy | Milwaukee, Wisconsin | Subscription: $1.00 per year | August, 1924 |

"Entered as second-class matter October 15, 1923, at the post office at Milwaukee, Wisconsin, under the act of March 3, 1879."

The Little Red School House! Americans, Stand By It!

His Nightmare   PUBLIC SCHOOL

"The children of the public schools turn out to be horsethieves, scholastic counterfeiters and well versed in schemes of deviltry. I frankly confess that Catholics stand before the country as the enemies of the public schools. They are afraid that the child that left home in the morning would come back with something in his heart as black as hell." So said Priest David S. Phelan, editor, the Roman Catholic Watchman, of St. Louis, Mo., all of whose sermons, writings, and utterances were blessed by the pope!

OUR NEXT ISSUE! WE PROPHESY THAT OUR SEPTEMBER NUMBER
WILL SEVERELY JOLT CERTAIN PROFESSIONAL POLITICIANS.

A Militant Americanism, Our Aim; A United Protestantism, Our Goal

FIGURE 3.1. Cover of Wisconsin Klan newspaper, *The Badger American*, August 1924.

"one of the vilest, most noxious Klan publications to receive a widespread circulation," which may be an understatement for a publication that venomously attacked black World War I veterans as "bloated with self-importance."[7]

Yet even the *Badger American* consciously aped many of the current publishing trends in its efforts to reach readers (see fig. 3.1). The newspaper humor column, critic Gilbert Seldes claimed in the 1920s, was "the most sophisticated of the minor arts in America." The articles of "colyumists" (in Seldes's formulation) like Don Marquis, Ring Lardner, and arguably H. L. Mencken himself were popular and influential mainstays of the major urban dailies. As such, it is unsurprising that the *Badger American* mimicked these features in its pages, drawing particularly on the tradition of popular dialect and vernacular humor that had long drawn readers to publications like the *Saturday Evening Post*. The regular column "Lissen Tu This," ridiculing Irish Catholics, appeared under the byline of one Q. Cluxton Clanning, while Jews were lambasted in a column called "The Jolly Jewboy." Where the appeal of content failed, the *Badger American* turned to *Daily News*–style tabloid sales gimmicks, including a promotion for a free "Wonder" telescope with every three subscriptions sold.[8]

These tendencies were even more pronounced among the largest and most widely circulated Klan publications. In many ways, these periodicals owed their success to one of the key publishing ideas of the 1920s. Like the newly founded *Reader's Digest* and *Time*, much of the Klan press offered news and features in capsule form, presenting a ready-made opinion. The *Searchlight* in Atlanta led the way. Dedicated primarily to reporting on the good deeds and charitable works of the Klan, features like "Ku Kluxin," a lighthearted roundup of local Klan activity, were typical. At the same time, these reports were mixed with short, reprinted news summaries and punchy populist attacks on the rickety schemes of venture capitalists in Georgia and restrictive "reform" politics—stances that, not coincidentally, also furthered editor Joe Wood's own political career.[9]

Indiana's *Fiery Cross*, controlled by a council of influential Klansmen,[10] similarly focused largely on self-flattery and on reprinting articles from popular publications around the country. The publication's purpose was not original reporting, editor Ernest Reichard argued, but to "give the American viewpoint" on news of the day, largely by reprinting political criticisms of immigration from major national publications. Vainly attempting to veil its anti-Catholicism in the language of "aliens" and "organized opposition," the newspaper consciously lurched toward the mainstream of American journalism. In a reflection of the split between the Klan organization and the lived ideology of the movement, these efforts apparently garnered the *Fiery Cross* "a number of complaints in certain sections because we refuse to say anything [overt] against the Catholics."[11]

Klan publications furthered these efforts toward at least a veneer of respectability with well-received forays into public-interest and lifestyle articles—a short history of the hatband, for example—side by side with the newspaper's anti-Catholic concerns. While this same press style could be found in any number of Klan publications, perhaps the most evident example of this approach was Minnesota's *Call of the North*. The St. Paul weekly mixed humor pieces (often reprinted from non-Klan publications, including the *Los Angeles Times*) and original poems with digested current events and longer articles on education, religion, and history to "stimulate constructive thinking." The *Call*'s content, claimed editor Peter J. Sletterdahl, was "newsy."[12]

This kind of "newsy" approach quickly proved popular with readers, which made Klan publications an attractive proposition for significant numbers of local advertisers. The *Searchlight* carried advertisements for a wide cross section of Georgia businesses, from shoe stores offering special discounts to Klan members to the powerhouse of Coca-Cola. The advertising director for the *Fiery Cross*, C. B. Salyer, boasted that the newspaper offered the best return on its display advertising (seventy-five cents per column inch) of any newspaper in Indiana. Whether or not that was the case, regional businesses flocked to advertise in the weekly. Some Klan periodicals clearly existed for little reason other than to carry advertising. The weekly *Kluxer* of Dayton, Ohio, regularly ran to more than fifty pages—more than half of which was advertising. The *T.W.K.* [Trade With Klansmen] *Monthly*, published in Alabama, weighed in at a hefty forty pages and generated sufficient revenue to print its advertising in tricolor.[13]

That so many businesses were willing not only to be associated with the Ku Klux Klan but to pay to advertise in the movement's publications points to the wide readership of these Klannish periodicals. Delivered directly to Klaverns and Klan officials, these newspapers were also carried on public newsstands and by newsboys on street corners across the country.[14] By 1923, *Dawn* boasted a circulation of fifty thousand. The five-cent *Searchlight* claimed to have over sixty-eight thousand readers and could be found at least as far west as Montana and at least as far north as Pittsburgh. The *Fiery Cross* went one better, with a paid circulation of over a hundred thousand throughout the Midwest. The paper was so popular in surrounding states that, in April 1923, the *Fiery Cross* announced plans to create additional "state editions" in Ohio, Iowa, and Illinois. The *Fellowship Forum*, meanwhile, boasted of being read by more than half a million people every week.[15]

This "newsy" business was a profitable one. As of March 1923, the *Fiery Cross* alone claimed to employ more than nine hundred newspaper vendors to circulate the publication throughout the Midwest. The Indiana newspaper also proudly listed more than a dozen newsstands in Indianapolis at which the publication was available. Some news vendors even took out advertisements to announce the availability of Klan publications at their establishments. A few—like "K.K. Kore, the Kluxer Newsman and his Leather Lunged

Newsboys"—flaunted their allegiance to the organization, but most operated from commonplace stalls.[16]

It is suggestive that much of the impetus for this success was commercial. Some sellers were certainly Klan members, and would even appear on street corners in their robes to pass out literature. Nevertheless, most "newsboys" were seemingly motivated more by financial than by ideological concerns. In June and August 1923, the *Fiery Cross* ran a competition offering a thousand dollars in prizes to those vendors showing the greatest gain in sales. The *Searchlight* allegedly paid well to distribute bundles of the newspaper to local newsstands for sale. One *Fiery Cross* salesman, Charles Holder of Indiana, told a local newspaper that he was a salaried employee who didn't "know anything about the Klan except what is in the paper," and claimed to be "as much at sea regarding it as you are." He had already sold almost a thousand copies in just one of the towns he was responsible for.[17]

Holder's sales were not out of the ordinary. The *Fiery Cross* broke down its sales agents into four categories, the highest-ranked of whom regularly sold more than a thousand copies. In Cleveland, more than a thousand copies were sold on a single corner in one Saturday afternoon. Some special issues sold even faster. One paper reporting on Klan-related murders in Louisiana (and absolving the Klan of all blame) managed to sell more than two thousand copies in a small Nebraska town. When the *Fiery Cross* issued an extra attacking the anti-Klan American Unity League, distributors "formed a steady stream into the circulation department until midnight." Corner sellers, meanwhile, "left the office with every pound of papers they could possibly lug" and "did not get a block . . . before having to return for more."[18]

These sales were not entirely without issue. Klan newspapers complained about "Irish" police who charged newspaper sellers with interrupting traffic, operating without a license, disturbing the peace, and "soliciting business in an offensive manner." One "newsboy," Eugene Leavengood, was arrested four times in ten days for selling the *Fiery Cross*—leading him to file a writ of prohibition against the local judge. Vendors in Cleveland claimed to have been "continually threatened by a ring of toughs and pugilists." Perhaps the most abused Klan newspaper salesman was Thomas Lowe of Cincinnati. Almost fifty, and with one leg amputated at the knee, Lowe was abducted and beaten on three separate occasions. Klan newspapers heavily publicized the assaults, emphasizing the vicious nature of anti-Klan activists willing to attack a "crippled news boy."[19]

Yet the fact that demand for these Klan publications was high enough and broad enough to warrant and sustain a widespread public distribution network is an important indicator that cultural tension did not denote cultural separation. Low-level clashes did not prevent Klan newspapers and magazines from being sold openly, publicly, and, most important, profitably. In doing so, the Klannish press largely avoided ghettoization. Members of the organization would have been able to find these publications through their Klaverns. The prevalence of public sales represented the appeal of the movement to a broader swath of the American public. Whether motivated by sympathy or curiosity, hundreds of thousands of Americans were engaging with the imagined community of the Klan on a regular basis. In finding a sizable audience both inside and outside of the organization for messages of a virtuous and heroic Klannish identity, these newspapers were a tremendously valuable form of propaganda.

That propaganda value also meant that the press was of key importance in 1923 in the struggle for control of the organization between founder William Simmons and his erstwhile successor, Hiram Evans. An effort at a bloodless coup—convincing Simmons to become the titular head of the Klan while relinquishing all control to Evans—backfired badly. Unhappy with his new position, Simmons had attempted to either retake his title as Imperial Wizard or create a rival Klan organization. In April 1923, even as the two factions went to court to sue for effective ownership of rights to the Klan organizational brand, the Klannish press fought a proxy war for the support of rank-and-file members.

To combat the loyalist *Searchlight*, which declared "there is only one Klan and Simmons is its head," Evans established the *Imperial Night-Hawk*. The new weekly was an oddity in the Klan press, clearly and expressly created to address members of the organization rather than the wider public. Unlike any other Klan publications, the *Night-Hawk* was not available on newsstands or street corners, or for purchase of any kind. Nor did it carry any advertising. It was distributed weekly to Klaverns around the country for free as "the house organ of your order." The *Night-Hawk* declared its sole mission to be to "promote the high ideals of the Klan," even as it engaged in attacks on the Americanism of Simmons and his supporters.[20]

The balance of power in the battle for the hearts and minds of Klan members lay with the *Fiery Cross*, the most widely read of the publications under Imperial control. After editor Ernest Reichard was ousted and replaced by Evans ally Milton Elrod, it became clear that the tide had turned decisively in the battle for control of the organization. Final victory against Simmons arrived in November 1923, when Evans supporters took control of the *Searchlight* as well. By then, however, the new Imperial Wizard had decided that control of the Imperial publications was not enough.[21]

Now secure in his position, Evans hoped to use the Invisible Empire as a power base for entry into national politics. To do so, the Klan head would need to appeal not just to members but to a wide coalition of white Protestant Americans. Evans had to reach beyond the organization to rally the broader movement. The fractious and fractured nature of the independent Klan press, though, represented a fundamental challenge to his political power. Nowhere was the federalized nature of the organization more evident than in the multiplicity of voices offered up by these publications. While they coalesced around a common culture, their failure to speak as one—to challenge and contradict the authority and decisions of Evans and his administration on many issues—represented an embarrassment to the Klan's ostensible leaders. As the Imperial Wizard explained to an interviewer, one of the greatest problems the organization faced was the "control of newspapers" that attempted to speak for the Klan without authority. High-ranking members, with no apparent sense of irony, even went so far as to complain that the use of the "hate programme" to increase circulation by these publications was tarring the good name of the Klan.[22]

By early 1924, it was clear to Evans that something had to be done. The solution presented itself in the unassuming form of Milton Elrod of Indiana. Despite somewhat unorthodox journalistic credentials, his backing of Evans had won him editorship of the *Fiery Cross* and a position among Evans's top lieutenants.[23] Now he would become the head of the Klan's new Bureau of Publication and Education. Elrod was responsible for "renovating Evans . . . and selling him as an impeccable product to the American people." To do so, he would have to take control of the Klannish press.[24]

Elrod set about his task with aplomb. While its ideas were nothing new, the bureau's aims and organization were thoroughly modern. Seeing the growing control of press chains and syndicates, Elrod declared the bureau to be a competitor to increasingly large wire services like the Associated Press. The Klan's new news-gathering service would operate as an alternative "national news service" for true Americans. The existing media, increasingly monopolized by a few outside interests, could not be trusted to supply the "vital facts" that the Klan wire service would provide.[25]

The notable success of the *Fiery Cross* had already moved the Klan press toward original reporting. Under Reichard, the Indiana weekly began to establish an organization of staff correspondents throughout the Midwest tasked with covering "every event of importance and happenings in, and of interest to, the citizens of the Invisible Empire, as well as to hundreds of thousands of 100 per cent Protestant American citizens." The Bureau of Publication and

Education would extend this network nationwide. In accordance with Evans's growing political aspirations, the wire service would have its base in the nation's capital, and allow any sufficiently patriotic periodical to carry the news provided by the new bureau.[26]

Under the direction of Elrod and the bureau, the *Fiery Cross* would become the official national newspaper of the Invisible Empire, supplementing the *Imperial Night-Hawk* as a mouthpiece for Evans's ambitions. To be effective in that role, it seemed to the organization's leaders that the *Fiery Cross* and the *Night-Hawk* would need to be the *only* Klan publications. All others would either be bought out, kowtow to Evans, or be run into the ground. As journalist Stanley Frost explained, Elrod's task was to "organize a string of Klan papers throughout the country which shall be under absolute control" and "reform or drive out the present sheets." Ex-Klansman Edgar Allen Booth described the process more colorfully, and perhaps more accurately, as "the strangling to death of papers opposing Evans." Either way, change was at hand.[27]

By 1924, there were already eleven state editions of the *Fiery Cross*, including the main Indiana publication, with a claimed circulation of over two hundred thousand. Elrod now planned to create a network of up to thirty state editions of the paper, estimated to reach a circulation of over seven hundred thousand and an actual readership of more than four million. Under strict central control, these state editions would carry "state news and editorial matter of state interests." The Bureau of Publication and Education would provide centrally distributed and approved "honest" news, "uncontrolled and unbiased." Such was their conviction that the success of the weekly was assured, Elrod and Evans also suggested that once the *Fiery Cross*'s national prominence had been assured, the Invisible Empire would establish three daily newspapers.[28]

The bureau's announcement of these plans came with more than a suggestion of hostility to all newspapers not a part of this official network, underlining once again the fractures between the Klan organization and movement. Independent publications, the *Night-Hawk* explained, although they had "rendered and are still rendering a great service to the organization," were expressions of "personal opinions and policies." Thus, the magazine argued, the "controversial matter" they often offered did not represent "the national Klan thought." If so desired, the bureau would supply papers with content if they "honestly desire the service and use it in the spirit which it may be given." It was time for the press of the Klan movement to fall in line or face the wrath of the organization's national leadership.[29]

As one of the newspapers that had rendered "great service" to the Invisible Empire, the *Call of the North* transitioned seamlessly into its new role as the *Minnesota Fiery Cross* without any interruption to its regular publication schedule. Although the paper was now credited to the Klan's own Empire Publishing Company, the switch had not even required a change in editor. The focus of the newspaper would remain on "news of the Klan arising within the borders of the Gopher state." If a distracted reader had not noticed the change of name when they picked it up, there was little to immediately point to the fact that it was technically a different paper.[30]

Others refused to go quietly. In September 1924, when its official state rival appeared for sale, the *Badger American* responded defiantly. "Many were under the impression that the *Badger American* would quit," an editorial explained, but "the only thing that would cause this publication to quit is lack of support." Having long proclaimed its autonomy from the national organization, the newspaper quickly jettisoned most of its Klan news and renewed its focus on anti-Catholic attacks. It was to little avail. As it moved away from the "newsy" style of the popular Klan press, and with an organization-approved competitor, the *Badger American* saw a steep decline in subscribers and the departure of most of the newspaper's advertisers. Shortly thereafter, the publication, which could once have claimed to be a major source of Klan power in Wisconsin and allegedly circulated from Alabama to Montana to New York, disappeared entirely.[31]

Similar scenarios unspooled across the country as the Klan flexed its financial muscle, and paper after paper was either bought up or forced out of business. Ex-Klansman Edgar Allen Booth called the process an "orgy of spending" that saw newspapers purchased "with reckless abandon." At the organization's 1924 Klonvokation (or annual conference), the national Klan's Finance Committee reported that twenty-one papers had been purchased for the oddly precise amount of $86,368.41. Booth estimated the cost in the "hundreds of thousands of dollars." The Imperial Wizard noted only that "putting the Klan press under control" had been a "difficult task." Whatever the price, "it was achieved and the achievement was of great value." The Klan's leaders felt no need to hide the fact that dissenting voices would be "discontinued at an early date."[32]

This process was anything but smooth, however. Evans first lost Elrod, whose departure from the Klan was surrounded by controversy, and then the name of the paper itself. The American Order of Scottish Clans, whose official publication was also called the *Fiery Cross*, finally won their lawsuit preventing the Klan from impinging on their copyright. The Invisible Empire

was forced to change the name of their official publication to the *Kourier*. In
an effort to save face, they did so while claiming that the change had always
been intended.[33]

At the same time, the organization faced public embarrassment from the
poor handling of the national expansion. In a number of the Invisible Empire's newspaper buyouts, the previous publishers never received the promised compensation. The lucrative *Kluxer* of Ohio, for example, sued the Klan
for two hundred thousand dollars in damages after it emerged that the reward
for halting publication was never paid. The bureau had refused a written con-
tract, as "they were all Klansmen together and Klansmen needed no written
agreement because Klansmen always did the things they agreed to do." In
their efforts to unify the movement behind Evans and the organization, the
Klan's leaders were producing dissatisfaction and dissension.[34]

Nonetheless, the bureau's campaign for control rolled on. By November
1924, even the *Searchlight*, the first paper taken over by Imperial Wizard Simmons, had been subsumed into the *Kourier* network. As an article in the last
issue explained, the *Searchlight* had actually been placed under the bureau
more than a year earlier. The intervening period had been dedicated to "per-
fecting a central organization," the newspaper boasted, but now "all that is
necessary" was complete. "Every section of the United States can be served"
by the Bureau of Publication and Education—"all radiating from a single
point, yet maintaining the local touch."[35]

To a remarkable extent, this was true. The Klan's leadership had succeeded
in building a national newspaper syndicate that would effectively dominate
the news much of its membership would read, and shape the public image
of the movement. In doing so, the new national weekly built on the example
of both its Klannish predecessors and the larger contemporary press landscape. The *New York Herald Tribune*, also established in 1924, would later
be described as "a Protestant paper," a publication not designed to appeal to
"the ethnic mix of the city." It was a description that the Klan's leaders would
happily have applied to their new newspaper. The *Kourier* represented a new
means for the organization to advocate for the Klan as a respectable mainstream movement in American society.[36]

Combining the sensationalism of the New York tabloids with the local
flavor of a state weekly, the Klan's flagship publication exemplified the porous
boundaries of cultural accommodation in the 1920s. The amalgamation of
the "newsy" style with the Invisible Empire's ideals had already proven highly
popular with a wide audience. The *Kourier* solidified that trend to significant success. By December 1924, there were sixteen different editions of the
newspaper. An eight-page weekly, sold for five cents, circulating in at least

twenty-one states, the newspaper syndicate claimed a paid circulation of one and a half million. This number was likely inflated, but even if the *Kourier* only sold a third of what the bureau claimed, the Klan newspaper was one of the most-read publications in the country. Although nowhere near a rival to the perennially best-selling *Saturday Evening Post*, which claimed a total readership of potentially ten million people, the *Kourier* seemingly far out-stripped the recently founded *Time* magazine, which claimed a circulation of fifty thousand.[37]

The front page of each edition of the *Kourier* was dedicated almost ex-clusively to Klan news from within the appropriate state or states. The or-ganization relied on individual Klaverns to supply these local reports. The Grand Dragon of Illinois, writing to one Klavern, suggested that "if you have a newspaper editor or reporter among your membership" or "someone who is fitted for such work," they should be appointed "*Kourier* correspondent." This correspondent would be given special credentials and instructions from the bureau. The nominated member would then be responsible for offering "details of happenings," or at least summarizing them for the capsule reports printed on the front page.[38]

The vaunted Bureau of Publication wire service supplied the rest of the edition's content, offering a centrally distributed selection of articles that of-fered a "newsy" mix. While Klan news from around the nation remained prominent, the *Kourier* also made a concerted effort to cover major national news and politics. Declaring that its service in providing the "truth" would allow for discussion of "serious problems by serious people," the Klan news-paper seemingly took its role in earnest. Lest anyone doubt the organization's commitment to compete with other digest news organizations, the *Kourier* supplemented its longer political coverage with a regular section titled "Im-portant News of the Week for Busy Readers." As well as the official editorials, which appeared without a byline, analysis of the week's happenings by Felix Free appeared in the "Current Comment" section. Even other newspapers commented on the apparent mainstream appeal of the reporting offered.[39]

A more unusual form of editorializing, owing a clear debt to one of the most popular columnists in the country, Don Marquis, was also featured in the *Kourier*. Appearing first in the *New York Sun* in 1916 and then in the *New York Tribune* from 1922 to 1925, Marquis's characters of Archy and Mehitabel had become favorites of thousands of readers. In creating these characters, the newspaper columnist earned favorable comparisons to Ben Jonson and Mark Twain. Archy, a cynical poet in the body of a cockroach, and Mehita-bel, an alley cat who claimed to be the reincarnation of Cleopatra, gave voice to Marquis's wide-ranging satires of modern life. The cockroach and the cat offered commentary in free verse on topics as varied as Lenin, radio broad-casting, and the place of humanity in the universe.[40]

Marquis was clearly no supporter of the Invisible Empire. The Klan made several appearances in his work—including as the Krew Krux Kranks in a column that ambitiously commented on both the inherent dangers of pa-triotic vigilantism and the Armenian genocide. The writers of the Bureau of Publication, though, were apparently enamored with Archy and Mehitabel. The regularly featured "Klan Ket" column in the *Kourier* aped Marquis, pre-senting social commentary under cover of the adventures of the official Klan kitten.[41]

The "Klan Ket" was far from the only feature in the Klan newspaper to stretch the definition of news. The Bureau of Publication and Education had astutely made sure to carry over some of the most popular features from the publications that the *Kourier* had supplanted, including the poetry of "Twi-light's Thinklings" from the *Call of the North* and the *Fiery Cross*'s "Sparks from the Fiery Cross" by John Eight Point. In a reflection of contemporary American journalism's affinity for "lifestyle" pieces, the bureau also made sure that the paper would appeal to the whole white Protestant family. "The Hearthstone of America" was a special section for female readers, includ-ing parenting tips and recipes that all too often featured cream cheese. Like the *Daily News* or the astoundingly popular new magazine *True Story*, the *Kourier* offered stories of the embarrassments and triumphs of its readers. The children, meanwhile, could turn to "A Junior Today—A Klansman To-morrow." On this page of juvenile Klannish news and "educational" guidance, youthful readers could also enjoy the "Chuckles!" section, which reprinted short jokes from other publications.[42]

There was no better example of the *Kourier*'s effort to position itself in the American cultural milieu than the crossword puzzle. Crossword puzzles had originally appeared in the *New York World* in 1912 to a relatively muted appre-ciation. By the time the *Kourier* was established, however, the crossword had become a national sensation. When the fledgling publishers Simon & Schus-ter released the first ever book of crossword puzzles in 1924, they sparked one of the fads that defined the 1920s. Even as the bureau created the Klan-nish press syndicate, the country's nonfiction best-seller list was dominated by crossword puzzle books. Readers of the *Kourier* were no exception to this puzzle mania. Thus, the Invisible Empire's weekly published a "Fiery Cross-Word Puzzle," presenting crosswords in a variety of uplifting shapes, includ-ing the Klan's blood-drop insignia, the Liberty Bell, and a Junior Klansman. It was such a success that the newspaper started offering a special crossword puzzle dictionary (Winston-Universal edition) as a reward for buying two subscriptions. The 1920s saw Klan members and opponents alike enjoying the thrill of unlocking the secrets of 7 Across and 42 Down.[43]

As the syndicate saw success, the Bureau of Publication and Education also extended its *Kourier* brand. In December 1924, the weekly *Imperial Night-Hawk* was scrapped and replaced by a new thirty-two-page monthly, the *Kourier Magazine*. Tasked with publishing "articles of an educational value rather than current news of Klan activities," the magazine explained that it would "deal with the deeper things of our national life." In practical terms, that meant filling the magazine with paeans to Protestantism, long discussions on the Klan's relationship with the virtues of Christianity, and numerous speeches and statements by Imperial Wizard Evans. The *Kourier Magazine* also highlighted subjects that the Bureau of Publication and Education felt were most important to Americans, publishing special themed issues on public education and the nature of patriotism.[44]

As 1925 began, with a central wire service and national newspaper syndicate to call its own, the Invisible Empire appeared to have triumphed. Although opposition undoubtedly remained, it was comparatively muted. Unlike earlier papers, the *Kourier*'s most visible face—its "newsboys"—went largely unmolested by both police and passersby, sold on newsstands and street corners across the country. Packaging Klannish ideals within contemporary press trends, the *Kourier* presented the Klan not as a violent and hateful vigilante group but as an appealing band of patriotic, law-abiding, white Protestants. In the *Kourier*, Evans had created a propagandistic information network that reached far beyond the organization's membership.

This triumph, however, was built on a fragile foundation. As with so many Klan achievements, the *Kourier* syndicate quickly crumbled. The first sign of trouble came with the disappearance of many of the state editions. At the beginning of 1925, the Bureau of Publication and Education had ambitiously patented the *Kourier* name in twenty-nine states, preparing for further expansion.[45] By the middle of the year, the *Kourier* was distributing only eight regional editions—all of which would soon be absorbed into a single national edition, the *National Kourier*. This last remaining vestige of the syndicate limped along for another year, but never regained its previous cachet. By 1927, the Klan's national newspaper network had disappeared.[46]

The *Kourier Magazine* was even less successful. Although directly circulated to Klaverns, the magazine had seemingly never decided whether it should appeal purely to members of the organization or to the wider movement. As a 1929 editorial revealingly explained, the magazine had attempted to be both the "official organ of the Order" and "the spokesman for the Klan to the alien world." This somewhat schizophrenic approach meant that they

could neither "fill the pages with inside Klan news" nor dedicate the publication to entirely "alien" subject matter either. This left a magazine that clumsily mixed overfamiliar restatements of Klan "principle and policy" in opposition to Roman Catholicism with features like "Klan Kiddies Korner" and the comic animal stories of Old Man Ganderspank. Cartoons, a short-lived adventure fiction section, and *True Story*–style essay competitions sat alongside castigations of Catholic influence in the public schools. The balance that had propelled the success of the *Kourier* weekly eluded the monthly. "The two purposes, each essential," the *Kourier Magazine* despaired, "got in each other's way, and each prevented a wholly satisfactory carrying out of the other.[47]

This was particularly evident in terms of revenue. With new members flooding into the organization, the Klan's leaders had decided that the magazine was valuable enough for outreach to subsidize as a loss leader. Breaking very sharply from publishing trends, then, the *Kourier Magazine* would be distributed free of charge *and* without any lucrative advertising. As the rate of new memberships began to slow, and existing members started to fall away, it became increasingly difficult to justify that decision. By February 1925, the magazine had begun to charge a one-dollar subscription to keep the publication afloat—"not done to make money, but to conserve the situation." The magazine's direct-mail circulation protected it from the vagaries of newsstand sales, allowing it to outlast the weekly newspaper. But as Klan membership, and therefore readership for the official magazine, fell precipitously, it proved an ultimately unsustainable model.[48]

In March 1929, the monthly became a quarterly. In April, the publication admitted it could not serve two audiences, splitting into a "Klan edition" and an "open edition," but it was already too late to stem the organizational collapse. With fewer and fewer members to sell to, the Klan edition was scrapped in 1930. The wider reach of the movement allowed the open edition to run until 1936, but it never gained the kind of readership that the 1920s had seen.[49]

As with the decline of the Klan organization as a whole, it is difficult to determine any single reason as to why the Klan's press network suffered such a precipitous collapse. Certainly, the Invisible Empire's rapid drop in membership after 1925 played a key role. The *Kourier* syndicate had reached its apex in late 1924, some six months after Congress passed the Johnson-Reed Immigration Act. Severely limiting "undesirable" immigration from southern and eastern Europe, the act also blunted some of the Klan's appeal to the wider nativist movement. While this alone was not responsible for the Klan's collapse from 1925 onward, this legislation undoubtedly had an impact—as did the arrest of Indiana Grand Dragon D. C. Stephenson for rape and murder in early 1925. An organization that had begun hemorrhaging members could hardly expect to retain the same kind of readership base that its newspapers had once enjoyed. Locked into a vicious cycle of decline, the weakened *Kourier* organization was unable to then staunch the steady stream of Knights abandoning their membership.

Even as its organizational base was eroded, the *Kourier* syndicate was unable to rely on its efforts to reach a wider audience. Much of this problem lay within. Imperial Wizard Evans's cornerstone achievement suffered from the same kind of mismanagement that had plagued the organization of the Invisible Empire since its inception. Edgar Allen Booth made reference to "the fighting, bickering, plotting and incompetency . . . going on behind the scenes." Lawsuits alleging broken promises and misdealing did not end with the *Kluxer* suit in 1924. Cases in Missouri and Iowa, among others, generated damning headlines in newspapers across the country.[50]

Reflecting the lasting division between the organization and the lived ideology of the movement, these management issues were exacerbated by the kind of independent publications the Klan's leadership had attempted to eliminate. Although the Bureau of Publication and Education had managed to either buy up or force out a large number of the *Kourier*'s predecessors, there was still significant competition from "unofficial" newspapers for the readers of the wider Klan movement. Milton Elrod returned to the publishing field with the *Daily American* in 1924 and the *National Democrat* in 1925. In an effort to repeat the success of the broad humor of Fawcett's *Captain Billy's Whiz Bang*, Klan members in Pittsburgh offered a more unusual take on Klannish publishing with the launch of their own "funny monthly," *Komic Klan Kracks*.

C. Lewis Fowler of New York City, a friend and close ally of William J. Simmons, attracted a significant following in 1924 and 1925 to his *American Standard*. Setting aside the reserve of the *Kourier*, Fowler used the pages of the *Standard* to wage a campaign against American Catholics and Jews that would have made the *Badger American* blanch. One historian has called it "a semimonthly of a particularly latrine nature." This underestimates a publication that claimed telepathic Jesuits had murdered President Harding. Even still, Fowler demonstrated that there was success to be had in publishing an independent alternative to the official Klan press and inspired a number of imitators.[51]

Making matters worse, as the organization itself collapsed, the *Kourier* not only had to compete with rival Klan newspapers, but also with publications established by new splinter groups. As contemporaries noted, "Offshoots of the Invisible Empire are undermining it." In California, for example, the new Knights of the White Cross Clan welcomed defectors to their ranks. Their

California Advance not only competed with the official Klan press for readers; it attacked the organization itself as a "dead issue."[52]

The Klan's leadership had themselves fostered some of these rivals for readership. The *Fellowship Forum*, one of the few semi-independents to survive the bureau's purge, clearly demonstrated that the Klan movement reached far beyond the members of the Klan organization. It was, without doubt, a Klan newspaper and openly espoused the Klan's ideology. Edgar Fuller, a former aide to Edward Young Clarke, claimed in 1924 that the Klan's leaders paid a thousand dollars a month to editor George Moore. Ex-Klansman Edgar Allen Booth similarly alleged that "money from the Klan treasury has poured with a lavish hand" into the *Fellowship Forum*. Even as he forced other flourishing publications out of business, Hiram Evans gave the *Forum* his official imprimatur, telling the newspaper, "I am anxious that you prosper in the work which you are doing." The Imperial Wizard noted that the weekly was "filling a niche peculiarly its own in the patriotic newspaper field." Similarly, Robbie Gill Comer, head of the Women's Klan, wrote to her members to enthuse that the *Forum* was doing "a very splendid piece of work" and encouraged Klanswomen to support the publication.[53]

That niche in the patriotic newspaper field was as a popular crossover publication, with appeal to both members and nonmembers across the country. The Grand Dragon of Oklahoma enthused that the *Forum* was the "best publication issued for the dissemination of pure Americanism" and "the principles of the Knights of the Ku Klux Klan," with the "possible exception" of the *Kourier* and *Kourier Magazine*. The value of the *Forum*, the Grand Dragon explained, was its ability to attract readers who eschewed official Klan publications. By reading the *Forum*, though, they would still obtain "the viewpoint and information we want them to have."[54]

The *Forum*, like the *Kourier*, took a "newsy" approach to providing that viewpoint. The weekly, which varied between eight and twelve pages long, declared itself "the LEADER in the field of Fraternal Journalism." In practical terms, that meant the same kind of mix of content found in the official Klan publications. Flattering news of Klan events and other fraternal organizations dominated the *Forum*'s pages, alongside longer articles on the evils of Catholicism and the benefits of Americanism. At the same time, befitting the newspaper's D.C. location, the *Forum* provided significant coverage of all the latest political news. By 1925, the ambitious weekly even had its own foreign correspondents.[55]

News pieces were supplemented by a variety of human-interest and lifestyle features. Reflecting the growing importance of photography in finding readers, the *Forum* regularly carried pictures of events of interest, from portraits of politicians to Klan weddings. The weekly's editor boasted the "wonderful" diversity of its reporting could rival any newspaper. In a long piece of self-reflection, the publication noted that while the majority of its content was "general news," readers could find plenty of information on Klan events and other fraternal affairs, "miscellaneous" news, "patriotic editorials," and a mix of regular features and special "promotion features." The weekly women's page, for instance, focused on fashion and food. Sympathizers to the movement could have learned how to serve "Klansman's Dream Toast," garnished with a pimento cross, at their next dinner party.[56]

As the Invisible Empire's official press network began to collapse in early 1925, the *Fellowship Forum* played an increasingly important role for the movement. Under the direction of publisher James Vance, the paper eagerly targeted Klan readers as a semiofficial rival that most likely hastened the *Kourier*'s demise. Walla Walla Klan No. 3 of Washington State declared that the paper was "of untold benefit to the Ku Klux Klan" and "one of the best mediums through which we can chronicle the things of interest to our members." Two Klans in Baltimore "went on record endorsing the work of *The Fellowship Forum*." The nearby Mt. Rainier Klan urged members to subscribe to "the Klan paper, the 'Friendship [*sic*] Forum.'"[57]

The *Forum*'s ability and willingness to take the place of the national publication as a respectable mainstream weekly was evident. The year 1925 saw state Klans pitted against each other in a competition to drive the *Forum* to five million readers. The massive national Klan parade through the District of Columbia that year was marked by the *Forum* with a front-page article by W. A. Hamlett, editor of the *Kourier Magazine*, and a specially commissioned poem, "I Am (the Ku Klux Klan)," by "Twilight" Orn, late of the *Minnesota Fiery Cross* and the "Twilight's Thinklings" column in the *Kourier*. At the end of the year, even as the *Kourier* faltered, the *Forum* published an article from Imperial Wizard Evans himself on the topic "What Christmas Means to Members of the Ku Klux Klan." By 1927, with the *Kourier* network defunct, the *Fellowship Forum*'s union with the Invisible Empire became official. The semi-independent newspaper of the Klannish movement was effectively folded into the organization. Readers were encouraged to save money with a joint subscription to the *Forum* and the *Kourier Magazine*.[58]

Ironically, it was this union of movement and organization that marked the beginning of the end for the *Forum*. It is telling that while readers flocked to a publication espousing Klannish ideology, significant sections of that readership were seemingly alienated by an explicit connection between the newspaper and the Klan. Although Vance would continue to publicly deny "Klan affiliations," the increasingly close ties between the publication and the

Invisible Empire had not gone unnoticed. In the eyes of many potential and existing subscribers, it was now a Klan paper, little different from the defunct *Kourier*. Certainly, other newspapers began to classify it as such. In 1925, the *Washington Post* had been happy to refer to the *Forum* as part of the fraternal Protestant press. By 1927, it was simply "a Ku Klux Klan publication."[59]

The Grand Dragon of Oklahoma had once trumpeted the ability of the *Forum* to attract readers who avoided Klan newspapers. That ability now seemed to disappear, and with it the readers. Nor could the *Forum* rely on Klan members to simply replace those numbers. The Klan itself was crumbling. Unable to maintain their official newspaper, there was little chance that the organization would be able to support the *Forum*. Although exact circulation figures do not exist, the *Fellowship Forum* had once boasted a circulation of somewhere between five hundred thousand and a million copies—a powerhouse of Klannish propaganda. By the beginning of 1928, it was "a starving little sheet."[60]

Although weakened, the *Forum* was not yet defunct. It had retained a surprising amount of its former power by diversifying into radio. More importantly, like the Klan organization, it regained a modicum of momentum with the news that there was a Catholic running for president. Governor Al Smith of New York had finally secured the Democratic nomination, and in so doing breathed fresh life into the Ku Klux Klan and its newspaper of choice. An anti-Prohibition Catholic, Smith was everything the *Forum* had fought against since its inception. The fact that he was a Democrat did not help— among the *Forum*'s major stockholders by this point were R. H. Angell, Republican Party chairman for the state of Virginia, and William G. Conley, the Republican nominee for governor of West Virginia. The *Baltimore Afro-American* went so far as to allege that the *Forum* was part of a coordinated appeal by Herbert Hoover's campaign to racial and religious prejudices in an attempt to break the Solid South of the Democratic Party.[61]

Whatever the strength of the official links between the *Fellowship Forum* and the Republican Party, there is no doubt that the *Forum* was one of the most vocal and influential voices of the anti-Smith movement. The paper filled its pages with attacks on the Catholic Church in general, and on Smith in particular. It also focused heavily on what the *Afro-American* called "scurrilous attacks" linking Smith with "Negro Equality."[62] Across the South, issues of the paper were distributed in rural districts "by the bale," allegedly at the expense of the anti-Smith organization. Virginia was flooded with copies, as were Alabama and Tennessee. Editor James S. Vance claimed that the *Forum* now had a readership of over a million, and publicly begged for funds to print an additional hundred thousand copies. Vance explained that if he could succeed in meeting the demand, he was "perfectly confident" the Solid South could be broken by those who believed that electing Smith would mean "Romanizing our Government." It is unclear whether he ever received these funds, but the *Forum* certainly "waxed opulent," in the words of the *Pittsburgh Courier*.[63]

Although it is impossible to determine how effective the *Fellowship Forum*'s anti-Smith campaign was, some measure of its impact is evident in the fact that Governor Smith was drawn to publicly denounce the paper on multiple occasions. During a radio address from Oklahoma, Smith answered some of the "senseless, stupid, foolish attacks" offered by the "notorious" *Forum*. At a speech in Baltimore before a crowd of over twenty thousand, Smith condemned "that gallant band of patriots known as the Ku Klux Klan" for "promoting the Republican candidacy." For "a sample of their handiwork," he encouraged the audience to read "their official organ," the *Fellowship Forum*. Every "contemptible" issue, Smith declared, contained "the most outrageous abuse that it would be possible to direct against a large body of American citizens." The *Badger American* would have been proud.[64]

On November 6, Herbert Hoover won forty states to Al Smith's eight. Among those that had gone for Hoover were Virginia, which had not gone to a Republican since 1872, as well as Tennessee, West Virginia, North Carolina, Florida, and Texas. The *Fellowship Forum* had won its victory against Smith and the threat of "Romanized government." But in its victory, the newspaper found defeat. Without an immediate threat like Smith's candidacy to inflate circulation, and without anti-Smith forces (whether official or unofficial) providing funding, the boom in the *Forum*'s fortunes soon vanished.

As with the *Kourier Magazine*, the *Forum* did not disappear immediately. The weekly continued to limp along until early 1937, but it had receded into irrelevancy. Without the Klan to lend it a crusade or a readership, the *Forum* had little to offer to its dwindling audience but run-of-the-mill histrionic diatribes against the publication's new enemies, Communists and Bolsheviks. The Invisible Empire disappeared from public view, and the *Forum*—like the *Kourier* before it—disappeared from newsstands. As it did so, it disappeared from popular memory. The Fiery Cross-Word, and all that it signified, were swiftly forgotten. In the process, we lost our understanding of what the success and squabbles of the "newsy" Klannish press revealed—the fluid cultural divisions of the period as Klan members and sympathizers railed against the press even as they adopted the trappings of the modern newspaper to promote a national identity of white Protestant heroism; the Invisible Empire's strained efforts to garner both visibility and respectability; and the shattering tensions between the Klan organization's leadership and the wider Klan movement.

4

The Good, the Bad, and the Best Sellers

The power of the printed page is so great that it is folly to ignore the influence of books and magazines.

MINNESOTA FIERY CROSS, May 23, 1924

The publication of *Civilization in the United States* in 1922 "made a considerable sensation," according to H. L. Mencken. Edited by Harold E. Stearns, a young friend and admirer of Mencken, *Civilization* was an ambitious consideration of "the problem of modern American civilization as a whole." Thirty-three commentators—many of whom had been suggested by Mencken, who also contributed a chapter on politics—offered what the Sage of Baltimore called a "sharply realistic point of view." Arthur M. Schlesinger, in his review of the collection, was less favorable in his appraisal. The noted historian and intellectual called it "supercilious" criticism, and complained that important subjects were treated "cynically and flippantly."[1]

Stearns's collection marked an early example of what one historian has referred to as the "new estrangement" of American intellectuals in the postwar period. As Louis Raymond Reid bemoaned in his chapter "The Small Town," the intellectual "may try to get in" to American cultural life, "but the doors are usually barred." Contributors like George Jean Nathan, Lewis Mumford, and Frederic C. Howe bemoaned the "unmistakably provincial" nature of American civilization. For many, there was no choice but to escape the "emotional and aesthetic starvation" of the United States for the virtues of the great nations of Europe.[2]

Much has been written on this avowed estrangement. Yet it is important to remember that, for all the discussion that surrounded the publication of *Civilization*, the collection had by 1924 sold less than five thousand copies in the United States, Canada, and England combined. Even in 1922, Schlesinger argued that "the future historian of American life" would find *Civilization* "valuable not as criticism of present-day civilization but as an aid to understanding a certain type of intellectual activity and outlook which is well represented in the persons of the authors." As Mark Greif has noted, generations of critics have retroactively canonized a pantheon of cultural masterpieces to serve contemporary needs. Doing so has simultaneously served to delimit popular understanding of "American literature." Too often, we have focused on the critics and not on the subject of their criticisms.[3]

Mencken divided the world of publishing between the books "that no one reads and those that no one ought to read." Best sellers are often the worst cultural survivors. In losing this work from analysis of the period, though, we lose the reading habits of the majority of Americans. By ensuring what might now be deemed middlebrow or lowbrow fare is folded into the historical record alongside more sophisticated works, we garner a far richer understanding of American culture and society. In following Erin A. Smith's cue to engage seriously with "bad" books, including the literary lowlights of the Invisible Empire, we garner greater insight into the Ku Klux Klan's ambivalent consumption of American literature and American literature's ambivalent consumption of the Klan.[4]

We need to understand the popular in American literature not least because more Americans were reading more books than ever before. The term "best seller" came into common use for the first time in the 1920s as the decade saw a literary boom in American life. Almost six thousand books were published in the United States in 1919. Ten years later, that number had increased almost 60 percent, fueled by a rise in the consumption of everything from hardbound scholarly works to inexpensive paperbacks, from reprinted classics to pulp fiction. The ranks of American publishing houses swelled, encouraging an increasingly literate population to devote their time to reading—romance novels and biographies of great Americans, mysteries and journalistic studies. The number of public libraries grew, as did the size of their collections and their use. The "average American" of the twenties apparently read seven books a year—buying two, withdrawing four from public or circulating libraries, and borrowing one from a friend.[5]

Even these growing numbers likely underestimate the number of books being produced and read by Americans in the 1920s. Before the First World War, an estimated 90 percent of books were sold outside bookshops. While that was beginning to change, there were still only around fifteen hundred book dealers in the United States by 1925, almost all of whom were found in large cities. For those outside major urban areas, door-to-door and mail-order sales were often the primary means of obtaining reading material. These alternative supply networks often make it difficult to obtain reliable information on the sales of certain titles, even as the decade saw major new avenues of distribution. The Book of the Month Club (BOMC) appeared in 1926, sending out almost five thousand copies of Sylvia Townsend Warner's *Lolly Willowes*, an English comedy of manners. The BOMC was soon joined by the likes of the Literary Guild, offering curated middlebrow fare to increasing numbers of American readers, and the Religious Book Club, as the number of religious books published increased dramatically.[6]

Just as there was no one type of distribution, there was no one type of publisher. For some, Horace Liveright was the emblem of this publishing boom, the "Ziegfeld of his profession." His firm, Boni & Liveright, was "the Jazz Age in a microcosm." Representing Ernest Hemingway, T. S. Eliot, Ezra Pound, William Faulkner, and Sherwood Anderson, among many others, he published seven Nobel Prize winners in a decade. Key members of the firm went on to found Simon & Schuster and Random House, shaping the future of American publishing.[7]

But Boni & Liveright was an outlier. In H. L. Mencken's estimation, most of the major firms dedicated themselves to "merchandising garbage that should make any self-respecting publisher blush." Established publishing houses tended to be bastions of conservatism, unwelcoming to African Americans and Jews, hostile to avant-garde or radical literature. At the same time, these companies were often looking for profits over Nobel Prizes. Hemingway might have brought plaudits, but—as trade publishers increasingly aware of the lucrative religious market knew—Giovanni Papini's *Life of Christ* was going to sell more copies.[8]

A publisher like Bobbs-Merrill arguably offers a far better understanding of the wider culture of the 1920s. The Indianapolis-based publishing house may not have attracted the same acclaim as Boni & Liveright, but it issued some of the most popular books of the decade. *Race or Nation* by Gino Speranza, which attracted praise from the Klan for its argument on the Anglo-Saxon underpinnings of American democracy, sat alongside adventurer Richard Halliburton's best-selling *The Royal Road to Romance* in the publisher's catalog. Felix Weiss's nativist tract *The Immigration Sieve* and Albert Wiggam's eugenicist *New Decalogue of Science* rubbed shoulders with Julia Peterkin's *Scarlet Sister Mary*. This groundbreaking novel offered an unsentimental depiction of African American life, attracted praise for the white author from W. E. B. DuBois, and won the Pulitzer Prize. Bruce Barton's *The Man Nobody Knows*, depicting a rugged Jesus as an example to modern businessmen, became one of the best-selling books of the twentieth century. All were published by Bobbs-Merrill.

When we look at this wider reading culture, we better understand the Ku Klux Klan movement's complex relationship with contemporary literary life—as consumer, creator, and subject. Popular perceptions of the Invisible

Empire make it easier to imagine Klan members simply as self-righteous cen-
sors with a propensity for burning books. To an extent, this was true. Like
many other groups, Klan members condemned "filthy fiction" and "salacious"
literature. A significant section of postwar literature did not meet with Klannish approbation. Stories of "unmarried mothers, concubines, free-lovers,
vampires, human wrecks," would, they claimed, "tear larger the hole in the
fabric of society" by helping corrupt the morals of the young. As the *American Standard* succinctly argued, "The reading of trashy novels and magazines
poisons the mind."[9]

This was not a fringe position to take. Many condemned the "lurid sensationalism" that could be found in the "diversions offered the shopgirl and
the clerk" in the 1920s, in the words of literary scholar Frederick J. Hoffman.
Leaders of the Catholic Church publicly declared war on "the moral offal that
passes for the best sellers of the day."[10] Methodist periodical *Zion's Herald* denounced postwar fiction as a "sea of filth." The New York Society for the Sup-
pression of Vice pushed for passage of a Clean Books Bill that would allow the
censorship of any publication containing even a single passage judged "filthy
or disgusting." The Salvation Army, the Knights of Columbus, the Y.M.C.A,
Rabbi Stephen S. Wise, and more came together to organize the "Clean
Books" crusade of 1923–25. Historian Paul S. Boyer called this effort "the most
far-reaching challenge to American literary freedom in the 1920s," if not in
the twentieth century. The Klan was far from alone in its blustery criticisms.[11]

If we are guided by this rhetoric of puritanism—and by the equally spiky
complaints of the Menckenians about "provincial" American culture—it is
tempting to imagine clear and immutable battle lines of cultural consumption. If we look less at rhetoric and more at the lived ideology of reading habits, however, then that cultural divide seems far less deep and far more fluid.
Ironically, Stearns's castigation of the state of civilization in the United States
points us toward one of the clearest indications that there were few clear-cut
divisions in these cultural debates. The concerns of Stearns were just one part
of a boomlet of books that promised "an assessment of the status of civilization to date," a "balance sheet" for the American people. Both Warren I.
Susman and James D. Hart have identified these reflections on postwar life
as one of the most widespread types of publication in the twenties. As Joan
Shelley Rubin has noted, the boom in both book production and readership
had made many publishers alive to the "journalistic and commercial opportunities" these kinds of books presented.[12]

Since no honest consideration of contemporary life in the Jazz Age was
complete without the Ku Klux Klan, the movement was an inescapable presence in these assessments of "civilization." The Lynds' groundbreaking social

study, *Middletown*, for one, was unable to provide a comprehensive view of modern life without frequent reference to the Invisible Empire. The same was true of Preston W. Slosson's *The Great Crusade and After*, Chandra Chakraberty's *The United States of America*, Philip Gibbs's *Ten Years After*, and more. At the same time, the diverse spectrum of opinion on the organization that could be found in these works—often presenting approval and disapprobation in the same book—underlines the shifting and sometimes contradictory tensions both between different cultural groups and within those same groups.

It is particularly notable, as in newspaper publishing, that it was not just an intellectual choice to discuss the Klan organization and its implications, but often a commercial decision. Book critics frequently focused on a volume's treatment of the Klan as representative of its general quality. *The Bookman*'s review of Slosson's *Great Crusade* singled out the University of Michigan history professor's discussion of the Klan movement as particularly praiseworthy. Chakraberty's *United States*, conversely, was chastised by the *New York Times* for an account of the Klan that "would hardly be accepted by any but a member of that order." At the same time, the Invisible Empire was central to *advertising* these narratives. Many publishers, realizing that the Klan was of considerable popular interest, specifically marketed their work as containing information on the organization. The George H. Doran publishing firm, for example, promoted *Ten Years After* as "ranging from the Dawes report to the Ku Klux Klan."[13]

Popular histories also underlined the importance of the Klan, often implicitly—and sometimes explicitly—endorsing the movement. John W. Burgess and William A. Dunning of Columbia University had argued extensively in the early years of the twentieth century that Reconstruction had to be considered as a tragic mistake, a Northern assault that upended an idyllic South and imposed racial tyranny. Their students continued to promulgate this "cheap and false myth," in the words of W. E. B. DuBois, through the 1920s. In doing so, these historians laid the groundwork for popular understanding of Reconstruction—and of the role of the Ku Klux Klan. The so-called Dunningite interpretation of the era, and particularly the work of Walter L. Fleming, described a besieged South in which the Reconstruction Klan could be understood only as saviors. The organization's violence was a justifiable response to the "monstrous" threat of the Freedmen's Bureau, the Union League, and black voters. As DuBois noted, to accept this mangling of history necessarily meant that white Americans would have to "embrace and worship the color bar as social salvation"—not just in the past, but in contemporary America. These historians effectively laid a mental framework for the revival of the Klan, allowing William J. Simmons to claim the mantle of Southern redemption. As far as both the organization's leaders and the wider cultural movement were concerned, the Klan had returned to save the United States once again.[14]

The idea that it was often the Klan's presence—contemporary and historical—in these books that attracted most interest from readers is underlined by the explosion of purportedly academic Klan analysis that appeared in print in the 1920s. These works explicitly appealed to a desire to learn as much about the workings of the organization of the Invisible Empire as possible. At the same time, much as many newspapers had done, they attempted to present a "balanced" view of the movement and its ideals. The Reference Shelf series, for instance, was created in 1923 to provide information on "timely subjects for public discussion." Its seventy-five-cent issue on the Klan collected twenty-eight articles, speeches, and excerpts from both books and official Klan documents, split roughly evenly between pro- and anti-Klan opinion.[15]

Similarly, Nutshell Publishing's *Catholic, Jew, Ku Klux Klan: What They Believe, Where They Conflict* came to the unusual conclusion that Judaism, Catholicism, and Ku Kluxism all had beneficial aspects. The booklet—either boundlessly optimistic or desperately wary of antagonizing readers of any faith—hoped that all three would be merged into "one glowing, 100-per-cent ideal for which we can all stand, without conflict and without prejudice." The highly popular Little Blue Book series, published by Emanuel Haldeman-Julius (at one time, H. L. Mencken's copyboy), offered multiple perspectives on the organization. *KKK: The Kreed of the Klansmen* condemned the Klan's "black wave of bigotry and reaction," while the far more positive *Is the Ku Klux Klan Constructive or Destructive?* included powerful defenses of the "law-loving, justice-loving, peace-loving" organization. An education in the issues of the day seemingly was not complete without a consideration of the Ku Klux Klan—both positive and negative.[16]

Longer works attempted to place the Klan within a wider context. In doing so, these books demonstrated the prominent but ambiguous place the Invisible Empire held within American popular consciousness. Published in 1924, *Five Present-Day Controversies* by Charles Jefferson, pastor of the Broadway Tabernacle in New York, considered the conflict between the Klan and Catholicism one of the major religious topics of the day, alongside the debates over evolution, the virgin birth, and biblical literalism. Jefferson sympathized with the Klan in its support for public education and its opposition toward the Catholic Church's "mistaken and mischievous" push for parochial schooling. He also understood the Klan's antipathy toward the "autocratic spirit" of Roman Catholicism. Nevertheless, he advised his readers to stay out of the Invisible Empire—a "dangerous movement" that "stirs up the very worst passions" and was, in the end, "futile." This analysis was so popular that Jefferson's chapter on the Ku Klux Klan was reprinted in expanded form the next year as a booklet.[17]

Charles Wright Ferguson's *The Confusion of Tongues*, published in 1928, considered the Ku Klux Klan as part of "the whole pageant of religious oddity in America." A Methodist pastor from Texas turned religious editor at Doubleday books, Ferguson concluded that the Klan was "a religion of the savage mind" best understood as "a malignant religious kult." What is notable about *Confusion of Tongues* is the company in which Ferguson placed the Klan. Readers could find the chapter "Ku Kluxism" nestled snugly between chapters on the Baha'i faith and liberal Catholicism. Other subjects included Christian Science ("The most that can be said . . . is that it has invested drugless healing with blue lights and incense"), Mormonism (a "menace" that flourished "without historical truth of any sort"), and atheism ("the most fervent and evangelical cult in the United States today").[18]

Many critics met Ferguson's comparison of the Klan to other popular religious movements with approval. Gilbert Seldes, one of the country's most influential cultural commentators, gave Ferguson's "cool, but not sneering, appraisal" of the Klan a highly favorable review in *The Bookman*. The book itself was popular enough that it was reprinted the next year under the title *The New Books of Revelations: The Inside Story of America's Astounding Religious Cults*. Doubleday, recognizing the book's main selling points, stressed in its advertising that the book gave "the complete lowdown on American messiahs, from the Mormons to the Ku Klux Klan."[19]

Ferguson's work demonstrates the odd kind of legitimacy that many of these educational and academic publications tacitly bestowed on the Klan movement. Horace M. Kallen's *Culture and Democracy in the United States*, in contrast, was an overt attempt to delegitimize the Invisible Empire's beliefs by presenting a compelling argument for the United States as an inclusive society. A German immigrant who had studied under William James and taught at the New School for Social Research, Kallen had for years criticized the concept of the "melting pot." He posited instead that true democracy involved "not the elimination of differences, but the perfection and conservation of differences"—a view that many Klan members would have agreed with. Where the two parted was that Kallen sought an America welcoming of those differences, while the Klan sought the exclusion of the different.[20]

The most significant section of the 1924 book, predominantly composed of reprints of Kallen's earlier work, was the new postscript (which the author advised be read first), "Culture and the Ku Klux Klan." Kallen warned against a popular "Kultur Klux Klan" as a singular illustration of the kind of antiheterogeneous thinking against which he had been railing for years. Thus, the postscript allowed Kallen to offer the most cogent explanation of his theory of societal inclusivity to date by defining it in direct opposition to Klannish philosophies—and, in the process, coining the phrase (although the idea predated it) of "cultural pluralism."[21]

The impact of *Culture and Democracy* was initially limited. Nicholas Roosevelt in the *New York Times* dismissed Kallen's book as offering "nothing new" and implicitly endorsed the wider Klannish movement, criticizing Kallen for advocating a position that would create a country in which "the hyphen is to be crowned king." By the end of the 1920s, though, the concept of cultural pluralism had already gained some traction. It would have long-term implications for America's post–World War II struggle with definitions of national identity. The Ku Klux Klan's cultural prominence had inspired the sharpening of an argument that struck at the heart of its beliefs, and would have an impact that far outlasted the organization's brief life cycle.[22]

While Kallen's work may have had a greater enduring influence, it was not the most popular work that emerged from the cottage industry of academic Klan analysis in the short term. That honor belonged to two books that heavily influenced early histories of the second Klan. Both John Moffat Mecklin's *The Ku Klux Klan: A Study of the American Mind* and Stanley Frost's *The Challenge of the Klan* were published at the apex of the organization's power in 1924, but provided widely diverging analyses of the Invisible Empire. The two studies—and the ways in which they differ—provide important insight into the heterogeneity and ambiguity of responses to the rise of the Ku Klux Klan and the fluid conflicts within American print culture.

Mecklin, a professor of sociology at Dartmouth, began gathering material for his book in early 1923 by "spending between three and four months in the South and Southwest, interviewing [Klan] leaders and members." The sociologist's study shrewdly questioned the fractured nature of the organization to consider whether the "real Klan" was represented by its hierarchical structures or its grassroots organization. For Mecklin, the Invisible Empire was at heart a "*local* organization." Its appeal lay in "moral idealism" more than in "hates and prejudices," which could "never account for the spread of the Klan." He criticized denunciations of the Invisible Empire for not providing "unbiased and critical" analysis of the organization and emphasized the wider influence of the Klannish movement, stressing that Klan members were "conventional Americans, thoroughly human."[23]

At the same time, many of Mecklin's arguments (which may also have been colored by the sectional nature of his research) owed a clear debt to the H. L. Mencken school of thought, in which "conventional Americans" were largely provincial "boobs." He considered the "strength" of the Klan to lie in the "more or less ignorant and unthinking middle class" found outside the cosmopolitan cities. The Ku Klux Klan was, at its heart, an expression of "the tyranny of the conventionally patriotic, often well-meaning but small-minded, mediocre man." Mecklin agreed with Klan members that the organization was an expression of true Americanism—but, for the sociologist, this Americanism was nothing to be admired.[24]

Publisher Harcourt, Brace emphasized in advertising that the study was "reliable" and written "clearly and calmly." Newspaper reviews echoed this idea, one critic greeting *The Ku Klux Klan* (in a review that sat next to a large advertisement for an upcoming Klan "Barbecue Wedding") as "practically the first reliable account . . . the first outstanding book on the subject published since the rise of the Klan." Similar appraisals appeared around the country, hailing the book's reasoned consideration of the Klan. William MacDonald in the *New York Times* went even further, praising Mecklin's work as "one of the most notable contributions to an understanding of the psychology and pathology of the American mind that has appeared for many a day." Before long, *The Ku Klux Klan* had become the standard text to consult on the Invisible Empire.[25]

While Mecklin attempted to offer a nuanced criticism of the Invisible Empire, Stanley Frost, a journalist, presented a cautious endorsement of the organization. Despite rumors that he was a friend of Milton Elrod, head of the Klan's newspaper bureau, Frost's *Challenge of the Klan*—published by Bobbs-Merrill—was not simply a propagandistic enterprise. The author, drawing an implicit line between the Klan movement and the organization, acknowledged the fear of many that "the mask, in its very nature, is a threat." He noted that the organization was inherently "irresponsible, uncontrollable, autocratic, and terroristic in form." He criticized the Invisible Empire's secrecy as "dangerous, destructive, creative of disunity and hatred." Yet, overall, he concluded that the movement was ultimately beneficial. The Klan had the potential to be "a great power for good or evil in every phase of life," and its "useful actions" seemed "on the whole to outnumber the harmful." To Frost, the organization may have been a bitter pill to swallow, but one that America needed to take.[26]

This hesitant backing of the Ku Klux Klan was the result, at least in part, of an attempt at "judicial reporting." *The Challenge of the Klan* was the expansion and elucidation of a series of articles that Frost had initially written for well-respected weekly *The Outlook*.[27] Instead of obtaining material from Klansmen at the local level, Frost relied heavily on information from the Klan's national leadership, primarily Imperial Wizard Evans. Indeed, large sections of Frost's book resemble nothing more than an extended interview with Evans. Taking the Klan leader at his word, Frost fell to some extent into the trap of confusing rhetoric with reality. Many of the journalist's conclusions echoed the Evans regime's positions—blaming the "violence and graft" of the organization on the Simmons administration, claiming that the Klan had fundamentally changed since Evans's rise to Imperial Wizard, overemphasizing the importance of the national leadership to determining the direction, success, and attitudes of the membership. Yet Frost, like Mecklin, found that the ultimate strength of the Klan organization resided in its wider movement appeal to the "ideals and aspirations" of the "most average man in America." Unlike Mecklin, Frost made clear his admiration for the kind of country that these average Americans had built. In the journalist's estimation, these ideals were not the product of the "ignorant and unthinking," but a reflection of the anxieties "which are distressing all thoughtful men."[28]

In shying away from Mecklin's psychosocial ideas about the reactionary "booboisie," Frost presaged the arguments of current historians of the Klan. The Invisible Empire was presented by Frost as a considered and almost utilitarian response to many of the issues that the "average" American faced in the 1920s: it represented an effort to offer a solution to "grave national problems" that were of "deep concern to all thinking Americans." In an indication of the Invisible Empire's status in modern culture, both Klan and non-Klan publications deemed Frost's argument "fair," "unbiased," and "instructive," although perhaps dealing "too generously" with "certain claims."[29]

The disparate analyses of Mecklin and Frost provide clear confirmation of the tensions present in the nonfiction of the 1920s, but also underline the heterogeneity and ambiguity of opinion that was present. Neither man was a polarized polemicist. There were no clear sides in these cultural struggles. And both suggested that—for both good and evil—the Ku Klux Klan was a significant factor in contemporary American life.

Not all work on the issue was as concerned with nuance, or with claiming legitimacy as academic study. The 1920s saw the creation of a minor cottage industry in the publication of anti- and pro-Klan books, often closely connected to newspapers. The Klan was not only subject, but actor in this ongoing literary discussion, as both Klan members and opponents became authors in an effort to shape the movement's cultural identity. Although there is no record of who purchased these literary efforts, the fact that there was enough of a market to support continued publication of these books is suggestive of the Klan's cultural relevance in the 1920s.

The first major contribution to this literature appeared in response to the attacks leveled against the organization by the *New York World* in 1921. Rushed to publication by the American Newspaper Syndicate, *Story of the Ku Klux Klan* by Colonel Winfield Jones claimed not to be a defense of the organization, but "an accurate description." This assertion was quickly undermined by the publisher's foreword, which falsely claimed that Jones was neither a Southerner nor a Klansman, in its attempt to portray him solely as a "trained and impartial writer." Jones, for his part, claimed to have persuaded a reluctant Imperial Wizard Simmons to allow him access to all Klan records, rituals, correspondence, and accounts.[30]

Given the contents of Jones's book, it is difficult to credit the idea that Simmons was all that reluctant. A little under half the volume was dedicated to lauding the Klan of the Reconstruction era for having "kept the negro quiet" and stopping the "tyrants" of the Freedmen's Bureau—an interpretation firmly within the popular Dunning school of opinion. The remainder of Jones's work consisted of fawning descriptions of Simmons, "the valiant leader of that band of forward looking patriots," and lengthy paeans to the reborn Invisible Empire as a worthy successor to the original Klan. These plaudits included an explicit attack on the *New York World*'s series, suggesting that the newspaper's coverage was masterminded by a vindictive Jewish cabal.[31]

Despite the dubious merits of Jones's work, it opened the floodgates to a veritable deluge of publications boasting of the movement's virtues and consolidating an imagined community of Klannishness. In 1922, C. Lewis Fowler, a Baptist minister from Atlanta and president of the city's Lanier University, published his semiofficial *The Ku Klux Klan: Its Origin, Meaning, and Scope of Operation*. Fowler was a close ally of Imperial Wizard Simmons, and his book parroted the Invisible Empire's official line, depicting the Klan as a positive force that fought to uphold law and order and defended American values. Similar notes were struck in short books by many of the Klan's traveling recruiters, including J. T. Renfro, a Baptist pastor and Klan lecturer from Texas; Reuben H. Sawyer, the Klan's "Grand Lecturer of the Pacific Northwest Domain"; and C. P. Roney, a Louisiana evangelist. The best-received of these was "Imperial Lecturer" Lester A. Brown's *Facts Concerning Knights of the Ku Klux Klan*, published in early 1923 and heavily promoted in Klan newspapers as "the most complete book of facts about this most wonderful of all American Organizations ever published."[32]

The Invisible Empire's newspapermen were no slower than the organization's lecturers in taking advantage of the reading public's apparent hunger for information on the Ku Klux Klan. By the middle of 1923, most of the major Klan newspapers had at least one affiliated book that extolled the positive nature of the organization's Americanism and detailed the insidious dangers of Catholicism. J. O. Wood of the *Searchlight* led the way with his *Are You A Citizen? A Handbook for Americans*. Ernest Reichard of the *Fiery Cross* published the remarkably similar *Americanism Plus*. Grady Rutledge collected his articles from *Dawn* in *The Flag-Draped Skeleton*, which, as the *Badger American* memorably described it, "rips the cloak of hypocrisy from Romanism, and shows the grinning, leering Harlot, with blood-dripping bony hands, feverishly pawing at everything that is American." Like the compilations of the lecturers, there was little in these short books that had not already appeared elsewhere, and they seem to have been rushed into print in the hope of a quick profit and increased circulation for their parent publications.[33]

Far more ambitious was an attempt in 1923 by Imperial Wizard Simmons himself to lay out the "truth" of the Invisible Empire in an almost three-hundred-page work entitled *The Klan Unmasked*. Attempting to counter criticism by the "uninformed," Simmons defensively denied that the Klan was an "anti" organization responsible for "fanning the flames of hatred" against any race or religious creed. Like other Klan authors, the Imperial Wizard focused on defining the group as a pro-white Protestant American fraternal organization that was "worthy" of the mantle of the original Klan. Simmons then promptly undermined his depiction of the Klan as a purely "pro" group, launching attacks on urban living, "hyphenated" Americans, immigration, parochial schooling, and unrestricted suffrage. Remarkably for a supposedly secret organization, two whole chapters were also devoted to explaining the terminology and symbolism of the Ku Klux Klan.[34]

Published amid Simmons's losing struggle with Hiram Evans for control of the Klan's national organization, this muddled defense of Klannish ideals and belabored justification for the organization's existence met with little success.[35] With its failure, and Evans's rise to Imperial Wizard, the Klan's national organization had by late 1923 moved away from the world of book publishing. Instead, the Imperial hierarchy refocused its efforts on pamphlets, supposedly penned by Evans, reaffirming the Klan's "100% American" stances on political topics ranging from "the menace of modern immigration" to the World Court to the "public school problem." Short, cheap to produce, and easy to distribute, the pamphlet offered the Klan's leadership a far more effective outlet for its propaganda.[36]

The Klan's national leaders, however, were not the only ones looking to promote the Invisible Empire. Unlike in the world of newspapers, in which local organs had been largely supplanted by a single official voice, the Klan leadership's withdrawal from book publishing was followed by independent ventures around the country. While official and semiofficial volumes dominated the early days of Klan publishing, 1923 onward saw an increasing heterogeneity in voices representing the Invisible Empire at all levels as lengthy and abstruse works of Klannish movement philosophy proliferated alongside shorter defenses of the Klan's organizational activities and attacks on the Catholic Church.

These "unofficial" books came from both local Klan officials and average Klan members, and were usually published by small local presses, often affiliates of a local newspaper. One of the earliest was Alabama Klan leader John Stephen Fleming's *What Is Ku Kluxism?* published by the *Masonic Weekly Recorder* of Birmingham, Alabama. The foreword boasted that Fleming "is not a scholar. He is not even a writer. He makes no pretension to being skilled in the art of coherently assembling statements of facts." Although this would usually be seen as something of a handicap to those with authorial aspirations, it was a badge of pride for many of the Klansmen who put pen to paper to defend their organization and their way of life.[37]

Underlining the cohesion of the wider cultural Klannish movement, these books tended to follow the same basic pattern. Even as they offered virulently bigoted arguments against foreign influence, they defended the "Pure Americanism" of the Klan and denied any hatred or wrongdoing on the part of Klan members. Any opposition to the organization was blamed on "scurrilous propaganda" that had led potential allies in the wider movement to wrongly turn against it. This unshakable belief—that the only reason a white Protestant American could be opposed to the organization was because they did not properly understand it—was the cornerstone of independent Klan publishing. Following the example of Simmons's *Klan Unmasked*, these independent authors defensively dismissed what they saw as the ungrounded fears of non-Klan members. Their work attempted to expound the organization's principles in such a way as to make the organization's opponents realize their mistake. Ironically, this more often than not simultaneously reinforced many of those original fears.

One of the best examples of this was *K.K.K., Friend or Foe: Which?* published in 1924 by Blaine Mast, the district attorney of Armstrong County, Pennsylvania. The purpose of the book, Mast explained, was to establish a "correct representation and interpretation" of the Invisible Empire in order to dispel a "great deal of misunderstanding." Throughout the book, Mast complained of "ignorant and misinformed folk" who wrongly characterized the organization. The Klan was not an enemy to anyone, Mast argued. It "does not oppose the Hebrew race." It was "a million miles from attempting to cause harm or to endeavor to defame the Roman Catholic Church." It was "not hostile to the colored race" and "desires to rend it all the help possible." In every case, though, Mast promptly undermined his own argument—declaring that the Klan was "tired of the outrages inflicted upon innocent girls by Hebrew libertines," decrying the "hypocrites" of the Catholic hierarchy, and denouncing the "unnamable crimes" perpetrated by "bad niggers."[38]

Endorsed by Sam Rich, King Kleagle of Pennsylvania, and advertised as "the work of a judicial mind" containing "no rabid, wild statements," the self-contradictory and self-defeating nature of Mast's work apparently went unnoticed by both the author and the Klan in general. The same lack of self-awareness could be found throughout many of these highly repetitive works from around the country. The same themes, the same arguments, the same defenses, of a heroic and virtuous Klannish identity could be found in Grand Klaliff E. H. Lougher's *Kall of the Klan in Kentucky* in 1924, in New Jersey Grand Dragon Arthur Bell's nationally popular *The Ku Klux Klan, or The Knights of Columbus Klan* in 1926 (issued by the California-based Q. Cluxton Clanning Publishing), and in Kleagle Paul M. Winter's New York–based *What Price Tolerance* in 1928.[39]

Regardless of the temporal or geographical disparity of these works, the Klannish cultural identity they presented was largely immutable, and it was rare for independent Klan publishing during the 1920s to deviate too far from this model despite its flaws. Nonetheless, a number of interesting variations on the theme appeared. George Estes's *Roman Katholic Kingdom and the Ku Klux Klan* and *Old Cedar School* delved into greater detail on specific anti-Catholic issues: the former focused on the Catholic Church's position as an "untaxable corporation," and the latter on public policy relating to parochial schooling.[40] Reverend Walter Wright's *Religious and Patriotic Ideals of the Ku Klux Klan* and Bishop Alma White's three-volume series placed a heavier focus on the Klan's Protestantism. Wright, a Texan Baptist, emphasized the nondenominational qualities of the Klan to unify Protestants, while White stressed apocalyptic concerns over the "Satanic power" of the Catholic Church and the "money-grasping Jew."[41]

A somewhat odder variation (although fully endorsed by the local Missouri Klan) came from E. F. Stanton, a self-professed "preacher, poet and musician," who seemingly took inspiration from Bruce Barton with his depiction of Jesus Christ as the "Great Klansman." Perhaps the most unusual contribution came from Leroy Curry, an American Legion official in Missouri. The first chapter of his fantastical *The Ku Klux Klan under the Searchlight,* for example, was an extended dream sequence in which Curry witnesses the prehistoric creation of a "Divine Klansman." Nonetheless, Curry still offered up the usual defenses and the litany of complaints against those "who do not believe in the pre-eminence of our American free institutions."[42]

Opponents of the Invisible Empire responded by publishing equally vehement denunciations of the organization. Usually drawing unfavorable comparisons between the modern Klan and its Reconstruction-era forebear, these books also often simultaneously endorsed the ideals and aims of the wider movement. The most common subset of these denunciations was a string of "exposés" by ex-Klansmen. The first hit bookshelves in 1922 and came, fittingly enough, from Henry P. Fry, the ex-Kleagle who had provided much of the information for the 1921 *New York World* series. Critical and bellicose, *The Modern Ku Klux Klan* is most striking for the highly conflicted attitude of Fry toward the Invisible Empire, and the implicit line drawn between the organization and the movement. The second Ku Klux Klan, for Fry, was a "monstrosity" whose use of secrecy "tended to inculcate lawlessness," and was unworthy of association with the heroic Reconstruction-era Klan. Fry claimed to have become "revolted" by "the spirit of religious and racial hatred which it inculcated." At the same time, he made clear his belief in the United States as "a white man's country," in which segregation better served both races. His opposition to the Klan's religious bigotry ultimately stemmed from Fry's fear that "it is splitting the white race into factions" when they needed to stand together against "the negro." As journalist William Pickens noted in the African American socialist magazine *The Messenger,* Fry "only pretends to expose and condemn the Klan in so far as it is a menace to white people."[43]

Yet Pickens still recommended the book to readers for the same reasons as many other reviewers—*The Modern Ku Klux Klan* was important for the information it revealed about a supposedly secret organization. It is clear from its critical reception that the book's main selling point was not Fry's arguments, but his willingness to share details of membership applications, to outline the theoretical command structure of the Klan, and to reveal the meanings of mysterious ranks like "Grand Goblins." A full guide to the "secret" Klan language and codes was provided, while the Ku Klux Klan oath was reprinted in its entirety. For readers of *The Modern Ku Klux Klan,* the Invisible Empire was invisible no longer in a book advertised as "more interesting than fiction"—a tempting proposition for readers who were bombarded daily with newspaper accounts of an organization that purportedly cloaked itself in secrecy.[44]

In both form and tone, *The Modern Ku Klux Klan* established a clear template for the books that followed it as ex-Klansmen competed to reveal the most complete, and most damning, "inside story." Lem Dever, previously publicity director for the Klan in Oregon, published *Confessions of an Imperial Klansman*. Edgar Fuller, former secretary to Imperial Kleagle Edward Young Clarke, wrote *The Klan Inside Out* (under the pseudonym of Marion Monteval) and *The Visible of the Invisible Empire*. William Likins, an ex-Klan newsman from Pennsylvania, published *Patriotism Capitalized*, *The Trail of the Serpent*, and *The Ku Klux Klan, or The Rise and Fall of the Invisible Empire*. Another ex-newspaperman, Peter Sletterdahl of the *Minnesota Fiery Cross*, wrote *The Nightshirt in Politics*, while ex-Simmons aide Edgar Allen Booth synthesized all the previous work to draw his own particular conclusions in *The Mad Mullah of America*. Simmons himself joined the trend, using *America's Menace, or The Enemy Within* to lambast Hiram Evans's "crafty methods." By the end of the decade, a dedicated reader of Klan exposés may well have had a better understanding of the rituals of the Invisible Empire than the average Klan member.[45]

The melodramatic tell-alls of the ex-Klansmen also combined to tell a specific narrative of innocent and decent god-fearing Americans tricked into becoming a secretive band of law-breakers by a conniving and greedy leadership. To a substantial extent, this was a self-serving story that often pointed to changes in leadership to justify the author's own membership and subsequent exit from the organization, while endorsing the values of the wider Klannish movement. At the same time, this argument subtextually underlined the fact that the author's decision to leave the Klan was less out of moral disgust than a change in fortunes or perceived slight. Despite its dubious foundations, this narrative was repeated so often that it contributed heavily to popular perceptions of the Klan at the time.

Whether a self-serving literary device or an expression of genuine disgust, these exposés uniformly featured ever more hyperbolic denunciations of the Klan's leadership. Fry, the earliest author, offered a mixed view of Simmons as "either insanely visionary or superlatively cunning." Dever excoriated the Klan's leadership as "mean and petty Kaisers of a queer and special type." Fuller attacked both Simmons's "physical laziness, mental inertia and moral insensibility" and Evans's "atrophy inside the cranium." Likins deemed Evans a "great American monster" and one of "the earth's most despised beings." Readers of these books learned not only the meanings of Klan codes and the true nature of Klannish ritual, but also how to hate the organization's leadership like only an embittered ex-Klansman could.[46]

FIGURE 4.1. Cover illustration for Ezra Cook's *Ku Klux Klan: The Strange Society of Blood and Death! Exposed!* (Racine, WI: Johnson Smith, ca. 1923).

Ex-members were not the only ones to put pen to paper to detail their disgust with the Invisible Empire. For the most part, other anti-Klan authors were no less hyperbolic than their Klannish counterparts, producing titles like *The Strange Society of Blood and Death* (see fig. 4.1) and *Liberty Dethroned*. At the same time, many of these complaints centered on a perception that the Klan organization did not live up to the ideals of the Klannish movement. Frank P. Ball of New York, for one, spent the majority of his *Faults and Virtues of the Ku Klux Klan* expressing his concern for the maintenance of white supremacy. His condemnation of the organization stemmed from a fear that Klan members were "guilty of the very worst kind of filthy, intimate social equality with the negroes and mulattoes."[47]

These anti-Klan jeremiads were also largely written by individuals with their own personal vendettas against the organization. *Liberty Dethroned*, for example, was written by A. V. Dalrymple, a staunch ally of "Ma" and "Pa" Ferguson, Texas politicians who were engaged in heated battle with the Klan for control of the state. Similarly, *The Ku Klux Kraze* was written by Aldrich Blake, executive counselor to Governor J. C. Walton of Oklahoma, who was impeached for having declared martial law in his state to combat the Klan. Many of these books represented individual grudges more than an expression of the Ku Klux Klan's status within the world of the 1920s.[48]

As important as it is that we recognize the existence of this pro- and anti-Klan material, we must also recognize that these tracts were not popular best sellers. While the rhetoric of *What Price Tolerance* or *The Strange Society of Blood and Death* might suggest cultural war, the lived ideology of the Klannish movement—what Klan members and their allies were actually reading—is more suggestive of a cultural spectrum that did not lend itself to clear divisions. The Ku Klux Klan was less interested in burning books than it was in having its members read them. "Have you read a book this week?" asked the *Fiery Cross*. If not, "your life may not have been so rich as it might have been," since "nothing adds so greatly to all the things that make life worth while as reading a good book."[49]

The Klan was particularly concerned with literacy rates in America, intertwining the issue with nativist concerns. Concerns over illiteracy, which *Dawn* called "a disgrace to the nation," were folded into the Klan's well-documented crusade for universal public schooling, claiming that Catholic parochial schools and poorly funded public education were responsible for dragging down literacy rates among American children. The *Kourier Magazine* even cited John Dewey on the "moral right of every child to have an education." Articles in the Klan's official publications criticized the United States as "a democracy which expends in a year twice as much for chewing gum as for school books." An educated citizenry, after all, was the only way to foster American democracy—and thereby avert a papal takeover.[50]

This passion for public school education led the Ku Klux Klan to also engage full-throatedly in contemporary debates over school textbooks. The primary focus of Klan members was, expectedly, rooting out perceived "Catholic propaganda" and "sectarianism." It was remarkably successful in this task. The Invisible Empire managed to have books removed from schools across America, including in Michigan, New Jersey, Indiana, Louisiana, and Georgia. In Tennessee, the Ku Klux Klan actually did burn the offending textbooks while charging admission to the bonfire to raise money to buy replacements.

A 1916 introduction to American history by Jennie Hall called *Our Ancestors in History* was one of the organization's favorite targets. Concerned that it would instill "a deep respect for Romanism in the hearts of the Protestant boys and girls," Klan members launched multiple attacks on the book between 1922 and 1925.[51]

Other Klannish concerns over schoolbooks found far more support in the wider movement outside the organization. The "New History" of scholars like David Muzzey and Charles Beard rejected "great man" interpretations of history in favor of socioeconomic analysis. This apparent diminution of the role of the Founding Fathers did not sit well with many. The attempt by some historians to take a more nuanced view of the American Revolution and the place of British policies further exacerbated the issue. In what historian Jonathan Zimmerman has termed the "textbook wars," more than twenty legislatures were by 1923 considering the regulation of "treasonous" textbooks. Wisconsin, for example, passed a bill banning textbooks "defaming or misrepresenting the heroes of the War of Independence or the War of 1812."[52]

These supposedly "unpatriotic" histories received criticism from a wide range of sources, including the American Legion, Mayor John F. Hylan of New York, the German American Steuben Society, the Hearst newspaper chain, and the Knights of Columbus.[53] Walter Lippmann observed in 1928 that it seemed "as if there were hardly an organization in America which has not set up a committee" on textbooks. The Ku Klux Klan was no exception. As early as 1923, *Dawn* had devoted more than a page and a half to denouncing the "venomous slanders" on Sam Adams that were to be found in *The Causes of the War of Independence* by Claude H. Van Tyne, a historian at the University of Michigan. The *Call of the North* hailed the work of the Veterans of Foreign Wars and Sons of the American Revolution to combat "not entirely satisfactory" textbooks.[54]

A clear indication of the fluidity of the boundaries in these cultural struggles came in 1927, when Mayor William "Big Bill" Thompson of Chicago launched his own investigation into what he called "pro-British, un-American propaganda." The notoriously corrupt and anti-Prohibition mayor found (much to his chagrin) that he had the full support of the local Ku Klux Klan on this issue—albeit nothing else. Gail S. Carter, Grand Dragon of Illinois, announced to reporters that the organization was in complete accord with Thompson's attempt to "drive King George from history text books." The *Kourier Magazine* agreed, welcoming Thompson's scrutiny of the books but criticizing the mayor for neglecting the "vast evil" of Catholic influence. The fact that attacks on "unpatriotic" textbooks nationwide, including Thompson's investigation, were also backed by American Catholic organizations was carefully ignored by the Invisible Empire.[55]

The reading program of the Invisible Empire encompassed far more than simply textbooks, however. There were plenty of best sellers that were eagerly endorsed by Klan publications and avidly read by members and nonmembers alike. Some of this literary enthusiasm stemmed from wider anti-Catholic sentiment, which reached far beyond the Klan's paying membership. The literary advertisement most commonly seen in Klan publications was for Helen Jackson's *Convent Cruelties, or My Life in a Convent*, first published in 1919. Jackson's anti-Catholic autobiography, which purported to detail the horrors of her life confined in a convent and her eventual escape, sold to a much larger readership than simply Klan members. Anti-Catholics across the United States paid their fifty cents to read her lurid tales, propelling the book to seven printings between its original publication and 1924.[56]

Authors like Lothrop Stoddard reached an even wider audience, and had an enduring influence on American popular thought. Walter White, then assistant secretary of the NAACP, alleged in 1923 that Stoddard was a member of the Invisible Empire, claiming "a reputable citizen of Atlanta in possession of secret Klan documents" as his source. White went so far as to name Stoddard as the Exalted Cyclops of Klan No. 1, Realm of Massachusetts, and claim that the author was tasked with leading the Klan's expansion into European countries. Stoddard denied any official affiliation with the Klan. Whether or not he was a dues-paying member, though, he was undoubtedly affiliated with the wider Klan movement. His ideas had a powerful effect on shaping the thinking not just of Klan members but also of what one biographer has called his "paradoxically broad yet elitist readership."[57]

Lothrop Stoddard's best-remembered work, *The Rising Tide of Color*, published in 1921, was an evaluation of race as "the basic factor in human affairs." Supplementing this first work through the decade with *The Revolt against Civilization*, *Racial Realities in Europe*, *Re-forging America*, and more, Stoddard offered a dire warning. What he identified as the "radical negro movement" in the United States was only part of a global shift in racial power. A growing race consciousness and racial militancy threatened the continued dominance of global white supremacy. For many in 1920s America, this was a compelling and chilling threat. President Warren G. Harding, for one, encouraged those concerned with the national and global "race problem" to read Stoddard. This was not an uncontroversial position, but it was a popular one for many—including Klannish readers.[58]

Telling as Stoddard's popularity was, it would be a mistake to reduce Klannish reading simply to ideological tracts. Klan members were more than happy to give their blessing to the westerns of Owen Wister and Zane Grey, classic adventures in the vein of Walter Scott and Alexandre Dumas, and the idyllic Southern romances of George Washington Cable.[59] Similarly, Klan members may have felt uncomfortable engaging with the "New History," but were encouraged to read popular biographies of "great Americans." The muscular Christianity of Teddy Roosevelt and Dunning-school depictions of Lincoln as a Southern hero who would never have endorsed Radical Reconstruction were particularly popular, as well as such classics of nonfiction as Macaulay's *History of England*, Jean-Henri d'Aubigne's *History of the Reformation*, and Erasmus's *In Praise of Folly*.[60]

Similarly, both Klan members and nonmembers shared a passion for advertising executive Bruce Barton's 1925 runaway best seller, *The Man Nobody Knows*, and its 1926 sequel, *The Book Nobody Knows*. Barton's work, which depicted Jesus and scriptural texts as a role model for the modern businessman, was widely ridiculed by contemporary critics. Many historians have similarly, as Erin A. Smith has noted, dismissed Barton as "a third-rate writer of boosterish prose who embraced a theologically empty and intellectually bankrupt consumerism." Yet hundreds of thousands of Americans not only read but loved Barton's books. Among these readers were Klan members, who rhapsodized that Barton must surely know Jesus personally to describe him so intimately.[61]

Klan officials and publications were certainly not reticent in endorsing these books and other suitable reading—much of which was seemingly published by Bobbs-Merrill. The *Fiery Cross*, in addition to its "Library Notes," ran regular book reviews and recommendations, while the *American Standard* offered its suggestions in "The Patriotic Bookshelf." The *Kourier Magazine* gave guidance to younger readers with its "Junior Klan Study Guide," and the *Kourier* network offered numerous reviews to help Klansmen find enjoyable and educational books. As the *Fiery Cross* explained, the reader should not "gulp down literature at random" but instead plan a well-balanced "intellectual diet."[62]

Klan leaders and members also worked actively to foster interest in (and financing for) public libraries to help allow Americans of all ages to access these reading materials. The *Fiery Cross* published a lengthy poem extolling the virtues of the library as "a teacher bigger than the schools." Like others concerned with the nation's "Americanism," Klan members championed the library's ability to teach recent immigrants about the wonders of the United States and, in the process, "make him an American." Even prisoners could benefit, with the Klan trumpeting the results of the installation of a library in the Pueblo, Colorado, jail. As the *Kourier Magazine* explained, anyone could become educated by reading "well-selected books."[63]

Klan publications, particularly in the North, often urged Klan members to visit their local libraries. The *Fiery Cross*'s regular feature "Library Notes" detailed the latest arrivals and events at the Indianapolis Public Library. In Chicago, all Klansmen were encouraged to "read and study and make the best possible use of the facilities in hand" as well as supporting any effort to improve the city's libraries. In Colorado, the Grand Dragon offered a more ambitious plan, suggesting that each individual Klan in the state create its own "Klan Circulating Library." Promising that it would not entail "a great deal of trouble and expense," the Grand Dragon emphasized that the library would pay "big dividends in the creating of a 'mind.'"[64]

The Klan as a literate public is perhaps best understood in the context of another Bobbs-Merrill author, John Erskine. His 1925 novel, *The Private Life of Helen of Troy*, a portrayal of Helen as a thoroughly modern vamp, was a highly acclaimed best seller quickly adapted for film. Yet Erskine's greater impact was as a Columbia professor who proposed the first full-scale "great books" curriculum. As Joan Shelley Rubin has noted, the "great books" program was, fundamentally, an "Americanization" program concerned with "the reassertion of white Anglo-Saxon Protestant superiority" in molding all Americans—including new immigrants—to fit "an existing white middle-class mold." It is not hard to imagine how the same impulses drove the creation of a canon of Klannish reading recommendations. Much like the Invisible Empire itself, the appeal of this "great books" ideology lay in "its capacity to provide familiar touchstones (self-reliance, character, Western civilization)" while bending to contemporary society's "heightened demands for information, social performance, and personal growth." In their concern with reading not only as a means of personal gratification and personal betterment but also as a cornerstone of an educated, literate, "Americanized" public, members of both the Klan organization and the wider Klannish cultural movement were engrossed in a wholly contemporary debate.[65]

Moving beyond the organizational rhetoric of "filthy fiction" to the lived experience of readers allows us to understand that members of the Ku Klux Klan movement seem to have shared in both mainstream concerns with modern literature and in mainstream literary tastes. At the same time, a consideration of the proliferation of "bad" books of the postwar period that concerned the Invisible Empire highlights the fact that many Americans shared a taste for reading about the Ku Klux Klan. Klan members and nonmembers alike battled in print to define public perceptions of the Klan—a literary Klannish identity. They did so in a disorganized and disordered process that played out predominantly at a local level, with little input and even less control from the organization's national leaders. That these considerations of the Klan and its place in contemporary society often offered mixed assessments reminds us how heterogeneous cultural reaction to the Klan was in the 1920s. Even as the Klan displayed ambivalent sentiments about American literature, American literature displayed ambivalent sentiments about the Klan.

5

Good Fiction Qualities

It occurred to the editors of BLACK MASK that the Klan and its mystic atmosphere
would make an excellent background for fiction stories and other Black Mask features.
It contains action, mystery, emotion, and other good fiction qualities.

BLACK MASK, May 15, 1923

The ambivalent relationship between American literature and the Ku Klux
Klan was, if anything, even more evident in the realm of popular fiction. The
Ku Klux Klan and its "good fiction qualities" appeared everywhere from the
Saturday Evening Post to Sinclair Lewis. Even as their image was commercialized and co-opted, Klan members and sympathizers put pen to paper to
promote a Klannish identity of heroic and virtuous white Protestantism. The
porous boundaries of cultural division saw Klan authors adopt a modern
pulp sensibility as modernist authors embraced nativism.

Many literary scholars have noted the appearance of the works of "God-
dard"—a portmanteau of Madison Grant and Lothrop Stoddard—in F. Scott
Fitzgerald's *The Great Gatsby*. Tom Buchanan extols the virtues of God-
dard's ideas at multiple points, warning that "civilization's going to pieces,"
that intermarriage threatened the American family, and that the "white race"
risked becoming "utterly submerged." It is fairly evident what Fitzgerald himself thought of Stoddard, as Nick Carraway notes the "pathetic" nature of
Buchanan's "impassioned gibberish." The endorsement of these "stale ideas"
is a means of underlining the fundamental character defects of Buchanan—
the wealthy, athletic, well-bred, and well-educated Midwesterner whose ar-
rogance and cruelty feature prominently in the novel.[1]

Those "stale ideas," though, are hardly limited in *The Great Gatsby* to Buchanan. Daisy, who fondly remembers her "white girlhood," ultimately remains with her deeply flawed husband rather than leave him for the ethni-
cally ambiguous Jimmy Gatz. Gatsby's own library prominently includes an
(unread) copy of the "Stoddard Lectures"—a travel series by John Lawson
Stoddard, Lothrop Stoddard's father. Jordan Baker's attempt to defuse Buchanan's rage with a reminder that "we're all white here," Lucille McKee's relief

at having avoided marriage to "a little kike," even Fitzgerald's own portrayal of Meyer Wolfsheim, the "small, flat-nosed Jew" who lapses into dialect, are all reminders of the nativistic and racialized modernism identified by Walter Benn Michaels.[2]

At the same time, in focusing on the racial undertones in Fitzgerald's work or the anti-Semitism of Hemingway or the "Anglo-Saxon chauvinism" of John Dos Passos, we risk losing sight of the wider cultural picture. The 1920s has long been celebrated as a decade of "exceptional richness" in the "flowering of the literary arts." The year 1922 alone—the year in which the world split in two for Willa Cather—saw the appearance of James Joyce's *Ulysses*, T. S. Eliot's *The Waste Land*, Claude McKay's *Harlem Shadows*, and Sinclair Lewis's *Babbitt*. It was a decade in which Fitzgerald, Faulkner, Dos Passos, Hemingway, and Wolfe published their first major works.[3]

While *Gatsby* may have been a critical success, however, its sales were modest. Similarly, James D. Hart has noted, many people in the 1920s may have been *talking* about Hemingway, but not that many people were *reading* Hemingway. William Faulkner was not quite as obscure as some have made him out to be, but his books were little read. It was only in the 1940s, as Mark Greif details, that critics retroactively rehabilitated him into the pantheon of great American novelists. If, then, we are to garner a more rounded understanding of the 1920s, we must consider the literary tastes of "America in the bulk," as *The Bookman* put it in 1923. And America in the bulk was not reading Hemingway or Fitzgerald. It was reading Jack London and Harold Bell Wright.[4]

A Disciples of Christ minister with a flair for "awkward, mawkish, and ingenuous" melodramatic fiction that was "both blatantly commercial and blatantly evangelical," Wright was excoriated by contemporary critics for his forays into "pseudo-literature." He was also one of the most popular novelists of the first quarter of the twentieth century, selling more than ten million books. Until 1926, he was the third most popular writer in the United States—with an audience that included a young Ronald Reagan, who claimed his baptism into the Disciples of Christ was prompted by reading Wright's *That Printer of Udell's* in 1922. Champions of heroism and morality in fiction like Gene Stratton-Porter were similarly popular. A flood of authors in the Jack London school of rough, red-blooded adventure, like Stewart Edward White and James Oliver Curwood, complemented the high sales of sentimental romantic fiction. Zane Grey, master of the western, remained one of the nation's top ten best-selling authors well into the decade.[5]

As in nonfiction, there was little here to differentiate between popular tastes and Ku Klux preferences. It was the department-store impresario John

Wanamaker, not a Knight of the Klan, who wrote to Zane Grey to praise his "distinctively and genuinely American" work that offered none of the "decadence of foreign writers"—though a Klan member would certainly have agreed. A notable example of this cultural continuum was prolific author Bernie Babcock's 1923 novel, *The Soul of Abe Lincoln*. In this romance spanning the length of the Civil War, President Lincoln played a crucial role in bringing two lovers—one, a spy for the North; the other, a nurse for the South—together. The *New York Times* described it as a "moving and appealing story" that was "well worth reading for its vivid and thrilling and historically accurate portrayal." The *Badger American*, a Klan newspaper, agreed, describing Babcock's book as "wonderful." *Dawn* went further, telling its readers that "every Klansman should read it, as it is the premier of historical novels of those times."[6]

If we are to understand the 1920s, then, we must understand it as the decade of both Fitzgerald and Wright. Yet condescension toward the aesthetic and stylistic failings on view in much of this literature too often colors scholarly understanding of the literary 1920s. As Erin A. Smith has persuasively noted, Wright is one of the more egregious absences from literary histories of the 1920s. His novels are among a host of other "bad books" that have been largely ignored by scholars. Following H. L. Mencken's cue, we have dismissed books that seemed not only to have been "primarily addressed to shoe-drummers and shop-girls," but also to have been "written by authors who *are*, to all intellectual intents and purposes, shoe-drummers and shop-girls."[7]

The great irony here is that Mencken himself was responsible for some of the most successful pulp magazines of the 1920s and 1930s—including *Black Mask*, which would afford the Klan its most striking appearance in the popular fiction of the period. In 1915, with their prestigious *Smart Set* struggling financially, coeditors Mencken and George Jean Nathan pseudonymously launched *Parisienne*. The new magazine saw glamorous heroines and aristocratic heroes swan about in short stories that had not made the cut for *Smart Set*, the location changed to the French Riviera in a cynical attempt to cash in on contemporary Francophilia. Noting its success, Mencken and Nathan followed in short order with *Saucy Stories*, a monthly collection of short fiction offering "the drama of poison and jealousy and the triumph of love." Shoe-drummers and shop-girls surely loved it.[8]

In 1920, Mencken and Nathan supplemented their collection of money-spinners by establishing *Black Mask*. One of the earliest pulp collections of detective stories, *Black Mask* quickly became one of the most popular "mystery magazines" on the market and would soon introduce what one historian has called "the greatest change in the detective story since Poe," pioneer-ing the "hard-boiled" fiction genre. Sold to the Pro-Distributors Publishing Company of Eltinge "Pop" Warner (also the publisher of *Smart Set*) and un-der the editorship of George W. Sutton, the magazine began to focus almost exclusively on detective stories.[9]

By 1930, the magazine had reached its peak circulation of over one hun-dred thousand, and was widely recognized as "the elite of the tough-guy fic-tion pulps." *Black Mask* defined the detective genre with stories from Dashiell Hammett, creator of Sam Spade and *The Maltese Falcon*, as well as the Thin Man and Continental Op stories; Erle Stanley Gardner, best remembered for the Perry Mason series; and, later, Raymond Chandler, author of classics in-cluding *The Big Sleep, Farewell My Lovely*, and *The Long Goodbye*. Preceding Hammett and Chandler to the pages of *Black Mask* was Carroll John Daly, one of the most popular pulp writers of the 1920s and creator of both the first hard-boiled private-eye story and the first successful hard-boiled private detective, Race Williams. Williams, in turn, made his very first appearance in *Black Mask* in the magazine's special June 1923 "Ku Klux Klan Number," an issue devoted to stories of the Invisible Empire.[10]

While Daly had sold his first story to *Black Mask* in 1922, it was not un-til 1923 that he began to perfect his super-tough style—and in the process forged the "hard-boiled" genre. Daly's story for the Klan issue, "Knights of the Open Palm," predated Dashiell Hammett's first Continental Op story by several months, though his writing did not bear comparison to Hammett's. One critic accurately deemed Daly "an artificial, awkward, self-conscious pulpster, endlessly repetitious, hopelessly melodramatic" with "no ability for three dimensional characterization" and "impossibly stilted dialogue." Never-theless, by virtue of being first, Daly's impact was significant. In creating Race Williams, who continued to be a major pulp attraction into the 1950s, Daly "set the boundaries for the [hard-boiled] code either to be observed or trans-gressed." Those boundaries were originally set in opposition to the Ku Klux Klan.[11]

"Knights of the Open Palm" was not a complex story. Only twenty pages long, it was concerned more with tough-guy wisecracks and two-fisted action than promoting a particular philosophy. Race Williams was tasked with in-vestigating the kidnapping of a boy who had witnessed a woman being tarred and feathered by the Klan, allowing Daly to quickly stake out an anti-Klan position without expository pontificating. Daly also clearly understood that the backdrop of the Klan was the main appeal of the piece, and exploited many of the widely known secrets of the Invisible Empire—its codes and sig-nals—as easy shorthand in building a suspenseful atmosphere.[12]

Williams's distaste for the organization's activities was made clear as he "searched" (mostly using his fists) a small, Klan-dominated town. At the same time, Daly managed to include a defense of the original Klan and a vaguely sympathetic nod to the Klannish protestation that "half the crime laid to their doors wasn't true." The story's anti-Klan message was also subverted somewhat by Daly's hard-boiled style. Williams engaged in precisely the violent vigilantism that was supposedly being condemned. While the Klan *organization* was being overtly criticized, Williams was in many ways emblematic of that larger cultural Klan *movement*.[13]

"Knights of the Open Palm" clearly emphasized entertainment over any kind of moral stand. In this, Daly was following the path *Black Mask* had laid out for him. In the magazine's advertisements for the issue, the editorial team had proclaimed absolute neutrality. Their reason for publishing an issue of Klan-based stories was instead that "the Ku Klux Klan—with its vital and far-reaching possibilities—has become almost a household word throughout the length and breadth of our country." The editors believed the organization would make "an excellent background for fiction stories," with its atmosphere of "action, mystery, emotion, and other good fiction qualities."[14] A note from editor George Sutton in the "Ku Klux Klan Number" itself explained further:

> We felt that the attempt to revive the old Ku Klux Klan—with new ideas and new purposes—was the most picturesque element that has appeared in American life since the war, regardless of whether we condemn its aims—whatever they may be—or not. And yet no magazine has used it as a background for fiction stories. A few wishy-washy articles have appeared against it, but nothing of an entertaining nature.[15]

Despite the long-term literary impact of Daly's story, it is this attempt by *Black Mask* to exploit the "picturesque" nature of the Ku Klux Klan that is most revealing. "Knights of the Open Palm" was only one of the thirteen original pieces published in *Black Mask*'s Klan issue, its luridly alluring cover by L. L. Balcom depicting a Klansman brandishing a smoking cross. Nine of these explicitly dealt with the Invisible Empire, and offered a spectrum of opinions on the organization. Daly's story was not even first billed. That honor went to the issue's longest piece, "Call Out the Klan," a "Complete Novelette of the Invisible Empire" by Herman Petersen, a prolific pulp author. Petersen's story, as well as his correspondence with George Sutton, the editor of *Black Mask*, offers a telling insight into the complex process of the co-option, commercialization, and sanitization of the Klan by popular fiction in the 1920s.

In February 1923, Sutton wrote to Petersen to request a "humdinger of a Ku Klux Klan story." This was a commercial decision, not an ideological one.

The magazine, Sutton explained, had already bought a Klan-based cover, and now they needed "a rip-snorting dramatic tale" to go with it. The pulp did not want a "controversial tale," but "if it must take sides it might lean a little toward the Klan rather than against it." Petersen, for his part, had no problem with this. As he explained in a letter to Sutton, "I may favor the Klan a bit—I lived south in 1917 and 1918—but I'll start no controversy."[16]

In "Call Out the Klan," Bruce Martin, a World War I veteran, returns to his Virginia home, where Klan members are stirring up trouble.[17] Martin considers the Klan little more than interfering "would-be reformers." His love interest, Lois D'Aprix, is a staunch defender of the organization: "If a man offends the Klan, he offends because he in some way has gone contrary to one of the great principles embodied in its constitution. . . . The Klan never gets the wrong man." When D'Aprix is apparently kidnapped by the Invisible Empire, Martin searches for her in the mountains, where he discovers the body of a dead Klansman. A group of Klansmen catch Martin and, believing him to have shot their dead member (the brother of their Grand Cyclops), prepare to lynch him. The sheriff arrives in the nick of time, informing the gathering that they have the wrong man, and the Grand Cyclops meekly submits to his authority. Rather than arrest him, however, the sheriff deputizes the Klan gathering, and instructs them to "call out the Klan."

In the tale's denouement, crosses are lit across the mountains to signal all Klansmen in the area, who ride out in search of D'Aprix.[18] Together with Martin and the sheriff, they rescue her from the troublemaker who has stolen Klan robes and been pretending to be a member so that his crimes would be blamed on the Invisible Empire. Martin then renounces his earlier opinions: "I'm sorry for the ill feeling I bore the Klan. Since last night I have come to view your organization in an entirely different light." With its virtue fully established, the story ended with the sheriff's decision to join the Ku Klux Klan.[19]

It is unclear whether Petersen had any direct connection with the Klan. In his correspondence with Sutton, he noted that "practically every incident in the whole yarn has been taken from newspaper clippings," implying no inside knowledge on his part. What is certain is that an official Klan propagandist could scarcely have done a better job at espousing the organization's merits. Petersen offered a thrilling conversion narrative that implicated readers in Martin and the sheriff's endorsement of the Invisible Empire. He also stayed true to his promise to Sutton and carefully stripped the organization of any controversy—at no point in the story was any sense of anti-Semitism, anti-Catholicism, or racial hatred even hinted at. Moreover, the plot device of having the Klan mistakenly thought guilty of a crime, only to be vindicated and

have some imposter unmasked as the true culprit, reflected widespread Klannish denials of any association with criminal misdeeds, and would become a
popular trope. Petersen's story presented the Invisible Empire, in a popular,
nationally distributed magazine, as a (generally) law-abiding adjunct to official law-enforcement, helping to punish evildoers and keep the peace. It was
the same view of the Klan that the Invisible Empire's leaders had long emphasized, the same imagined heroic self-image that bound an otherwise fractured and localized organization and appealed to a wider cultural movement
of Klannishness. With just enough mystery and action to make it attractive,
the Ku Klux Klan was a "picturesque element" indeed.[20]

The remainder of the stories in the *Black Mask*'s "Klan Number" continued to mine the organization's "good fiction qualities." In "The Color of
Honor" by Richard Connell (soon to become famous for his story "The Most
Dangerous Game"), a Klansman discovers that he's actually of mixed race and
subsequently helps a Northern black voting rights activist escape from the
rest of the Klan. In "T. McGuirk—Klansman" by Ray Cumming, a "humorous tale" of the Klan, McGuirk (a petty criminal and one of *Black Mask*'s favorite recurring characters) joins the Klan and uses it as a cover to rob a rich
loafer, but offers no real opinion on the organization. A "historical" article
on Reconstruction took the Dunning school line, firmly endorsing the first
Klan while condemning carpetbaggers as "human scum." Robert Lee Heiser's
"Devil Dan Hewett" was avowedly "neither for nor against the Klan" but "just
a fine BLACK MASK yarn" with "a lot of the KKK action."[21]

The overwhelming response to publication of the special issue prompted
Black Mask's editors to establish a "Ku Klux Klan Forum" in the next three
issues to allow readers to have their say. Having been "literally flooded with
mail," this "only open, free, absolutely unbiased discussion" ran heavily in
favor of the Invisible Empire. Klan members were certainly pleased: "Others
together with myself bought the magazine and gave it away, so personally I
can account for six sales that would not have been made were it not for the
significance of the issue." But even nonmembers responded favorably to the
pulp magazine's "picturesque" use of the organization. Not counting those
who explicitly identified themselves as members of the Klan, the letters published in the *Black Mask* ran two to one in favor of the Invisible Empire.[22]

This pro-Klan outpouring is not altogether surprising. Virtually all the
stories and features in the issue (including Carroll John Daly's Race Williams
story) had either explicitly or implicitly endorsed the "100% American" ideals
of the Klan movement, whether or not they supported the organization's activities. This division of sentiment was made abundantly clear in the story
"Hoodwinked" by Newton Fuessle, published in the following issue because

of lack of space in the "Klan Number" itself. Although the story detailed one businessman's turn against the Klan, it was their activities, not their aims, with which he disagreed. As Fuessle wrote, "He realized that, while the ideals of the Klan might be right, certainly their practices that he had been able to observe at close range were wrong."[23]

E. R. Hagemann, the preeminent chronicler of *Black Mask*, noted that "one gets the distinct impression that *Mask* supported and upheld the Klansmen and that it favored their racism and vigilantism. No other argument seems logical." This idea is underlined when we also consider the readership that *Mask* was trying to foster. Joseph T. Shaw, *Black Mask*'s editor after 1926, wrote that the pulp's reader was "vigorous-minded; hard, in a square man's hardness; hating unfairness, trickery, injustice, cowardly underhandedness." This reader would be "not squeamish or prudish, but clean, admiring the good in man and woman," "responsive to the thrill of danger, the stirring exhilaration of clean, swift, hard action." Those who read *Black Mask* were "always pulling for the right guy to come out on top." Shaw's characterization of his readers could have been lifted directly from a Klan recruitment pamphlet. In fact, the *Imperial Night-Hawk* had encouraged Klan members to purchase the special themed issue, claiming that the mayor of New York was attempting to suppress *Black Mask* to prevent publication of anything favorable to the Klan.[24]

Two studies of hard-boiled fiction have expanded on this relationship between detective stories and the Klan. Erin A. Smith makes the case that hard-boiled fiction functioned as an imagined community that addressed a need for male sociability that would once have been found in the saloon. Detective fiction concerned itself with "work, manliness, and the embodiment of class and social position in dress, speech, and manners"—all concerns shared by the imagined community of the Klan movement. Sean McCann has taken this argument further, making the case that the Invisible Empire itself rose to prominence "championing a social fantasy that closely resembled the mythology implicit in hard-boiled crime fiction." Both "railed against class parasites and social decadence," both "spotted the signs of corruption," and both saw vigilante justice as "the only effective response to social ills." Given their common touchstones, it seems reasonable that scholars might find considerable support for the Klan within *Black Mask*'s readership of hard-boiled detective fiction, and to find considerable appreciation for the world of detective fiction among members of the Klan.[25]

This mutual admiration, though, was not limited to the rough-and-tumble world of the mystery pulps. To some extent, the very existence of the Invisible Empire was built on chivalric romances in the vein of Sir Walter Scott that lionized the Reconstruction Klan and an idealized Old South. These stories had arguably done even more than the Dunningite historians to forge a new national consensus on Reconstruction and Southern identity. As K. Stephen Prince has argued, Southern writers were able to "win with the pen what they had lost with the sword." In reinventing the period as proof of the dangers of "wrongheaded northern intervention," in Prince's words, these Reconstruction novels secured Northern complicity in Southern racial thought. In celebrating the racial violence of Southern white men in the past, popular novelists shaped a contemporary white supremacist masculinity that welcomed the resurgent Klan movement of the 1920s.[26]

This was not a one-sided literary struggle. Albion Tourgée's *A Fool's Errand*, published in 1879, had achieved tremendous success as an anti-Klan novel that lionized the Union League and Northern Republican "carpetbaggers." But Tourgée's book disappeared under a flood of Southern authors who acclaimed the Klan's role in liberating the South from the heinous rule of the Radical Republicans. N. J. Floyd's *Thorns in the Flesh* came first in 1884, followed by Thomas Jefferson Jerome's *Ku-Klux Klan No. 40* in 1895. Their somewhat lackluster efforts were significantly overshadowed by the publication of *Red Rock* in 1898 by Thomas Nelson Page, one of the most celebrated of the Southern "magnolias and midnight" romantic authors, and then *Gabriel Tolliver* in 1902 by Joel Chandler Harris, best known for his popular Uncle Remus stories.[27] The genre reached its apex, however, with Thomas Dixon Jr.[28]

Dixon's "Reconstruction Trilogy"—*The Leopard's Spots* (1902), *The Clansman* (1905), and *The Traitor* (1907)—was key in creating the romantic myth of a heroic Reconstruction Klan that had fostered a fertile atmosphere for the organization's rebirth. Although his writing left something to be desired, Dixon's breathless narration of the Klan's night-riding heroics garnered him millions of readers. The *Atlanta Journal* hailed *The Leopard's Spots*—in many ways, an explicit refutation of *Uncle Tom's Cabin*—as "an epoch-making book." The novel would go on to sell over a million copies and establish Doubleday, Page & Co. as a major publisher. When *The Clansman* was published in 1905, Firmin Dredd noted in *The Bookman* that it was "a very poor novel, a very ridiculous novel," but "a novel which very properly is going to interest many thousands of readers, of all degrees of taste and education." Dredd was not wrong—the *Clansman* sold an estimated forty thousand copies in just ten days. Those readers, in turn, were inculcated into a literary public centered around the idea that the Klan had "saved" the South.[29]

These pro-Klan novels generally followed the same basic, highly successful formula. Each told the story of a sterling example of Southern manhood who fought unscrupulous carpetbaggers, suppressing their attempts at "stirring up racial strife." In the process, these Southern gentlemen would usually find great romantic and/or financial success. Simplistic and repetitive, these narratives of Klannish heroism nonetheless found fertile ground both in the popular imagination and in the work of many historians at the turn of the century. Literary scholar Walter Benn Michaels credits Dixon's work with helping to rewrite American definitions of "whiteness" and "American" in the early twentieth century. Joel Williamson has similarly argued that Dixon had more impact on the lives of modern Americans than some presidents.[30]

Contemporary observers certainly noted the influence these novels had on the national white imagination. African American author Joel Rogers, for one, argued in 1923 that popular writers had given the original Klan "a clean bill." Their romanticized view of the Invisible Empire had taken root in both the popular mind and the academic community, leaving Americans ready and even eager for a revival of the organization. Novelists had to bear, in Rogers's estimation, "a great deal of blame" for the success of Simmons's efforts. In many respects, the new Invisible Empire owed its existence more to a fictionalized ideal of the Reconstruction Klan than it did to the brutal reality of the Southern night riders.[31]

Yet, that same year, Thomas Dixon appeared at the Century Theatre in Detroit at an anti-Klan meeting organized by the American Unity League to condemn the resurgent Invisible Empire as "the acme of stupidity and inhumanity." Although he made sure to praise the Reconstruction Klan as "the bravest and noblest men of the South," Dixon's criticism of the Klan revival was unremitting. The author was particularly concerned that the organization's anti-Semitic and anti-Catholic sentiments undermined racial unity. Like Henry P. Fry, he feared any division that would leave whites weakened in the unceasing competition with other races. He saved his harshest words for the Invisible Empire's opposition to immigration, arguing that the Klan's plan to "meet the humble immigrant of today with a mask and dagger and push him back to hell" denied America's heritage as a nation of immigrants. "If this is 100 per cent Americanism," Dixon told his audience, "I for one spit on it."[32]

It is a reflection of the fluid tensions of the cultural 1920s that Dixon, that professional Southerner, was also arguably the most important voice of anti-Klan fiction in the postwar period. The frenzied adulation with which Dixon described the valiant efforts of the Reconstruction Klan as a stout band of Southern patriots obscured an important fact. The author believed that the organization had accomplished its task and had been rightfully dissolved. *The Traitor*, published in 1907, told of the dangers of a Klan that was reconstituted after the organization's leaders had ordered it to disband.[33] Having already achieved its purpose of protecting the South from Reconstruction, the aimless Klan was turned to petty ends, pitting "faction against faction, neighbor against neighbor, man against man," and leading to "martial law, prison bars and the shadow of the gallows."[34]

This theme was reinforced in Dixon's 1912 novel, *The Sins of the Father*, which harped on the idea that the Invisible Empire was an inherently "dangerous institution" that gained its virtue in its "absolute obedience" to "an intelligent and patriotic chief." Without that leadership, the organization would degenerate into "a reign of terror by irresponsible fools." Although in both books the "good" Klan is ultimately able to take control of the "bad" Klan and force it out of action, Dixon's disapproval of a Klan revival was clear.[35]

As the second Klan rose in power through the early 1920s, then, it seemed obvious to the author what he needed to do. In the summer of 1924, Dixon published *The Black Hood*, explicitly warning the revived Klan to disband. The story of a Reconstruction Klavern that outlives its purpose, *The Black Hood* returned to the themes and heavy-handed preaching of *The Traitor*, forcing additional lectures on religious tolerance and the dangers of anonymity into already labored dialogue. The revived Klan of the book—whose white robes are replaced, without any attempt at subtlety, with a black hood— abused the power of the organization, leading to score settling, attempts to "regulate the private life of individual men and women," and a disintegration into "a weapon of religious persecution." The "criminal folly" soon descended into violence. To rule out any misunderstanding, Dixon underlined his hamfisted sermonizing about the awful dangers of the Klan with the deaths of both a crippled Jewish boy (the son of a Polish immigrant bearing "a remarkable resemblance to Hoffman's Christ") and the boy's dog.[36]

As the *New York Times* remarked, although the book's attempt to discourage membership in the resurgent Klan would "seem a good purpose," it did not make this a good book. The *New York World* noted that the novel was "a book of intensely melodramatic quality" that seemed to have been written "in a good deal of a hurry." The book's sales seem to have reflected this point. Nonetheless, Dixon had made his point. The *World* review commended *The Black Hood*'s "rebuke and condemnation" of the reborn Klan's "worst possible impulses and auspices." The author reiterated his arguments to interviewers during a press tour, calling the Klan's disguise "a provocation to violence and disorder" and the organization "a menace to American democracy." The original Clansman would remain a vocal opponent of the Invisible Empire until its collapse.[37]

Dixon was not alone in channeling his antipathy toward the revived Klan into fiction. Walter White's *The Fire in the Flint*, for example, presented a sorely underrepresented African American viewpoint on the organization that scandalized many white Southerners. White, who worked for the NAACP as "an investigator and reporter of racial violence" (and who would head that organization from 1931 until his death in 1955), hoped to promote "a literature and art that told a truth about African Americans and made no concessions to stereotype." In White's words, "Writing about Negro life as it really exists" was a subject "as yet practically untouched." *The Fire in the Flint* was his attempt to rectify the situation by depicting the struggles of African Americans living in a Georgia plagued by the violence of the Ku Klux Klan.[38]

Just as much a message novel as Dixon's *The Black Hood*, *The Fire in the Flint* was redeemed by its journalistic attention to detail and its realistic dialogue. Although the book was his first foray into fiction, White understood that the best means of communicating his meaning was through an engaging plot and effective characterization rather than lectures shoehorned into the discussions of his characters. *The Fire in the Flint* is particularly successful at conveying White's argument for black group consciousness as the prerequisite for an end to discrimination, particularly in Southern farming, as well as a need to debunk the idea that lynchings were somehow justified by imagined "outrages" against white womanhood. White was also able to convincingly present an unflattering portrait of "stodgy, phlegmatic, stupid citizens" with "a natural love of the mysterious and adventurous and an instinct toward brute action." For White, this group as a whole comprised the racially charged Ku Klux Klan, without nice distinctions between members of the organization and sympathizers to the wider movement. *The Fire in the Flint* even managed to summon up some small measure of sympathy for Klansmen as "creatures of the fear they sought to inspire," living in "constant dread" that African Americans would prove themselves the equal, if not the superior, of white men.[39]

White's ideas were embodied in the novel by the character of Kenneth Harper, a black doctor returning home after attending college and serving in the First World War. Harper's involvement with a black tenant farmers association (which draws the ire of local Klansmen, including the sheriff and other local landowners and officials) stimulates a growing awareness of himself as an affluent black man in the South. That process is hastened considerably when a gang of white men rape Harper's sister, pushing Harper's brother, Bob, to kill several of the rapists. Bob, pursued by a mob bent on lynching him, then kills himself.[40] The Klan, in turn, murders Harper—ostensibly to prevent him from avenging his family, although in large part because of his success in organizing local black farmers to resist the poor treatment they have faced at the hands of white landowners—and successfully avoids any repercussion for the crime by falsely claiming that Harper had assaulted a white woman and been lynched.[41]

White's unflinching condemnation of antiblack violence and his aspersions on the "honor" of white womanhood were rooted in his experiences touring the South for the NAACP, where he had observed firsthand white reaction to black labor movements.[42] Concerned that the novel would offend white Southerners and hurt sales, publisher George H. Doran rejected *The Fire in the Flint*. White refused to downplay the severity of the situation in the South and weaken his stance. To one correspondent, he wrote that he "would destroy the manuscript before I would submit to emasculation which would kill the effectiveness of the novel." Instead, White took it to Alfred A. Knopf, one of the few progressive major publishing houses, which issued it in late 1924 to great success.[43]

The book sold well (helped in no small part by White's use of NAACP branches to build a distribution network and boost sales), and was received with great acclaim by many Northern and black critics, who praised the book for both its message and its literary merit. Joel Rogers used the pages of *The Messenger* to praise its "rough-hewn, Rodinesque vigor and its crisp, tense narrative." *The New York Times* called it "an inevitable novel" that "deserves serious consideration." *The Independent* declared it "a cry of the oppressed" and an "indictment of white civilization." W. E. B. DuBois, writing for *Crisis*, called *The Fire in the Flint* "a stirring story and a strong bit of propaganda against the white Klansman and the black pussyfoot." The *Baltimore Afro-American* listed it among its best books of the year, and tried to convince White to let the newspaper serialize it.[44]

Even some Southern white critics commended *The Fire in the Flint*. A. S. Bernd of the *Macon Telegraph* reviewed it favorably, losing the newspaper a number of subscribers. Lawrence Stallings, a Georgia native, wrote an overwhelmingly positive review lavished with criticism of his home state that was published in the *New York World* and widely republished by sympathetic newspapers. Stallings called the plot "a melodramatic story, garish and hysterical," but conceded that White's case "is so fiery a one of truth" that "overstatement is almost necessary to a fighting book."[45]

A more typical Southern response came from the *Savannah Press*, which published an editorial review of *The Fire in the Flint* entitled "A Book of Lies," and was similarly widely republished—although in most cases it was republished by Northern newspapers as an example of Southern intolerance. The *Press*, carefully avoiding any mention of the Klan, called the book "the worst libel we have seen on the South and Southern men and women." With no apparent irony, the paper accused White's book of encouraging "unfair prejudice." The novel's claim that nine out of the ten "trifling" women who claimed to have been raped by African Americans were actually just trying to save their reputations, and were willing to see a man lynched to do so, attracted the most criticism. Even white Southern liberals reacted with dismay to such an idea, as *The Fire in the Flint* had suggested they would. The *Press* called it a "palpable, outrageous lie" and "a deadly insult to the women of the South." With characteristic restraint, the newspaper implicitly threatened White with violence if he ever returned to Georgia.[46]

Few novels dealing with the Klan had the same kind of literary merit as *The Fire in the Flint*. As with nonfiction publishing, the decade saw the creation of a cottage industry of polemical novels arguing the wonders and dangers of the Klan organization. These were often widely read, but have been largely forgotten as (per Erin A. Smith's formulation) "bad books." The *New York Times* commented in 1926 that "controversial matters" like the Klan were "very rarely . . . presented with the breadth of vision and insight which is imperative for their genuine success." Worse, "the controversial matter spoils in most instances what might otherwise prove to be a good narrative." This is all too true. Yet what we must not forget is that sufficient people were reading these novels to compel the *New York Times* to bemoan their quality, even as these books offered disparate and heterogeneous definitions of Klannish identity for popular audiences.[47]

The year 1922 did not just see the publication of *Ulysses* and *Babbitt*. Texas academic Hubert Shands's *White and Black*, published by Harcourt, Brace, also reached shelves that year. The story of Bob Robertson, a young white Texan preparing to leave for college who became embroiled in the lives of the tenant farmers on his family's plantation, Shands's novel was really a clunky diatribe against the methods of the Invisible Empire. The Klan, the novelist argued, "disregarded every civil right of a citizen," substituted "the savagery of a mob for ordered judicial processes," and would plunge society "back into barbarism."[48]

Concerned primarily with the "dangers" of fraternization between the races, the Texan used the novel to underline his support for a "non-partisan, non-sectarian organization" that would promote "racial purity." Shands's issue with the Klan was not its ideas, but the "outrages" perpetrated by the organization in pursuit of its admirable aims. In this, the novelist's approach was similar to anti-Klan nonfiction like Henry Fry's *The Modern Ku Klux Klan*, attacking the organization while promoting the movement's racial ideology. This conflicted attitude was reflected in reviews of the book. Burton Rascoe in the *New York Tribune* deemed Shands's story "an elementary tale" but a "frank picture." A decade later, the novel was remembered by critic Herschel Brickell as "fiction primarily concerned with the race question." *White and Black* understandably garnered more attention for its message than for its half-baked plot.[49]

Tar and Feathers by Victor Rubin, a Chicago newspaperman, was not much of an improvement. The 1923 novel described the ethical awakening of Robert Hamilton, a young Georgian, the grandson of a Confederate captain, and heir to an extensive cotton plantation. Returning home after World War I, Hamilton joins the "Trick Track Tribe," where he meets William J. Simmons's fictional counterpart. By the novel's end, though, the Georgian has been disabused of the organization's worth by his true friends, a Catholic soldier and Jewish doctor.[50]

An effective argument against the real-life Klan's official propaganda, Rubin's novel met with some success, and was rushed into a second printing by his publisher, Dorrance & Company of Philadelphia. Once again, however, the book's true appeal seems to have resided not in its story but in its message—combined with the Klan's seemingly ever-present ability to attract public attention. Reviewers noted that *Tar and Feathers* kept "the interest sustained," but it was the "timely enough, and incidentally worthy enough," theme of the book that would "justify its publication." Much the same was true of Ellen Corrigan Scott's *That Fool Moffett*, the story of a lapsed Catholic whose lack of faith loses him true love, and who ends up married to the anti-Catholic daughter of a Klan lecturer. A tedious debunking of various myths spread by the Klan, framed within an exaltation of the "moral superiority" of "inviolable Catholic marriage law," *That Fool Moffett* offered little in the way of plot, and even less in the way of enjoyment.[51]

Literary merit took a backseat to propagandistic intent. The same was true of most pro-Klan novels. If historical fiction had endorsed the idea of Klan as savior, the organization's continued appearance in contemporary American fiction served to endorse the movement's supposed virtues. Most of this writing was extraordinarily mediocre, yet was nonetheless able to find an audience. In doing so, Klannish authors situated a localized and federalized organization within a largely uniform cultural identity that was reproduced nationally, as books from around the country drew readers into an imagined community of white Protestant heroism. Thus, we must consider 1922 not only the year of *Ulysses* and *Babbit* and *White and Black*, but also the year of Egbert Brown's *The Final Awakening*, a thoroughly bad book.[52]

As Brown explained in a foreword, the "sole idea and intention" of the novel was "to convey to the alien world, from a Klannish standpoint, the true attitude of the organization." Given that aim, it is unsurprising that *The Final*

Awakening was marked by shoddy dialogue and awkward characterization. It is also unsurprising that the "true attitude" Brown claimed to present was one that attempted to divorce an imaginary heroic Klannish identity with (theoretically) wide appeal from the violent bigotry of reality. This fictional Klan had no hatred toward Catholics, Jews, or African Americans, but merely a desire to see laws enforced and "Americanism" reign supreme. To that end, Brown told the story of Roger Wilson, a Catholic and the stepson of a bootlegger. Over the course of the novel, Wilson slowly realized the error of his opposition to the Klan, renouncing both his stepfather and his religion, while Brown bolted on a romantic subplot with the sister of a Klansman for good measure. In the process, the Klan saved local African Americans from themselves by shutting down the (white Protestant) bootlegger, whose whiskey was rendering them useless to their white employers. The novel also saw the organization kidnap and beat a (white Protestant) doctor responsible for a string of botched illegal abortions resulting in the death of multiple young Jewish women.[53]

The Klan was thereby presented as the savior of morality, without regard to race or religion, with all violence in the novel leveled only against other white Protestants and done so to protect other groups. Simultaneously, Brown reinforced bigoted frames of understanding—African Americans as the only group weak willed enough to fall under the power of the bootlegger, Jewish women as the only clients of the abortionist. In both disclaiming and appealing to intolerance, Brown crafted a poor story but an effective call for new members. As the *Fellowship Forum* described it, "If you are NOT a Klansman now, you will want to be one after you have finished reading it."[54]

The novel's link to the Klan organization is almost as murky as the book's plot. While Brown claimed to have no official connection with the Invisible Empire, his book was published in the Klan stronghold of Brunswick, Georgia, by Empire Distributors, a common nom de plume for Klan publishing ventures. Certainly, *The Final Awakening* parroted the organization's official line. Most novels of the Klan movement, though, were clearly produced independently of any control from national leaders of the Invisible Empire. Despite their disparate and uncoordinated origins, they offered an aesthetic of Klannish movement identity far more cohesive than the federalized organization itself—a consumable cultural identity in which signifiers of the cross and hood denoted white Protestant virtue rather than violence and hatred.

That heroic self-identity was further reinforced in 1923 with the publication of *Harold the Klansman* by George Alfred Brown. *Harold* was certainly not devoid of the sermonizing that had plagued *The Final Awakening*. Like Egbert Brown, George Brown made clear the fact that the book had been written to provide "reliable information" about the Klan, and devoted pages of stilted dialogue to issues of papal infallibility and parochial school education. Unlike Egbert Brown, George Brown displayed a fairly deft hand at characterization and melodramatic plotting. The novel saw the eponymous Harold save his sweetheart's family business from ruin at the hands of a greedy bootlegger and his Catholic, Jewish, and African American allies. By joining the Klan, along with all of the other leading citizens, Harold was able to clean up his unnamed western town, while also proving the Invisible Empire's worth to his beloved. Historian Wyn Craig Wade has gone so far as to call the plot "engrossing," although that may be overstating the case.[55]

While it was not going to knock Gertrude Atherton's *Black Oxen* from the top of the best-seller list, *Dawn* called *Harold the Klansman* "a story that both entertains and instructs." The *Badger American* extolled it as "a volume that is without precedent in the fields of literature," written "in a beautiful, sincere manner" that "sounds the tocsin for a greater service to America." The *Jayhawker American* raved that it was "a great social novel destined to make its impress on the thought of Americans" and would prove to be "one of the great historical novels of this generation." It certainly struck a chord with sympathetic readers, who kept *Harold the Klansman* in reprints until at least 1927.[56]

A similar attempt at entertaining Klan fiction promoting a sanitized definition of Klannish identity appeared in early 1924, printed by Ohio's Patriot Publishing Company. *Knight Vale of the K.K.K.* by William Andrew Saxon told the story of Fairfax Vale. A vigorously anti-Klan crusader in the employ of a vicious Catholic state governor (clearly modeled on Oklahoma's governor J. C. Walton), Vale came to realize the error of his ways and joined the Invisible Empire. Over the course of the novel, Saxon managed to include complete reprints of the "Klansman's Creed" and of an alleged Knights of Columbus oath. He also displayed an interesting strand of defensiveness about the Klan's anti-Semitism, claiming that Catholics were the real anti-Semites. On the whole, though, the Klan author seemed far less interested in the idea of furnishing reliable information than in presenting an adventure story with a byzantine plot. *Black Mask*'s influence was evident in the increasingly standard conversion narrative and in a denouement lifted almost wholesale from "'Call Out the Klan," as Catholics framed the Klan for the kidnapping of Vale's sweetheart.[57]

Even as the Klan's power as a national organization began its rapid decline, movement authors continued to churn out message novels of dubious literary merit. *The Son of a Klansman* by Albert Gaffney bypassed the allegory of the allegorical novel and simply stated in the foreword which character personified the modern Ku Klux Klan and which personified political corruption, the Klan's ultimate enemy. The tangled melodrama *100%* by Albert Wentz (under the subtle pseudonym of Kenneth Kenelm King) was little better, as the usual criticisms of Catholics, Jews, and African Americans took the place of most dialogue. Wentz's *100%* was at least able to distinguish itself through the bizarre nature of its plot, which included rape, murderous nuns, baby strangling, and the revelation that the Catholic proscription of meat on a Friday was actually a conspiracy to slowly poison the Protestant population with arsenic-laced foodstuffs.[58]

Startling as the content may have been, these polemics are primarily useful in understanding how Klan members and sympathizers defined themselves. They are less useful to our understanding of the wider cultural 1920s than the ways in which the Invisible Empire's presence infiltrated novels with less propagandistic concerns. This most often meant following the same model as many newspaper editors or the editors of *Black Mask*—to increase sales by exploiting the "picturesque" atmosphere presented by the Klan while leaving the organization itself largely incidental to the plot. The purpose was entertainment rather than judgment. Thus, these stories often implicitly legitimated and promulgated the aims and ideas of the wider Klan movement.

Even H. L. Mencken's lofty *American Mercury* was not beyond co-opting the Klan into its short stories, albeit to lambast the very idea of Americanism. In David Purroy's "On the Lam," the detective hero complained that leads were "as scarce as Jews at a KKK pig roast." Somewhat more substantially, "Ku Klux" by W. A. S. Douglas saw a Polish-born war veteran driven insane by the Klan's subversion of American values. Perhaps most effectively, the *Mercury* featured one of mystery writer (and close friend of Mencken) James M. Cain's earliest stories. In 1928, six years before *The Postman Always Rings Twice*, eight years before *Double Indemnity*, thirteen years before *Mildred Pierce*, Cain published "Trial by Jury." The short dialogue sketch saw jurors deliberating their verdict in the case of a man who had murdered a Klansman in self-defense. After bribing the simpleton Klansman in their midst to offer a favorable account of their deliberations to his organization, the jurors ultimately vote to soften the conviction to manslaughter, and leave, paying lip service to "Citizenship . . . Patriotism . . . All like of that" as they do so. The only kind of Americanism that seemed to matter, to Cain, was the kind that might get you targeted by the Ku Klux Klan.[59]

Similar ideas were offered by James Stevens, another friend and protégé of Mencken, best known for his tales popularizing Paul Bunyan as an American folk hero. In 1924, Stevens published "Uplift on the Frontier" in the *Mercury*, mocking the "simpletons" lured by the "childish excitements" offered by the Klan. Three years later, his novel *Mattock* would take similar aim at such excitements in a thoroughly Menckenian excoriation of prejudiced and ignorant Americans who made mealymouthed professions of Christian faith. These tendencies were made flesh in his protagonist, "upright honest Christian" Parvin Mattock, who soon succumbs to temptation—in the form of drink, gambling, cigarettes, and French whores—when he joins the army. His self-righteous attitude also propels him into a role as an informer inside his unit, looking for Bolshevist influence in "the grand, new, patriotic, religious, upliftin' American game of snoop, spy, frame up, and stool."

A postwar religious awakening puts Mattock back on the straight and narrow—married to a reverend's daughter, taking a lead in the local American Legion, and, best of all, becoming an official of the Kansas Ku Klux Klan. The Invisible Empire barely features in the plot, but Mattock's membership is the effective climax of the novel, as Stevens used it to display the ignorance and hollow faith of such men. Critics praised the "imperceptible irony" and "superb detachment" of the novel. Stevens's "solid and humorous" novel painted the Klansman as an ultimately pathetic figure, continually struggling for "decency."[60]

Stevens was not the first to take such satirical aim. Journalist James Henle's *Sound and Fury* (which beat Faulkner to the title, minus a few definite articles, by five years) was published by Knopf in late 1924. Henle's book focused on the plight of George "Goody" Guthrie, whom the *New York Times* called "an individual knight gallantly leading a lost cause against a ruin and a havoc of regimented democracy and industrial materialism." For Henle, the Ku Klux Klan (which included the local mayor and chief of police) was the personification of soul-sapping regimentation, "the most typical product of America and 100 per cent Americanism," who "merely went one step further than the prohibitionists." It was with no small symbolism that the novel ended with a mob of Klansmen murdering Guthrie.[61]

This satirical attack on not just the Klan organization but the wider Klan movement and the effort to impose an alien morality on individuals like Guthrie was received with mixed reviews. Some lavished praise on a "distinguished" novel filled with "true and sham-smashing observation and comment" that made the book "decidedly good and decidedly out of the ordinary." Others complained that Henle's work was "platitudinous and unconvincing" and that the Klannish climax was "too dramatic." Nonetheless, *Sound and Fury* offered a notable critique of the Invisible Empire for its vicious enforcement of a hectoring moralism.[62]

Henle's lament for the decline of rugged American aristocratic individualism in the face of conformism and conventionality owed no small debt to Sinclair Lewis, who also incorporated the Klan into his controversial 1927 best seller *Elmer Gantry*. The self-serving attitude of the eponymous antihero toward the Invisible Empire was the perfect example of the evangelical minister's disingenuousness. Lewis presented the Klan as a political problem for "many of the most worthy Methodist and Baptist clergymen," who looked favorably on the organization. Gantry's own inclination in the novel is as a member of the Klannish movement, favoring the desire "to keep all foreigners, Jews, Catholics, and negroes in their place, which was no place at all." That enthusiasm is tempered by his awareness that there are "prominent people, nice people, rich people," who oppose the Klan organization. As such, Lewis's antihero takes a typically Gantry-esque stance: "It seemed to him more truly American, also a lot safer, to avoid the problem." The hollowness of Gantry's conviction is reflected in a statement on religious liberty so generic that it pleases both Klansmen and their opponents—the approach many real clergymen, as well as newspaper editors and authors, had taken. The Klan's part in *Elmer Gantry* was short and incidental to the plot, but operated as ideal shorthand for Lewis, allowing the author to explicate his scathing condemnation of American moral hypocrisy in a nutshell.[63]

This approach reached its apogee with the bizarre but much-admired 1927 novel *Half-Gods* by Murray Sheehan, which took Lewis's satirical approach but added a fabulist twist. A professor of journalism at the University of Arkansas, Sheehan set the story in the small town of Roosevelt, Missouri.[64] There, the Durnan family's old black mare gives birth to a centaur, whom the family names Dick. This "half-god" then spends the rest of the novel struggling between an honorable barbarism, symbolized by ancient Greek art and culture, that allows him to occasionally encounter Pan and wood nymphs, and the crude civilization of the small town that he longs to be accepted by—a conflict none too subtly embodied by his own dual biology. Even as Dick's innate nobility is vulgarized over the course of the story by contact with the ignorant bigots who populate the town, one of Durnan's sons, Daniel, is drawn to higher cultural aspirations, embodied by the town's recently arrived artistic free spirit, a married Frenchwoman named Lolla Delacourt.

In the novel's denouement, Dick—whose struggle took on an increasingly sexual nature, torn between dalliances with mares and a growing attraction to humans—abducts a young woman. In response, the Klan (including the town's reverend, its leading businessmen, and Durnan himself) springs into action. Instead of tracking the centaur, however, the posse soon heads for Delacourt's home. The Frenchwoman having obtained a reputation for "ungodly thinking and loose morals" (symbolized by her affinity for "dirty" art like Greek statues), the moralizing mob moves to burn down the house, with or without Delacourt inside, as a lesson to those "who thought to contra-vene . . . the customs of common decency and American virtue."[65]

After several members suggest that burning the house would be bad for the town's reputation and, by extension, their businesses, the Klansmen limit themselves to burning a cross. "It is one thing," the mob is reminded, to have a Klan "serving admirably to keep in order the black dwellers" and the "mean citizens of no import." It was quite a different matter if the Klan became "de-structive of property values" and injurious of "those with bank balances." With the abduction completely forgotten, the Klan dissipates back into the night. Dick, who is almost instantly henpecked by his abductee, returns the girl the next day with little recrimination. By the novel's end, Delacourt has been forced out of town, Daniel has left for better things in California, and the men of the town have finally accepted Dick as one of them.[66]

With its fashionable criticism of a reactionary and unenlightened "boo-boisie," *Half-Gods* was received with critical acclaim as a "daring and satirical story" that offered "humor, tragedy, satire and gross realism." Praising *Half-Gods'* ability to illustrate the idea that small-town religion was "not a refine-ment of the spirit" but "an emotional outlet for stunted souls and dreary lives," reviews hailed the book as an "odd tour de force" in which "the Klan adds its bit to the shallow performance." As many reviews of the novel pointed out, the Invisible Empire's place in the book was not as a plot point. Instead, the organization embodied the townsfolk's inability to understand that morality should be "acquired from within, rather than applied from without."[67]

The town's success in replacing Dick's youthful ideals with their own standards (unable to find middle ground between "salacious" and "rigor-ously moral"), though, illustrated the enduring power of Klannish moralists. A short story in the best-selling *Saturday Evening Post*, "Tar and Feathers" by George Patullo, further underlined this point. Patullo's story, ostensibly a satirical barb in the vein of Sheehan et al., explicitly endorsed the ability of the Klan to "put the quietus on a lot of evils" in the postwar period. The real problem of the "mask and shroud" organization, the piece argued (alongside national advertisements for Pepsodent and Buster Brown Shoes), was that it allowed "riffraff" to join and subvert the organization to their own purposes. Ultimately, the local Klavern in the story disbands—save for the heroic "true" Klansmen who set out to punish those who had subverted the movement.[68]

Even this mild criticism was blunted in the work of many authors who, like *Black Mask*, saw only good literary (and commercial) material in the "childish excitements" identified by James Stevens. *The Ku Klux Ball* by Glenn Gordon, published in 1926, is a significant example of the trend. Gordon's run-of-the-mill story aped Petersen's "Call Out the Klan," as a local Klavern rescues the Catholic main character from his kidnappers, who are falsely posing as Klansmen. Yet the Invisible Empire remained fairly incidental. The novel was predominantly concerned with the niceties of the "younger set," worried more with the etiquette of when the Victrola should be turned off than with the Klan. When the *New York Times* described the book as "a story of the Klan," the author wrote to the newspaper to make the telling complaint that the organization was "unimportant" to the novel, and was "used merely as a background to justify the title and popularize the book." Gordon was not interested in presenting an argument for or against the Klan. The Invisible Empire was simply a selling point.[69]

Much the same was true of a series of adventure novels published through the 1920s that often lauded the Klan. Cyril "Sapper" McNeile's *The Black Gang*, a tautly plotted thriller originally published in England, was widely serialized in the American press and published in the United States by the George H. Doran Company in 1923. McNeile's story was the second of what would become a highly popular nineteen-book series. His formidable protagonist was Bulldog Drummond, an ex-military man and unorthodox private detective, and acknowledged model for Ian Fleming's James Bond.

Although the novel was set in England, the heroic Black Gang was an overt heroic fictional Klan equivalent. Drummond, secretly the head of the group, led the Gang to foil the malevolent plans of a group of Jewish Bolshevik spies (who also dabbled in white slavery and drug peddling), largely by kidnapping and flogging the evildoers. For Drummond (and, by extension, McNeile), the ends more than justified the brutal means—just as they had for John Carroll Daly and Race Williams in *Black Mask*. As the head of Scotland Yard argued in the novel, the Black Gang's methods "were undoubtedly illegal," but "the results were excellent."[70]

The organization's similarity to the Klan was not lost on American readers. The *New York Times* commented that McNeile "has apparently taken for his model a Konklave of the Klan as its most loyal adherents imagine it to be." This did not stop the *New York Times* reviewer from praising the book's "spectacular and daring adventures." The *International Book Review* noted that the Klan analogue's adventures would make even "the most jaded reader of crime stories" bound to "sit up and take notice." McNeile wasted no time on sermonizing. *The Black Gang* was simply an adventure novel that used the Ku Klux Klan as a model for its heroic protagonists, reinforcing the Klannish self-image that polemical novels had worked so hard to promulgate. This exploitation of the Klan's cultural prominence certainly did not seem to hurt the book's success.[71]

Novelist Ridgwell Cullum's *The Saint of the Speedway* similarly featured a lightly disguised Invisible Empire as a heroic vigilante organization. Published in 1924, again by George H. Doran—who had rejected White's *The Fire in the Flint*—Cullum's Klan analogue added character to the novel while remaining largely incidental to the plot itself. Cullum himself was a popular author of the Jack London school of rough outdoor adventure and red-blooded romance. Like many of his Alaska-set adventure stories, *The Saint of the Speedway* told a fairly familiar story of an indebted family set to lose their farm until a rough-hewn man sweeps into town to romance the daughter, save the farm, and set all things right. Cullum's minor twist in this book was the reveal of the rugged hero as the Chief Light of the local Clan. Although depicted on the book's striking cover as possible villains and drawn, without any pretense otherwise, as Klansmen (see fig. 5.1), the Clan served throughout the book as a civilizing moral force that defended the weak while punishing those outside the law, including gamblers and drug dealers.

While Cullum spent little time dwelling on the nature of the organization, preferring to push on with his narrative, he made clear his admiration for the "passionate exasperation" of a Klan movement desirous of a world "made safe for decent democracy," and "prepared to purge it without regard to the rest of the world's opinions." The *New York Times* met this exaltation of Klannish

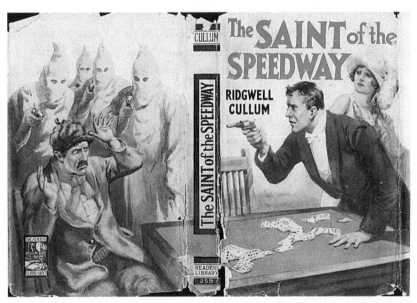

FIGURE 5.1. Book jacket for the Readers Library edition of Ridgwell Cullum's *The Saint of the Speedway* (New York: George H. Doran, 1924).

philosophy with praise in a review that clearly demonstrated an understanding that the "Clan" was "an organization very similar to the Ku Klux," making for a "real mystery" filled with "dramatic and thrilling" adventure. Bruce Gould in the *New York Herald Tribune* agreed. The introduction of the vigilante organization "when quicker measures are needed than those provided by the processes of law" made for "plenty of action and somewhat of mystery." *The Bookman* called it "as possible as it is exciting."[72]

One of the most popular adventure novelists of the period was Rex Beach, part of the flood of self-consciously masculine melodrama of the early twentieth century, alongside Stewart Edward White and James Oliver Curwood. His action-packed oeuvre made him one of the most popular writers in America, selling more than three million books by 1926. He had also earned the mockery of H. L. Mencken, who ridiculed the "gaudy tales of a Rex Beach, with their bold projections of the Freudian dreams of go-getters, ice-wagon drivers, Ku Kluxers, Rotary Club presidents, and other such carnivora." The Sage of Baltimore was not far wrong. Beach's brand of escapist fiction was exactly the kind of middlebrow literature that the American public—including Klan members—adored. The *Fiery Cross* had, for example, particularly praised Beach's *Flowing Gold* in 1923.[73]

Beach, for his part, offered the same conflicted attitude on the Klan as many other writers of the period. Where the adventure novelist was approving of the movement's "100% American" aims, he was critical of the organization's methods. This was particularly clear in Beach's 1927 novel, *The Mating Call*. Leslie Hatten, the poor but noble Southern protagonist, reiterated throughout the novel that he could not support "secret influence or mob violence." At the same time, he had no objection to "the principles of the Klan advocates."[74]

Those patriotic and moralistic Klannish principles were omnipresent themes in *The Mating Call*, even as Beach largely elided any idea of the violent implementation of those principles. The growing presence of the local Klan (which included local luminaries such as the judge, clergymen, and several of Hatten's friends) was a constant source of interest for the characters, and one of the primary topics of conversation. The only direct action taken by the organization, however, was limited to a threatening note—and even that note was revealed to be the work of an impostor.[75]

The Invisible Empire's role in *The Mating Call* was ultimately inconsequential. The Klan did not even warrant a mention in the *New York Times* review of the book, which praised Beach's "detail and colorful description." Will Cuppy in the *New York Herald Tribune* noted the novel's "exciting bouts with the Ku Klux Klan," but they were only one aspect of Beach's "first rate cinematic mystery." The Invisible Empire was there purely to add flavor to the plot. As one review tellingly noted, the book had "a dash of Ku Klux Klan to give it spice."[76]

In examining these varied fictional representations of the Klan, we see clear exemplars of the fluid cultural continuities and conflicts of the period. Even as the organization's secrecy was criticized, the carefully cultivated air of mystery and excitement that surrounded the Invisible Empire made it a popular backdrop for crime and adventure stories. Satirists like Sheehan tried to highlight the threat of the Klan, often by tying the organization to an identity of toxic Americanism—an identity that the Klan itself embraced. At the same time, popular authors like Herman Petersen and Rex Beach implicitly legitimized the organization in their work and often explicitly championed the aims and ideals of the wider Klan movement.

Whether it was the "good fiction qualities" identified by *Black Mask* or the "spice" in a Beach novel, the Ku Klux Klan found itself widely commercialized and sanitized in popular fiction in the 1920s. In divorcing the fictional Invisible Empire from its more unsavory aspects, these stories often echoed the cultural identity of Klannish heroism promulgated by Klan propagandists. Around the country, working largely independently of the Klan organization, these enthusiastic amateurs hammered home a largely uniform vision of white Protestant virtue in polemical novels like *Harold the Klansman* and *Knight Vale of the K.K.K.* Yet these "bad books" have often been absent from literary studies of the period. Henle's *Sound and Fury* disappeared from the historical record, and Faulkner's *The Sound and the Fury* was written in. In the process, we have forgotten the significance of the Invisible Empire as both hero (or at least antihero) and villain for a mass literary audience in the 1920s. As the Klan consumed popular fiction, popular fiction consumed the Klan— and neither was entirely sure what to make of the other.

6

Just Entertainment

One splendid field for our efforts is the movies. The screen offers the best possible opportunity for propaganda.

SEARCHLIGHT, November 15, 1924

Go fuck yourself.

EUGENE O'NEILL to unknown Georgia Klansman

The theatrical entertainments of the 1920s displayed the same commercial hunger for a dash of Ku Klux Klan to add spice. The Invisible Empire was not just featured on the front page of newspapers across the country, but also in *Variety*, alongside stories on George M. Cohan and Mary Pickford. As the entertainment trade publication noted, "A touch of the Ku Klux Klan that serves as a thrill" was a key feature in a "successful screen production." Just as on the page, commercial productions on the stage and screen offered mixed assessments of the Klan organization, but frequently served to sanitize and legitimize the wider Klan movement. The ambiguous attentions paid the Invisible Empire often furthered the conceptions of a heroic white Protestant identity shaped by local Klan members and individual sympathizers, who appropriated popular dramatic forms even as the organization denounced those same entertainments.[1]

This hostility was perhaps best exemplified by the reaction to Eugene O'Neill's acclaimed but divisive *All God's Chillun Got Wings*. It had already caused a rift between H. L. Mencken and his coeditor, George Jean Nathan, over whether it warranted publication in the *American Mercury*—though that was an argument over quality. The content proved even more problematic. O'Neill's 1924 play told the story of Jim Harris, an ambitious young black man, who marries Ella Downey, an insecure white woman. In the face of Harris's struggles to become a lawyer, Downey feels increasingly inferior to her husband, despite her "superior" skin color. Coming to equate Harris's efforts to pass the bar exam with the efforts of African Americans to "pass" in white society, Downey attempts to undermine his career at every turn. Ultimately, her growing prejudice drives her insane.[2]

Even before *All God's Chillun* opened, Klan publications complained of the "nauseating and disgusting" nature of the interracial production, arguing that the play should be suppressed lest it "stir the negroes of the country to violence." Members of the cast, including star Paul Robeson, received a deluge of intimidating letters allegedly written by Klan members. The Long Island Klan threatened to bomb the theater if the play ever opened. O'Neill himself was the target of a number of explicit death threats. One, sent from Georgia on official Klan stationery, warned O'Neill that he would never see his sons again if the play opened. The playwright responded by scrawling "Go fuck yourself" across the face of the letter and mailing it back to the Georgia Klan.[3]

Despite the extremism evident in these threats, the Klan's general reaction was firmly within the American mainstream. As O'Neill later remembered, it seemed "as if all the feeble-witted both in and out of the K.K.K. were hurling newspaper bricks in my direction." The *Pittsburgh Courier* noted that the play lay at the center of "a veritable storm of pro and con discussion," while critic Heywood Broun commented on "the most violent sort of controversy" surrounding the production. One study of *All God's Chillun* claimed that so much newsprint was dedicated to the play that the clipping service cost more than the sets. The *American Mercury* lamented the number of "half-wits" responsible for a "copious flood of ga-ga" about the play. From the American Legion to a Princeton faculty member to the Salvation Army to half the Southern newspapers, the Ku Klux Klan was in "respectable" company.[4]

This was not an unusual alliance. Although their criticisms of theater tended to be more overtly racialized, the concerns of Klan members fell generally within the mainstream of American moralizing. Even as the organization's leaders bemoaned the "degenerate sensuality" of the "vicious and depraved" stage, Catholic periodicals like *The Sign* complained of "vile plays" that violated "every canon of morality and common decency." Booth Tarkington took to the pages of *Collier's* to dismiss most of the 1926–27 season's plays as "sheer dirt." Even as Broadway solidified its theatrical prominence, New York's 1927 Theater Padlock Law banned "obscene, indecent, immoral or impure" productions. The city's mayor declared his vehement opposition to "disgusting or revolting degenerate plays." The mayor of Boston, meanwhile, instituted a theatrical "Code of Morals" and was empowered to revoke theater licenses "for any reason whatsoever."[5]

The same was true in film, where the industry saw a series of scandals stir public outrage—most notoriously the arrest of Roscoe "Fatty" Arbuckle for manslaughter in 1921. As the presiding judge in Arbuckle's first trial noted, "We are not trying Roscoe Arbuckle alone. . . . We are trying present-day morals, our present-day social conditions, our present-day looseness of thought and lack of social balance." These concerns were similarly present in a letter sent by Pittsburgh Klan No. 1 to popular fan magazine *Movie Weekly* in 1923. "High morals, clean living, respect for religion and our flag" and "respect for law and order" in films, the Klan argued, would help the country produce "he-men and patriotic womanly women." The alternative was "cigarette-smoking devils who love poodle dogs more than they do babies."[6]

It was difficult for *Movie Weekly* to disagree. Reprinting the Klan's letter in its entirety, the magazine was forced to admit that "we find ourselves in accord with many of the sentiments expressed in this communication." Indeed, writer T. Howard Kelly encouraged "right-minded citizens of this country in all levels of life" to "applaud the order for such a stand." Although disavowing the organization's "secret methods" and intolerance, the magazine implicitly endorsed the wider Klan movement and argued that in fighting for high morals and clean living, "we can work shoulder to shoulder with Ku Kluxers." Many did just that, as local efforts to fight "indecent motion pictures" around the country—including the appointment of Will Hays as president of the Motion Picture Producers and Distributors of America—intertwined with Klannish efforts to subdue the "corrupting influence" of cinema.[7]

Their success in this was most notable in the attacks leveled against Charlie Chaplin, and particularly his 1923 short *The Pilgrim*. Prefiguring later Nazi criticism, Klan members accused Chaplin of being Jewish and using his popularity to make the "crowning insult" to Protestant clergy. "For a long time," the *Searchlight* argued, it had been generally known that "a deliberate attempt was being made by certain Jew picture-show magnates" to "ridicule the Protestant ministry." *The Pilgrim*, in which Chaplin played an escaped convict who poses as a parson in a small Texas town, was the final straw. In a widely publicized move, the Klan of Walla Walla, Washington, persuaded the mayor to have all showings of the picture canceled. Inspired by this example, Klans in Iowa, South Carolina, West Virginia, Indiana, Pennsylvania, and New York launched similar successful protests to have Chaplin's film suppressed.[8]

These condemnations, though, represent only one part of the multifarious cultural tensions over representation and race on the stage and screen in the 1920s. Our understanding here, as in the world of the book, has often been blinkered by cultural condescension. As Gilbert Seldes noted at the time, "In America no one cares for revues except the unenlightened millions who pay to see them." Much as theatrical plaudits may have gone to the likes of Maxwell Anderson or O'Neill, many more theatergoers went to see Rachel Crothers's *Nice People* laud the virtues of hard work and rural life over modern society—and many more than that went to see the smash hit *No, No, Nanette*. Revealing of the cultural tensions of the time, the slender plot of the light comic musical was propelled along by the spending habits of a wealthy Bible publisher. H. L. Mencken, meanwhile, complained that the movie business was built upon "a foundation of morons," turning "bad novels and worse plays" into films that they had to sell to "immense audiences of half-wits." To an extent, this was true. Just as there were plenty of "bad" books, there were plenty of "bad" plays and films. And just as with bad books, plenty of these bad films and plays attempted to exploit the commercial possibilities of the Klan—even as the Klan movement attempted to exploit the propagandistic possibilities of the stage and screen.[9]

While the total number of theaters in the country declined after 1915, and competing attractions gained steam, the United States remained a nation enthralled by the stage in the 1920s. Broadway's importance as a multimillion-dollar industry was cemented as the number of shows staged rose from 192 in 1920 to a peak of 268 in the 1927–28 season. This was not, however, where most Americans found theatrical entertainment. Outside of New York, local stock companies surged in importance. Offering cheap tickets to comfortingly old-fashioned comedies and melodrama, these theaters became the "principal venues for dramatic entertainment" for much of the country. In localities that couldn't sustain a stock company, popular itinerant "tent shows" offered affordably priced melodramas, classics, light comedies, adaptations of popular novels, and variety performances. By 1925, some four hundred traveling tent shows plied their wares in sixteen thousand communities, selling almost eighty million tickets—twice as many as "legitimate" theater. As Russel Nye has noted, these were audiences looking for "just entertainment; if you wanted culture, you didn't go."[10]

Motion pictures, meanwhile, were soaring in popularity. By 1926, more than fifty million people paid admission to more than twenty thousand movie theaters every week. Following the example of the Roxy in New York, which grossed more than a hundred thousand dollars a week in its first year of operation, most sizable urban areas had their own specialized "picture palace" with an average turnover of three to four films a week. Smaller towns may not have had such luxurious surroundings to watch in, but showed an equally inexhaustible appetite for film, fed by nickelodeons, itinerant movie shows, and popular church and community screenings. To keep up with this demand, the industry produced an average of seven hundred pictures a year. In 1930, *Fortune* magazine hailed the growth of the motion picture industry—particularly with the introduction of sound in 1927—as "beyond comparison the fastest and most amazing revolution in the whole history of industrial revolutions." Moviegoing was quickly becoming an almost universal recreation.[11]

One of the most important steps in this rise of American cinema was the release of *The Birth of a Nation* in 1915, directed by D. W. Griffith. Based on Thomas Dixon's 1905 novel, *The Clansman*, *The Birth of a Nation* was the story of the Stoneman family in the North, headed by abolitionist Austin Stoneman (loosely based on Thaddeus Stevens), and the Cameron family in the South. At the beginning of the story, love blooms between the children of the families, but the Civil War soon tears them apart. Following the assassination of Lincoln, and with the urging of his treacherous mulatto protégé Silas Lynch (the monster to the abolitionist's Frankenstein), Stoneman leads the charge to impose punitive measures on the Reconstruction South. The ensuing outrages inflicted on the South under Lynch's direction compel Ben, the eldest Cameron son, to form the Ku Klux Klan, although it costs him his relationship with Elsie, Stoneman's daughter.

In the film, the abuses of Reconstruction reach their height when Flora Cameron, Ben's sister, jumps to her death to avoid the advances of a brutish freedman. Ben and the Klan hunt the culprit down and murder him. The freedman's body is dumped at the house of Silas Lynch, who furiously attempts to suppress the heroic efforts of the Klan. When Lynch confesses that he also intends to wed Elsie, even Austin Stoneman is forced to concede that he does not favor total equality. In the film's climax, Ben Cameron and his Klansmen defeat Lynch's militia and save Elsie. On the next election day, order is restored to the South by armed and mounted Klansmen who prevent African Americans from voting. The film ends with the double marriage of Phil Stoneman to Margaret Cameron and Ben Cameron to Elsie Stoneman, symbolizing the reunification of the nation.[12]

D. W. Griffith's groundbreaking adaptation of Dixon's novel was a technical masterpiece. It was also a national phenomenon. Setting records for the longest and most expensive film made to that point, *The Birth of a Nation* was the most popular film of the silent era, perhaps "the most widely seen single cultural document of the industrial age." One film historian has called it "the world's greatest motion picture, if greatness is to be measured by fame." Louis Menard has estimated that by 1926 over one hundred million people had seen Griffith's portrayal of the Klan. *The Birth of a Nation* created a new kind of audience for a new kind of moviegoing experience. And the film's impact reached even further—not least in providing early work to later Hollywood stalwarts like Raoul Walsh and John Ford, and early success to Louis B. Mayer's fledgling distribution network.[13]

The importance of this tale of the Reconstruction Klan to the Ku Klux Klan of the 1920s has been dealt with at length in studies of the organization and is difficult to overstate.[14] It is an exaggeration to say that the film was the sole motivator behind the birth of the second Klan, but *The Birth of a Nation* did play a uniquely important role in popularizing and publicizing the organization. In remaking history into a morality play, the film carried the message of the Dunningite historians and turn-of-the-century novelists to a vast new audience. By portraying Reconstruction as a tragic mistake, the film wiped the sins of the first Klan clean. In this, *The Birth of a Nation* built on two of Griffith's earlier works, *His Trust* and *His Trust Fulfilled* (both 1911), in which a faithful slave protected the family of his Confederate master from the depredations of Northerners. The director himself was open in his desire to rework the past on screen. The time was nigh, Griffith declared, "when the children in the public schools will be taught practically everything by moving pictures" and "will never be obliged to read history again."[15]

In rewriting (or rewhiting) history, Griffith and *The Birth of a Nation* also labored to remake the present. The epic film was, as Davarian Baldwin has noted, as much about contemporary racial uncertainty as Reconstruction itself—a Stoddard-like warning to a new imagined community of whiteness to stem the rising tide. In transporting viewers into a world of racialized righteousness, Amy Wood argues, Griffith made lynching itself into an act of sensationalized melodrama. Audiences saw racial violence not as the barbarity of a frenzied mob, but as the necessary action of stoic white heroes. Contemporaries agreed. Thomas Dixon claimed that "every man who comes out of one of our theatres is a Southern patriot for life." A more somber assessment came from NAACP lawyer Morefield Storey, who believed that white people who saw the film "will want to kill every colored man in the United States." It is doubtful that the Klan of the 1920s could have achieved the success it did without the influence of *The Birth of a Nation* on public opinion and its endorsement of white vigilantism.[16]

The Birth of a Nation was, without a doubt, the urtext of the revived Klan. Too often, however, we allow Griffith's groundbreaking film to dominate any discussion of cultural Klannishness. To do so is to forget that, as film scholar Tom Rice adroitly observed, there is life after *Birth*. It is also to forget that racism was, in the words of Thomas Cripps, the "normal intellectual baggage" of much of the popular entertainment of the day. Before *The Birth of a Nation*, Griffith had worked for the American Mutoscope and Biograph Company, the studio responsible for *Watermelon Feast* (1896), *Dancing Darkies* (1896), *Hallowe'en in Coontown* (1897), and *A Nigger in the Woodpile* (1904), among others. In producing these films, Biograph was only extending the persistent themes of theatrical minstrelsy from the stage to the screen, and from the nineteenth into the twentieth century.[17]

Within this context, it is unsurprising that Klan members and sympathizers would be able to find plenty of cultural fare more suited to their palate than *The Pilgrim*. While the movement's publications did not engage in film and theater criticism in the same way as they did for the printed word, Klaverns across the country staged "clean, wholesome comedy-dramas" and screened pictures that met with the movement's favor throughout the 1920s. Supplying "clean and legitimate entertainment" became a valuable component of the Invisible Empire's public face and recruitment efforts, extending the imagined identity of heroic Klannishness into new media. This had become particularly apparent by the beginning of 1925. As membership in the Klan organization began to fall, the Klan movement identity was reinforced in theater and film.[18]

The national organization had little to do with these entertainments, and would never engage with the stage and screen in any systematic way. These productions were overwhelmingly local and regional creations. At the forefront of amateur theatrical efforts were not national leaders, but individual members of the Women's Klan, who staged short plays and skits so frequently that many local Klaverns would have their own "play committee." These wholesome and often comic playlets, including such titles as *Foolish Frolic*, *Mrs. Sullivan in Politics*, and *The Comical Country Cousins*, emphasized Klan beliefs but rarely mentioned the organization itself. Similarly, Klans across the country took the lead in exhibiting films for the local community, often offering free matinees for children. Some Klans even went so far as to buy their own projectors. As the *Wisconsin Kourier* noted, movies were "the regular thing" and "greatly enjoyed by the entire membership."[19]

A particular favorite was the 1920 film *The Face at Your Window*, produced as part of the government-sponsored Americanism Committee's efforts to promote patriotic values. Distributed by the Fox Film Corporation, the picture was a parable of compassionate capitalism. The story of a Bolshevik agent's attempts to stir up trouble among Russian immigrant factory workers, the film showed that the genially paternalistic factory owner faced little difficulty in quashing employee concerns. When his less amiable counterpart dismissed their demands entirely, he started a riot. *The Face at Your Window*'s climax saw the American Legion called in to establish the peace and find a reasonable (and patriotic) solution to the Bolshevik's troublemaking.[20]

Klan members around the country embraced the film and repeated screenings quickly turned it into a highly successful propaganda tool. Although the heroes of the picture were members of the American Legion, they were dressed in Klan-like uniforms and Klan recruiters were quick to claim that the film actually showed the Invisible Empire saving the day. Often pairing showings with a talk by a Klan lecturer, Kleagles would force membership applications on attendees at the end of the film. As the King Kleagle of Tennessee noted, *The Face at Your Window* was a "wonderful picture" and of "wonderful value to us" in trying to convert movement enthusiasm into organizational membership.[21]

Even more than the Fox film, screenings of *The Birth of a Nation* played a central role in the organization's propaganda efforts. The unmatched spectacle of the picture remained incredibly popular with both Klan members and the general public. A 1924 run of the nine-year-old film in Chicago, for example, saw record attendance. A showing in Richmond drew the entire two-thousand-strong local Klan. Recruitment drives were often launched with a Klan-sponsored exhibition of the film. Outside the theater, Klansmen distributed pamphlets and membership applications. Proceedings from the film showing were ostentatiously donated to local charities or churches. The tactic proved spectacularly successful. It was no coincidence that Klaverns often saw the largest increase in local membership following a showing of *The Birth of a Nation*. As Klan advertisements for the film noted, "It will make a better American of you."[22]

Unsurprisingly, the stage production of *The Clansman*, which had been adapted by Thomas Dixon for a very successful touring production in 1905, was also a popular choice. In Maryland, in an early effort at cross-promotion, a revival of the melodrama was directed by the wife of James S. Vance, editor of the *Fellowship Forum*. An Arkansas Klan, meanwhile, cannily combined the play with an initiation ceremony, swearing new members into the organization as part of the drama. Nor was *The Clansman* the only literary adaptation to find favor. For those wanting to see the modern Klan on stage, *The Martyred Klansman*, a widely redistributed pro-Klan pamphlet about the death of a Klansman during a riot in Pennsylvania, formed the basis of a three-act drama praised for "giving non Klan members a better idea of the order." Similarly, a five-act adaptation of the popular 1923 novel *Harold the Klansman* quickly proved itself another Klannish favorite.[23]

These productions were not a structured effort, nor a reflection of an organized drive toward recruiting members for the Invisible Empire. The relationship of Klan members to popular entertainment often had little to do with the organization's leaders. Klannish entertainment was fundamentally localized. Yet the productions promulgated a Klan identity—an imagined community—that was largely uniform on a national level. With minor variations, these theatrical and filmic endeavors recycled the same tropes present in Klan fiction. The organization, these entertainments argued, was a mis-understood guardian of Americanism and an upholder of law. Allegations of criminality were the result only of wrongful accusation—often of foreign elements pretending to be Klan members to discredit the organization. The most popular narrative was that of conversion, as the audience's surrogate in the production shed their opposition to the Invisible Empire to espouse the virtues of the movement.

In original productions on both stage and screen, it was local Klaverns and individual Klan members and sympathizers who took the lead. *The Mysterious Way*, a "Comedy-Drama" written by Missouri Kleagle Floyd P. Lee, was staged in towns throughout the Midwest in 1923. Lauded as "a power-ful lesson in Klankraft," the play gave audiences the opportunity to watch an idealized Klavern meeting, portrayed by Klansmen in full regalia. J. Lamb Perry's *The Flaming Cross* met with sufficient success touring in Kansas and Texas in 1924 to be revived as *The Light* for a Midwest tour the following year. Outdoing Griffith's rewriting of history by reinterpreting well-known historical events to trace the Klan's roots to the Boston Tea Party, Perry's play delivered on its title by closing with an on-stage cross burning.[24]

By far the most striking of these theatrical endeavors was *The Invisible Empire* by New York playwrights Edward E. Rose and Charles F. Park. A murder mystery set in the "evil stronghold" of a treacherous Bolshevik, somewhere in the Georgia mountains, *Invisible Empire* was billed as an unofficial sequel to *The Birth of a Nation*. Although details of the plot are scarce, the *Chicago Tribune* noted that the production contained all the expected "persiflage and laughter and comedy relief, and shrieks in the dark," with additional "disser-tations on patriotism and the Klan." After the Invisible Empire was framed for murder, the heroic Klansman saved his sweetheart from the clutches of the racialized villain, who was posing as a Japanese prince. The secret Bolshevik was killed by his own trick cane. The organization's good name was cleared, proving that the Klan waged only "honorable warfare" and could not be held responsible for "unauthorized crimes."[25]

A moderate success in its short time touring in Alabama and Georgia, the play began to garner wider attention when the Central Amusement Company production arrived in Chicago for a run sponsored by the local Klan. *Dawn* breathlessly promised "the most talked of play" in America. A series of articles and advertisements lauded the "strictly all New York cast"—heroine Renita Randolph and villain Bennett Southard were indeed familiar, albeit minor, Broadway stock actors. The "scenic production of unusual beauty" and the music from members of the Chicago Symphony were also featured heavily in promotional materials. The box office was promptly "swamped with mail order requests for tickets," according to *Dawn*, which advised its readers to buy their tickets soon. The anti-Klan American Unity League (AUL), meanwhile, somewhat predictably campaigned to have the show banned from the city.[26]

Despite the AUL's efforts, the play opened on December 30, 1922, in a theater surrounded with uniformed policemen, with additional plainclothes detectives in the audience. The AUL's protests had not been entirely in vain, however. The overwhelmingly pro-Klan audience found to its chagrin that the final scene of the last act—the play culminating in a Klan gathering at the foot of Stone Mountain—had been censored. The audience, according to one theatergoer, left the theater muttering darkly. *Dawn*'s review of *The Invisible Empire* reflected this mood of discontent, complaining that "Protestants have been double crossed" by an alien element.[27]

The production itself was met with unsurprising acclaim by the Klan publication, which found that "the play in its entirety is to be praised from every standpoint." For the next several issues, the newspaper ran select reviews from readers who agreed on the "dandy" nature of the "superb" show, and called on every "100% American" in Chicago to attend and extend the play's run for a year. Despite *Dawn*'s best efforts, though, *The Invisible Empire* ran only for the three weeks it was scheduled, and does not seem to have been revived—perhaps because, as the *Chicago Tribune*'s review noted, "it is a pretty bad play."[28]

Klan members and sympathizers also launched enthusiastically into filmmaking. Requiring greater organization and expenditure than most theatrical endeavors, many of the Invisible Empire's forays into motion-picture production never came to fruition. This was particularly evident whenever the national leadership attempted to exert its influence. The existence of a planned "elaborate and costly . . . screen spectacle," *Yesterday, Today and Forever*, was revealed by the *New York World* in 1921. Although producer Clifford Slater Wheeler (a New York Kleagle) apparently had the backing of Imperial Wizard Simmons and Imperial Kleagle Edward Young Clarke, with a proposed budget of four hundred thousand dollars, negotiations over the film ultimately came to nothing.[29]

Similarly, *Armageddon*, announced in 1923, proved little more than an ambitious pipe dream. The "stupendous spectacle dealing with the modern-day Klan," which its producers had hoped would be directed by D. W. Griffith, never materialized. The same was true of the 1927 announcement of *The Trail of the Serpent*, an "epoch-making" film adaptation of the serialized story run in *Fellowship Forum*. The Klan newspaper's efforts ultimately amounted to little more than an advertisement calling for "fine Protestant women" to audition for roles. Edward Young Clarke created the Twentieth Century Motion Picture Corporation in 1925—beating Joseph Schenck and Darryl F. Zanuck to the name by seven years—but his new company was largely moribund.[30]

More successful were local filmmaking efforts to promote the movement, like *The Fifth Horseman*, a seven-reel melodrama released in 1924. Written and directed by Texas Klansman E. M. McMahon, who also found success composing Klan sheet music, *The Fifth Horseman* told the story of an idealized Klan fighting the insidious influence of a gang of bootlegging radicals. Shorn of any racial or religious ideological baggage, the group was never identified directly as Klansmen in the picture, although the inference was clear, and the organization was named explicitly in advertising materials. This flattering portrayal was a minor success, and the film toured extensively with private showings throughout the country—even making it as far north as Maine. Despite the organization's localized and federalized structure, the national Klan movement united within the imagined community of stoic white heroism presented by the film.[31]

A similar picture was presented to Klan members and sympathizers in the 1923 film *The Toll of Justice*, written and directed by Corey G. Cook and made in Columbus, Ohio, with the help of local Klansmen. *The Toll of Justice* told a familiar story of a good Protestant wrongly accused of a crime in which the Klan is falsely implicated (in this case, framed for murder by a gang of bootleggers and dope fiends). Once again, the Invisible Empire heroically rides out to clear its name, save the girl, and bring the real criminals to justice. The massing of the Klan was given particular dramatic heft by filming some scenes at an actual Klonklave, at which some estimated two thousand members were present (although later publicity materials tried to pass it off as twenty thousand). Extra spectacle came from some early special effects—a villainous master of mesmerism who could shoot lightning from his fingertips—and from a number of impressively staged aerial stunts, complete with wing-walkers and plane crashes. *The Toll of Justice* was not some bargain-basement propaganda play.[32]

Although it is impossible to say precisely how successful the film was, *The Toll of Justice* garnered wide publicity and continued to be exhibited around the Midwest until at least 1925. Though it dealt with the Klan, its producers attempted to sell it as "not strictly a Klan picture" but "merely as a photoplay" for public entertainment. *Movie Weekly* had ballyhooed the "patriotic" film after it was first announced. Writer T. Howard Kelly took to the popular magazine's pages to declare that "all the screens of this country" should show the film "in an effort to enlighten Americans with regard to their least un-

derstood secret organization." *Variety* ran several pieces on the film, presenting news on the Klan production alongside pieces on Robert Benchley and
Lillian Gish. The *Fiery Cross* hailed it as "one of the most spectacular screen
dramas ever produced."[33]

As with *The Fifth Horseman*, the film's financial success was limited by the
venues in which it could be exhibited. As Kathryn Fuller-Seeley has noted,
there were distinct regional variations in 1920s moviegoing, most noticeable
outside urban areas. The rural South, in particular, saw "the lowest density
of movie theaters of any other region." The well-connected network of small
towns in the Midwest, conversely, hosted a thriving community of avid film-
goers. Distribution of *The Fifth Horseman* reflected that fact. Though the film
was originally announced to be booked in over twenty states, screenings outside the Midwest were rare.[34]

These regional distribution issues were further exacerbated by the increasing control of vertically integrated major studios over the majority of movie
theaters. Although community screenings and "church shows" remained a
viable market, both were—like most independent exhibitors—rapidly losing
ground to increasingly powerful producer-distributors. Wary of the effects
on their profit margin, Hollywood studios were both hostile to independent
distribution and careful not to take too strong a stance on the Invisible Empire. The widely varying standards and often capricious nature of local and
state censorship boards also made it difficult to guarantee that a film could be
shown. Without studio support, screenings in theaters tended to be private
affairs orchestrated by the local Klan rather than part of a wider distribution network. In many cases, *The Toll of Justice* was exhibited primarily at
large Klan gatherings or through existing church and community screening
networks.[35]

Anti-Klan pictures faced a similar problem. Studios were as wary of criticizing the Klan as they were of celebrating it, leaving these pictures sparsely
exhibited without a major distributor. The 1922 film *The Hooded Mob* (also
released as *After Dark, Men in Masks*, and *Law and Order*), which "pans the
entire Klan," made little impact. The melodrama depicted the abduction and
whipping of an innocent Catholic by masked men. Fear of angering the Klan
(and of controversy in general) left "no-one . . . anxious to handle the picture."
The film's divisive subject matter also meant it faced issues of censorship, often failing to garner a license to exhibit. *Knight of the Eucharist* (later retitled
The Mask of the Ku Klux Klan) faced similar issues that same year. A creation of Creston Feature Pictures, an avowedly Catholic production company,
Knight of the Eucharist was twice refused a license to exhibit in New York

because of the likelihood "it would arouse antagonism against a certain class of people." Where it could be exhibited, the picture was screened in seminaries and Catholic school auditoriums.[36]

More popular was the work of prominent African American filmmaker Oscar Micheaux, whose pictures owed their success to the fact that their ideological tendencies took a backseat to a compelling narrative. The 1920 eight-reel drama *The Symbol of the Unconquered* generated publicity with the story of Van Allen, an African American man in the Northwest, and Eve Mason, a recently arrived heiress, whom Allen protects from white swindlers. When those same swindlers, the Knights of the Black Cross (a thinly veiled Klan analogue), attempt to run Allen off his oil-rich land, he rallies the local community to fight back. "The biggest moments of the photo-play," the *New York Age* noted approvingly, "are when the night riders are annihilated, a colored man with bricks being a big factor."[37]

Glowingly reviewed by the *Chicago Defender*, *The Symbol of the Unconquered* created "a wonderful amount of comment all over the East." In late 1921, the film was re-released to capitalize on the soaring public interest in the "haggard splendor" of the organization. Micheaux's brother told newspapers that the "new demand" for the film could not be estimated. The prolific filmmaker returned to the Klan theme in his 1924 film, *A Son of Satan*, described by advertising materials as "a hair-raising, side-splitting story of a haunted house with a colored man locked in while the Ku Klux Klan are holding conclave." Micheaux's search to increase both "political awareness and his box office receipts" represented a remarkable achievement, but one that was often crippled by censor boards that objected to the "realism" of the "race hatred" shown. "Every scene or subtitle calculated to produce friction between the races," the Virginia censor board warned, would be "eliminated."[38]

Censorship was not the only problem. Klan films like *The Toll of Justice* were also hobbled by the same kind of backroom squabbles that plagued the Klan organization more generally. The original production company for *The Toll of Justice*, C. & S. Pictures, was financially struggling and had to be bought out by the Ohio Klan before the film was finished. The Klan members then distributed *The Toll of Justice* as the Miafa Pictures Company—a popular Klan acronym meaning "My Interests Are For America."[39] Miafa, in turn, went into receivership in 1924 and sold the rights to a group of Columbus businessmen, who formed Arthur C. Bromberg Attractions. The film may have been reaching sizeable audiences, but, without a major distributor to back it, did not seem to be a financial success.[40]

The Traitor Within, released in 1924, fared somewhat better with its financing. In April 1923, the Cavalier Motion Picture Company was incorporated in Delaware with a capital stock of one million dollars. The president of the company was C. Lewis Fowler, a leading Klan lecturer and writer and longtime ally of Imperial Wizard Simmons. Vice president J. E. D. Smith was the Kleagle of Buffalo, while the Reverend Oscar Haywood, a popular traveling lecturer for the Klan, served as treasurer. Doing the majority of the work as the secretary of Cavalier was Roscoe Carpenter, reportedly "the high muck-a-muck" of the Invisible Empire in Lyons County, Indiana. This pedigree notwithstanding, Carpenter told reporters that the Klan was "in no-wise interested" in Cavalier Pictures, "either officially or otherwise."[41]

It may well be true that the national Klan had no financial interest in Cavalier. Fowler had left the Klan's leadership after Simmons was deposed, and Haywood reportedly resigned his position. Cavalier, conversely, was most certainly interested in the Klan. The company had initially announced that its first picture would be *A Portrayal of the Life of Abraham Lincoln*, but that project never materialized. Instead, Cavalier's first and only production was *The Traitor Within*, accurately advertised as "the super-Klan film," and prominently featuring footage of the Klan's 1923 "magnificent parade" through Fort Wayne, Indiana. No print of the film survives, and plot details are scarce, but *The Traitor Within* seems to have revolved around Klan efforts to combat political corruption.[42]

As with other Klan-centered films, *The Traitor Within* was predominantly exhibited in churches and schools throughout the Midwest, with occasional forays into local movie theaters. Klan publications greeted the production as "a motion picture of great educational value." This "most spectacular display" purportedly offered so many thrills that during a run in Illinois a Klan nurse was "present at each performance to render service if necessary." Again, no quantifiable data survives on how successful the film was, but it did remain a significant draw through at least the end of 1925.[43]

Although Klan members comprised the bulk of the audience for these entertainments, they did also actively attract sizable non-Klan crowds. In the unlikely case that any non-Klan patrons attended these productions for a clever plot or nuanced character development, they would most likely have been disappointed. The real draw seems to have been the continued public interest in the Klan organization. Just as it sold newspapers and fueled a minor literary industry, the promise of revelations concerning the nominally secretive Invisible Empire drew patrons to these shows. Nor were distributors and exhibitors reticent about using this allure to drum up business.

Advertisements for *The Mysterious Way* promised that audience members would "Know the Truth" and, like *The Flaming Cross*, relied on the lure of a scene showing the inner workings of a full-regalia Klan Klavern. *The Fifth*

Horseman was billed as an "exposé of the order." *Movie Weekly* hailed *The Toll of Justice* as a means of revealing the Klan's "secret purposes and innermost workings." Even the only notable anti-Klan play of the decade, *Behind the Mask* by ex-Kleagle C. Anderson Wright, was reliant on the promise of "many startling revelations" about the Invisible Empire to (unsuccessfully) try to draw an audience. Publicity for *The Traitor Within* asked, "What Do You Know About the Ku Klux Klan?" and "Is the Ku Klux Klan Guilty or Not Guilty of all the Crimes and Vices Laid at Their Door." Only attendance at the film—with "Klan Oath Exposed"—would tell you. Advertisements for *The Invisible Empire* in non-Klan newspapers were particularly blunt—"It Tells You About the Ku Klux Klan." These promotions clearly understood the kind of attraction these entertainments held.[44]

Most tellingly, the same kinds of advertising techniques were used even for productions that did not actually feature the Ku Klux Klan. As *Exhibitor's Trade Review* noted in 1923, "Any idea which is suggestive of the type of activities which characterize the Ku Klux Klan, has an appeal to the general public at this time." Similarly, *Exhibitor's Herald* observed that "anything smacking of the mysterious and seeming to point to the KKK attracts considerable attention." The *Three Musketeers*, starring Douglas Fairbanks, was teased in 1921 with only the words "All for one and one for all" to draw parallels with similar Klan phrases. The same year saw a minor western retitled *The White Masks* to capitalize on the "advertising value" of the Klan. C. B. McDonald drew attention to his 1923 vaudeville revue in New York by printing pamphlets warning that "the K.K.K. is coming"—the Keith Komedy Karnival. In Boston, Leon J. Rubinstein similarly attracted crowds to the film *Three Ages* by promising the K.K.K.—Keaton, Keaton, Keaton.[45]

Many others offered more than just the promise of the Klan, as the image of the organization was appropriated for commercial entertainment. As in the world of fiction, popular portrayals of the Klan were carefully shorn of any ideological baggage for maximum commercial potential in the emerging consumerist society. The Invisible Empire's presence represented only an easy means of signifying mystery and excitement. In co-opting this image, these productions often sanitized the organization and functioned as an implicit endorsement of the wider Klan movement.

Not all of these portrayals were flattering. On the stage, the cabaret heartily embraced mockery of the Invisible Empire. One producer's "very novel, timely, and striking" bit in his new show had to be jettisoned after he discovered how many other productions were already incorporating similar Klan-themed musical numbers. Eddie Cantor, one of the best-known performers of the day, used Klan-based patter in his vaudeville act. By late 1923, Cantor's

Klan bit had become so popular that it sparked a minor controversy as a number of other performers plagiarized the joke.[46]

While Cantor may have been the bigger name, arguably the most culturally significant of these Klannish appearances was in the play *Processional*. Written by future Hollywood Ten blacklistee John Howard Lawson and produced by the influential and innovative Theatre Guild, the play ran for ninety performances at the Garrick Theatre in New York in 1925. A self-conscious effort by Lawson to create a new theatrical method that would "express the American scene" in its vaudevillian "native idiom," *Processional* was described by the playwright as a "jazz symphony of modern life." The overtly political and often absurdist plot, one reviewer noted, could be replicated "by reading the headlines of any sensational American newspaper from cover to cover." In such a play, an appearance from the Ku Klux Klan was an inevitability.[47]

Very loosely based on labor disputes in Mingo County, West Virginia, *Processional* was set in a West Virginia mining town during a strike. The first act saw tensions grow between the miners and the soldiers sent in to break the strike. In the second act, a miner, Dynamite Jim, kills one of the soldiers in a struggle. Going on the run, Jim rapes Sadie Cohen, the daughter of a Jewish shopkeeper. Caught by the combined forces of the soldiers and the local Ku Klux Klan in the third act, Jim is taken offstage, where he is strung up to a tree and blinded.[48]

In the final act of the play, in what one theatergoer referred to as "The Ballet of the Ku Klux Klan," the Klan returned to the stage in full regalia to persecute the now-pregnant Sadie Cohen for her allegedly loose morals. The plutocrat responsible for the miners' woes, now an eight-foot-tall King Kleagle, led the Klansmen. In rhythmic, lyrical chants, the group proclaimed that they were "Native-born Americans, Patriotic Protestants, regular citizens" who had "taken the oath to exterminate foreigners."[49] Their task, according to their leader, was to "clean up the dirty foreigners, make 'em kiss the flag! Skin the Jews, lynch the niggers, make 'em kiss the flag!" Adopting a Christ-like pose, one outstretched arm on the American flag and the other on the cross, the King Kleagle declared that the Klansmen must give Sadie "Christian punishment."[50]

Although Sadie was saved from her punishment by her father, disguised in Klan robes, Lawson turned the end of *Processional* into a disturbing and sardonic parody of happy endings. In a grotesque reworking of *The Face at Your Window*, the Klan puts down the strike. The plutocrat reappears on stage, sans robes, to quash any bad publicity and declare a peaceful reconciliation. His mealymouthed protestations of patriotic values are undermined by a side exchange that reveals he plans to have the strike leaders murdered later. Finally, the blinded Dynamite Jim returns and marries Sadie in a "jazz wedding."[51]

Reviews of *Processional* were mixed. On the one hand, the conservative mainstream of critics found little to like. Walter Winchell said that he had never seen anything so bad—and that was "being kind." Alexander Woollcott declared the play "pretentious" and "boring." More liberal-minded critics, like Gilbert Gabriel of the *New York Telegram-Mail* and Heywood Broun of the *New York World*, on the other hand, greatly admired Lawson's work. Stark Young of the *New York Times* called *Processional* "creative and streaked with genius" with "a strange, fresh, young, robust, half brutal pathos unique to our drama." Robert Benchley went even further, taking to the pages of *Life* to favorably compare the play to *Othello*.[52]

Almost every review, favorable or not, made prominent reference to the last act's "mock dance of the Ku Klux Klan." As Stark Young understatedly phrased it, the "Ku Klux scene dropped into a poor tone indeed." Gilbert Seldes liked the Klan scene, but criticized the "pretensions" of the production. Thornton Wilder declared that the last act "approached greatness." "What," the playwright asked in a question that defined the cultural tensions of the 1920s, "could be more attractive than a play that intermingles strips of vaudevillian patter, exciting drama and burlesque, a Klux Klan ballet and a Negro song and dance?"[53]

Good or bad, *Processional* certainly made an impact. Louis Bromfield in *The Bookman* called it "the most interesting" play in New York. Playwright Elmer Rice praised Lawson's "brilliant effectiveness" in creating "a psychograph of America." Edna St. Vincent Millay and Ogden Stewart placed an advertisement in the *New York World* calling *Processional* "one of the most thrilling plays ever written." In *Vanity Fair*, John Dos Passos proclaimed the play a groundbreaking abandonment of the fourth wall. At a sold-out public discussion of the play hosted by the Theatre Guild in February 1925, "debate ranged strongly" with "violent speeches" on both sides. Fanny Hurst and Dorothy Parker were among the voices present championing Lawson's work.[54]

One newspaper in the Midwest, attempting to summarize the controversy, called Lawson's show "the play all America loved to argue about." The *St. Paul Minnesota Pioneer Press* referred to *Processional* as "the most irritating and the most questioned, discussed and defended of all plays." Debate over the show's merits lasted for so long that when it moved to a short run on Broadway, Alexander Woollcott reversed his initial review. Although "gauche and brash and at times cheap," the *New York Sun* critic wrote, *Processional* contained "a rare and exhilarating quality of beauty and high excitement."

The Ku Klux Klan was one of the most memorable parts of one of the most discussed plays of the 1920s.[55]

Yet *Processional* was also largely unrepresentative of the ways in which the Klan was represented in more popular entertainments. On stage, "a dash of Ku Klux Klan for spice" was a more common phenomenon. Willard Mack's *Raw Law* in Los Angeles added the Klan to the "usual Mack tradition" of "much pulling of guns." A British music-hall show saw a noblewoman and naval officer taken captive by the Klan, but freed through comic means. These efforts were typified by *The Gorilla*, a successful touring "mysterious melo-drama" that featured the Invisible Empire as just one of many plot points. As the play's press materials put it, the show contained "a playwright in love with the tenant's niece, two detectives, a butler, a locked chest, a dead sailor, the Ku Klux Klan, screams, pistol shots, sliding panels, and the inevitable reporter."[56]

This trend was even more pronounced on the screen, where sanitized representations of the organization further served to normalize and even glorify the Klan. The "novel and timely" 1921 Hal Roach comedy short *Law and Order*, for one, showed a local district attorney organize his own—highly unsuccessful—Klan to fight local car thieves. But the emphasis was on the ex-citement added by the trappings of the Klan, not its ideology. As Rice astutely observes, "The representation of the Klan appears secondary to the Klan costume." Thus, in two other Hal Roach comedies, the popular "Our Gang" members actually joined idealized Klan analogues: in 1922's *Young Sherlocks*, the crime-solving J.J.J.'s; and in 1923's *Lodge Night*, the Cluck Cluck Klams, who foil a gang of criminals.[57]

Newsreels placed Klan rallies on the same level of "momentous" event as Marconi demonstrating wireless or celebrated racehorse Man o' War winning the Kentucky Derby. The fictionalized Invisible Empire made appearances in the Harold Lloyd comedy *An Eastern Westerner* (as "masked angels"), in the "Torchy" comedy *Ghosts* (in which Klan robes played a central part in a farci-cal elopement), and in the Fox comedy *The Chauffeur*. In the westerns *The Prodigal Judge*, *Big Stakes*, *The Night Riders*, and *Shadows of the West*, a Klan or Klan analogue appeared as a nonviolent vigilante force. The Pathé cartoon *The Wayward Dog* drew "a lot of laughs" with a canine Klan.[58]

Rather than appearing as bigots leading a lynching (which would never have made it past most censorship boards), the Klan was generally depicted as a moralistic organization dedicated to law enforcement. The 1928 screen adaptation of one of the most popular novels to use the Klan as background color, Rex Beach's *The Mating Call*, was so hesitant to offend that it did not even name the organization, referring to it simply as "The Order." Nonetheless, reviews noted that the Invisible Empire was "an interesting and vital part of the picture" and enthused over the "more or less accurate exposé of the workings of the Klan." Exploiting public interest in the group was far more important than taking an ideological stand.[59]

The best expression of this tendency to exploit the Klan image for commercial entertainment was the 1922 film *One Clear Call*. Loosely based on the 1914 book of the same name by Frances Nimmo Greene, the mawkish melodrama told the story of two friends in a small town in Alabama—one a doctor, the other a dying bootlegger and gambler—divided by a woman. Among the many changes the First National production made to Greene's book was the introduction of a group of Klansmen who led the charge to shut down the bootlegger's gambling establishment and possibly kill the proprietor, but were dissuaded by the doctor. Although the doctor reprimanded the Klan members as cowards for wearing masks, the wider Klan movement was implicitly presented in the film as an admirable force for justice.[60]

Producer Louis B. Mayer, who had made his first fortune from the New England distribution rights to *The Birth of a Nation*, clearly recognized the commercial value of the Invisible Empire to *One Clear Call*. As one exhibitor noted, it was "a good picture, with a misleading press sheet." The Klan's effort to shut down the gambling joint was only one facet of the story, lasting only a few minutes, but the organization took primary place in efforts to market the production. Newspaper articles highlighted the "nightly ridings of the Ku Klux Klan," while advertisements placed the Klan's name above that of the picture—"We Present the Ku Klux Klan in A Screen Drama Ever to be Remembered." One exhibitor happily "played it while the newspapers were full of K.K.K. stuff" so that "the Ku Klux end of the picture drew them in fine." In some towns, exhibitors even engaged local Klansmen to publicize the film, or ran it in a double bill with the Klan's own *The Toll of Justice*. The only judgment made on the Klan was its entertainment value. *Variety* hailed the film as having "everything that goes to make a successful screen production"—which included a "wandering boy and blind mother bit, comedy, and a touch of the Ku Klux Klan that serves as a thrill."[61]

While *One Clear Call* was perhaps the most successful commercial exploitation of the Ku Klux Klan, the pro-Klan stage production *The Awakening* was an even more evident embodiment of the porous cultural boundaries of the 1920s. Producer-writer-director-star James H. "Jimmy" Hull of Port Arthur, Texas, began staging annual "home-talent" amateur shows in the Southwest in 1915. It was not until 1924, though, that Hull struck upon his biggest success. *The Awakening* combined a thinly veiled rehash of *The Birth of a Nation*'s story of Reconstruction with music, comedy, and "very beautiful women in somewhat abbreviated costumes"—all staged with the help of local Klan members.

Patricia Bradley has observed that in many ways the stunning success of the Ziegfeld Follies lay in the production values dedicated to "Glorifying the American Girl." The emphasis "on opulence, on breathtaking technique, on light and color," dazzling with sex appeal, brought in mass audiences. *The Awakening* was a Follies for the rest of the country. An almost three-hour spectacular, Hull's show was described in one early review as "a variety of dramatic situations." The vaudevillian revue combined songs and dances, tableaux, "plantation-day melodies, many of which have long ago been forgotten," and jazz music. The play's "scenes of the past and present" presented audiences with an "undeniable touch of patriotism and a beautiful love story running throughout." It was the perfect vehicle for the second Klan, and a pure expression of the cultural contradictions that marked the postwar period.[62]

The Awakening was first staged in Beaumont, Texas, in May 1924, in a production sponsored by the local Dick Dowling Klan No. 25 and its female counterpart (see figs. 6.1 and 6.2). The mammoth spectacle, with a cast of over three hundred locals, ran for a week of sold-out shows and reportedly raised over ten thousand dollars for the local Klan. A month later, it opened in nearby Port Arthur with a cast of over four hundred, where its entire run of nine days sold out before opening night. The *Port Arthur News* rhapsodized

FIGURE 6.1. "The Awakening"—A James H. Hull Production for Beaumont Klan No. 7—KKK, Beaumont, Texas, May 12, 13, 14, 15, 16, 17, 1924. Photo by Reeves. 1924. Image retrieved from the Library of Congress, https://www.loc.gov/item/2001695587/.

FIGURE 6.2. "The Awakening"—A James H. Hull Production for Beaumont Klan No. 7—KKK, Beaumont, Texas, May 12, 13, 14, 15, 16, 17, 1924. Photo by Reeves. 1924. Image retrieved from the Library of Congress, https://www.loc.gov/item/2001695592/.

over the "fire, originality, genius and devotion," the "great inspiration," and the "magnificence, opulence, magnitude, vastness" of the show. The play not only conveyed "the ideals of the Ku Klux Klan, their allegiance to their country, and their high ideals of womanhood, of home, and of right," it did so with blackface minstrels, high-kicking chorus girls, and lavish musical numbers that would not have been out of place in a New York cabaret.[63]

After the Port Arthur run, *The Awakening* went on the road in productions sponsored by local Klans and manned by local actors. Playing to "crowded houses" and rave reviews in Dallas, Birmingham, Atlanta, and Tulsa, Hull's production had made its way to Virginia by 1926. In Norfolk, the "dazzling" and "astounding" production broke all local attendance records and had to run for an extra week. The profits from the estimated twenty thousand ticket sales went to a building fund for a new Klan meeting hall. In Richmond, the show may have featured an early appearance by the Andrews Sisters. When the show arrived in Roanoke shortly after, it drew an opening night crowd of twelve hundred. As local Thelma Deel, then sixteen years old, later recalled, her whole family auditioned to be in the show. No matter that the play was held under the auspices of the local Klan. "Of course we said yes. . . . We were all in it."[64]

In February 1927, *The Awakening* arrived in Washington, D.C., now with a cast of over five hundred, ranging from "tiny but distinctively talented tots"

to women in blackface as "oldtime darkey-dancing . . . mammies." King Kleagle Louis A. Mueller gave the show the organization's imprimatur, appearing
nightly to lead the oath in a scene depicting the first ever Klan initiation.[65]
Although the "combination of melodrama and revue" met with a mixed
review from the *Washington Post*, the show's weeklong run at the Belasco
Theatre was successful enough that it returned for another week a month
later. The *Washington Herald* called it "a dramatic musical extravaganza of
the very highest type." The *Fellowship Forum* attributed the play's success to
its "real patriotic, Protestant, American" nature and its thrilling portrayal of
"the white-robed host of liberators." The "miles of bare knees" and "acres of
shimmering shoulders" on display almost certainly did not hurt either.[66]

As Lewis A. Erenberg has noted of the New York cabarets, the chorus
girl formed the backbone of the revue, and *The Awakening* was no different.
The "Diamond Chorus," which featured Hull wearing a 112-pound rhinestone
costume and backed by sixteen "beautiful co-stars" in much skimpier ver-
sions of the same outfit, was singled out for particular praise. Hull's show cul-
minated in Charleston, West Virginia, in the summer of 1927. With most of its
lead roles openly populated with "local talent by the Ku Klux Klan," and a cast
of nearly six hundred, the show's five-night appearance was greeted by the
Charleston Gazette as a "stupendous and gorgeous musical-spectacle-drama."
During its run, Imperial Wizard Hiram Evans came to deliver a public address and see the much-discussed show for the first time. Unfortunately, no
record can be found of his opinion on the rhinestone-studded extravaganza,
but it is suggestive that this seems to have been the last time *The Awakening*
was staged.[67]

The creation of an entertainer without formal links to the Klan, propelled
to success by local Klan members and sympathizers rather than any official
support, *The Awakening* underscores the split between the Klan organization
and the Klannish cultural movement. The production offered little of the dignified respectability that the organization's leaders so desperately craved. In
many ways, not least its miles of bare knees, it was seemingly the epitome
of the "degenerate sensuality" in modern entertainment denounced in the
rhetoric of the Invisible Empire. Yet at heart it was a deeply conservative production, appropriating modern musical and theatrical forms—plus some sex
appeal and a little dazzle—to promote the same reassuring narrative of white
Protestant Klannish heroism that productions like *The Fifth Horseman* and
The Toll of Justice had carefully cultivated.

The Awakening reflected the complexities of the Klan's ambivalent and
sometimes ambiguous relationship with modern popular culture. At the same
time, it was "just entertainment"—and by all accounts entertaining enough

to draw a vast audience. A 1929 article promoting a new show by Jimmy Hull claimed that the theatrical producer had attained "national importance" with the "great dramatic success" of *The Awakening*. While that success was more regional than national, the play was purportedly seen by over a quarter million people, with perhaps "the biggest run of any home talent production ever presented in America." That feat provides valuable insight into the Klan movement's position in American popular culture in the 1920s. Even as the organization's image was appropriated for mass entertainment, the lived ideology of the Invisible Empire's cultural engagement reached far beyond rhetorical condemnation. Both critics and supporters of the Klan saw value in the spectacle of a song-and-dance number featuring the Invisible Empire. There was room for long-legged showgirls in the imagined community of Klannishness, just as there was room for a thrilling "touch of the Klan" in a Louis B. Mayer picture.[68]

7

That Ghastly Saxophone

Sheet music and phonograph records are among the few artifacts which afford insight into the inarticulate Americans of the twentieth century.

H. F. MOONEY

We have the best organization
In this whole world of nations
That's why we have our Ku Kluxers
We have our Ku Klux Klan today.

KLAN SONGBOOK SELECTION, to be sung to the tune of "Yes! We Have No Bananas"

In 1925, after renting the local opera house to hold a rally and entertainment, the Klansmen of Ocean Grove, New Jersey, found that the same establishment was to host a performance by Paul Robeson two nights beforehand. Despite being assured that Robeson was "one of the highest musical exponents of his race," according to the *Baltimore Afro-American*, Klan representatives met the news "with disdain" and launched a protest. After failing to force the venue to cancel the concert, Klan members conceded the need to share the space. Even as the piano was being tuned for Robeson, the *Afro-American* reported, amplifiers were being erected for the Klan rally. In another illustration of the fluid divisions of the period, while neither may have cared for the other, Paul Robeson and the Invisible Empire shared the same cultural—and physical—spaces in the 1920s.[1]

Popular music is, as Gilbert Seldes argues, "a clue to the social history of our time." Sigmund Spaeth has similarly suggested that "what America has sung . . . is the people's own record of our history." The 1920s were undoubtedly a crucial time for the development of music in America, in both form and content. Edison's phonograph, Berliner's flat disc recordings, and the domestic radio set transformed the consumption of music. As Philip K. Eberly has noted, it was now possible to speak credibly of truly "popular" songs. Arnold Shaw has argued that the decade saw "a group of new tonalities" enter American music, "fixing the sound and the forms of popular music" until the rock revolution of the 1950s. It was the time, in the words of music historian Nicholas Tawa, for Americans to discover the country's "authentic voice"—in blues, on Broadway, from Tin Pan Alley, and, most of all, in jazz, the "rich and permanent fusion" of black and white American music. "Hot sounds" coming out of New Orleans and Kansas City enthralled audiences ready to shake off the musical styles of the prewar period—"an antidote to conformity, boredom, custom, tradition."[2]

Yet the popular understanding of the 1920s as, in F. Scott Fitzgerald's formulation, the "Jazz Age" is arguably the most deeply engrained and most pernicious of the cultural myths surrounding the postwar period. Jazz has become a signifier of "the end of an earlier era and the transition to a modern one," even as "the music itself and the circumstances under which it was performed embodied social change." Arguments over jazz in the 1920s, as Kathy Ogren persuasively suggests, then become used as a synecdoche of larger arguments over national identity in the postwar era. To overstate the extent to which jazz represented a wider transition to modernity, however, is to lose the ambiguity, ambivalence, and compromise of the era. To understand the cultural 1920s, we must fully appreciate both the inter- and intragroup tensions of the period. Jazz, for example, actually represented one of the very few subjects upon which H. L. Mencken, the *New York Times*, and the Ku Klux Klan could theoretically agree.[3]

"The number of genuine music-lovers in the United States," Mencken argued, "is probably very low." You could tell the number of "tone deaf" Americans from the crowds who could "not only sit through the infernal din made by the current jazz-bands," but "actually like it." For Mencken, the "hot sounds" of Jazz Age America were akin to "the sound of riveting." In this opinion, he found a diverse slew of allies.[4]

Significant sections of American society were openly hostile to jazz. The Reverend Dr. Percy Stickney Grant of New York City, for one, called it "a savage crash and bang." Anne Shaw Faulkner, national music chairman of the General Federation of Women's Clubs, took to the pages of the *Ladies' Home Journal* to ask whether jazz put the sin in syncopation. This upstanding American, writing in one of the most popular publications of the day, noted that the music stimulated "the half-crazed barbarian to the vilest deeds." Both Faulkner and Fenton T. Bott of the American National Association of Masters of Dancing claimed to have evidence that listening to jazz actually caused brain damage, causing the young to become rowdy, if not to entirely lose their ability to tell right from wrong. The Ninth Recreation Congress, led by critic Sigmund Spaeth and Professor Peter Dykeman, among a host of other cultural highfliers, declared "war" on jazz. The *New York Times* was compelled to complain that jazz "offends people with musical taste already formed," especially when it made use of "that ghastly instrument," the saxophone.[5]

The Klan's condemnations of jazz were, therefore, hardly exceptional—although the organization's rhetoric leaned more toward overt anti-Semitism than most critics, who were more concerned with the music's black roots. Isaac Goldberg, writing in Mencken's *American Mercury* in 1927, described jazz as "musical miscegenation" between "the American Negro and the American Jew." Klan members perceived a double threat in this alliance, and the publications of the Invisible Empire attacked "Jew-monopolized jazz" as part of a concerted campaign to "lower the standard of morals" by inflaming "animal passions." Jewish "songs that rock with sex," full of "sensual jazz rhythms," would destroy "the moral fiber of American pulchritude."[6]

Nor were the organization's criticisms limited to jazz. Broadway songs, "written and published by Jews," were "the limit of inanity, filthy suggestion, and vulgarity." Like jazz, Broadway tunes transmitted the "low and degrading influence" of Jews into the homes of morally upright Protestants. Music on the vaudeville stage, the *Fiery Cross* complained, made "sly sport" of "all the worthwhile things in life." Critics of opera, meanwhile, sounded a familiar anti-Catholic refrain. "A foreign, alien expression, with a far-reaching influence for evil," their arias allegedly broadcast a "poisonous taint" of Romanism.[7]

Not all of these attacks were verbal. Dance halls often found themselves subject to protest by Klansmen and allied groups. Klan members in Michigan and Wisconsin passed resolutions barring all dancing at any function held under Klan auspices. In some areas, Klansmen patrolled to monitor for infractions. Institutions that repeatedly flouted warnings about inappropriate dancing might find themselves victims of property damage and arson. Dancers in Oakland, New Jersey, were left "panic-stricken" after Klansmen allegedly exploded several bombs outside a charity ball, leaving burning crosses at the front and rear.[8]

If we accept the Klan's rhetoric that the organization represented a unified bloc of resistance to jazz and all that it supposedly represented, though— that is, that the cultural signifiers of the hood and the saxophone were diametrically opposed—we lose the reality of the contemporary ambiguities. Per Spaeth, scholars have often seen jazz as the "inevitable music" of a new era, an "ideal expression of complete freedom from convention" in an "unrestrained society." Yet jazz was in many ways still restrained. Even as the Cotton Club played host to talent like Louis Armstrong, Bessie Smith, and Duke Ellington, the nightclub's stage saw scenes of the "Old South" or "darkest Africa." As Philipp Blom has noted, all too often, "Harlem nights became show nights for the Nordics." Even those white Americans who celebrated jazz frequently tended to do so in a way that reinforced racial tropes, enthusing over the ability of the music to express the "more intense" traits of "carelessness" and unthinking "instinctive qualities" of African Americans.[9]

At the same time, it was a music that no one seemed able to successfully define. Popular understanding of what could be considered jazz broadened. A white mainstream consensus formed around a "jazz" that would encompass all up-tempo dance music—what Eberly calls "razz-ma-tazz music." While we may better remember Armstrong and Ellington, the decade's self-proclaimed "King of Jazz" was a white man named, with no small irony, Paul Whiteman. And following the example of musicians like Whiteman, Klan members were among the many white Americans who picked up instruments and formed "jazz" bands of their own.[10]

It should not be surprising that an organization like the Ku Klux Klan would make use of music. Most big tent revivalists traveled with a music leader, and some had a full musical entourage. As Josh McMullen has noted, music and singing were frequently identified as the most popular features of revival meetings, while revival musicians became well-known personalities in their own right. Billy Sunday, for one, traveled with band members, singing groups, and soloists. His music director, Homer Rodeheaver, even recorded albums of revival music to allow the message to reach a wider audience. Little wonder, then, that the Invisible Empire would follow a similar path—so similar that Rodeheaver would also play an important part in the recording of Klan music.[11]

What may be more surprising was the kind of music that Klan members integrated into their organizational life. In addition to the significant role that organizationally sanctioned music played in official Klan rituals, performances of unofficial musical pieces quickly became commonplace at regular Klan gatherings. As in other popular entertainments, this was an almost entirely unstructured process, with little to no oversight from the organization's national leaders. Rather, the Klan's relationship with music offers a telling insight into the wider movement's involvement in contemporary popular culture.

The Klan of Lagrange, Oregon, hailed their Klavern's musicians as "a real inspiration" to their meetings, while an assembly might be brought to order by the singing of "Hail, Hail, the Gang's All Here." Klaverns of the Women's Klan were even more evidently enthused by musical entertainments. The minutes of the WKKK of Denver, for example, record the organization of an "Entertainment Committee" that had members contribute to a regular musical revue. Selections for the piano (which the Denver Klan had assiduously raised money to buy) might be interspersed with solos by local musicians, songs by a choir, or even outside performers. On one notable occasion, the ladies of the Klan were entertained by the Berry family—Razz, Huckle, Blue, and Straw.[12]

As the popularity of this Klavern music with members became evident, Klans across the country increasingly began to feature musical entertainments at larger public meetings and rallies through the early 1920s. Klan parades, to heighten the deliberately ghostly atmosphere, initially featured no music but the pounding of drums, while naturalizations might feature chanting and sacred music a cappella. When these events moved to shed their mysticism, Klannish musical attractions were at the forefront of the shift. As early as 1921, the *New York World* reported that Klansmen at an initiation in New Jersey "took the edge off the solemnity" by playing "popular airs." The Klan repertoire included "Ain't We Got Fun," a hit foxtrot published that year, which Sigmund Spaeth called "the perfect theme song for the carefree young people of the twenties"—including members of the Invisible Empire.[13]

Bands, choirs, orchestras, and other musical groups quickly became a staple of events. As membership grew, and Ku Klux Klan demonstrations and rallies became ever more ostentatious, each local Klan attempting to outdo the other, music became a requisite. A Klan picnic without a performance of some kind began to seem distinctly underwhelming. To be a truly successful event and draw a sizable crowd, at least three or four different groups needed to perform. An initiation in Minnesota reportedly stood out "to a marked degree" because of the skillful performance of "patriotic, religious, and popular numbers." A Los Angeles naturalization centered around a dramatic rendition of "Rock of Ages" that saw all lights extinguished, save for a single spotlight on the cross. In stark contrast to the muted drumming of earlier marches, a planned parade by New York City Klans featured twenty-five bands.[14]

By 1924, these musical entertainments had often begun to dominate reports of otherwise quotidian Klan events. A story in the *Searchlight* on a Ku Klux Klan lecture in Kansas, for example, was headlined "Klan Quartette Provides Music." Notices advertising Klan events increasingly featured the appearance of musical groups, and in ever-larger type. It soon became clear that these performances were sufficiently popular to draw crowds even without the additional enticement of Klan parades, lectures, initiations, or picnics. Recognizing the appeal that they held for members and nonmembers alike, the Invisible Empire was quick to exploit the allure of these musical entertainments.[15]

Even as they policed the same behavior in nonmembers, Klans increasingly began to stage concerts and dances. In 1922, an Illinois Klan played host to three hundred people at a "Harvest Jubilee" where "dancing predominated the evening." A 1924 "musical entertainment" by the Milwaukee Klan attracted nearly a thousand people. By 1925, local newspapers breathlessly advertised the Klan's concerts and dances as major events. One open-air concert, in Missouri, allegedly drew a crowd upward of ten thousand. In some locales, Klan dances were such a fixture of the social scene that attendance was reported on the society pages. A "Ku Klux Mask Ball," thrown by Chicago Klan members to celebrate George Washington's birthday, satirized the organization's supposed obsession with secrecy by having all Klansmen unmask "at the mystic hour of midnight." In western Pennsylvania, a Klan-sponsored foxtrot competition descended into chaos after dancers bumped into one another, resulting in seven arrests. If any other organization had been responsible, local Klan members would doubtless have pointed to the event as proof of creeping Jewish and Catholic immorality.[16]

Klans were occasionally forced to turn to outside bands to provide music for these events. In Kansas City, the local police band played for a Klan convention. In California, the Downey Klan hired bandleader Caesar Mattei after determining he was both Protestant and a Mason. Klaverns even sometimes hired African American musicians to perform. At one event in Virginia, local members explained that they had "danced to the music of Negro musicians" only after ascertaining that the only other band available was from the Knights of Columbus. An Alabama Klan purportedly managed an accomplished African American bluesman, Burl "Jaybird" Coleman, and hired him out to play at events across the South.[17]

For the most part, however, the Invisible Empire found its musicians among its members. A survey conducted by the music trades in 1925 saw a remarkable increase in the sale of musical instruments, a development that they attributed to the twin phenomena of radio and jazz. More and more Americans aspired to become musicians, and Klan members were no exception. As musical entertainments at Klan events became ever-greater attractions, Klaverns around the country—including Junior Klansmen and members of the Women's Klan—formed increasingly well-trained and professional bands. Resembling popular contemporary big band "jazz" acts like Paul Whiteman, these groups usually featured a mix of cornets, clarinets, drums, and even the dreaded saxophones. In a clear example of the separation between the organization's rhetoric and the lived ideology of movement members, Klaverns openly referred to their groups as jazz bands without eliciting any comment. Members of the Women's Klan of Clarksburg, West Virginia, for one, noted that they were on their way to forming "a fairly good jazz orchestra" but were still in need of "a good trombonist" and a trap drummer.[18]

Friendly rivalries sprang up as Klans competed to have the largest and most polished band in the area. Anything with less than twenty members was a disappointment. If the Klan was to play big band, then its bands would be the biggest. Popular Klans, such as those in Los Angeles and Detroit, formed groups with anywhere from sixty to a hundred members. The Women's Klan of Texas organized a 150-piece band "credited with being the largest and best trained organization of its kind in the United States." Chicago's Mammoth Klan Band aspired to become "the world's largest band" with six hundred members, although it does not appear that membership of the group ever reached more than a highly respectable two hundred.[19]

With Klannish musical performances continuing to gain favor, Klan bands increasingly represented the attractive public face of the Invisible Empire, garnering regional, and even national, popularity. Belatedly realizing the significance of this outreach, the organization's leaders struggled to take control. By 1924, the national Klan had introduced a money-spinning regulation band uniform—an impressive variation on the usual robes, with gold silk–embroidered lyres and a purple satin cape, which could be purchased only through official channels (see fig. 7.1). By 1928, the organization had created the new official position of "Musiclad" to regulate musical entertainments. In all of this, though, the Klan's leaders were trailing far behind the existing success of musical members at the local level.[20]

The Mammoth Band toured extensively throughout the Midwest and provided music for a wide variety of events. The Chicago Heights Klan Band claimed to be "the most famous musical organization in the Middle West." The Junior Klan band of Evansville, Indiana, spent more than thirteen weeks on the road in 1925, traveling over four thousand miles and "giving concerts all along the route." The two-hundred-piece Denver Klan Band, performing in full regalia, was popular enough to throw a public recital at the city's ten-thousand-seat Cotton Mills Stadium in 1925, selling tickets for fifty cents.

FIGURE 7.1. Band in official regalia, Klan Field Day, Ridgway, Pennsylvania, October 1924. Photographer unknown.

While contemporary rhetoric may have described bloc resistance, the reality was that Klan bands played jazz—and they did so for mass audiences.[21]

As this popularity might suggest, Klannish music was not limited to staid hymns and piously patriotic classics. These songs were certainly central to the Klannish catalog. "America" and "The Star Spangled Banner" were staples of Klan meetings. The official *Musiklan* was comprised exclusively of such standards, including "Battle Hymn of the Republic," "Just As I Am," and "Rock of Ages." "Onward Christian Soldiers" was effectively adopted as the organization's anthem. "The Old Rugged Cross" was an unsurprising favorite at cross burnings. Nonetheless, these selections represented only one small part of the Klan's repertoire.[22]

At the most basic level, Klan members expanded their musical range by rewriting the lyrics to well-known tunes, allowing whole crowds to sing along. Many relied on traditional standards. "Onward Christian Soldiers" remained prevalent. "Let the Fiery Cross Be Burning," an 1870s religious song adapted by North Carolina Grand Dragon (and superior court judge) Henry A. Grady, became a popular Klan number. With no apparent sense of irony, the abolitionist tune "John Brown's Body" found itself twisted into "The Klansman's Jubilee Song."[23]

Other lyricists adopted less pious but no less classic melodies. "The Ballad of Casey Jones" was one of the most common choices, with interpretations including "A Friend Worth While," which mocked evolutionary theory, and "The Klansman's Friend," which explained that the Klan "do not aim to harm" but only wanted law and order. "Mary Had a Little Lamb" similarly became the anti-Catholic ditty "Rome Has a Little Pope," who was "full of dope" and planned to take control of the schools.[24] "Huckleberry Doo" became "My Huckleberry Jew," which accused its subject of greed, low morals, and trafficking in white slavery. "You," the "Huckleberry Jew" was warned, "better keep a sheeny's place." Any tune that members could be assumed to know was put to use.[25]

What is perhaps most significant about these rewritten songs is how many used popular modern tunes. Contemporary hits like Billy Rose's 1923 smash "Barney Google" (often adapted into "Barney Google, Klansman," to criticize Google's fat "Irish Jew" wife) were clearly familiar to Klan members. "I'm Forever Blowing Bubbles," first published in 1919, inspired a number of Klannish rewrites, most variations on "I'm Forever Burning Crosses." By far the most popular of these songs was "Yes! We Have No Bananas." Given its ubiquity in American life after being popularized in 1923, it is unsurprising that the melody to the novelty hit was well known to Klansmen. Spaeth called it the "all-time top in the school of musical nonsense." Journalist Mark Sullivan noted that "Yes! We Have No Bananas" was heard "from almost every lip" and sung "more often than all the hymns in all the hymnals of all the churches combined."[26]

Little wonder, then, that Klansmen contorted the nonsense song to their own ends, producing wide-ranging variations. "Yes! We Have Our Ku Klux-ers" took a positive stand "for free speeches—free presses, White supremacy—Just laws and liberty." "Yes! The Klan Has No Catholics" focused instead on criticizing "that Dago Pope in Rome." The *Badger American* had condemned the song as the work of "two Jewboys," containing "neither rhyme nor reason," but Klannish songwriters apparently felt comfortable assuming Klan members knew the tune well enough to sing along. Although the rhetoric of the Invisible Empire might have decried the debauched "sewage" of modern music, its members were clearly listening.[27]

The Klannish movement was also creating music and, in doing so, rein-forcing an imagined cultural community of white Protestant heroism. Simply bastardizing popular songs of the day to include commendations of Klannish virtue and condemnations of alien vice was not enough to satisfy a grow-ing demand for Ku Klux Klan musical entertainment. Instead, the men and women of the organization turned progressively toward original Klan com-positions. These songs promulgated the same tropes of virtuous self-image that were also enthusiastically promoted on page, stage, and screen. The only difference was that the message was set to an upbeat tune.

These highly localized creations were once again far removed from any official oversight or control, yet promoted a largely uniform national com-munal identity. Many of the original compositions dealt with a range of issues important to the Klan movement. "The Klansmen's Kall," by George Zterb of Ohio, was a heartfelt ballad on the merits of public schooling. "We Are the Ladies of the Ku Klux Klan" added a feminist note, praising the WKKK fight against "the immorality of man." A New York songwriter extolled the merits of the Klan's fight against political graft, foreign agitators, and the "Boozeshe-vik" in "American Means the Klan (When We A-Marching Go)." The Frank Harding Music House of New York City published "The Ku Klux Klan Song," which called for keeping the Bible in education. "I'm a Klansman (Hoo-Ray!)" from Emory Sutton of Los Angeles insisted simply that "we stand for all that's right."[28]

Others sounded the familiar refrain that the Klan was not responsible for the heinous actions attributed to it. As Francis Roy's song "They Blame It on the Ku Klux Klan" had it, the Klan was wrongly found "responsible for ev'ry little thing that's done" from "Florida to Oregon." J. Owen Smith's 1923 song "The Fiery Cross on High" stated that Klansmen stood "for obedience to the law and freedom." New Jersey's Kenneth Paterson similarly observed that the Klan stood for "respect for the home and laws" in his 1924 song, "KKK (If Your Heart's True, It Calls to You)." Moving hesitantly away from some of the more hateful language that marked the co-opted popular tunes sung at Klan meetings, the movement's lyricists attempted to reinforce the Invisible Empire's self-image and public image as a "pro," not an "anti," movement.[29]

These original compositions were primarily produced and distributed as sheet music. Many were self-published, but the growing market for Klan music also gave birth to a number of larger publishing houses that specialized in Klannish odes. The profitable nature of this enterprise was reflected by the high quality of the sheet music that was published. Collections of rewritten songs were, for the most part, ramshackle affairs, clearly turned out by a local printing shop at the cheapest possible rate. Ku Klux Klan originals were an entirely different affair, boasting lavishly illustrated covers, predominantly in color. These covers often featured the Klan marching in lockstep with Uncle Sam, as in E. M. McMahon's "We Are All Loyal Klansmen," or rushing to his rescue. Many others depicted heroic visions of Klansmen, alone or in groups, or majestic burning crosses. The Thompson Music Company cannily consolidated its brand (and saved money) by repeatedly using the same cover of a Klansman astride a rearing horse, defiantly raising a fiery cross in his hand. The striking image was copied by a number of smaller publishers.[30]

The care taken in publishing these Klan songs meant that they would not—and did not—look out of place when placed on the rack next to non-Klan musical publications. In fact, the widespread sale of this sheet music offers a clear indication of the porous boundaries of American cultural life in the 1920s. The National Association of Music Merchants had bemoaned the use of "smut" and cursing in jazz music, but clearly did not consider "Klan" a four-letter word. Klan sheet music was available in stores across the country, with major suppliers of Klannish music located in Kansas City, Denver, Indianapolis, Pittsburgh, and several upstate New York towns. For those who were not conveniently near a store, music was often sold at public events and Klan meetings. The sale of sheet music by mail was perhaps the most common means of distribution.[31]

Newspapers in towns and cities across the United States regularly carried advertisements for Klannish sheet music, both by individual songwriters and by larger publishing houses. Clearly, there was demand for these original Klan songs outside of those who read the Klan press and would have seen the advertisements there. Newspaper advertising was also hardly the only means used to sell sheet music by mail. The lucrative nature of this business, especially for larger publishers who carried a wide range of pieces, is suggested by the professional—and sizable—catalogs produced by two of the most prominent publisher-distributors: the International Music Company and Lutz Music Printing.

The Reverend Paul S. Wight, "nationally known Bible teacher and gospel singer," ran the International Music Company of Buffalo, New York. Under the title *American Hymns*, the company printed a handsome collection of lyrics to Klan covers of popular tunes. Distributed at "special prices to Klaverns and dealers," this was a canny piece of advertising disguised as altruism. The pamphlet contained not only lyrics for Klan sing-alongs but also a full listing of the thirty different songs that Wight sold as sheet music, alongside details on how to order. The Lutz Music Printing Company of York, Pennsylvania, run by H. A. Lutz, onetime "personal representative" of Imperial Wizard Simmons, focused more openly on self-promotion. Alongside the thirty different songs listed for sale as sheet music, Lutz printed gaudy advertisements. Most were for the compositions of the publisher's most prolific songwriter, Abe Nace, owner of a local music store.[32]

Sheet music was not the only thing Wight and Lutz sold. While a printed score seems to have been the primary means of distributing Klan music, there was an increasingly large market for an alternative method of consuming these songs—the phonograph. Record players had a devastating impact on "the active piano-playing generation" in the 1920s. They offered music on demand, requiring no skill, no practice, and no effort. Sheet music sales had declined accordingly, and prices dropped precipitously. At the same time, the phonograph was becoming a multibillion-dollar business with the growth of a new recording industry—one that would propel the intersectional popularity of both jazz and Klan music.[33]

A Detroit-based effort to manufacture and sell Klan phonograph records was characterized by historian Kenneth Jackson as "amusing." Certainly, the Cross Music and Record Company never actually produced a record. Detroit Kleagle Ira W. Stout seemingly organized the enterprise to fraudulently sell stock and bilk potential recording artists, although the group did also tour extensively and publish several original numbers in sheet-music form. Less "amusing," though, were the remarkable number of musicians who did successfully record, market, and sell Ku Klux Klan phonograph records across the country. At the forefront of these endeavors, and emblematic of the cultural complexities of the 1920s, was the Gennett Records studio in Richmond, Indiana.[34]

Starr Piano, owned by the Gennett family, had begun manufacturing phonographs in 1916. A year later, to complement growing phonograph sales, the Gennetts established their own recording label. By 1920, the company was producing around three thousand phonographs and three million records annually. Although small compared to major record manufacturers like Victor and Columbia, the Indiana label carved out a profitable niche as one of the larger second-tier companies. Initially reliant on a Manhattan recording studio, Gennett built its own facility in Richmond in 1921.

As the preeminent chronicler of Gennett Records, Rick Kennedy, has noted, the majority of the studio's recording artists were simply "obscure musicians passing through rural Indiana." Not all would remain obscure. Native Hoosier Hoagy Carmichael originally recorded "Stardust" at the studio. Key figures in the nascent jazz and blues scene made early recordings at Gennett. Bix Beiderbecke, Louis Armstrong, Jelly Roll Morton, and Blind Lemon Jefferson all recorded at the Indiana studio—as did members of the Ku Klux Klan. The sharing of physical space with the Klan was not limited to Paul Robeson. Some of the greatest African American jazz and blues musicians of the 1920s shared a recording studio with the Invisible Empire.[35]

Although these jazz and blues recordings were musically important, their significance did not necessarily translate into profits for the Gennett label. It was private contracts and commercial recordings that kept the company afloat. Clients included Sears, Roebuck & Company,[36] the Salvation Army, and the Ku Klux Klan. Rick Kennedy has posited that this diverse client list reflected the family's "business pragmatism." One family member, Richard Gennett, recalled simply that the company released Klan recordings "because they paid us. That was all. We did a lot of vanity records for all kinds of people." The company's location in the Klan stronghold of Indiana, combined with the fact that it employed (like many companies in Indiana at the time) a number of Klansmen, led Gennett to become a linchpin in the Invisible Empire's musical efforts.[37]

Ku Klux Klan recordings made at the Gennett studio appeared under a number of different labels. Certainly the most prolific of the Indiana studio's Klannish recording artists was singer-songwriter Wilbur Rhinehart. With the help of his brother Charles, Rhinehart ran the 100% label. Often with the backing of pianist Hattie Buckles, the brothers issued recordings of covers like "Barney Google, Klansman," and "Onward Christian Klansmen" that continued to reinforce a unified cultural identity and community of Klannish virtue. A typical example, "There'll Be a Hot Time, Klansmen," an adaptation of "There'll Be a Hot Time in the Old Town Tonight," dedicated one verse to asserting that crimes the organization were accused of were "a fake" and another verse to exulting in the Klan's 1924 political victories. Residents of nearby Muncie, the brothers also ran the 100% Publishing Company, one of the state's most important Klan sheet-music publishers.[38]

HKS Records and the Wake Up label, both recorded at Gennett, operated under the auspices of two groups of Michigan Klansmen. Homer Rodeheaver, the gospel impresario and music director for Billy Sunday, lent out his Chicago studio for Klan recordings, releasing the titles through Gennett on his private label. A variety of Klan recordings, including the popular "Wake Up America (and Kluck, Kluck, Kluck)," were issued by James D. Vaughan of Tennessee, a songbook publisher known as "the father of southern gospel music," on his Gennett-produced label.[39] Indianapolis Klan publisher The American released a series of popular Klan tunes in 1924 and 1925 on the KKK and Hitch labels, including "The Bright Fiery Cross," "Mystic City," and "Why I Am a Klansman." The Indiana Klansmen were so convinced of the quality of these "leading Klan hits of today" that they sent sample copies to Thomas Edison in 1924 in hopes of gaining wider distribution. Edison, for his part, dismissed them as "trash," although he did note that "Why I Am a Klansman" had a "fair tune."[40]

Much as with Klan sheet music, sales of Klan recordings were an indication of the complex relationship between the Invisible Empire and modern mass culture. Klan-made phonograph records could be found in music stores across the nation. The KKK label even had its own Acme Record Shop in Indianapolis. Salesmen and local distributors took out advertisements in both the Klan and mainstream press, selling recordings by mail. The *Danville Bee* of Virginia, for one, regularly carried announcements of the latest Klan records, while the *Joplin Globe* of Missouri was frequently used to promote the work of local songwriter Billy Newton and his Klannish melodies. Both the Lutz and Wight catalogs offered more than twenty double-sided phonograph records, a mix of original tunes and rewritten classics, selling at around a dollar each.[41]

As significant as these Klan songs are in fully understanding the cultural milieu of the 1920s, an even clearer indication of the ambiguities and contradictions of popular entertainment in the period comes from the embrace of the Klan by songwriters outside the organization. World War I had seen an outpouring of new patriotic songs to capitalize on the moment. The 1920s saw an even greater prevalence of "event songs" as songwriters on Tin Pan Alley jostled to create the latest hit. It is hardly surprising, then, that a number of novelty songs attempted to capitalize on public interest in the Invisible Empire. As the 1921 song "There's a Bunch of Klucks in the Ku Klux Klan," by Sam Coslow and Leon Friedman, noted, "a certain society" was being provided with "notoriety" by constant coverage in the daily papers. Coslow and Friedman's tune was widely advertised as a "timely and sensational hit."[42]

"Klucks" was perhaps the least flattering of these novelty songs, complaining that the Klan's "awful hoke" made them an "awful joke." Many others, however, implicitly favored and normalized the Invisible Empire. As on page, stage, and screen, the commercial exploitation of the Klan in music reinforced the Klannish community in many ways. While the organization came in for criticism, the ideals and aims of the wider movement were sanitized and often celebrated for a mass consumer public.

The 1922 song "Ku Ku (the Klucking of the Klan)" by Billy Frisch of Tin Pan Alley's Hitland Music, released by OKeh Records in 1923, provides a prime example of this tendency. The song clearly indicated its anti-Klan sentiments, referring to the "awful sight" of Klansmen on the march, mocking the "gobble of the Goblin Man," and warning listeners that the Klan would "call 'round in their nighties" and tar and feather them. At the same time, any real sense of menace was undermined by the bouncy, jaunty tune, while Frisch seemingly endorsed the Klan's choice in victims. If you were a landlord who "tries to profiteer," a drinker of "home-made beer," or if you beat your wife, the song warned, you would soon hear "the Klucking of the Klan" as it came for you. Even as the song jeered at the organization's tactics, it endorsed the movement's morals.[43]

A popular upbeat tune entitled "Daddy Swiped Our Last Clean Sheet and Joined the Ku Klux Klan" had similar issues. Written by Helen Marcell of the University of Kansas, the song was intended to lampoon the organization. In the most cutting line of the novelty number, Marcell noted that "Daddy took the pillow case to cover up his head," but "he soon found out that it would smother him instead." Nonetheless, the fact that it also endorsed many of the movement's aims meant the song soon began to become popular with Klan members and sympathizers. The sheet music was offered for sale in Klan publications, and Marcell's composition was recorded at the Gennett studios and released under the KKK label (see fig. 7.2). By 1927, the touring Klan production *The Awakening* prominently featured the song, receiving "loud applause" whenever it was performed. Marcell's intent in writing the song did not seem to matter. "Daddy Swiped Our Last Clean Sheet" had become a bona fide hit with the Ku Klux Klan.[44]

The majority of these novelty songs took a similar tack. The organization's violence and vigilantism were condemned even as the lyrics implicitly reinforced the idea that the Klan stood for law and order, and its victims somehow warranted their fate. This tendency was particularly apparent in the proliferation of Klan "blues" songs. Illustrative of the often-ironic tensions of the cultural 1920s, these popular songs fused the racial stereotypes of nineteenth-century "coon" songs with contemporary rhythms appropriated from black musicians.

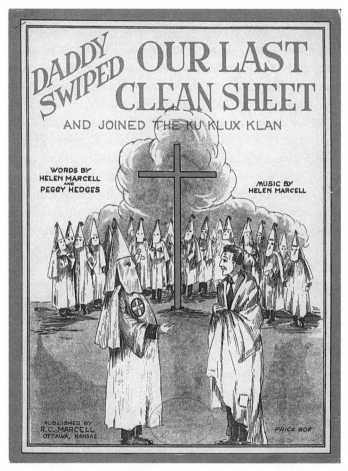

FIGURE 7.2. Cover illustration for Helen Marcell's "Daddy Swiped Our Last Clean Sheet and Joined the Ku Klux Klan" (Ottawa, KS: R.C. Marcell, 1924).

The "coon song" fad, from the mid-1880s until the early 1910s, had seen hundreds of songs published that combined earlier tropes of blackface minstrelsy with a Jim Crow desire to enforce racial hierarchies. African Americans, these songs proclaimed, were marked by ignorance and indolence, lust, dishonesty, and irresponsibility. Worse, the "coon" represented an active threat to white Americans. Prone to drinking and gambling, he was also inextricably associated with the physical threat of black violence. In song after song, the straight razor became the signifier of an uninhibited savagery.[45]

These stereotypes continued well into the 1920s and 1930s in songs like "Pickanninies' Heaven" and "Georgia Gigolo"—and in songs about the Klan.

Most often, these songs took the point of view of an African American in the South. Mingling cartoonishly exaggerated Negro dialect with classic blues chord progressions, these songs explained exactly why their subjects actually deserved to be punished by the Invisible Empire. In "Those Dog-Gone Ku Klux Blues" by John Douglas Lewis, for one, the song's narrator is threatened by the Klan after "loafing around" and brewing alcohol, and flees, leaving "my woman and my booze." Warren D. Ownby's "De Ku Klux Klan Gwine to Git You Ef You Don't Watch Out" told the story of a black preacher in Alabama who used the threat of the Klan to scare his parishioners into good behavior. While containing elements of criticism, these songs were recognizably favorable to Klannish aims and to the law-enforcing image that members of the organization were keen to promote. This became particularly apparent when Klan songwriters began to adopt a similar narrative and melodic device in their own work, including Billy Newton's "Ku Klux Steppin' Blues" and Charles A. Arthur's "Those Good Old Ku Klux Blues."[46]

The earliest, and most successful, of these novelty blues songs was "The Ku Klux Blues" by popular Southern songwriters Al Mars and Clarence Krause, published in 1921. Mars and Krause told the overfamiliar "coon" story of Sambo Rastus, who liked to "roam around, with a razor in my hand," "loved to fight both night and day," and enjoyed shooting craps. After a visit from the Klan, though, Rastus reformed and vowed to be "as good as Abraham." Several well-regarded African American bands actually adopted the song as a regular number, while Gus Creagh's Orchestra recorded it for See-Bee Records.[47]

The Invisible Empire's most influential and lasting interaction with American musical culture was not, however, as the subject of novelty songs. It was as a catalyst in the revival of "old-time fiddling" and the development of the new "hillbilly" genre. Many in the 1920s, including novelist Andrew Lytle and tycoon Henry Ford, bemoaned the decline in the popularity of classic rural fiddle music. Klan members apparently shared not only the car manufacturer's anti-Semitism but also his musical tastes. The Invisible Empire proved itself a high-profile aficionado of "old-time" music, with fiddlers often providing the entertainment at Klan events. This appreciation for the genre also translated into active support.[48]

Although the musical style was popular with Klan members as a whole, the story of the Invisible Empire's influence on the "hillbilly" genre is best understood within the context of the story of one man—Fiddlin' John Carson, one of the most successful and talented white Southern musicians of the 1920s. Carson was a native of Georgia, and his career was intertwined with the second Klan from the very beginning. In 1913, he wrote "Little Mary Phagan," demonizing local Jewish industrialist Leo Frank, who had been falsely accused of killing Phagan. By 1915, when Frank was lynched by a precursor to the soon-to-be-reborn Klan, Carson's song had already become recognized as a "classic murder ballad" popular with the Southern working-class community.[49]

Thanks largely to his participation in the annual Georgia Old-Time Fiddlers' Conventions, Carson's popularity in the state steadily grew. By 1922, when he became one of the first Southern fiddlers to appear on radio, Carson had already joined the Ku Klux Klan. His membership is hardly surprising. According to music historian Patrick Huber, Carson was "deeply immersed" in Georgia's populist politics, alongside many of the Invisible Empire's leading lights. One biographer, Gene Wiggins, defends Carson as "probably not an ardent" Klansman, but the musician was certainly a valuable ally of the organization. Klansman Clifford Walker, soon to win election as governor of Georgia, hired Carson in 1922 to play at political rallies across the state. Historian James C. Cobb notes that the fiddler was a frequent presence at Klan events in Georgia.[50]

Carson's membership in the Klan certainly did not seem to hurt his career, which took a major step forward in 1923. Producer Ralph S. Peer of OKeh Records (which had also issued Billy Frisch's "Ku Ku") arrived in Atlanta, looking to be "the first of any major company to record traditional artists of either race in the South." Peer, an emblem of the dynamic cultural currents of the 1920s, was already credited with sparking the boom in African American "race records" after recording Mamie Smith in 1921. Now he was in search of material that he thought would appeal to rural and rural-minded markets. He found it in Fiddlin' John Carson. By 1924, Carson's records were so popular that the company began to advertise the Klansman and similar artists as "a new and discrete genre of American commercial music." Trafficking on romanticized ideas of a preindustrial South, Carson's recordings marked the beginning of what was initially known as "Hill Country Music."[51]

The trend that Carson started was turned into a cultural juggernaut by the 1925 Fiddlers' Convention in Mountain City, Tennessee. Fiddle contests of this type had emerged in the 1890s, making them, in the words of Patrick Huber, "a comparatively modern and largely urban phenomenon." Fiddling aficionado Henry Ford backed some of the most prominent of these conventions and created a prize for national fiddle champion as a means of spurring interest in the genre. In doing so, he "set the woods and hills and plains afire with competitive rage" throughout the 1920s. Similarly, the Ku Klux Klan sponsored a number of local and regional competitions.[52]

The Invisible Empire's association with these "old-time fiddling" contests reached its apex with the Mountain City Convention in May 1925. Cosponsored by the Buster Brown Shoe Company, the event began as a fund-raiser for a local farmer but quickly grew much larger. Much of this may have been due to the convention's "liberal cash prizes." Whatever the reason, the Ku Klux Klan's Mountain City Convention managed to attract, according to one historian, "every old-time musician who ever was or hoped to be," a collection of performers that even Ford's national conventions could not match. Competitors included Carson, Edgar Hickam, Ralph Story, Charlie Bowman, Waits "Whiskers" Wiseman, Demp Harris, Al Hopkins and his brothers, Ralph Chinouth, and Smokey Davis.[53]

A Klan lecturer, the Reverend J. C. Reynolds, opened the convention with a "very fine" address. The local newspaper reported that the music offered was "the best ever heard" in the region and declared the event a "great success." Bob Cox, biographer of Charlie Bowman, has argued that this is an understatement. The collection of talented performers, many of whom were already well-known to radio listeners, attracted an above-capacity crowd. With the auditorium filled to overflowing, old-time music enthusiasts were left "standing on cars and sitting in windows," anywhere they might be able to hear the fiddlers. Dudley Vance won the grand prize, with Bowman taking second and Uncle Am Stuart third.[54]

Quite apart from its immediate success, the Mountain City Convention also left such an impression on the "hillbilly" genre that it is still widely remembered among music scholars—even though its Klannish connections are often conveniently forgotten. One of the event's most significant legacies was in marking the spectacular rise of the band that lent its name to the genre, the Hill Billies. The group, which was initially comprised of Al Hopkins, Joe Hopkins, John Rector, and Alonzo Alderman, had already made several recordings for Ralph Peer and OKeh earlier in the year. At the fiddling convention, they "made their initial reputation." They also met and recruited Charlie Bowman, which marked a major turning point for the group. Infrequent appearances on the District of Columbia's WRC radio station soon became four- or five-hour stints. Radio success parlayed into sales and increasingly popular tour dates. By 1927, the Hill Billies were playing at the White House Correspondents' Dinner in front of President Calvin Coolidge. The Ku Klux Klan had launched a phenomenon.[55]

It is a mistake, though, to assume that the Invisible Empire's association with this "old-time" music represents a consolidated resistance to modernity. For one thing, the launch of that hillbilly sound was caught up in the development of a modern consumerist music culture of phonographs and radio. For another, an appreciation of skillful fiddling does not erase the fact that Klan members enjoyed a wide swath of popular songs of the day, including novelty nonsense like "Yes! We Have No Bananas." In a process largely divorced from organizational control or sanction, they were also performing in widely popular jazz bands. While the organization declaimed modern musical miscegenation, Klan musicians appropriated rhythms and melodies from black performers to promote a virtuous white Protestant identity. Published, recorded, and sold around the country, these songs could be—and were—purchased by members and nonmembers alike. At the same time, the organization's image was hungrily, if inconsistently, consumed by a music industry looking for sales. The imagined community of the Klannish movement was reinforced even as members reveled in the same popular culture as most other Americans. In the new tonalities of the 1920s, the hot sounds of jazz harmonized with the razzmatazz of the Ku Klux Klan.

PBS—The Protestant Broadcasting System

Astronomers have observed a vast white area on Mars. The Ku Klux Klan may now be expected to set up a radio station.

CHICAGO DEFENDER, August 26, 1922

William S. Paley began the 1920s "half student, half playboy." By 1930, he had graduated to playboy tycoon. Propelled by the soaring stock market, he took control of the Columbia Network in September 1928. In New York, he combined the business mania of the Coolidge years with the "giddy hedonistic" pursuits of the Jazz Age city. Frequenting the lavish Casino nightclub, hosting elaborate and glamorous parties, he threw himself into what one biographer called a "sybaritic time of nightclub hopping and theatergoing." Even as he pursued a string of socialites and film stars like Louise Brooks, he began to build the Columbia Broadcasting System (CBS) radio network to compete with the fledgling National Broadcasting Company (NBC). As he did so, this fixture of the New York nightlife found himself in business with the Ku Klux Klan. The ambivalent embrace of the Klan and pluralist mass culture extended into the rise of radio.[1]

Radio, like the second Klan, was a true product of the postwar era. Although the technology had arrived with the turn of the century, it was not until after World War I that the radio boom began—and what a boom it was. In November 1920, with radios in less than 1 percent of American homes, station KDKA aired what is commonly cited as the first scheduled commercial broadcast. Radio listeners had previously been limited to hobbyists with a deep knowledge of receiving crystals. Even as the second Klan began its rise, commercially manufactured radios became widely available for the first time, massively expanding the potential radio audience.

A Radio Corporation of America (RCA) official recalled that "demand developed with an intensity that industrial America had never before experienced." Half a million radios were sold in 1923; almost four million in 1925—roughly the same number of members in the Invisible Empire that year;

then over six million in 1926. The cost of sets declined even as choice proliferated. Consumers were no longer restricted just to RCA equipment, with the ability to purchase the Mercury, the Newport, the DeForest Radiophone, and more. By the end of the decade, more than 45 percent of homes had at least one radio set. Some seventy-five thousand listeners in 1922 had become more than twelve million households, comprising an estimated forty million listeners, by 1930. In the process, radio broadcasts became social events. Families, friends, neighbors, and communities gathered to listen, on porches and in front yards, outside stores, and at special "radio parties." Broadcasting had become a billion-dollar industry.[2]

This remarkable rise has marked radio in the mind of many historians as the first truly modern mass medium. Marshall McLuhan, with typical bombast, declared radio to be "a subliminal echo chamber of magic power to touch remote and forgotten chords." While this may be overstating the case somewhat, radio arguably did more than any previous system to create a common culture, consumed by a national audience. Michele Hilmes and Susan J. Douglas have masterfully detailed the impact that radio made on the United States, disrupting the cognitive practices of a visual culture that suddenly found itself in an auditory world.[3]

Radio connected Americans as part of a vast listening public. Broadcasting bridged divides between rural and urban, bringing the country together in common cultural consumption. By the end of the decade, even more than newspapers, radio was able to construct a *national* audience, an imagined community of listeners who reveled in the "chance to feel that they were connected to others." One of those connections was with the Ku Klux Klan. Radio broadcasting would allow for the reinforcement of an imagined Klannish community in the vast unseen radio audiences across the country—a literal Invisible Empire.[4]

With millions more Americans buying radios, turning on, and tuning in every year, the demand for broadcasters soared. In 1922, there were thirty stations on the air. By 1923, there were more than five hundred. Not all were successful. More than two hundred new stations joined the airwaves in 1923, but almost three hundred closed. A key factor in this success, though, was content. All of these stations needed material. Michele Hilmes has astutely argued that as the rise of the Klan coincided with the development of radio broadcasting, the idea that "these two sets of phenomena were hermetically sealed off from each other requires a greater effort at explanation than the opposite assumption." This was not just mutual exploitation. This was mutual development.[5]

It is even easier to lose historical understanding of broadcast material than in the case of other forms of entertainment. The same cultural snobbery was

present, exacerbated by the inherently ephemeral nature of early radio. H. L. Mencken complained that the occasions when he had been able to listen to "anything even remotely describable as entertainment" were few and far between. More often, he found "rubbish." The early days of radio turned largely to the familiar—to vaudeville and musical comedy, to Broadway revues and Tin Pan Alley novelty numbers. Broadcasting from largely improvised studios, deadening sound with thick carpets, drapes, heavy furniture, even potato sacks, stations filled time with a wide variety of acts and entertainments, including the Ku Klux Klan.[6]

As with newspapers and newsreels, the interest generated by the Invisible Empire made the organization attractive to radio broadcasters looking to draw listeners. August 1923 marked the first reported appearance on the new medium by Imperial Wizard Hiram Evans, who delivered an address "to the Klansmen of the Nation" from station WOQ in Kansas City, Missouri, "heard within a radius of 1,000 miles." Evans's address to the Alabama state Klan convention in 1926 was carried on Birmingham's WBRC station "in one of the city's first night radio broadcasts." In Virginia, WDBJ and WTAR aired speeches by Evans and the proceedings of the state convention. Station KLZ of Denver, Colorado, gave time to speeches "honoring Klan notables." Pennsylvania's WPRC broadcast a special address by Evans on the "malign influence of the Roman Catholic Church" and the Klan's opposition to the World Court. In a move indicative of how far the Klan had shifted from attempting to cultivate an air of mystery, Louisiana station KFFY aired a Klan initiation from the county fair, including the order's theoretically secret oath.[7]

Significant as these appearances were, the organization's leaders once again lagged far behind the wider Klan movement in the adoption and exploitation of radio. By the mid-1920s, members of local Klans could already be heard on broadcast stations across the country. WLW in Cincinnati billed a forty-five-minute segment by the Hamilton County Klan in 1924 as "one of the first ever Klan programmes ever broadcast from a government [licensed] radio station." It was certainly not the last. These appearances usually consisted of either lectures by Klan state officers or, increasingly, light entertainment provided by Klan musicians. KFPW in Missouri, for example, proved a friend to the Klan with its broadcasts of Ozark Klan Band concerts, consisting "mostly of patriotic selections." James D. Vaughan, the prolific Klan music publisher, owned station WOAN in Tennessee and made it available for the use of Klan lecturers.[8]

Without any real oversight or organizational structure, these appearances were generally sporadic and irregular. Some stations, though, offered their listeners more consistent Klan programming. Klansmen appeared on WBAP in Texas, operated by the *Fort Worth Star-Telegram*, throughout 1923. A Klan concert aired in February could reportedly be heard as far away as Oregon. By December, the combination of "novel stunts" and "interesting information" in the Klan broadcasts had apparently made them popular enough for the station to feature the organization as their holiday entertainment. Listeners to WBAP rang in the New Year with a "Ku Klux Klan concert."[9]

The Invisible Empire found an even more influential ally in KFKB of Milford, Kansas. Originally established in 1923, the station had by 1925 become one of the most powerful broadcasters in the Midwest. In 1929, *Radio Digest* named KFKB the most popular station in the country after the broadcaster received more than a quarter of a million votes. Founder and operator John R. Brinkley was a "true early innovator" of radio, being among the first to air an almost full-time broadcast schedule. He was also one of the country's most successful medical hucksters. KFKB had been built with the money Brinkley earned offering goat gland transplants for sexual revitalization. Much of the station's programming was used to offer dubious medical advice and peddle patented "medicines."[10]

Perhaps recognizing a kindred spirit in the Klan movement, Brinkley featured local Klan members on KFKB on a fairly regular basis in 1925. The first of these broadcasts, an all-night affair on February 28, was publicized by Klan periodicals as "the first time such a program has ever been arranged over the radio." The experimental lineup included lecturers, monologists, Klan quartets, musical selections, and the Junction City Klan's jazz band—the superbly named Whiz Bang Orchestra. Listeners were encouraged to write in "in order to determine just what benefit such programs would be."[11]

Some audience members were not taken with the Kansas station's decision to provide the Invisible Empire with airtime, and a number of "threatening letters" were sent to KFKB. One disgruntled listener wrote to the Department of Commerce's radio office to complain about "broadcasting under government license the false, malicious, and un-American propaganda" of the Klan. Klan members and allies of the movement, in contrast, hailed the broadcast as "a smashing hit" and boasted that positive responses were "pouring in" from across the country. According to one Klan newspaper, the station received over two hundred long-distance phone calls praising the event, while Milford's small Western Union office was forced to bring in extra operators in order to receive all the congratulatory telegrams. A Kansas newspaper reported that one of the telegrams commending the program was signed by the entirety of the Emporia fire department. Certainly, the program was a sufficient success that KFKB immediately scheduled a repeat performance, while Brinkley took to the airwaves to excoriate those who had threatened violence against the station for broadcasting the Klan.[12]

Klan members were also listeners, and they found plenty to draw them to the early days of radio broadcasting. Some worried that the new medium, like the "Romanized, Jew-censored daily newspaper," would become a tool of un-American interests. The *Kourier Magazine* ran multiple articles warning of the "Romanist and anti-American propaganda" spread by radio. The *Kolorado Kourier* demonstrated the organization's usual disregard for facts, alleging that Catholics owned two-thirds of broadcasting stations. The paper warned that "the possibilities for ruining America" were "greater through air [wave] control than in any other one thing." One Klan, in Batavia, New York, went so far as to boycott all General Electric products after the Knights of Columbus appeared on the company's radio station. The *American Standard*, meanwhile, launched attacks on the "highly offensive" material broadcast on the radio.[13]

Even the *Standard* had to admit, however, that radio had "quickly become a subject of first importance." While there was plenty they could take offense at, the Klan publication also acknowledged the broadcast of "entertainment of high quality." An officer of the Women's Klan in Wisconsin was more effusive in her praise, telling members, "I should like very much to know that every Klan family in the land, had a radio. Used rightly, they are a gift from God." Many did not need the encouragement. Klan members were hardly immune from soaring American enthusiasm for radio.[14]

Despite dire warnings of Catholic control, enough Klan members had expressed interest in the new medium by 1922 that the *Searchlight* introduced a regular radio column, "devoted to items of general interest to radio 'bugs.'" Later that same year, the newspaper offered a hearty recommendation of several technical books aimed at amateur radio enthusiasts. At a Wisconsin Klan's New Year's Eve celebration, a large radio was the featured attraction, supplemented by a box supper and lecture. Craig Fox notes in his study of Michigan Klansmen that half those who owned radios in the town of Fremont were Klansmen. Fear of offensive material infiltrating their homes was clearly not enough to dissuade the men and women of the Klan from adopting this new technology.[15]

Seemingly the Klan's most favored broadcasting station was WHAP of New York City. WHAP was founded by Augusta E. Stetson, a Christian Scientist who had been expelled from the church for "perverted sexual teaching."[16] She retained a sizable following, including the wealthy William H. Taylor, who financed the construction of WHAP in 1925. Stetson's station was char-

FIGURE 8.1. From Paul M. Winter's *What Price Tolerance* (Hewlett, NY: All-American Book, Lecture and Research Bureau, 1928), facing p. 53.

acterized from the outset by the same kind of cultural snobbery offered by Mencken and his coterie. This attitude initially manifested itself in the same self-conscious intellectual refinement that marked much of radio's early programming. Educational offerings, high culture and art, respectable drama—this was the order of the day for many stations. Much of WHAP's airtime was dedicated to lectures by Ivy League professors and classical music performances that included members of the New York Philharmonic Orchestra.[17]

By mid-1926, the veneer of civility had been stripped away. The academics had gradually been phased out, replaced by fuming lecturers who did not bother to cloak their nativist beliefs and bigoted arguments on religious differences and race relations. Leading this pack was Stetson's personal secretary, Franklin Ford (see fig. 8.1), who was made WHAP's station manager. Ford presented a "News Digest" program three times a week, as well as a special lecture on "political Romanism" every Saturday. He filled his broadcasts with so much anti-Catholic and anti-Semitic vitriol that Sol Bloom and Samuel Dickstein, two of New York's congressional representatives, launched a campaign to have WHAP removed from the airwaves. As Ford gradually replaced more and more of the station's musical programming with these kinds of lectures, the *New York Herald Tribune* optimistically noted that "not many broadcasters devote 40 per cent of their weekly schedule to editorial talks, and it is doubtful that many broadcasters ever will." The WHAP broadcaster's "jeremiad of . . . claptrap" made him something of a pioneer in the field of talk radio.[18]

Ford denied he was a Klansman, and there is no evidence of a formal affiliation—he was a part of the Klannish movement, not a member of the organization. Informally, the bonds between the WHAP announcer and the Invisible Empire were clear. Ford often used his addresses to promote the Klan and its ideas. One of his most popular Saturday lectures, broadcast in April 1927, was entitled "Why Rome Fights the Ku Klux Klan." In it, Ford made the case that "no genuine American" could object to the Klan, which was "an agency of highest value for American welfare" and a "tremendous influence for good." These lectures were reprinted in their entirety every week by the *Fellowship Forum*, a Klan publication.[19]

Ford also had close ties to Paul Winter, head of the Ku Klux Klan in Queens. A widely circulated booklet by Winter, *What Price Tolerance*, contained a lengthy hagiography of Ford. The Klansman hailed the broadcaster as a "vitriolic thunderer" and quoted his opinions on Catholicism in politics at length, including the idea that "radio is doing, and will continue to do a great work" in freeing those enthralled to the Pope. Ford, for his part, often appeared at Klan events with Winter, lecturing on the evils of the Roman Catholic Church. At some Klan events, the WHAP front man was a draw on par with Imperial Wizard Evans, with whom he shared the stage on multiple occasions.[20]

Klan members were certainly not hesitant in embracing WHAP. As early as 1926, the *Fellowship Forum* praised "gallant old WHAP" as one of the few stations spreading "our message." Lecturers appeared on the station to exalt the Klan and its ideals. By 1929, the *Kourier Magazine* referred to WHAP as one of "our radio stations," commending its ability to "make Americans think." The Klan publication instructed members to tune in to WHAP and send financial contributions where possible. Klansmen were also encouraged to spread the word to other radio owners, and to invite friends and neighbors with no radio to listen with them.[21]

Yet WHAP was not the Ku Klux Klan radio station that many of the organization's members wanted. The Invisible Empire was far from alone in this desire. Although the majority of early broadcast stations were owned and operated by companies, fraternal groups across the country had eagerly welcomed the potential of radio for spreading their message and boosting their membership. A wide variety of churches had embraced the airwaves. Klan members were determined to get the Invisible Empire a foothold on the air as well.[22]

The most sophisticated and stable stations were those built as a means of increasing sales by radio manufacturers and dealers, who accounted for roughly 40 percent of the total station ownership. Many other stations were run by educational institutions and newspapers, which could afford to subsidize the new medium. The significant financial outlay required to establish and operate a broadcast station was a major obstacle for many, including the Klan. Given this impediment, it would seem reasonable that the national leadership—with access to the organization's sizable finances—would take the lead in this process. In reality, though, the Klan's efforts to conquer the world of broadcasting would see the efforts of local Klaverns and sympathizers achieve the greatest success. The split in radio once again reflected the power of the wider movement to construct a national Klannish community where the organization failed.[23]

Initially, the Invisible Empire's national leadership considered establishing a centrally controlled network of stations that would supplement the *Kourier* newspaper syndicate as a national propaganda outlet. In 1924, two years before NBC became the first national network in the United States, the Klan reportedly considered "extensive plans for a system of stations throughout the country." That project was temporarily abandoned: radio was still a fledgling medium, with crowded airwaves, and control of the newspapers was the national leadership's primary objective. By 1925, more of the Klan's officials had awakened to the possibilities presented by radio, and the Invisible Empire sought once again to build a "chain of stations." As newspapers noted at the time, the system would be "unique in the United States broadcasting field." While many organizations owned one or two small transmitters, "no body of this nature has ever considered a group of stations that would cover all or a section of the country." The Klan's ambition had vaulted it to the forefront of radio innovation.[24]

Like many of the Ku Klux Klan's grand plans, however, its ambition to broadcast outstripped its ability. With the Klan's organizational power already on the wane in 1925, the national "Protestant Broadcasting System" never seems to have progressed any farther than the planning. Instead, as with so many other cultural endeavors, Klannish broadcasting was left to members across the country who aimed to establish their own radio stations. In 1925, the King Kleagle of New Jersey (which had been mentioned as a potential home base for the national broadcasting system) declared his intention to erect a Klan station "from which matters of interest to the organization may be broadcast." The state's Klan even went so far as to purchase a tract of land from RCA that housed a Marconi wireless station. While it is unclear what went wrong, no broadcasts were forthcoming. By 1926 the land had been put to use as a Klan-only summer resort. In Iowa, the Des Moines Women's Klan did successfully establish a radio station, NSSA, and an accompanying newsletter, *The Iowa Broadcaster*, in 1926. For some reason, neither enterprise seems to have made much of an impression. The station did not even manage to garner a mention in the official Klan press. As the Klan's national membership continued to fall and its power weaken, it seemed as though the organization would never achieve its dream of a Ku Klux Klan broadcaster.[25]

The *Fellowship Forum* of Washington, D.C., came to the organization's rescue. With the *Kourier* syndicate already in rapid decline, the *Forum* represented the Invisible Empire's only remaining power base in the world of newspaper publishing. Newspapers constituted one of the largest and most powerful corporate interests invested in broadcasting. As Chicago newspaperman William Hedges noted in 1924, radio provided a powerful tool for a newspaper to promote itself, to "[pour] inoffensively its name into the willing ears of thousands of listeners." The *Forum* was a natural choice to get the Klannish voice on the air.[26]

In 1926, the *Forum* printed a "flood of letters" from around the country encouraging the publication to erect its own broadcasting station. Homer B. Summers of Illinois, in a typical example, called on the newspaper to "get some Protestantism on the air." In response, the newspaper declared that it was open to donations to finance the construction of a new home for the publication, complete with radio transmitter. As of May, the newspaper began publishing the names of contributing individuals and organizations as a mark of thanks. Supporters would have to hurry. The newspaper declared that it intended to break ground on the project with a "patriotic fete" on July 3.[27]

The response from the Ku Klux Klan and the Klannish public was immediate. A "tremendous gathering of Klanspeople" in Michigan, for instance, resolved to support the *Forum*'s radio project in every way possible, including enlisting a hundred thousand new subscribers. In the newspaper's first published list of donors, contributions from thirty states were listed, with an overwhelming majority sent by Klan members and affiliates. In at least one state, the Women's Klan circulated a bulletin informing members that "no unit is in any way compelled to contribute," but they would "miss an opportunity to help make history" by failing to donate.[28]

The national head of the Women's Klan, Imperial Commander Robbie Gill Comer, wrote an open letter to the *Forum* to inform readers, "I very much favor this project and believe that a Broadcasting Station would be of infinite value." To that end, she pledged to "cooperate in any way possible" and would push a "hearty response" from her members. In June, a similar letter arrived from Imperial Wizard Hiram Evans to "heartily endorse this movement" and underline "the urgent need of such an instrumentality." The Klan's head also donated a thousand dollars to the cause, and encouraged "every sincere American" to give "every possible financial assistance."[29]

Despite this impressive show of support, the *Forum*'s publisher and editor, James Vance, soon realized that he had overestimated how quickly the newspaper would be able to raise the necessary funds. As 1927 began, the *Forum* had raised over $110,000—short of the $160,000 needed. Nor was the lack of funds the only problem. In late January 1927, the newspaper announced that Congressman Henry Rathbone (R-Illinois) had agreed to become the head of the new radio station's advisory board. In the wide publicity that followed concerning "the radio broadcasting station to be erected by the Ku Klux Klan," Rathbone quickly denied any affiliation with the Invisible Empire and distanced himself from the *Forum*. Then, in April, the newspaper was informed by experts that a transmitter tower on a downtown D.C. property would be unworkable. As such, extra funds had to be raised to buy land outside of town as a dedicated site for the radio station. Vance's hectoring letters took on a new tone of urgency for a "great 60-day drive," a "regular CYCLONE OF ACTION," to raise the money. The initiative was spearheaded by a contribution from the Klan's favorite broadcaster, Franklin Ford.[30]

The most serious blow came in June. The prospective broadcasters had found a site in Virginia, near George Washington's home at Mount Vernon, and purchased it. On June 11, the cornerstone of the radio building was finally laid, almost a year behind schedule. A few days later, the *Fellowship Forum* received word that a broadcast permit was required to begin construction. Not only did the *Forum* still not have a permit, but it was not likely to receive one any time soon. If they had been able to raise the funds in 1926, the transmitter would likely have been completed in short order, but the extended fund-raising meant that construction had not begun before Congress passed the Radio Act of 1927. Previously, under the Radio Act of 1912, stations had operated under license from the Department of Commerce with minimal oversight. Now, a newly formed Federal Radio Commission (FRC) had the power to decide whether to grant a station a broadcast license based on "public interest, convenience or necessity," as well as to regulate broadcast frequency and power.[31]

This legislation effectively transformed broadcasting into a federally regulated public arena, as some forms of radio were deemed more worthy than others. Although the FRC was explicitly prohibited from directly censoring broadcasters, its licensing power meant that it was able to wield considerable power over programming. As well as the ability to deny a license to a new station, it could also refuse to renew an existing station's license. Since these licenses normally expired within six months of issuance, broadcasters the FRC deemed unacceptable could soon find themselves off air. John R. Brinkley of Klan-friendly KFKB had his right to broadcast removed in 1930 after the FRC found that the station "no longer met proper standards" and Brinkley's dubious medical advice was not "in the interest of the listening public." Outspoken broadcasters like Norman Baker of Iowa's KTNT and Reverend Bob Shuler of Los Angeles's KFEG met similar fates. New York City's WEVD, a Socialist station, was forced into a lengthy appeal to retain its license.[32]

With new federal oversight that looked unfavorably on stations that were "undesirable and obnoxious to . . . religious organizations" and that outright forbade the airing of "obscene, indecent, or profane" material, some newspapers simply reported that the *Fellowship Forum* had been denied a license to broadcast. The reality was somewhat more complicated. Construction had been halted because the newspaper did not *yet* have a permit. A letter from Commissioner Orestes Caldwell of the FRC to Vance noted that while the *Forum* was welcome to apply, "the commission has on file 300 applications for new stations, for which it is unable to find wave lengths." No new permits could be issued until other stations ceased broadcasting, to prevent overcrowding of the airwaves. Thus, Caldwell wrote, he could give "very little encouragement looking toward a wave length on which to operate on in the future." Numerous publications reveled in the Klan's lack of foresight.[33]

Caldwell's letter elided the fact that the *Forum* had actually registered an application for a broadcast permit in April.[34] After receiving the Klan publication's request, local radio supervisor G. E. Sterling wrote to the Department of Commerce to strongly recommend denying the *Forum* a permit:

> Confidential inquiries concerning this publishing company indicate that the above concern is connected with the Ku Klux Klan and that it is their policy to denounce in their publication, the Catholic Church. . . . It would seem on the strength of the above that it is safe to assume that this applicant, should a broadcast station be erected and licensed, would carry on religious propaganda to the extent that it would be questionable whether such a station would be in the interest of public convenience, interest and necessity.[35]

To support his point, Sterling wrote, he was "endeavoring to obtain a copy of its most radical publication in which religious attacks are published" and would forward his findings to the department. He also recommended that if "a station of this class" were to be licensed, it should be placed in a band wave "consistent with the type of material to be broadcast," with an emphasis on the minimizing of interference with the "more desirable class of programs"—a common practice, in which favored stations (generally those owned by large corporations) were given access to the 400-meter band, while others were relegated to the crowded 360-meter band. In May, Sterling sent several issues of the *Fellowship Forum* on to his superiors, highlighting what he considered the most egregious religious attacks. Almost all the pieces were reprints of Franklin Ford's radio addresses over WHAP.[36]

It was only with this information in hand that Caldwell wrote to Vance in June to inform him that the *Forum* should not expect a broadcast permit any time soon. Contrary to what many anti-Klan publications around the country gleefully reported, the Invisible Empire had not technically been "denied a license." The FRC had nonetheless effectively postponed the *Forum*'s debut indefinitely. The Klan would have to take its turn in the glut of applications.

Vance was not one to take this news peacefully, and began to look for alternatives to speed the process along. By July, he had found his answer. In an effort coordinated by the *Forum*'s attorney, ex-Congressman Charles I. Stengle (D-New York), the *Forum* agreed to buy station WTRC in Brooklyn—and the station's broadcasting license—from the local Republican club that operated it. If the FRC would not grant the *Forum* a permit until another station freed up a portion of the broadcast spectrum, then Vance would simply buy an existing permit.[37]

The *Forum* quickly filed the necessary paperwork to have ownership of WTRC's bandwidth officially transferred. In the application, Vance stated that the *Forum*'s primary mission would be to broadcast lectures on "Religious, Educational, Fraternal, Agricultural, and Patriotic" subjects. This would be supplemented by musical programs intended to foster "higher moral, spiritual, educational, and patriotic standards." The station, Vance boasted, "is asked for by 100,000 American citizens." Asked how the station would be financially supported, Vance coyly named "fraternal and patriotic services."[38]

At the end of July, the Department of Commerce finally issued a permit for the *Fellowship Forum* to begin construction of its new transmitter and studio. Although the *Forum* was "a recognized organ of the Ku Klux Klan" and "members of the commission regard the new station as having Klan leanings," the FRC also decided to issue a permit that would allow broadcasting to begin on August 15 under the name WTFF. The *Forum*'s new station would retain WTRC's power restrictions and undesirable frequency. The Klan would be broadcasting at 1,470 kilocycles, and with only 50 watts of power, so listeners would have to tune their radios to "the extreme lower end" of the dial where "squeals will probably be heard" unless the rheostats were properly adjusted. Nonetheless, the Klannish movement now had its own radio station—and with it the imprimatur of the federal government.[39]

Vance exulted that the FRC had "granted us everything which we asked for." Despite the station's limited range, the commission's decision made national news. To head off any potential backlash, the newspaper's executives told reporters that the station would "not be Klan controlled" or "dominated by the Klan," despite the fact that "many Klansmen read the *Forum*." Vance similarly contended that the *Forum* was not "primarily a Ku Klux Klan organ." He could not deny that the newspaper and its radio station "could properly be described as 'pro-Klan.'"[40]

Any doubts about where the *Forum*'s allegiances lay would be quickly assuaged by an examination of who had contributed to the construction of the radio station. Of the more than two thousand organizations that had donated to the newspaper's campaign, over 90 percent were local Klans or Klan affiliates, including the Women's Klan, the Junior Klan, and the Krusaders, the association for foreign-born Klansmen. Among the more than twenty-eight thousand individuals who donated, the Klan represented a similar proportion among those who declared an affiliation. Certainly, other fraternal groups sympathetic to the *Forum* had contributed—including the Independent Order of Odd Fellows, the Knights of Malta, and the Woman's Christian Temperance Union. It is also important to remember that by this point the Klan's organizational power had waned significantly on a national level. This did not alter the fact that the new radio station's executives, particularly Vance, knew their greatest strength and support lay with the Invisible Empire.[41]

At the end of August 1927, WTFF began broadcasting experimentally until the *Forum*'s new transmitter was fully operational. "Test programs of sacred and patriotic music" were aired for an hour every Tuesday, Thursday, and Sunday evening. In October, after more than a year of fund-raising and months of bureaucratic wrangling, WTFF, "the Patriotic American Radio Broadcasting Station," formally began broadcasting. The *Forum* claimed that properly tuned radios had managed to receive WTFF as far north as Ontario, as far west as Cleveland, and as far south as Georgia. The Klan movement finally had its own radio station on the air. Even so, this was not enough for Vance. By the end of the month, the station's manager had applied to the FRC to boost WTFF's power from fifty watts to a fantastic fifty thousand, which would make the station one of the three most powerful in the United States.

As the *Washington Post* noted, "The request for so great an increase in power" indicated "the desire of the pro-Klan organization to be heard over a large portion of the United States."[42]

In November, Caldwell wrote to Vance to inform him of the FRC's decision. Although WTFF would remain in the undesirable portion of the spectrum, moving to 1,480 kilocycles, the station's transmitter was approved to start broadcasting at ten thousand watts. Vance used the front page of the *Forum* to declare that WTFF would switch to the new power level as soon as possible, so as to best serve "the militant Protestant American army." The editor also devoted no little space to celebrating the station's triumph over "the bitter opposition of our enemies." The minor opposition that WTFF met, however, was far from bitter. The FRC reported that "few protests had been received" about the power increase. The *Kourier* exulted that "all liberty-loving Americans" were behind the station.[43]

The power increase transformed WTFF from a fairly minor local broadcaster to a national outlet. The station began transmitting at ten thousand watts at the beginning of 1928. WTFF was now the fifth most powerful radio station in the United States. It was by far the most powerful station in the mid-Atlantic region. Letters praising its programming arrived from as far north as Nova Scotia, as far south as Havana, as far west as California, and as far east as England. The Klan movement had become a pioneer in high-powered low-frequency broadcasting. Not only had the FRC found nothing obscene, indecent, or profane in allowing the Ku Klux Klan on air, the movement was now broadcasting coast-to-coast under government imprimatur. Hilmes has argued that early radio's position as a federally regulated entity made it a semipublic institution, responsible for education on a par with schools, churches, and government. The Invisible Empire now had not only the cultural weight of government regulation behind its message, but also the ability to create both local and national publics, potentially reaching millions of American homes.[44]

Representative of the continuities that marked the cultural landscape of the 1920s, the Klan broadcaster was largely unremarkable in its programming. A special New Year's Day lineup to mark the power shift was listed by the *Washington Evening Star* as the best radio programming of the day, offering the usual mix of "musical entertainment, religious sermons, and patriotic addresses." Although clearly Klan-approved, the broadcasts varied little from those of the majority of other broadcasters. Most consisted simply of suitable musical selections and lectures by a variety of individuals, rather than singularly Klannish programming. The newspaper editor estimated that the station spent roughly four hours each week on "entertainment," four hours on religious material, and two hours each on educational, agricultural, and fraternal matters. The only significant variation from a growing norm was that WTFF did not air commercials.[45]

The average station filled its programming with music and variety acts. Dance bands, transmitted live from hotel ballrooms, became a staple of the airwaves. Classical music and "old-time" tunes remained popular. Radio was soon a key arbiter in determining "popular" music. As one longtime Tin Pan Alley writer lamented, "The gal in Kalamazoo don't buy sheet music any more." Increasingly, she didn't buy phonograph records either. Radio was becoming the primary means of musical consumption for many Americans—and the Klan movement was no exception.[46]

According to the schedule published by the *Forum* at the beginning of 1928, WTFF dedicated Sunday evenings to musical numbers "specially suited to a Sunday," climaxing in a gospel sermon. Monday, Wednesday, and Friday evenings saw "varied selections" of music, "serious and humorous readings," and "patriotic addresses." Vance also offered up the station to any members of Congress who wished to take advantage of its services, free of charge. Many accepted, happy to take advantage of the high-power transmitter's ability to reach both their home state and a national audience. A bipartisan parade of politicians passed through the studio, from the progressive Senator William Borah (R-Idaho) to Senator "Cotton Tom" Heflin (D-Alabama) to Congressman Albert Johnson (R-Washington), cosponsor of the 1924 Immigration Act. Broadcasts might range from a local monologist to vaudeville acts to an outline of the current political situation by a sitting senator. The diverse musical offerings gave listeners both "Old Time melodies" and novelty acts cashing in on the craze for Hawaiian music, and much more.[47]

At the same time, WTFF did not shy away from its Klan connections. Every Friday night was set aside as a special "Fraternal Night." The Invisible Empire's local music troupes, particularly the choirs of the Fairfax County, Virginia, Klan and its Women's Klan affiliate, appeared frequently. Klan lecturers and lectures approving of the Klan's activities and ideals were popular mainstays of the station's programming. Imperial Commander Robbie Gill Comer's portrait was hung in the WTFF studio, the first picture to adorn the new facility's walls, to mark the notable contribution of Klanswomen to the Forum's fund-raising campaign. The *Kourier* printed lengthy paeans to WTFF's "great patriotic fraternal program" and "important mission." After the power increase, Klan leaders from around the country, including the head of Indiana's Women's Klan, made pilgrimages to Virginia to appear on the station. A fairly typical evening on WTFF saw talks from Congressman Ewin

Davis (D-Tennessee) on farm relief and from Gail S. Carter, Grand Dragon of Illinois, on public schools.[48]

Yet WTFF would ultimately falter and fail. In large part, that was because even as the station reached the airwaves, it was already outdated. The problem was not the programming, which seemingly successfully appealed to a broad audience. The problem was revenue. As radio audiences had become more sophisticated and discerning in their entertainment choices, many companies quickly learned how to monetize their broadcasting. An AT&T station aired the first "commercial" in 1922. The company introduced sponsored programming in 1923. By 1925, an increasing number of stations used short commercial "spots" to finance their operations. By 1928, the practice of selling a minute of airtime had become common.[49]

This commercialization of the airwaves had made radio broadcasting big business. As such, it had begun to attract heavier investment and greater corporate involvement. Even before WTFF had received its license, independent radio broadcasting was in decline. In 1926, as the *Forum* had struggled to raise the money to build a transmitter and studio, David Sarnoff and his fellow executives at RCA had been building a new, permanently connected radio system using the AT&T telephone network. That year, the new corporate conglomerate of NBC hit the airwaves. In a process hastened by the 1927 radio legislation, the widely varying voices of independent stations began to disappear in the "public interest." In their place came the general-purpose programming of the network, centralized in New York and distributed across the country.[50]

That centralization had also made it far easier to fund broadcasting from the regulated and standardized sale of advertising time. In this, WTFF was a proud outlier. As the *Forum* asserted, the station "owes allegiance to none." It was "not affiliated with any 'chain' system." The broadcaster would remain true to ideals of Americanism. In doing so, it refused to "solicit or broadcast advertising programs." WTFF, the *Forum* declared, would never "advertise or promote the sale of horse-collars, razor blades, or whiskered cough drops."[51]

It was possible to take that kind of stand against advertising as long as the newspaper could afford to support the broadcasting arm as a promotional tool. But the Klan's membership was collapsing, and the *Forum*'s circulation had begun a severe decline. Vance had to do something if his entire operation were not to collapse, and he refused to demean his greater purpose with radio commercials. So, in October 1928, a little more than fourteen months after WTFF's first broadcast, the editor launched a rebranding effort in the hope of making up his revenue shortfall. Vance wrote to the FRC to declare that he would soon "change the policy and improve the quality of all pro-

grams flowing through the microphone of Station WTFF." To mark "separat-
ing the past from the future," he requested that the station's name be changed
to WJSV. This "new" station would carry religious programming only on
Sundays and devote the remainder of its time to the same kind of general-
purpose programming offered by the fledgling networks. Asked whether
WJSV "would continue to run as a pro-Klan station," Vance told reporters
that it would not.[52]

In November 1928, WTFF became WJSV. Klan broadcasts all but disappeared from the air, although their motivating sentiments remained—the
station continued to broadcast vicious attacks on 1928 Democratic presidential candidate Al Smith throughout the transition. The holding company that
owned both the radio station and the *Fellowship Forum*, the Independent
Publishing Company, was soon approached by a "new country-wide network
now being formed," the American Broadcasting Company (ABC), about selling the station. Vance refused.[53]

The station continued to limp along, but could not last for long. By 1932,
with the *Forum* weakened, the Klan all but defunct, and still refusing to carry
advertising, the Independent Publishing Company could no longer absorb
the financial loss of operating WJSV. Instead, it accepted a new offer—from
Jazz Age impresario William S. Paley and CBS. Starting with only sixteen affiliates to NBC's fifty, the new network had grown rapidly since 1928. By 1930,
there were forty-nine affiliates in the CBS family, but the network needed
more. And so it was that in 1932, Paley, that fixture of New York nightlife,
leased the Ku Klux Klan's valuable high-power transmitter to carry the network's programming. In 1935, CBS bought the station outright. The Invisible
Empire's foray into the world of early radio was over.[54]

Though easily forgotten, the formative years of broadcast radio had been
molded by the same world that propelled the Ku Klux Klan to prominence.
Even as Klan members traveled widely to use radio to spread their message
on stations around the country, a blackface minstrel performer from Chicago
named Wendell Hall used similar itinerant appearances to make himself the
first national radio star. While CBS sought to expand its reach, the network's
The Majestic Theater Hour made stars of George Moran and Charlie Mack,
the "Two Black Crows." By 1929, radio audiences could switch back and forth
from the Knights of the Ku Klux Klan to the antics of the Mystic Knights of
the Sea on NBC's new blackface sensation *Amos 'n' Andy*. In a symbol of the
irregular cultural divisions at the heart of the 1920s, the show's theme was
Joseph Carl Breil's "The Perfect Song"—the love theme from *The Birth of a
Nation*. Radio and the Klan did not exist in separate worlds. Rather, they
were often uncomfortably closely entangled. Once again largely divorced

from organizational control, Klannish broadcasters found audiences around the country, an Invisible Empire of the airwaves. While the Klan movement's active participation in the world of radio may have been short-lived, it left a lasting mark. What started as WTFF still operates today in the nation's capital as WTOP, broadcasting traffic and weather on the eights.[55]

9

Invisible Umpires

The Ku Kluxers are going to have their own baseball league next year and we suppose they will use invisible umpires.

WISCONSIN SUPERIOR TELEGRAM, March 1924

Sport—like popular novels, songs, and films—offered another stage on which the nation's postwar cultural psychodramas played out. Perhaps no story gripped Americans in the 1920s more than the battles of Jack Dempsey and Gene Tunney. In 1926, when Tunney beat Dempsey for the world heavyweight boxing title, newspapers dedicated almost as much space to the fight as they had to the armistice that ended World War I.[1] The *New York Times* alone gave over nearly thirteen pages to the fight. Congress adjourned early to allow lawmakers to attend, joining Henry Ford, Al Jolson, and a bevy of other national notables. More than three hundred thousand people listened on a special radio hookup organized by NBC's David Sarnoff. A year later, the Tunney-Dempsey rematch was aired coast-to-coast on eighty-two radio stations, drawing an estimated fifty million listeners—or 45 percent of the U.S. population. When Dempsey knocked down Tunney in the infamous "long count," NBC broadcaster Graham McNamee's breathless coverage reportedly resulted in eleven deaths from heart failure.[2]

As the Dempsey-Tunney mania demonstrated, boxing—and sport in general—had become a popular obsession for a wide cross section of Americans by the mid-1920s. While its wider significance is often overlooked in histories of the period, sport was a central pillar in the creation of the new mass society that bound the nation in a common cultural identity. The spectacle of sporting achievement provided popular melodrama to a rapidly growing mass audience. Members of the Ku Klux Klan were no exception. Yet the clash between the Klan's rhetoric on boxing and the lived ideology of the movement is another telling example of the Invisible Empire's complex and ambivalent relationship with a modern pluralist mass culture.

The growing popularity of boxing was a remarkable reversal from prewar trends. Between the turn of the century and the end of World War I, boxing had been widely viewed as "more a crime wave than a sport." Fixed fights, brutal tactics, and fatalities in the ring all served to discredit boxing in much of the public mind. State after state outlawed the sport as even proponents of the pugilistic arts were forced to acknowledge that the situation had become untenable. At the time of the Dempsey-Tunney fight, it was illegal to even transport films of boxing matches across state lines.[3]

The New York Klan newspaper the *American Standard* attacked boxing as a "brutal and crooked business." It had become a "rotten spot in American life" and "an injurious influence to American children and youths," appealing only to "savage blood-lust and hate." When the Maryland Athletic Club's boxing arena was burned down in 1923, most local residents believed it to be the work of the Klan, which had allegedly threatened to destroy the venue. Similarly, when the Klan of Marion, Ohio, purchased a new meeting place in 1924, its first act was to cancel a prizefight that the property's previous owners had scheduled. As the local Kleagle explained, "Clean athletic contests will be sponsored by the Klan, but no prize fights."[4]

Boxing was theoretically a ripe target for nativists like the Ku Klux Klan, who complained that the sport was "almost entirely in the hands of Jews and Roman Catholics." As an avenue to success with comparatively fewer barriers of religious and racial bigotry, boxing was particularly popular with second-generation Jewish Americans. Through the 1920s, Jewish boxers dominated prizefighting in the United States, closely followed by those of Italian and Irish heritage. The management, promotion, and training of fighters also saw Jewish Americans take "disproportionately prominent roles." These boxers, who often remained closely attached to the same neighborhoods in which they had been raised, were a source of ethnic pride and pushed for the acceptance of the immigrant communities they represented. In particular, Benny Leonard, the lightweight champion of the world from 1917 to 1925, was, according to historian Peter Levine, a "folk hero" to East European Jewish immigrants and their children.[5]

Equally obnoxious to the Klannish sensibility was the notable place of African Americans within the ring. As one historian of interracial boxing has suggested, black boxers "were competing in a sport where their mere involvement scraped white insecurities." Around the turn of the century, the burgeoning talent of African American boxers like Jack Johnson and the appeal of the sport to a predominantly immigrant male urban working-class crowd had allowed for a weakening of the color line. Boxing became one of the few professional sports in which African Americans were allowed to excel prior to the Second World War.[6]

The 1908 victory of Jack Johnson over white Canadian Tommy Burns for the heavyweight title—a fight in which Johnson taunted and humiliated Burns in front of a white audience—and his crushing 1910 defeat of the "Great White Hope" Jim Jeffries upended notions of racial superiority. As a result of these performances and his well-publicized romances with white women, Johnson became "the central sexual and racial scapegoat of the era." His victories irredeemably sullied boxing's reputation among many whites. With such a public preponderance of Jewish and Catholic involvement, and with the racialized specter of Johnson's "unforgivable blackness" (in the words of W. E. B. DuBois) looming over it, it would seem inevitable that the Klan would condemn boxing.[7]

Yet among the nation as a whole—including members of the Invisible Empire—the popularity of pugilism was rapidly increasing in the 1920s. Many Americans had learned to box while serving in the military during World War I and carried a newfound appreciation for boxing back into civilian life. The newly formed American Legion reflected this changing attitude, promoting fights in many areas. The Klan was little different. In Indiana, for example, the *Fiery Cross* boasted of the "leading exponents of the fistic arts" who were plying their trade at nearby Fort Benjamin Harrison. The organizer of these military bouts had "succeeded in lifting the boxing game to a higher plane," and was allegedly reviving considerable interest in the sport.[8]

By 1924, Junior Klans were encouraging amateur boxing matches as a means of manly development. With the Klan headquarters in Georgia leading the way, it was soon a regular occurrence for boys across the United States to lace up their gloves. At the end of regular meetings, a makeshift gym was erected, and members made "the Klavern ring with leather-pusher thuds." The indoor sport was particularly popular among Junior Klansmen with the encroachment of the winter months, when outdoor activities were restricted.[9]

The apex of the Invisible Empire's involvement with boxing came in the Klan stronghold of Colorado. In 1925, the Denver Klan staged its First Annual Ku Klux Klan Boxing and Wrestling Tourney.[10] Over eleven days (with no bouts on Sundays) at the Klan's own Cotton Mills Stadium, 250 fighters competed in eight different weight categories. To broaden appeal, each night's program was preceded by tumbling acts and live music "to add zest," while promotional materials heavily emphasized the respectability of the event with the fact that "women are especially invited."[11]

For the majority of the eleven days, the sports page of the *Denver Post* was dominated by banner headlines promoting the Klan tournament, with full results of every bout and extensive details of the best fights of each night. The *Post*'s enthusiasm for the event reached fever pitch with its claim that a battle between Mike Verant and Jack Dale was "one of the greatest comeback fights ever staged." Although the *Post* always made sure to highlight the Klan's role in organizing the competition, the Invisible Empire's involvement in organizing a major sporting event seems to have drawn little comment and even less criticism. The newspaper focused solely on the boxing itself and not on what the event suggested about the Invisible Empire's place in Colorado life.[12]

This incongruous disconnect was particularly noticeable in the January 25 edition of the *Post*. The front cover was dominated by news of the bloody Klan riot at Herrin, Illinois, that left four dead.[13] The sports page was dominated by the "A1 program" of the Klan's boxing tournament, which was "unmarred by one instance of inferior sport." Whatever was happening in the larger world, it seems, it did not immediately affect the Klan's place in American sporting life.[14]

With the *Post*'s enthusiasm and the Klan's showmanship behind it, the tournament was a notable success, drawing crowds of between three thousand and four thousand most nights. Notable spectators included prominent local boxing enthusiast Clarence Morley, a Klansman and the newly elected governor of Colorado. The event was such a triumph that organizers declared their intentions to hold monthly Klan boxing shows "featuring some of the best mitt slingers in the country," but no evidence can be found that this plan came to fruition. Nor was the Denver Klan ever able to equal its accomplishment. By 1926, a vicious internecine battle within the Colorado Klan had left the organization moribund. The second (and final) annual Klan boxing tournament was overshadowed by the Denver Athletic Committee boxing tournament and received scant attention.[15]

In the meantime, though, boxing had become big business in America—and for the Ku Klux Klan. The "sweet science" had become sufficiently popular that the Klan of Danville, Illinois, was allegedly able to fill a lecture hall to the rafters, with hundreds still left outside, when it invited a boxer to deliver a public lecture. The sportsman met with a "lively and friendly welcome," and the audience expressed their approval of his talk on the "Golden Rule" in an "emphatic manner." In a revealing insight into the fluctuating cultural boundaries of the 1920s, that boxer was the unforgivably black Jack Johnson.[16]

The least well understood of the Invisible Empire's cultural endeavors, the Klan movement's relationship with sport offers perhaps the most significant insight into the complexities of American cultural life in the 1920s. Sports represented a unique expression of both American and Klannish identity. As such, they offered an important tool of legitimization. Rather than proclaiming the Klan's all-American nature, Klan members were able to demonstrate it. Involvement in sports was a notable means of outreach and self-promotion, of constructing and reinforcing the imagined community of the heroic and virtuous Invisible Empire. It was also very much an outgrowth of the genuine enthusiasm of Klan members—everyday American men and women—for boxing, basketball, and, above all, baseball.

In this, the Klan movement was no different from the majority of Americans of the era. Sports had a good claim to being the most popular of the popular arts in the 1920s. Historians have long described the postwar period as "sports crazy." In 1922, the *Literary Digest* proclaimed the decade to be "a new golden age of sport and outdoor amusements." The amount of space that newspapers devoted to sport increased from less than 1 percent in 1880 to nearly 16 percent by 1923. Baseball and boxing became radio staples. The "ballyhoo" that accompanied this "golden age" pushed athletic events to the forefront of the nation's mind. Even the reliably misanthropic H. L. Mencken—who complained, "I . . . hate all sports as rabidly as a person who likes sports hates common sense"—privately harbored a fondness for baseball as "the best game ever invented" and spent his childhood as "a violent fan for the Orioles."[17]

In the process, sports fandom raised athletes to an often-mythic status, creating popular folk heroes whose names still resonate today. Dempsey and Tunney in the ring. Knute Rockne and the Notre Dame football team. Johnny Weissmuller, swinging from Olympic swimmer to movie Tarzan. Bobby Jones dominated the world of golf, even as Bill Tilden became an icon on the tennis court. And all the while, the big bat of George Herman Ruth grew the legend of the "Babe."

If we remove these sporting legends from their contemporary context, though, we lose the complex reality of the cultural 1920s. Even if we look only at the burgeoning world of professional baseball, it is evident that we cannot clearly divide the world of the Klan from the world of modernity. Player/manager Tris Speaker of the Cleveland Indians—who hailed from the same small town in Texas as Imperial Wizard Hiram Evans—was alleged to be a member of the organization. Fellow Hall of Famer Rogers Hornsby of the St. Louis Cardinals was widely understood to be a citizen of the Invisible Empire. Ty Cobb of the Detroit Tigers, one of the best ever all-around baseball players, may or may not have been officially affiliated with the Klan. A virulent racist, he was undoubtedly sympathetic to the wider Klan movement in the 1920s. His fellow Georgian Roy "Dizzy" Carlyle is probably best remembered now for purportedly hitting the longest measured home run ever. He was certainly a member of the Ku Klux Klan, even as he played for the Washington Senators, the Boston Red Sox, and the New York Yankees—alongside Lou Gehrig and Babe Ruth.[18]

This reality was not restricted to professional sports. Growing interest in athletic competition spurred greater participation at all levels of society as organizations across the United States formed sports teams and sponsored events. The Ku Klux Klan was no exception to this trend. Klan teams sprang up all over the country, playing baseball, basketball, and other sports. And in doing so, the movement thrived within the mainstream of American sporting life. Even as they espoused the rhetoric of cultural war, members of the Invisible Empire competed peaceably with other Klan teams, other Protestant fraternal organizations, Jewish teams, Catholic teams, and even African American teams.

Sport in the 1920s itself presents a telling paradox. Segregation in sport often served as a reminder and symbol of enduring racial division. Yet as a mass institution of modern national identity, sport was a pillar of the American civil religion and a key tool of immigrant assimilation. Sport, in the words of historian Peter Levine, was a "middle ground," a "significant cultural institution" that "encouraged . . . enthusiasm for full integration into American life." Levine was referring specifically to the Jewish immigrant experience, but his observations apply to a broad range of "fringe" groups, from Mormons to the House of David. Anyone who "played the game" theoretically had the opportunity to assert their place in American society. Sport allowed the men and women of the Invisible Empire to come together to reinforce the virtuous imagined identity of the Klannish community. They could prove both to themselves and to the world at large that the Klan movement was to be celebrated, not feared.[19]

It is revealing both of the fractured nature of the Klan organization and of the extent to which Klannishness was already embedded in the American mainstream (and vice versa) that this was seemingly a largely unconscious process. The Invisible Empire's forays into the world of athletics were sporadic and haphazard. Sports results were never prominently featured in Klan publications. Klan athletic teams were never organized within any kind of uniform structure or subjected to some kind of national regulation. Sport was rarely a focus of the organization's official activities. Some events (or simply plans for events) were obviously intended to draw as much attention as possible. On the whole, though, such games tended to be the exception. Newspapers, Klannish or otherwise, rarely highlighted the Invisible Empire's sporting endeavors. On the occasions Klan games did attract notice, the commentary elicited tended to be heavily weighted toward the mechanics of the sport rather than toward any deeper ideological context.

This haphazard engagement meant that sport was often not a shining beacon of achievement for the Ku Klux Klan. Even as attendance at college football games doubled, the closest the Invisible Empire came to Knute Rockne was causing a riot with the Catholic students of Notre Dame. In 1925, the first race at the Klan's own auto-racing stadium in Denver was won by Ralph De Palma—a world speed record holder, a winner of the Indianapolis 500, an Italian immigrant, and, as the *Colorado Springs Gazette* gleefully reported, a Catholic. There is no record of the Klan reaction to De Palma's win of the four-thousand-dollar prize, but, as the *Gazette* described it, "smiles are the order around sporting circles of Denver."[20]

The world of basketball was a little more welcoming to the Invisible Empire. Although most professional basketball teams in the 1920s hailed from New York, New Jersey, and Pennsylvania (where, like boxing, the sport was dominated by second-generation Jewish Americans), it was in the Midwest that passion for the amateur game reached its peak. As Phillip M. Hoose has written, basketball was an "epidemic" in Indiana, played in every available space. Fittingly, the Klan's basketball teams seem to have been most successful in Indiana, Ohio, and Michigan, although viable Klan teams could also be found in Illinois, Iowa, Pennsylvania, and California.[21]

Local observers were initially skeptical of the Klan's involvement with the game. The most pressing question for the *Kokomo Daily Tribune* was, "How're they gonna shoot baskets with their masks on?" Nonetheless, Indiana, Ohio, and Michigan were all home before long to a sufficient number of Junior Klan basketball teams that by 1924 they were each able to organize large statewide tournaments. Their respective champions then battled for top interstate honors. The winning team stood to receive a special Ku Klux Klan trophy, and gold medals would be awarded for sportsmanship and for the most valuable player.[22]

Klan members and sympathizers from all over the Midwest gathered to watch and play basketball. Local newspapers offered a subdued response. The *Logansport Pharos-Tribune* best encapsulated the seeming apathy, reporting simply that "another basketball tournament has been announced to the already long list of tourneys held in Indiana." The Klan may have been involved, but the prospect of another round of basketball games apparently offered little novelty or surprise. The tournament would be reported on much as all the others were—local newspapers cheering their respective hometown teams and lamenting their defeats—with little or no editorial comment on the fact that it was the Klan that was competing.[23]

On the afternoon of April 5, Kokomo beat Elwood to become state champions. A few hours later, the interstate championship was settled as Kokomo was thoroughly beaten by New Philadelphia, the Ohio state Klan champions. Indiana newspapers lamented the loss, but the Junior Klan had found acceptance into Indianan sporting life. The change was most noticeable in the initially dismissive *Kokomo Daily Tribune*. By the end of 1924, the newspaper was taking the *Indianapolis Star* to task for having ignored the Kokomo Junior Klan's victory at the basketball tournament in its annual roundup of Indiana's 1924 state champions. Hometown pride seemingly trumped any qualms the newspaper may have had about the Invisible Empire.[24]

By 1926, no team reflected the widespread popularity and acceptance of Junior Klan basketball more than the Xenia Klan of Ohio, composed of "a number of well known players," including "several ex-high school luminaries." Competing against teams from seven other cities, the Xenia Junior Klan won that year's state championship. The local newspaper, the *Xenia Evening Gazette*, excitedly reported the Klan's victories, praising the team's "fine floor games." Despite this powerful performance, the Xenia's team dominance did not extend into the 1927 season (the last year that the championships were held), when the Lima Junior Klan's players took top honors.[25]

Unlike some teams, the Xenia Junior Klan did not confine itself to competing only with other Klans. Little attention seems to have been paid to its organizational affiliation as both the local newspaper and other teams treated the Junior Kluxers as just another youth basketball team (albeit a successful one with a strong record) in a town filled with them. When a new independent basketball team, the Xenia Celtics, was formed in February 1926, their first order of business was to challenge the best teams in the city—including the Xenia Eagles, the National Guard team, and the Junior Klansmen. An even greater indication of the Junior Klan's integration into the city's sporting life came in March of that same year. When another local team, the Xenia Buckeye Big "5," were unable to secure the court at the local high school to play a game, the event was shifted to the local Klan "tabernacle" to play on the Xenia Junior Klan's floor. The fact that the Buckeye Big "5" was an all African American team seems to have evinced little mention.[26]

The incorporation of these Junior Klan teams into the Midwestern basketball community is a significant indicator of the extent to which the Klan movement was invested in American cultural life in the 1920s. Like other Midwesterners, the Junior Klansmen were swept up in the phenomenon that basketball represented in that section of the country. As Robert and Helen Lynd noted in their study of the Midwestern Middletown, "more civic loyalty centers around basket-ball than around any other one thing."

The cheering crowds were not divided by their beliefs. "North Side and South Side, Catholic and Kluxer, banker and machinist," all came together to support the local team.[27]

That enthusiasm was even greater when it came to baseball. Sports historian Steven Riess has argued that baseball in the 1920s was "probably more successful in helping socialize and integrate Americans than ever before." A Utah team, the Salt Lake City Mormons, helped the church "prove its American character" without surrendering its community identity. The Christian Israelites of the House of David fielded one of the most popular and successful barnstorming baseball teams of the decade, an "evangelistic tool" that promoted the group's "religious acceptability."[28] Ku Klux Klan members were, to a significant extent, just another group of "athletic assimilationists."[29]

But not everyone took the idea of the Klan playing baseball entirely seriously. Dr. Harry Emerson Fosdick, minister of New York's First Presbyterian Church, declared that "the millennium will come when the Ku Klux Klan and the Knights of Columbus play a baseball game with a negro umpire for the benefit of the Jewish employees of Henry Ford at Zion City." Walter Dill Scott, president of Northwestern University, was more optimistic, telling "a story of a friend who said he would not be surprised if some day the Knights of Columbus would play a match ball game with the Ku Klux Klan, with a colored umpire, and the gate receipts going to Jewish charities." A correspondent in the African American *Chicago Defender* joked about the game being for the benefit of the Young Men's Hebrew Association. The socialist African American magazine *The Messenger* declared that such a game, with the proceeds going to a Jewish orphan asylum, would be the very definition of "good old-fashioned Americanism." The joke was repeated so often, with slight variations, that as early as 1923 the Klan's *Imperial Night-Hawk* referred to it as an "old chestnut," while fake tickets for these imaginary games were sold as novelty items (see fig. 9.1).[30]

What those who jested about such matters did not realize was that members of the Invisible Empire were busily engaged in attempting to organize exactly those kinds of games. In July 1924, perhaps inspired by the "old chestnut," Colonel Evan Watkins, Klan pastor and lecturer of Youngstown, Ohio, challenged the Knights of Columbus to a baseball game during an upcoming Klan picnic. As far as the Klan organization was concerned, the Knights of Columbus were a fundamentally subversive force, out to bring the United States under papal domination. The Columbians saw the Klan as little more than organized thuggery designed to crush Catholicism in America. Yet, as Watkins explained in the invitation, a "colored referee" and "2 Jewish friends on the gate" would be features of the matchup so that the game "ought to take

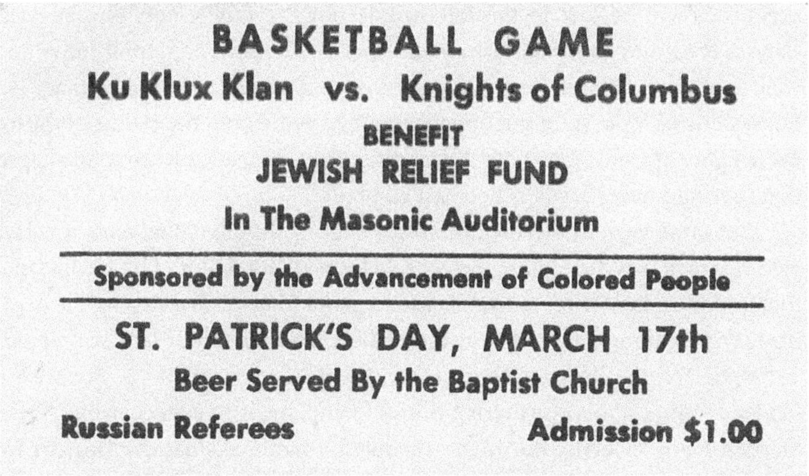

BASKETBALL GAME
Ku Klux Klan vs. Knights of Columbus
BENEFIT
JEWISH RELIEF FUND
In The Masonic Auditorium

Sponsored by the Advancement of Colored People

ST. PATRICK'S DAY, MARCH 17th
Beer Served By the Baptist Church

Russian Referees   Admission $1.00

FIGURE 9.1. Popular joke item: a ticket for an unlikely event, ca. 1924.

out of the day all the usual sting of bigotry which the enemies of the Klan usually attribute to it."[31]

These were not simply abstract references to the oft-repeated imaginary game. The umpire was identified as Claude Johnson, a "well known negro athlete."[32] The takings from the game, which would be donated to charity, were to be handled by Max Brunswick, a "Jewish lawyer." An Associated Press report on the invitation was picked up by newspapers across the country. The *Chicago Defender* headlined its article, "Scorekeeper Should Add Casualties to Box Score Columns." No casualty report was ever needed though, as the Knights of Columbus declined the invitation.[33]

A similar situation arose a year later in Orange, Texas. Local newspapers reported that the Orange chapters of the Ku Klux Klan and the Knights of Columbus would play a charity baseball game to benefit the town's school, said to be in dire financial straits. One report claimed that Imperial Wizard Hiram Evans and two Catholic cardinals would sign the balls for the game. Another suggested that music at the event would be provided by the Orange Negro Band and that ticket sales would be handled by members of the local Jewish community. Reactions to the announcement ranged from bemused to approving. One newspaper compared the game to the biblical prophecy of Isaiah "that the wolf shall dwell with the lamb," and unimaginatively joked that the umpire would be a rabbi and an African American would serve as batboy. At the other end of the spectrum, the *Hutchinson News* declared that the game represented the "real cooperation" of "opposing factions" uniting "for the good of all." Similarly, the *Mexia Daily News* declared that "religious prejudices will be cast to the four winds" for the public benefit. *The Mes-senger*'s dream of good old-fashioned Americanism was apparently alive and well. Despite these high hopes, the game once again failed to materialize. The flurry of news reports on the "much-heralded game" and the claims of the lo-cal Knights of Columbus notwithstanding, the Orange Ku Klux Klan alleged that they had never actually been asked to play.[34]

That same year, in Sterling, Illinois, a slightly different challenge was lev-eled. There, it was the Sterling Browns, "a local all-star colored baseball team," that issued an invitation to the Klan for a game to be played during the orga-nization's outdoor celebration at the end of July 1925. The Klansmen appar-ently rejected the Browns' offer of "a real battle" in favor of playing a team fielded by the Illinois Northern Utilities Company. Instead, according to the Sterling *Daily Gazette*, the Klan scheduled a game against the Browns for Labor Day weekend.[35]

It is unclear whether that game ever came to pass, but an analogous matchup—one of the few Klan sporting events to receive any real historical analysis—was held in Wichita, Kansas. In June 1925, the Wichita Monrovians, "Wichita's crack colored team," played local Klan No. 6. The Monrovians were a particularly successful African American semipro team. Popular and profit-able enough to own their own ballpark, they had just returned from a barn-storming tour of the state. The Klan, conversely, had recently been ruled to be operating illegally in Kansas by the state supreme court, a serious blow to the organization. Nonetheless, the two teams (it is unclear which approached the other) came to an agreement to meet on the baseball diamond.[36]

To "get away from all possible favoritism," two well-known local amateur umpires were selected to score the game—"Irish" Garrety and Dan Dwyer, both Irish Catholics. Fearing the combination of elements could result in trouble, the local newspaper warned that "strangle holds, razors, horsewhips, and other violent implements of argument will be barred." Whether because of or despite the threat of violence due to "the wide difference of the two organizations," the local newspaper predicted that "the novelty of the game will attract a large crowd of fans." Both teams promised that "all the fans will see is baseball," and the game did indeed go off without a hitch. The Monro-vians defeated the Klan ten to eight in a "close and interesting baseball battle." And that was an end to it. Although it was described as the "best attended and most interesting game" held that day, the matchup was not apparently so much more fascinating than any of the other baseball games as to warrant anything other than a two-sentence report on the mechanics of the game. If Fosdick was right, the millennium had come. Yet the game seemed to stir little interest—both at the time and among historians ever since.[37]

Those few who have remarked upon these games have viewed them largely as novelties, usually publicity-seeking stunts in an effort to boost membership. Brian Carroll argues that the fixture was "a Klan ploy to curry favor with the public at large and the black community especially." Jason Pendleton dismisses it as "anomalous." William Jenkins situates Reverend Watkins's invitation in the context of a crumbling Ohio Klan, riven with infighting and driven to desperate lengths to rebuild its popularity.[38]

This interpretation does have its merits. It does seem as if a number of these unorthodox baseball games were the actions of Klaverns whose power had faded. They were apparently relatively few and far between, and a reasonable case could be made that the proposals for the games were done for publicity purposes. Klans that had passed their apex were grasping at straws in an attempt to put themselves back into the public eye and regain the influence they once had. But this explanation fails to answer convincingly how the Klan hoped to use the game as a recruiting tool. Staging the event to disassociate the organization from the "sting of bigotry" might "curry favor" with the local black community, or provide a patina of respectability. But in almost every other medium, from newspapers to radio, declining Klans made efforts to energize the core movement to boost membership rather than engage in the earlier politicking of the national leadership. By engaging—and potentially losing to—an African American team in a sport that was still largely segregated nationwide, the Wichita Klan organization would surely have run the risk of alienating their base, and actually losing members. Either way, the game certainly did nothing for the Klavern's long-term prospects. If the event was a recruiting tool, it was not a particularly effective one.[39]

Moreover, the dismissal of these games as anomalies or publicity stunts is reflective of a larger issue in how we have understood the Klan and the 1920s more generally. Concentrating on narratives of organizational affiliation means that we lose the wider implications of these games for the construction and reinforcement of Klannish community and identity. These games were far from an anomaly, and are revealing of the Klan movement's relationship with American culture. On the baseball diamond, the cultural scripts of Klan propaganda took life. Nowhere was this more obvious than in the noteworthy success of Klan amateur sandlot baseball teams.

As attendance at professional baseball games stayed above ten million throughout the decade, more and more Americans were no longer content to simply watch. They began to play as well. Most major cities supported at least two or three different sandlot leagues, largely divided up between well-meaning but lackluster amateurs and more polished semiprofessional teams. Atlanta, for instance, had five amateur baseball leagues in the 1924 season, each featuring at least six teams. Companies, churches, or charities—organizations of every kind put together nines to take to the field in cities and towns across the country.[40]

The first Klan sandlot team seems to have been formed in the organization's stronghold of Indiana. In March 1923, the *Fiery Cross* announced the creation of the Indiana Travelers Ball Team, composed of "ex-league players," and boasted that it would be "one of the strongest semi-professional teams in the central states." A month later, another Klan newspaper noted that "a dozen or more" Klans in Indiana had established teams, with challenges between them "flying thick and fast even this early in the season." Despite the press excitement, none of these teams seem to have made much impact.[41]

The next Klan team appeared a year later in Imperial Wizard Hiram Evans's home state of Texas. It was also something of a failure. The team from Fort Worth caused an initial flurry of national publicity when it was established. Much of this interest stemmed from the fact that it had been admitted to the Fort Worth Amateur Association league, which also included a team fielded by the Knights of Columbus. As newspapers across the country excitedly reported, the regular schedule for the season would call for several games between the two teams. Even more color was added to the story with the report that the Klan's field was bounded by a Jewish cemetery and a Catholic hospital.

Team manager Steve Ellis told the United Press that the Klan team would be no different from any other in the league. The uniforms would feature a fiery cross on a white background, and the team's caps would be marked with the letter *K*, but "the only player to wear a mask on the field will be the catcher," Ellis announced. A month after the team formed, a campaign event by Felix D. Robertson, the Klansman attempting to win the Democratic nomination in the Texas gubernatorial campaign, featured a game between the Klan players and the local American Bodies team. Trying to boost attendance, the campaign billed it as "one of the biggest ball games of the season" and "a battle that will be worth seeing" between two well-matched teams. Outside of those advertisements, though, the Klan team received little publicity and, despite Ellis's best efforts, left little impression.[42]

A Klan team formed that same year in Atlanta met with considerably more success. The fact of the Invisible Empire's involvement drew little attention. It was just one of the forty-six sandlot teams playing each weekend. The Knights of Columbus had already been playing in the Spalding League, the most prestigious of the city's five amateur leagues, for years. The Klan players found themselves in the Dixie League, otherwise known as the City League, competing against teams fielded by the Peachtree Road Presbyterian

Church (which neighbored the Klan's Imperial Palace), the First Methodist Episcopal Church of Atlanta, the Western Electric Company, King Hardware, the Tech Rehabs, Georgia West Point, and the Georgia Railroad and Power Company.[43]

The Atlanta team bore the imprimatur of the Klan organization and the Imperial Wizard. Its manager was T. J. McKinnon, one of Hiram Evans's top lieutenants, known to be "head of the secret service department," as well as manager of the organization's lucrative printing and regalia business.[44] Perhaps more importantly, the Klan players were actually good. By early July, the *Atlanta Constitution* described a victory for the Klansmen over the Tech Rehabs as "one of the closest and best games so far this year." At the end of the month, a rematch between the two teams was eagerly anticipated, and did not disappoint, with "brilliant fielding" displayed by both sides.[45]

Both games between the Klan and the Tech Rehabs received more attention than one of the Invisible Empire's nonleague games in late June. Since it had no bearing on the pennant race in their respective leagues, little note was paid at the time to the June 30 game between the Ku Klux Klan and the Knights of Columbus. A confrontation between the two organizations might well have been expected to end in bloodshed. Yet the two sides met with equanimity. Drawing a "good crowd," the game was described as "clean and fast." The Knights of Columbus, generally regarded as the superior team, found themselves outmatched on this occasion by "the heavy hitting of the battery of the K.K.K." No violence was recorded, on or off the field. The Klan and the Knights of Columbus may have feared, distrusted, and hated each other, but they were apparently capable of meeting peacefully. For all the jokes made about the improbability of such an engagement, the cultural complexities of the period were made manifest on the ball field.[46]

Revealing as this meeting was, contemporary commentators in both the Klan and non-Klan press were far more interested in the fact that the Klan team won the Dixie League that year. In celebration, McKinnon threw a lavish "barbecue and entertainment" at his home, where all the players were presented with individually engraved miniature baseballs made of gold. Klan player Eldon Carlyle's brother, "Dizzy" Carlyle, praised the team as "one of the best amateur teams in the south." An *Atlanta Constitution* report on the event (reprinted wholesale by the *Searchlight*) explained that everyone present "came away with most pleasant memories of the occasion."[47]

Overlooking the apparent incongruity of the game against the Knights of Columbus, it could be argued that the success and acceptance of a Klan baseball team were to be expected in Atlanta, birthplace of the second Klan. It is difficult to make the same case about the Klan baseball team that came to prominence later the same year—in Los Angeles, California. The L.A. Klan baseball team made its initial appearance in August 1924. The *Los Angeles Times* seemed unsurprised by the Invisible Empire's incorporation into the city's sporting life, noting only that a large crowd was expected at their first game. Despite an inauspicious start to the season, the *Los Angeles Times* soon remarked that the Klan was playing "good consistent baseball." Less than two months later, Los Angeles Klan No. 3 had also organized a team.[48]

Much as in Atlanta, the Klan teams were received like any of the sixty or so other amateur and semipro teams that played around Los Angeles every weekend. Only particularly interesting games warranted more than a short report and a full box score in local newspapers. Klan No. 1 and No. 3 were treated no differently—including having their names printed for all the city to see. The L.A. Klan's record was relatively pedestrian, and, for the most part, the Klan's games did not draw any special attention. The Invisible Empire was not so invisible when it reached the sports pages, but it was also seemingly not that remarkable.[49]

There was a singular exception to this. In October 1924, Los Angeles Klan No. 1 played a three-game charity series. Their opponents were the local chapter of the Independent Order of B'nai B'rith, the oldest Jewish service organization in the world. Although Jews were not, for the most part, vilified by Klannish rhetoric to the same degree as Catholics (and particularly the Knights of Columbus), anti-Semitism remained a significant part of the Klannish worldview. As far as most Klan publications were concerned, Jews were fundamentally un-American, as well as materialistic, economically rapacious, and (depending on which Klansman you asked) willing allies or dupes of the international Catholic conspiracy. American Jews, for their part, did not hold Klan members in much higher regard.[50]

Despite these wildly differing worldviews, the two teams managed to arrange to peaceably face each other on the ball field. Nor was it just any sandlot diamond. The games were played at Vernon Ball Park, home to the Double-A Vernon Tigers team and able to seat a capacity crowd of ten thousand. Adding to the unique quality of the games was the fact that the B'nai B'rith had somehow been convinced to play the Klan to benefit the city's Crippled Children's Christmas Fund. Reality was beginning to far outpace the joke.[51]

Newspaper coverage of the series completely ignored any clash of creeds. Instead, the *Los Angeles Times* exulted that the matchup was a "corker" with both teams "playing fast ball." Adding to the excitement, the Klan and the B'nai B'rith had won a game apiece by the time of their final meeting on October 19. Those two games had been "hotly contested," with victories only coming after the games had gone into extra innings. The matchup was expected to draw a large crowd—not for any novelty value, but because the clash of well-matched teams "should be hotter than ever." It was simply a matter of baseball.[52]

In May 1926, Creth Bailey Hines, a junior member of National Capital Klan No. 2 and a student at the Georgetown School of Foreign Service, organized a sandlot team in Washington D.C.—"believed to be the first in the East."[53] Hines was a sporting-minded young man. Inducted into the Georgetown Athletic Hall of Fame in 1927 for his remarkable skill with the javelin, he went on to represent the United States at the 1928 Olympics in Amsterdam alongside Johnny Weissmuller. The Klan team, Hines boasted, was "capable of taking on the best."[54]

Local newspapers were again initially skeptical. The *Washington Evening Star* made references to the need to "doff their white robes in favor of baseball uniforms." As in Atlanta and Los Angeles, however, press coverage of the Klan players quickly came to resemble that of any other local sandlot team. Home to the organization's national offices and to a sizable but largely nonviolent local Klan, the District of Columbia was neither a Klan stronghold nor a center of opposition. Few there seemed to mind the Klan's place in the sandlot leagues. The *Star* went so far as to call 1926 "the most successful sandlot baseball season in Washington's history." By the beginning of the 1927 season, the Klan was considered to have "one of the strongest teams in the district." Newspapers reported on the Klan nine's "winning rampage" and "triumphant march." Garnering twenty-five wins in thirty starts, the Invisible Empire was a viable challenger for the District of Columbia's 1927 independent unlimited baseball title. The Klan nine had "trounced some of the best teams in and around Washington, creating quite a few upsets in their lists."[55]

It would be naive to think that there was no element of publicity seeking to the Klan baseball team. Novelty games had long been used by evangelists and others for promotional purposes. Billy Sunday, as an ex-player himself, was particularly keen on the technique. In 1917, he had organized a team to compete with Hollywood celebrities, including Douglas Fairbanks, in a game umpired by Mary Pickford and Charlie Chaplin. And for the Capital Klan, baseball was the linchpin of one of their most successful public events—an annual charity benefit game against the D.C. chapter of the nativist Junior Order of United American Mechanics.[56]

In 1926 and 1927 (the annual tradition was not a long-lived one), the two teams met on the field at Clark Griffith American League Stadium, then home to the Washington Senators. Takings from the gate went to the Mechanics' orphanage in Tiffin, Ohio, and to the Klan Haven orphanage in Harrisburg, Pennsylvania. In 1926, the game drew a crowd over six thousand strong to

see the Klan team defeat their opponents. In comparison, two months earlier the stadium had played host to the much-anticipated first congressional baseball game in over ten years, which attracted a crowd of roughly four
thousand—and that had included the draw of the Republican team riding on
a live elephant. The 1927 Klan game drew only a little over three thousand
spectators—still a respectable crowd, but an obvious indication of the Invisible Empire's waning popularity. What is notable, however, is not how much
publicity these games garnered for the ailing Klan, but how little publicity the
rest of their games received, and how little the Klan courted it.[57]

In September 1927, the baseball team of National Capital Klan No. 2 faced
the Hebrew All-Stars. The game against the all-Jewish team—including Abe
Povich, brother of sportswriter Shirley Povich—had been organized by local doctor and Jewish sandlot baseball star Carl "Ikey" Dreyfus.[58] The Klan,
after scoring all its runs in the first inning, held the All-Stars at bay until the
seventh inning, when heavy rain meant the game had to be called. The Invisible Empire beat the Hebrew All-Stars four runs to none, and the closest either side came to violence was three beanballs, all likely unintentional. Local
newspapers barely found the game worthy of note. The *Washington Evening
Star* gave the game less than an inch of column space.[59]

This was not the only "anomalous" game for the D.C. Klan. The Klan
nine played against at least three different Catholic teams on multiple occasions. Less than a month after Creth Hines formed the team, the Klan played
"Wee-Willie" Glascoe's Shamrocks, all Irish Catholics, losing badly. Later in
the season, the Klan not only played the St Joseph's Catholic Church team, it
also joined them to successfully petition for amalgamating leagues from the
District of Columbia, Maryland, and Virginia. The next time that the Klan
met the Shamrocks, toward the end of the 1926 season, the Klan bested them
by a single run, thirteen to twelve, in what newspapers described as "a big
game" for "two hard hitting teams." The game was not "big" for any religious
or political reasons, but rather because "both teams are still hopeful of grab-
bing the unlimited crown." When the Klan played St. Mary's Celtics in June
1927, the game was met with no more or less interest by the newspapers than
any other pairing. It was "a spirited game" in front of "a large crowd," characterized by "a brilliant pitchers battle" that the Celtics won, two to none. The
Post even described, without any apparent irony, how a "snappy double play"
by the Celtics put an end to "a threatening Klan rally."[60]

A fuller consideration of the Klan movement's engagement with baseball, then, undermines an understanding of these kinds of sporting events
as anomalies. It is also difficult to make a case for them as publicity stunts.

Time and again, these athletic competitions proved to have little actual publicity value for the Klan organization itself. Although it is impossible to know
for sure, none of these ventures seem to have been particularly successful
in recruiting new members to the Ku Klux Klan or even in preventing current Klansmen from leaving. The Monrovians game did not prevent the ongoing collapse of the Kansas Klan. The L.A. baseball teams did nothing to
hurt the organization's image, but their ability to draw new members was
seemingly negligible. The rapid decline of the D.C. Klan was not stemmed
by their games against the Shamrocks or the Hebrews. Engaging Jews and
Catholics (especially the Knights of Columbus) on the sports field not only
risked embarrassing defeat, but also undermined Klan rhetoric of inherent
and unbridgeable differences. Far from increasing the Klan's numbers and
strengthening their ideals, these games were more likely to alienate those who
believed that Catholics and Jews represented a clear and present racial, religious, and political danger.

If we move away from the narrative of organizational affiliation and disaffiliation, the participation of Klan members in public sporting events becomes
more understandable and makes for a revealing insight into the movement's
place in American cultural life in the 1920s. Not least, the Klan's ongoing
commitments in tournaments and leagues belie the importance that many
contemporaries—and many historians—placed on an organizational *need* for
secrecy. Members of Klan teams in cities and towns across the country had
their full names published on a regular basis in the sports pages of major
newspapers, in souvenir programs, and on scorecards. The open nature of
these events meant that members of the public could see as many unmasked
members of the so-called Invisible Empire as they wished. The managers of
the L.A. and D.C. baseball teams, like the managers of most other sandlot
teams, regularly put notices asking for games in the newspaper—notices that
gave not only their name, but often their address and telephone number. The
Washington Evening Star might have scoffed at the idea that Klansmen would
doff their hoods for baseball uniforms, but that is exactly what they did, as
team photographs published in that same newspaper showed. Klan sportsmen were some of the most visible members of the Invisible Empire.[61]

The motivating idea behind a thousand contemporary editorials and the
passage of a number of local antimasking laws was that when the hoods were
removed and members exposed to the light of day, the Klan would shrivel
and collapse. Fearful of mainstream disapproval, members would shed the
fringe organization for societal respectability. The "mediocre men," "cowards,"
and "weaklings" who made up the Klan (per John Moffat Mecklin) would

abandon the "glaring historic anachronism" without the shield of anonymity. Their identity known, they would bow to the judgment of the "high-minded and independent members of the community."[62]

None of these assumptions seemingly held true for the members of Klan sports teams. Rather, their ability to operate freely in the world of amateur sports underlines the fact that there were no clear delineations between a cultural "mainstream" and a Klannish "fringe." Despite their overt institutional affiliation, players for Klan teams found little hindrance to playing for a variety of other organizations as well. Members of the Xenia basketball team and the Atlanta baseball team saw successful collegiate sporting careers. Steve Ellis of the Fort Worth Klan became player/manager for the Texon Oilers, leading the successful semipro team to victory in the 1928 sixteen-state *Denver Morning Post* championship. Bill Howser, pitcher for the D.C. Klan, went on to play for the Chambersburg Maroons in Pennsylvania. When the Maroons won their league, the *Washington Post* ran a picture of Howser with his teammates, openly identifying him as an ex-Klan player in a story celebrating the success of a local native. Creth Bailey Hines, founder of the D.C. team, went on to a minor league career in Florida. The decision to not only affiliate but openly identify with and play for the Invisible Empire seemingly carried little consequence for any of these men.[63]

From the Denver Klan's boxing tournament to the Junior Klan basketball team of Xenia to the Los Angeles sandlot baseball teams, sport offered another avenue for the construction of a unified identity. These sporting events helped project the heroic, inclusive vision of the pro-Protestant, pro-white, pro-American Klan that underpinned the imagined community of the national Klannish movement. But to dismiss these forays into the world of sport as merely a propagandistic concern—a conscious effort to attract members—is to ignore the importance of differentiating between the organizational rhetoric and the lived ideology of the wider movement. The average Klan member needed no Imperial officer to tell them to enjoy baseball, or to be caught up in their community's fervor for basketball. While issues of legitimization, of assimilation, of Americanization, and of publicity may all have percolated through the conscious and subconscious minds of Klan members, the Invisible Empire's engagement with the world of sport was ultimately a reminder that Klansfolk were not strange, otherworldly creatures. Tentative as their embrace of the new mass culture of the 1920s was, Klan members shared the same ordinary interests as other Americans. In doing so, they became part and parcel of the emerging pluralist mass culture of the United States.

Epilogue

The Most Picturesque Element

I am aware that the net effect of it might be to argue that Klansmen and Klanswomen are ordinary, two-footed human beings, without either tails or horns. But I am afraid that after all this is just what they are.

CHARLES MERZ, *The Independent*, February 12, 1927

Klannish culture left behind no great works, no aesthetic marvels—no reason to be memorialized. And not only were such cultural products not remembered, they were often actively and aggressively forgotten. By the end of 1928, the Ku Klux Klan organization was all but defunct as a national power, and the movement had begun its precipitous slide from public consciousness. Out of public sight, and increasingly out of mind, the "spice" of the fictional Klan held less appeal as the Invisible Empire lost its cultural relevance and commercial cachet. The multifarious depictions of the second Klan that reflected the spectrum of America's cultural response to the organization in the 1920s largely disappeared. Klannish protestations of the organization's virtue fell out of favor. Public interest faded. Like the organization itself, the efforts to capture or capitalize on the Klan would soon be consigned to obscurity, relics of a misbegotten decade. Our cultural memory is short—especially when it comes to things we would rather forget.

With no literary titans like Hemingway, Fitzgerald, or Faulkner to memorialize it, the once thriving subgenre of Klannish fiction was quickly forgotten. By 1965, the hit song *Daddy Swiped Our Last Clean Sheet* had become an out-of-context historical curio, an oddity for newspapers to reflect on and find "rather amusing." In 1957, members of the third iteration of the Klan formed a softball team in Chattanooga, Tennessee. The *New York Times* declared that "in the long history of the Klan's nocturnal activities," this was "the first instance in which the terroristic organization sought to 'advertise' openly its cause to the public through the widely popular method of fielding a ball team in a friendly contest with umpires and the accepted rules of the game." In 1947, when the *Port Arthur News* ran a profile of theatrical producer

Jimmy Hull, the Ku Klux Klan's involvement in Hull's success had been ex-
pediently forgotten. In his decades as a producer of amateur shows and one
of the "leading tent-show impresarios," the *News* noted, *The Awakening* had
been Hull's largest and most popular production. Rather than mention the
show's Klannish subject matter, or the involvement of Klan members in staging, performing, and attending the show, the newspaper noted only that it
had been shown under the auspices of undefined "men's and women's service
clubs" across the country. Such convenient historical amnesia is typical. The
ghosts of the Invisible Empire were seemingly quickly exorcised.[1]

It is indicative of our selective memory when it comes to the Ku Klux Klan
that there is one cultural manifestation of the organization that has managed
to retain a hold on both the popular and the scholarly imagination. For three
weeks, beginning June 10, 1946, radio listeners heard the story of a multieth-
nic youth baseball team and its star pitcher, Chinese American Tommy Lee.
Unfortunately, youthful jealousy of Lee had blossomed into prejudice, and
the team had attracted the attention of an organization of professional bigots.
Fortunately, the team was managed by Jimmy Olsen, Superman's best friend.
And for sixteen episodes, listeners thrilled to the superhero's struggle with the
thinly disguised Klansmen of the "Clan of the Fiery Cross."

In just the past fifteen years, the story of Superman and the Klan has appeared in a young adult nonfiction book, in the best-selling *Freakonomics*,
as a story on the public radio show *This American Life*, and in the Comedy
Central show *Drunk History*. It is not difficult to understand why the radio
serial has been far better remembered than the ambiguity and ambivalence
displayed in the 1920s. For one thing, the serial itself offered a familiarly reassuring condemnation of the organization. Here, unlike in the 1920s, Silas
Bent's claim that the press offered unqualified opposition to the Klan rang
true—*Daily Planet* editor Perry White excoriates them as "lunatics in night-
shirts" and "hate-mongering ghouls." The "Grand Imperial Mogul" of the
Clan openly admitted that it was simply a means of fleecing the weak and
gullible. Superman himself, embodiment of truth, justice, and the American
way, told listeners that the "intolerant bigots" of the Klan were simply un-
American: "They don't judge a man in the decent American way by his own
qualities."[2]

More than that, the show also reinforces a comforting popular myth about
the ability of American cultural heroes to defeat the evils of the Klan—both
within the world of the Superman story and in reality. The "Clan of the Fiery
Cross" story represented an overt piece of anti-Klan storytelling that met
with significant commercial success, primarily in increased ratings for the
radio show. This was something that narratives dedicated to discrediting the

Invisible Empire in the 1920s signally failed to achieve. More than that, the Superman story purportedly represented a successful attack on the recruiting efforts of the real life Ku Klux Klan. As such, it became a key part of the Stetson Kennedy mythos.[3]

In the telling and retelling of the legend of Superman's fight with the Klan, the reality of Stetson Kennedy's contribution has become blurred. In Kennedy's narrative, he personally—and at great risk—infiltrated one of the more powerful Klaverns of the 1940s. He proposed the idea of fighting the Klan to the producers of the Superman serial, and allegedly supplied them with the Klan's own secret "code words" for inclusion in the story—all the better to strike at the absurdity of the real-life Klan. It was this story that *Freakonomics* uncritically repeated, and which was depicted on an episode of *Drunk History*.[4]

The reality is somewhat more murky, and it is oddly apropos that the best consideration comes from Rick Bowers's study, aimed at young adult readers. As the authors of *Freakonomics* noted after their book met with criticism, Kennedy seems likely to have infiltrated a few meetings himself but appears largely to have relied on information garnered from a mole known only as John Brown, whom Kennedy "handled" for the Anti-Nazi League and the Anti-Defamation League (ADL). It seems unlikely that it was Kennedy's suggestion that sparked the Superman serial, but producers did receive information from Kennedy via the ADL. That information may or may not have included secret "code words" of the Klavern, but, as anyone who has listened to the show can hear, it does not seem those "code words" were actually aired as part of the serial. The Man of Steel definitely fought the "Clan." Everything else about the story appears to be up for debate.[5]

Again, though, it is easy to understand *why* we would be drawn to the Kennedy story. This version of events is inherently appealing. As Mark Gagliardi recounted on *Drunk History*, it seems as though racism and intolerance could be easily overcome by one courageous man simply revealing "the childish, dumb shit that these guys would do." With their own children poking fun at their antics, "thanks to Stetson Kennedy, the Klan was defeated." In the face of reasoned ridicule by civilized society, the Ku Klux Klan would surely crumple—a deeply reassuring narrative. It is far more flattering to remember the Klan as kooks and crazies, un-American anomalies, brought down by brave men and women representing the American way. While Superman did not save the day until 1946, the remembrance of his radio heroics allows us to imagine the existence of clearly defined adversaries in a struggle for America's future. We can comfort ourselves that the Ku Klux Klan of the 1920s was little more than an aberration in our progress toward modernity.[6]

When we look at the postwar period more closely, it is evident that all these efforts at self-delusion really leave us with is an incomplete understanding. As historians of the Invisible Empire have come to agree, the men and women of the Klan were far from aberrant and far from marginal. This awareness is strengthened and deepened when we recognize the Klan not only as a social and fraternal organization but also as a deeply rooted cultural movement. The lack of permanence of Klannish cultural "ephemera" should not be mistaken for a lack of significance.

Far from having to choose between the Invisible Empire and other leisure activities, many Americans inextricably combined the pursuits. When we move away from a singular focus on the paying membership of the Klan organization, and the vagaries of the rise and fall of that membership, we better appreciate the cultural clout of the Klan movement. Members of that wider movement produced newspapers, created books and films, staged plays, recorded jazz music, built a radio station with national reach, even fielded baseball teams against Jewish and Catholic opponents. They did so largely divorced from—and often in contention with—the organization's leadership, an organic expression of a lived ideology.

Ironically, these local efforts reflected what, in many ways, bound together members of a supposedly national organization. Klannish newspapers insisted the Invisible Empire was not an "anti" organization of bigoted vigilantism, but rather a law-abiding and law-enforcing union of white, native-born, Protestant, patriotic "100% Americans." Klannish authors promoted the same idea. Whether in (supposed) nonfiction like Blaine Mast's *K.K.K., Friend or Foe: Which?* or in novels like George Alfred Brown's *Harold the Klansman*, the Klan was consistently depicted as a heroic defender of "pure Americanism" that had been unfairly maligned by scurrilous propaganda. On stage and screen, in *The Invisible Empire* and *The Fifth Horseman*, wrongful accusations were discredited and the stoic white heroism of the Klan celebrated. The musicians of the Invisible Empire reinforced that image in songs like "Wake Up America!" sold as sheet music and phonograph records and broadcast around the country. Across media, the cultural signifiers of the Klan—the cross and the hood—became a consumable cultural identity of white Protestant virtue. A fractured and federalized organization united behind this heroic self-image, an imagined community of Klannishness.

This communal identity was no frail flower, wilting in the face of scorn. Newspapers, novels, cartoons, songs, and plays all heaped ridicule on the "childish, dumb shit" of the Klan of the 1920s. Yet within "the thickest bombardment of custard tarts," in George Jean Nathan's words, the organization prospered, and the movement grew. It should be no surprise that Klan sportsmen felt comfortable in having their names and faces splashed across newspapers and programs. So what if newspapers ran stories that alleged Klansmen had committed crimes of violent hatred? Everyone knew—from reading stories like Herman Petersen's *Call Out the Klan* or listening to songs like Francis Roy's "They Blame It on the Ku Klux Klan"—that it was really criminals and Catholics to blame. For as much as the robes of the organization may have been stained with blood in reality, the signifier of the robe remained unsullied as an emblem of virtue for the movement. Klansmen couldn't be criminals—they stood for law and freedom and America. Newspapers, novels, cartoons, songs, plays, and films from all around the country cultivated a bedrock of belief in an unassailable identity of Klannish valor.[7]

In promulgating that image, the men and women of the Klan movement demonstrated their immersion in contemporary popular culture. The cultural Klan strained to make the Invisible Empire visible. To disseminate their propagandistic message, they consciously and unconsciously appropriated the culture around them, even as the organization denounced that culture. The ambivalent and often conflicted embrace of jazz, tabloid newspapers, pulp fiction, and more reflected the reality that rhetoric denied. The men and women of the Klan were thoroughly modern Americans, both a part and a product of postwar society, who simultaneously resisted and helped to create modern American culture.

As we recognize the Klan's ambivalent consumption of modern culture, we must also recognize modern culture's ambivalent consumption of the Klan. A complex and inconsistent mix of antagonism and accommodation, the mass culture of the 1920s—from newspapers to movies to radio—offered audiences around the country multifarious and heterogeneous popular representations of the Klan. While many declaimed the Invisible Empire as an existential threat to the nation, others sanitized and normalized the organization, whether for reasons of profit or principle or both. These tensions were present both between apparently antithetical groups and within those same groups, even within individual responses. Shifting alliances and porous boundaries made a mockery of cultural partitions between supposed incompatibles.

The Knights of the Klan navigated the same cultural terrain as most Americans in the 1920s. Though their robes were white, the daily existence of the organization's members was drawn in shades of gray, nothing quite so clear-cut as polemicists on either side insisted. Tempting as it is to depict the postwar decade as a Manichaean struggle between the forces of progress and reaction, the reality of American cultural politics is far more ambiguous.

When we reevaluate the period through the lens of the Invisible Empire, we find a pattern of coexistence and compromise that fundamentally challenges our ability to draw stark divisions. The twenties were a decade in which a touch of the Ku Klux Klan could serve not simply as a threat but also as a thrill, as a bit of spice, as the "most picturesque element" in an emergent pluralist mass culture.

Acknowledgments

Acknowledgments are a tricky beast. At what point does a project really begin, and how far back must the thanks go? So, let us begin with a blanket acknowledgment of all who have played a part in this process—even if there is not enough room to name you, know that you are appreciated.

I began research for this book at George Washington University. I am eternally in debt to Leo Ribuffo, adviser and fearless foe of historical cliché, even if I still think "whilst" is a perfectly valid conjunction. My thanks and respect also to Eric Arnesen, Ed Berkowitz, and Richard Stott for their feedback and help. Denver Brunsman provided a model for teaching and collegiality that I can only hope to emulate.

Materials for the project came from archives around the country, and it is impossible to thank all those institutions individually, but I want to express my gratitude to librarians and archivists around the United States—and around the world—for the vital work they do. Much of this book was researched and written in one of the many reading rooms of the Library of Congress. It is an unsurpassed institution, and I will not soon forget reading about the Klan chasing a centaur while glancing up at the Jefferson Building dome.

Support has come from a wide variety of institutions and individuals, all of whom deserve praise and gratitude. Christy Regenhardt, Chris Brick, Mary Jo Binker, and the Eleanor Roosevelt Papers Project helped support me through the doctorate, financially and intellectually. To Eleanor Roosevelt herself, I say thank you for the inspiration your life and work still provide, although I wish your handwriting were easier to read.

Academia can often be a forbidding environment, and so my great thanks go to all in the History and Geography Department at Columbus State

University (especially Amanda Rees) for their collegiality and great generosity of spirit. Particular thanks go to Gary Sprayberry for both hiring me and then encouraging others to hire me. On the collegiality front, I must also thank the visiting lecturers at Georgia State University—Will Bryan, Rachel Ernst, Jay Watkins, Carolyn Zimmerman, Bryan Banks, Allyson Tadjer, and Deanna Matheuszik—for their companionship and support, and their feedback in developing this book.

This manuscript was completed at the Bill and Carol Fox Center for Humanistic Inquiry at Emory University, and I am grateful to Keith Anthony, Martine Brownley, Colette Barlow, and Amy Erbil. The Center's ongoing commitment to support work in the humanities is a vital task, and is much appreciated by all their fellows. It is certainly appreciated by me.

Tim Mennel, my editor at the University of Chicago Press, has been an invaluable help. Rachel Kelly has been a great source of support. The excellent feedback from the anonymous reviewers of the manuscript challenged assumptions and helped shape and clarify my arguments.

A portion of chapter 9 is drawn from my article "Invisible Umpires: The Ku Klux Klan and Baseball in the 1920s," which was published in *NINE: A Journal of Baseball History and Culture* 23, no. 1 (2015), and is reprinted with permission from the University of Nebraska Press.

Thanks are due for the moral and immoral support offered by my Anglo-American swirl of friends and family, including Annah Slack, Margie Navas, Chris Culig, Nate Jones, Daniel Leighton, Burns Eckert, fellow Ribuffites Andrew Hartman and Christopher Hickman, the entire Washington Nationals franchise and especially those seated in section 401, and those paragons of nontoxic masculinity David Lindfield, Luke Henning, Tom Cherry, Nick Taylor, Michael Koutas, and Laurence Stellings.

My love and thanks to my extended family—to Dick and Martha, Katie and Steve, and Elizabeth and Will. To my grandparents. And, most especially, to my parents, Chris and Stella. From them comes my love of reading, my interest in history, and my desire to fight for a more just society. None of this is possible without them.

And also Christina, I guess.

This book is dedicated to her.

Notes

Chapter One

1. The allegation had come from columnist Drew Pearson in committee testimony a few months earlier. *New York Times*, June 26, 1947, October 29, 1947.

2. *New York Times*, October 29, 1947.

3. *New York Times*, October 28, 1947; *Washington Post*, October 28, 1947; Horne, *Final Victim*, 28, 30, 32.

4. Lawson, *Processional*, v; Fisher and Londre, *Modernism*, 384; *New York Times*, February 1, 1925; *Chicago Tribune*, January 18, 1925.

5. Jackson, *Klan in the City*, 4–7; Alexander, *Klan in the Southwest*, 3; MacLean, *Behind the Mask*, 4, 14; Pegram, *One Hundred Percent*, 7.

6. Jackson, *Klan in the City*, 7–10; Lay, *Hooded Knights*, 7; Alexander, *Klan in the Southwest*, 7; Tucker, *Dragon and the Cross*, 70; Pegram, *One Hundred Percent*, 8.

7. Jackson, *Klan in the City*, 10–11; Newton, *Ku Klux Klan*, 371–72; Pegram, *One Hundred Percent*, 9–10; Hohenberg, *Pulitzer Prize Story*, 336; *Elyria Chronicle-Telegram*, March 4, 1999.

8. *New York World*, September 6, 1921–September 26, 1921.

9. *New York World*, September 8, 1921, September 27, 1921; *New Orleans Times-Picayune*, September 22, 1921; Streitmatter, *Mightier Than the Sword*, 113–14; United States Congress, House of Representatives, *Hearings on the Klan*, 6–7.

10. *Call of the North*, February 15, 1924; Chalmers, *Hooded Americanism*, 38; Jackson, *Klan in the City*, 12; Blee, *Women of the Klan*, 21; Streitmatter, *Mightier Than the Sword*, 114–15; Pegram, *One Hundred Percent*, 10; Fuller, *Visible of the Invisible Empire*, 19; *American Mercury*, June 1925; Knights of the Klan, *Meeting of Grand Dragons*, 93, 95.

11. Jackson, *Klan in the City*, 12; Newton, *Ku Klux Klan*, 373–74; Pegram, *One Hundred Percent*, 60.

12. Jackson, *Klan in the City*, 12, 16; Newton, *Ku Klux Klan*, 375–77; Pegram, *One Hundred Percent*, 17–18.

13. Chalmers, *Hooded Americanism*, 108. For the best study of the female auxiliary, see Blee, *Women of the Klan*. For the best analysis of the Klan's parochial school fight, see Pegram, *One Hundred Percent*.

14. Jackson, *Klan in the City*, 145–46, 154; McVeigh, *Rise of the Klan*, 187–89; Chalmers, *Hooded Americanism*, 171–72; Pegram, *One Hundred Percent*, 206–7. For the best treatment of the Stephenson case, see Tucker, *Dragon and Cross*; and Lutholtz, *Grand Dragon*.

15. *Washington Post*, November 2, 1930; Jackson, *Klan in the City*, 252; Blee, *Women of the Klan*, 175; Rice, *Klan in Politics*, 91; Cash, *Mind of the South*, 340–42; Newton, *Ku Klux Klan*, 17.

16. Much of the early consideration of the Klan was inspired by the work of John Moffat Mecklin in what became known as the "Mecklin thesis." The sociologist's 1924 study of the Klan, *The Ku Klux Klan: A Study of the American Mind*, emphasized the "uninformed" and "unthinking" nature of Klan members "reared in obscure towns and country places." Mecklin's ideas found purchase in a number of influential post–World War II texts. Richard Hofstadter wholeheartedly endorsed Mecklin's interpretation of the Klan in *The Age of Reform*. Placing "uncultivated" and "gullible" small-town Protestants at the center of the Klan's membership, Hofstadter buttressed the concept of the Klan as a senseless and instinctive reaction to imagined evils with his own ideas on status anxiety. Although less willing to speculate on the motivations of Klan members, John Higham's *Strangers in the Land* similarly stressed that the movement was an outgrowth of postwar "emotional ferment" in the small towns and "ordinarily tranquil countryside." It was not until the late 1960s, with the publication of Charles C. Alexander's *Ku Klux Klan in the Southwest* and Kenneth T. Jackson's *Ku Klux Klan in the City*, that Mecklin's ideas were fundamentally challenged. Focusing on analysis of local Klan activities and surviving membership rosters rather than the bluster of the Klan's national leadership, these studies began to reshape the understanding of who joined the Klan and why. Robert A. Goldberg's 1981 study of the Klan in Colorado and William D. Jenkins's 1990 work on the Klan in Ohio's Mahoning Valley built on the idea that the interwar Klan garnered members from across the socioeconomic spectrum. Nancy MacLean criticized this work for minimizing the role of violence in the Klan's impact. Even MacLean, though, was compelled to acknowledge that "the core elements of Klan ideology were not as aberrant as one might imagine." Scholars coalesced around Shawn Lay's "civic activist school," which suggested that the Klan "bore a remarkable resemblance to other locally oriented political and social movements in American history," albeit in unusual garb. A slew of local area studies have reinforced this conclusion, with minor variations, best reiterated in Pegram's wide-ranging survey of the Klan's rise and fall, which places particular emphasis on the importance of the organization's concern about public education (Mecklin, *Ku Klux Klan*, 14, 82, 99, 103, 107; Hofstadter, *Age of Reform*, 293–96; Higham, *Strangers in the Land*, 286, 291; Alexander, *Klan in the Southwest*, 18; Jackson, *Klan in the City*, xi, 251; Moore, *Citizen Klansman*, 11; MacLean, *Behind the Mask*, 187; Lay, *Hooded Knights*, 6, 188; Blee, *Women of the Klan*, 102).

17. Lawrence Grossberg, "History, Politics, and Postmodernism," in Morley and Chen, *Stuart Hall*, 157–59.

18. Denning, *Cultural Front*, xvii, 26, 63, 67, 202.

19. Denning, *Cultural Front*, xvii, xx, 26, 63, 67, 202.

20. Pound, *Kulchur*, 184; See Nash, *Nervous Generation*, 1970 and 1990. Gilman M. Ostrander, "The Revolution in Morals," in Braeman et al., *Change and Continuity*, 137–38; Gist, *Secret Societies*, 43; Schlesinger, "Nation of Joiners," 20; Erickson, "Kluxer Blues," 56. For an example of strong recent scholarship, see McGirr, *War on Alcohol*.

21. Levine, *Unpredictable Past*, 191, 196, 201, 205.

22. Cather, *Not under Forty*, Prefatory Note; Jackson, *Klan in the City*, 18; Coben, *Rebellion against Victorianism*, 136; Alexander, *Klan in the Southwest*, 32; Jenkins, *Steel Valley Klan*, ix; Kyvig, *Daily Life*, 166.

23. Kyvig, *Daily Life*, 156; Douglas, *Terrible Honesty*, 20; Fass, *Damned and Beautiful*, 3; Miller, *Supreme City*, 47; Denning, *Cultural Front*, 39, 42.

24. Levine, *Unpredictable Past*, 296; Rubin, *Middlebrow Culture*, 33.

25. Nye, *Unembarrassed Muse*, 4; Frederick Hoffman, "Fiction of the Jazz Age," in Braeman et al., *Change and Continuity*, 310, 322; Weaver, "Klan in Wisconsin," 40–41; Grossberg, "History, Politics, and Postmodernism," 157, 159.

26. Denning, *Cultural Front*, 42; Lears, *No Place of Grace*, xiii–xv, 6; Susman, *Culture as History*, 76, 97.

27. Chapman, *Prove It on Me*, 6–7; Davarian Baldwin, "New Negroes Forging a New World," in Baldwin and Makalani, *Escape from New York*, 16; W. Fitzhugh Brundage, "Kingdom of Culture," in Brundage, *Beyond Blackface*, 2–4, 14; Baldwin, "Our Newcomers to the City," in Brundage, *Beyond Blackface*, 171.

28. *Motion Picture News*, January 13, 1923.

29. Chalmers, *Hooded Americanism*, 38; *Waterloo Evening Courier*, September 13, 1927.

30. Mencken, *Damn!* 32–33; Rodgers, *Mencken*, 181; Nash, *Nervous Generation*, v, 5–32; Miller, *New World*, 1, 175; McParland, *Beyond Gatsby*, ix–x.

Chapter Two

1. Anderson, *Imagined Communities*, 35–36; Marchand, *Advertising the American Dream*, xx, 12; Hilmes, *Radio Voices*, 6, 11; Tarde, *Public and Crowd*, 278, 281, 284.

2. *American Mercury*, March 1926; Bent, *Newspaper Crusaders*, 138–39, 154; Scharlott, "Hoosier Journalist," 122; Moseley, "Invisible Empire," 75–76; *Imperial Night-Hawk*, July 11, 1923; *Fellowship Forum*, July 21, 1923; *Call of the North*, July 27, 1923, January 25, 1924; *Searchlight*, October 4, 1924.

3. *Yale Review*, June 1920.

4. Lynd and Lynd, *Middletown*, 471–72; Sumner, *Magazine Century*, 2, 57, 61–62, 72; Drowne and Huber, *American Popular Culture*, 189–90.

5. Baldasty, *E. W. Scripps*, 4–5; Kyvig, *Daily Life*, 190–91; Miller, *New World*, 329.

6. Miller, *New World*, 329–30; Peterson, *Magazines*, 313.

7. Douglas, *Golden Age of the Newspaper*, 231–37; Burnham, *Bad Habits*, 35–36; Drowne and Huber, *American Popular Culture*, 189–90; Brazil, "Murder Trials," 165; Dumenil, *Modern Temper*, 72–73; Bohn, *Heroes & Ballyhoo*, 5–6; Douglas, *Terrible Honesty*, 18; Miller, *Supreme City*, 358; Weaver, "Klan in Wisconsin," 92.

8. The original seventeen papers that carried the series were the *St. Louis Post Dispatch, Boston Globe, Pittsburgh Sun, Cleveland Plain Dealer, New Orleans Times-Picayune, Houston Chronicle, Dallas News, Galveston News, Seattle Times, Milwaukee Journal, Minneapolis Journal, Dayton News, Toledo Blade, Oklahoma City Oklahoman, Fort Wayne News-Sentinel, Syracuse Herald,* and *Albany Knickerbocker Press.* An eighteenth paper, the *Columbus* (Georgia) *Enquirer-Sun,* began printing the articles several days later.

9. Fry, *Modern Klan*, vii, 223–24; Boylan, *World and the 20s*, 5, 61, 63; Streitmatter, *Mightier Than the Sword*, 112–13; Harrell, "Klan in Louisiana," 54; Jackson, *Klan in the City*, 12–13; United States Congress, House of Representatives, *Hearings on the Klan*, 8–9; *The Crisis*, October 1921; *New York World*, September 1, 1921, September 6, 1921, September 7, 1921, September 19, 1921, September 21, 1921, September 24, 1921; *New York Times*, June 28, 1958.

10. *New York World*, September 7, 1921, September 8, 1921, September 10, 1921, September 11, 1921, September 13, 1921, September 16, 1921; *New York Times*, September 7, 1921, June 4, 1925; Chalmers, *Hooded Americanism*, 38; Streitmatter, *Mightier Than the Sword*, 115; Jones, *Story of the Klan*, 95. Reprinted editorials included the *Pittsburgh Sun,* the *Bronx Home News,* the *Plain-*

field (NJ) *Courier-News*, the *Chattanooga Times*, the *New York Times*, the *Boston Post*, the *Buffalo Courier*, and the *Duluth Herald*.

11. House of Representatives, *Hearings on the Klan*, 56, 75, 141–42; Jones, *Story of the Klan*, 95; *Broad Ax*, September 24, 1921; *Oakland Tribune*, October 12, 1921; *Washington Post*, October 13, 1921; *Racine Journal News*, October 15, 1921; *Fellowship Forum*, December 15, 1923.

12. Knights of the Klan, *Meeting of Grand Dragons*, 94; *Call of the North*, February 15, 1924.

13. Even in Klan strongholds like Texas and Indiana, and the reborn Klan's home state of Georgia, newspapers leveled sharp criticism at the organization. Most of the major dailies in Dallas held well-earned reputations as "implacable foes" of the Klan, as did the *Houston Press*. In Indiana, the *South Bend Tribune* was "notorious" among Klan members for almost daily front-page articles that the organization deemed "perfidious attacks upon the Invisible Empire." Atlanta's *Wesleyan Christian Advocate* condemned the "un-American and thoroughly undemocratic" nature of an organization fueled by "demagogic drivel." Other liberal Protestant periodicals like the *Northwestern Christian Advocate* and the *Presbyterian Advance* followed the Atlanta publication's lead to try to distance themselves from the Klan. Sherwood Eddy took to the pages of *Christian Century* to label the Klan as a "travesty" of Americanism and a "prostitution" of Protestantism (Morris, "Saving Society," 77–78; Bent, *Newspaper Crusaders*, 141; Scharlott, "Hoosier Journalist," 128–29; Baker, *Gospel*, 105; Melching, "Klan in Anaheim," 178; Hatle and Vaillancourt, "Minnesota's Klan," 363; Randel, *Century of Infamy*, 192–93, 196; White, *Autobiography of William Allen White*, 630–31; Johnson, *White's America*, 342–43, 375–77, 385; Hoffman, *The Twenties*, 382–83; *Fiery Cross*, January 5, 1923, February 2, 1923, July 6, 1923; *Atlanta Constitution*, August 4, 1921; *Literary Digest*, October 1, 1921; *Mexia Evening News*, April 5, 1922; *Fellowship Forum*, November 3, 1922; *Christian Century*, July 6, 1922, August 10, 1922; *Call of the North*, February 15, 1924; *Literary Digest*, September 24, 1921; *Baltimore Sun*, September 11, 1921; *Portsmouth Herald*, January 6, 1923; *Searchlight*, January 20, 1923; *Dawn*, February 3, 1923; *Chicago Tribune*, September 16, 1921, September 22, 1921, November 27, 1923; *Los Angeles Times*, June 15, 1922, August 19, 1924, August 26, 1924; *Atlantic Monthly*, July 1922; *The Forum*, February 1923; *Leslie's Weekly*, September 10, 1921, September 18, 1921, October 15, 1921; *New Republic*, September 21, 1921; *Nation*, September 14, 1921, November 15, 1922; *Bakersfield Californian*, December 26, 1922; *New York Times*, July 21, 1923, November 6, 1923, March 19, 1924; *Washington Post*, July 21, 1923; *Bridgeport Telegram*, July 21, 1923; *Imperial Night-Hawk*, August 8, 1923; *Dawn*, October 6, 1923; *Pittsburgh Courier*, November 3, 1923; *Thomasville Daily Times-Enterprise*, November 5, 1923; *Atlantic News-Telegraph*, January 7, 1924; *Chicago Defender*, February 2, 1924; *Searchlight*, July 12, 1924, July 19, 1924; *San Antonio Light*, December 11, 1938).

14. *Collier's*, January 27, 1923; *New York World*, September 8, 1921, September 15, 1921, September 26, 1921; *New York Tribune*, December 17, 1922, November 27, 1923; *Pittsburgh Courier*, January 20, 1923, November 3, 1923, November 17, 1923, May 17, 1924, June 21, 1924, June 28, 1924; *Washington Post*, December 11, 1922; *Chicago Tribune*, December 27, 1922; *Buffalo Commercial*, September 17, 1921, September 20, 1921; *Buffalo Express*, September 19, 1921, September 27, 1921; Lay, *Hooded Knights*, 41; Wade, *Fiery Cross*, 161; Knights of the Klan, *Meeting of Grand Dragons*, 95–96; *Call of the North*, February 15, 1924; *Nation*, January 3, 1923; *North American Review*, June-August 1926; Nathan, *Autobiography*, 175–76.

15. Salesman William R. Toppan claimed that after his name was published, many of his previous customers (primarily those in groups targeted by the Klan) "wholly refused and still do refuse to have any transaction, acquaintance or discourse with me." J. William Brooks, an undertaker, claimed that after being named in the pages of *Tolerance* "practically all of his cli-

ents . . . deserted him" and his business was "nearly ruined." Augustus Olsen, one of the rising stars of Chicago's business world, was forced to step down from his position as president of the Washington Park National Bank after depositors withdrew thousands of dollars (Craine, "Klan Moves North," 17–18, 20; Jackson, *Klan in the City*, 104; Goldberg, "Unmasking the Klan," 39–41; *Broad Ax*, August 19, 1922; *Chicago Defender*, September 2, 1922; *New York Times*, December 8, 1922; *New Castle News*, December 9, 1922; *Mansfield News*, December 10, 1922; *Fiery Cross*, December 29, 1922, January 5, 1923; *Dawn*, January 27, 1923; *Tolerance*, July 8, 1923, July 15, 1923).

16. The signature on Wrigley's application form was a copy of the signature that adorned the wrapper of Wrigley's gum—and which did not resemble Wrigley's actual signature. W. J. Winston, the Klansman who had passed the application form to *Tolerance*, soon admitted that it was a forgery. Wrigley's lawsuit ignited long-held differences among members of the AUL board. Patrick O'Donnell, who wrote the article naming Wrigley, was convinced of the millionaire's Klan affiliation and had published over the objections of other members of the editorial staff. With the backing of AUL treasurer Robert Shepherd, O'Donnell refused to allow *Tolerance* to print a retraction, and attempted to dismiss those who disagreed. When Grady K. Rutledge, the president of the publishing company and executive secretary of the AUL, and assistant editor Lionel Moise attempted to publish the retraction anyway, they were allegedly removed from the premises by force by Shepherd and his son. Rutledge promptly sued for an injunction against the newspaper, while Moise filed suit for assault and battery. For several weeks, the newspaper was forced to cease publication until the judge overseeing the case agreed to take on an advisory position that would allow him final decision over what articles *Tolerance* could print until the suit was settled. By March 1923, *Tolerance* was back in print, but continued to struggle. Lawsuits continued to mount—for twenty-five thousand, fifty thousand, and even one hundred thousand dollars. Butcher Harry Junker, for example, also sued the AUL for fifty thousand dollars, claiming that being named as a Klansman had cost him all his Catholic customers. Junker, however, was only awarded a single dollar in damages. The editorial infighting had lent credence to the Klan's charges that the newspaper's attacks on the organization were nothing more than the "venom and virulence" of "Mad Pat" O'Donnell, the "prophet of hate." Circulation collapsed to less than forty thousand. By the end of April, *Tolerance* and the AUL were forced to file for bankruptcy, listing assets of $4,000 and obligations of $475,000. The newspaper's subscription solicitor was arrested for allegedly bombing the businesses of Klansmen. In May, the Klan further hamstrung the beleaguered organization by suing to prevent the publication of membership lists that had allegedly been stolen from the Klan's Indiana headquarters. The newspaper continued to limp along until the beginning of 1925—mainly through a series of countersuits against the Klan—but circulation had fallen to less than five thousand, and *Tolerance* would never regain its short-lived effectiveness as a Klan opponent (Craine, "Klan Moves North," 20–23; Goldberg, "Unmasking the Klan," 40–41; Jacobs, "Catholic Response," 95; *Chicago Tribune*, February 3, 1923, February 6, 1923, February 8, 1923, February 9, 1923, February 20, 1923, February 24, 1923, March 16, 1923, May 12, 1923; *Los Angeles Times*, February 6, 1923; *Appleton Post-Crescent*, February 16, 1923; *Fiery Cross*, February 16, 1923, March 2, 1923, March 9, 1923, March 16, 1923, April 6, 1923, April 13, 1923, April 27, 1923, February 23, 1924; *New York Times*, February 16, 1923, June 29, 1924; *Burlington Hawk-Eye*, March 20, 1923; *Sandusky Register*, March 20, 1923; *Dawn*, March 24, 1923, April 7, 1923, April 14, 1923, April 21, 1923, May 17, 1923, June 16, 1923; *Washington Post*, April 22, 1923; *Badger American*, August 1923, December 1923; *The Kluxer*, October 20, 1923; Deposition of Harry Junker, *Harry Junker v. American Unity Publishing*, S-388057, Cook County Superior Court, 1923).

17. Hohenberg, *Pulitzer Prize Story*, 336, 348; Scharlott, "Hoosier Journalist," 128; Wade, *Fiery Cross*, 202; Jackson, *Klan in the City*, 47, 115; Streitmatter, *Mightier Than the Sword*, 115, 120–24; *Washington Post*, May 14, 1923; *New York Times*, May 14, 1923, January 10, 1941; *Imperial Night-Hawk*, May 23, 1923; *Badger American*, September 1923; *Chicago Tribune*, December 1, 1926; *Literary Digest*, September 24, 1921; *The Spectator*, February 17, 1923; *The Forum*, November 1924; *Montgomery Advertiser*, July 4, 1927; *Baltimore Afro-American*, May 26, 1928; *Atlantic Monthly*, May 1928.

18. The award committee would also later cite the *Enquirer-Sun*'s work in fighting the passage of a law banning the teaching of evolution, its exposure of governmental malfeasance, and its opposition to lynching (*Thomasville Daily Times-Enterprise*, March 22, 1921, March 29, 1921; *Chicago Defender*, May 7, 1921; *Leslie's Weekly*, October 15, 1921; *New York World*, September 10, 1921, September 15, 1921; *Leslie's Weekly*, October 15, 1921; Hohenberg, *Pulitzer Prize Story*, 336; Wade, *Fiery Cross*, 202; Moseley, "Invisible Empire," 58, 85; Mugleston, "Julian Harris," 284, 286–87, 289–90; Lisby, "Julian Harris," 8).

19. Moseley, "Invisible Empire," 85; Mugleston, "Julian Harris," 290–3; Lisby, "Julian Harris," 1; Hohenberg, *Pulitzer Prize Story*, 69, 336; *The Forum*, July 1926; *American Mercury*, August 1926; *Leslie's Weekly*, October 15, 1921; *Chicago Defender*, June 17, 1922, May 15, 1926; *Baltimore Afro-American*, May 8, 1926; *Topeka Plain Dealer*, May 14, 1926; *Broad Axe*, May 15, 1926; *The Sign*, September 1927.

20. Knights of the Klan, *Meeting of Grand Dragons*, 8, 93; *Call of the North*, February 15, 1924; Chalmers, *Hooded Americanism*, 38; Morris, "Saving Society," 111; *The Spectator*, February 17, 1923.

21. Booth, *Mad Mullah*, 106–7, 207–8; Scharlott, "Hoosier Journalist," 128.

22. Knights of the Klan, *Meeting of Grand Dragons*, 96; *Dawn*, June 2, 1923.

23. *New Menace*, May 8, 1926; *Rail Splitter*, December 1925; *New York World*, September 15, 1921; *Dawn*, January 13, 1923, December 1, 1923, January 5, 1924, February 2, 1924; *Winnfield News-American*, July 21, 1922, July 28, 1922, January 26, 1923; *Los Angeles Times*, July 1, 1922; *Oakland Tribune*, October 20, 1922; *Tipton Daily Tribune*, September 27, 1922; *San Antonio Express*, September 27, 1922; *Washington Post*, August 31, 1924; *Decatur Daily Review*, September 8, 1924; *Bridgeport Telegram*, October 20, 1924; *Washington Post*, September 13, 1925; *Sandusky Star-Journal*, October 30, 1922; *Massillon Evening Independent*, May 23, 1922; Harrell, "Klan in Louisiana," 46, 175; Jackson, *Klan in the City*, 191; United States Congress, House of Representatives, *Hearings on the Klan*, 10; Fry, *Modern Klan*, 114.

24. *New York Evening Post*, December 20, 1920, December 27, 1920, January 6, 1921, January 14, 1921, January 20, 1921, January 29, 1921, February 5, 1921, February 19, 1921, March 10, 1921; Horn, *World Encyclopedia of Cartoons*, 71–72.

25. *Imperial Night-Hawk*, January 23, 1924; *Call of the North*, February 8, 1924; *Fellowship Forum*, February 16, 1924; *Fiery Cross*, May 25, 1923; *Searchlight*, November 8, 1924; *Roanoke Times*, December 2, 2001; *Wisconsin Kourier*, February 6, 1925; *Harrisburg Daily Reporter*, October 1, 1924; Jacobs, "Catholic Response," 277; Lalande, "Klan in Oregon," 45–46; Moore, *Citizen Klansman*, 26.

26. *Imperial Night-Hawk*, July 4, 1924; Mugleston, "Julian Harris," 289; Morris, "Saving Society," 89; Scharlott, "Hoosier Journalist," 128; Goldberg, *Hooded Empire*, 152; Cocoltchos, "Klan in Orange County," 32, 162; Fox, *Everyday Klansfolk*, 143; Abbey, "Klan in Arizona," 16.

27. Kyvig, *Daily Life*, 191; Peterson, *Magazines*, 23–24.

28. Marchand, *Advertising the American Dream*, xvii, 20.

29. Albert Lasker had begun working as an office boy at the respected Lord & Thomas Agency in 1898. By 1910, he had become the advertising firm's sole proprietor, leading it to

become "one of the largest and most successful advertising agencies of its time," representing Kleenex, top-selling toothpaste Pepsodent, Sunkist, and Lucky Strike cigarettes. Lasker pioneered the idea of in-house copywriting by advertising professionals, and created the position of account executive. Moore, *Citizen Klansman*, 98; Fry, *Modern Klan*, 22; *World's Work*, May 1923; *New York World*, September 7, 1921; *Chicago Tribune*, August 16, 1921, August 19, 1921, February 4, 1922; *New York Tribune*, September 7, 1921; *Galveston Daily News*, September 23, 1921; "Albert Lasker," *American National Biography Online*; Shotwell, "Public Hatred," 102; Marchand, *Advertising the American Dream*, 32, 35.

30. *New York Tribune*, September 7, 1921; *New York World*, September 7, 1921, September 11, 1921, September 16, 1921; *Washington Post*, October 12, 1921.

31. *El Paso Herald*, February 14, 1922; *Imperial Night-Hawk*, April 4, 1923, July 4, 1923; *Fiery Cross*, May 11, 1923; *Joplin News-Herald*, January 23, 1923; *Searchlight*, October 7, 1922, November 11, 1922; *Kourier Magazine*, May 1925; *Fiery Cross*, March 9, 1923; *New York Times*, June 2, 1923; *Fellowship Forum*, December 13, 1924; *Washington Post*, September 11, 1925; *Bradford Era*, April 26, 1927; *Oakland Tribune*, June 25, 1930; Chalmers, *Hooded Americanism*, 219; Feldman, *Klan in Alabama*, 31; Lay, *War, Revolution, and the Klan*, 104.

32. Some of McCall's gruesomely elaborate schemes included luring Richardson to a doctor's office, murdering him, and cutting the body into pieces for Klansmen to carry away in different directions; locating a local pit of quicksand to throw the editor into; or organizing a grand jury and subpoenaing Richardson to appear so that a sharpshooter in a nearby building could kill him.

33. *Baltimore Afro-American*, December 17, 1920, September 9, 1921, April 4, 1925; *Chicago Defender*, December 18, 1920, September 2, 1939; *Savannah Tribune*, December 25, 1920; *The Messenger*, September 1921; *Broad Ax*, June 11, 1921; *New Orleans Times-Picayune*, September 22, 1921; *Negro Star*, June 2, 1922; *Pittsburgh Courier*, March 28, 1925; *Call of the North*, October 5, 1923; *Coshocton Tribune*, September 3, 1922; *Savannah Tribune*, September 14, 1922; *The Messenger*, October 1922; *Connersville News-Examiner*, March 14, 1923; *Los Angeles Times*, July 11, 1926; *Chicago Tribune*, July 9, 1926, July 10, 1926, July 12, 1926, July 16, 1927, August 9, 1933; *Lowell Sun*, July 17, 1926, July 28, 1926; *Charleston Daily Mail*, July 25, 1926; *Bluefield Daily Telegraph*, July 23, 1926; *New York Times*, July 26, 1926; *Kokomo Daily Tribune*, February 22, 1927; *Bridgeport Telegram*, March 10, 1927; Scharlott, "Hoosier Journalist," 126–27; Lisby and Mugleston, *Someone Had to Be Hated*, 139.

34. Lynd and Lynd, *Middletown*, 475; Peterson, *Magazines*, 23, 26.

35. Meeting Notes, July 14, 1924, July 21, 1924, Ku Klux Klan Carlock Unit No. 71 (Carlock, Ill.) Records, Manuscript Collection No. 903, Box 1, Folder 3, Manuscript, Archives and Rare Book Library, Emory University, Atlanta, GA; *Tulsa Daily World*, September 8, 1921; *South Bend Tribune*, February 1, 1923; *Fellowship Forum*, May 12, 1923; *Fiery Cross*, May 25, 1923; Davis, "Klan in Indiana," 319; Scharlott, "Hoosier Journalist," 127.

36. *South Bend Tribune*, February 1, 1923, March 9, 1972; Lisby, "Julian Harris," 8; Mugleston, "Julian Harris," 287; Davis, "Klan in Indiana," 319; Scharlott, "Hoosier Journalist," 127.

37. *The Independent*, December 20, 1924; *Imperial Night-Hawk*, April 23, 1924; *South Bend Tribune*, March 9, 1972; Davis, "Klan in Indiana," 320; Mugleston, "Julian Harris," 289–90; Fry, *Modern Klan*, 19; Morris, "Saving Society," 83, 86, 88–90, 324.

38. *Imperial Night-Hawk*, May 30, 1923.

39. *Pittsburgh Courier*, July 28, 1923.

40. *New York Times*, November 8, 1923; *New York Age*, December 25, 1920; *Cleveland Plain Dealer*, November 16, 1923; *Savannah Tribune*, January 1, 1921; *Washington Bee*, January 1, 1921,

January 15, 1921; *Hutchinson Blade*, February 5, 1921; *Topeka Plain Dealer*, February 25, 1921; *Negro Star*, October 21, 1921; *Baltimore Afro-American*, December 9, 1921, October 31, 1924, May 22, 1926, August 20, 1927; *Broad Ax*, January 1, 1921; *Chicago Defender*, January 14, 1922, September 2, 1922, November 17, 1923, November 10, 1928; *Cleveland Gazette*, January 8, 1921, February 19, 1921; *Pittsburgh Courier*, April 7, 1923, April 14, 1923, June 30, 1923, September 1, 1923, September 22, 1923, June 14, 1924, August 23, 1924, February 28, 1925; *Opportunity*, January 1923, September 1923; *The Crisis*, November 1922, February 1924; Goldberg, "Unmasking the Klan," 37; Morris, "Saving Society," 85, 91; Bent, *Newspaper Crusaders*, 139; Streitmatter, *Mightier Than the Sword*, 111; Scharlott, "Hoosier Journalist," 124–25; Moore, *Citizen Klansman*, 26; Melching, "Klan in Anaheim," 178; Abrams, *Cross Purposes*, 79.

41. This was a priority shared by much of the black press, including *The Crisis*, the *Pittsburgh Courier*, and others. *Savannah Tribune*, July 27, 1922; *Pittsburgh Courier*, August 23, 1924; *The Crisis*, May 1924; *The Messenger*, March 1921, September 1921, October 1921, November 1921, February 1922, June 1922, July 1922, September 1922, October 1922, December 1922, January 1923, February 1923, April 1923, August 1923, October 1923, December 1923, March 1924, December 1924; *America*, February 2, 1921; *Broad Ax*, February 5, 1921, August 19, 1922; *American Israelite*, April 20, 1922; *Daily Jewish Courier*, February 5, 1925; *The Tablet*, December 3, 1922; *New York Times*, December 1, 1922, April 15, 1923; *Searchlight*, December 16, 1922, September 3, 1924; *The Appeal*, January 27, 1923; *American Ecclesiastical Review*, January 1924; *Jewish Press*, August 14, 1924; *True Voice*, July 3, 1925; *Fiery Cross*, April 2, 1923; *Our Sunday Visitor*, 1920–28; *The Sign*, August 1921, September 1924, August 1926, November 1926, April 1928; *Fellowship Forum*, November 10, 1923; Jacobs, "Catholic Response," x, 139, 140–42, 145, 149–50; Dumenil, *Modern Temper*, 278–79; Schuyler, "Klan in Nebraska," 240, 247; Goldberg, "Unmasking the Klan," 37–38; Diner, *Almost Promised Land*, 96–97; Feldstein, *Land That I Show You*, 228; Davis, "Klan in Indiana," 58.

42. *Call of the North*, February 15, 1924; *American Mercury*, November 1924.

43. *Chicago Defender*, August 6, 1921; *Washington Post*, December 5, 1920; *Chicago Tribune*, August 17, 1921; *New York Times*, June 8, 1924; Shotwell, "Public Hatred," 78.

44. *Albert Lea Evening Tribune*, September 5, 1923; *Call of the North*, September 7, 1923; *Prattsville Progress*, September 24, 1925; *Birmingham Age-Herald*, June 28, 1924; *Birmingham News*, June 27, 28, 1924; Feldman, *Klan in Alabama*, 31; Snell, "Magic City," 214; Shotwell, "Public Hatred," 76.

45. Showalter, "Payne County," 265; Morris, "Saving Society," 77, 92; Payne, *Big D*, 95; Alexander, *Crusade for Conformity*, 83; Shotwell, "Public Hatred," 76; Safianow, "Konklave," 333.

46. *Colorado Springs Gazette*, July 5, 1923; *Searchlight*, July 5, 1924; *Dawn*, June 2, 1923; *Imperial Night-Hawk*, May 30, 1923; *Kokomo Daily Tribune*, January–July 1924; *Oxnard Daily Courier*, July 28, 1923; *Oakland Tribune*, August 23, 1924; *American Mercury*, February 1928; Moore, *Citizen Klansman*, 94; Blee, *Women of the Klan*, 168; Newton, *Klan in Mississippi*, 74; Schwieder, "Klan in Northwest Iowa," 300; Weaver, "Klan in Wisconsin," 92, 156; Moseley, "Invisible Empire," 24; Shotwell, "Public Hatred," 76, 79; Goldberg, "Klan in Madison," 38.

47. *New York Times*, January 28, 1921; *Birmingham Post*, January 28, 1921; *Birmingham Age-Herald*, January 28, 1921; *Washington Post*, December 3, 1922; Shotwell, "Public Hatred," 75; Snell, "Masked Men," 207–8.

48. *Searchlight*, February 18, 1922, May 27, 1922, August 5, 1922; September 2, 1922, September 9, 1922; Lutholtz, *Grand Dragon*, 61; Shotwell, "Public Hatred," 76, 80; Jacobs, "Catholic Response," 136.

49. *Knoxville News*, May 30, 1922; *Searchlight*, June 3, 1922.

50. *Searchlight*, June 3, 1922; *Lancaster Examiner-New Era*, October 30, 1923; *Indianapolis News*, July 2, 1923; *Indianapolis Star*, July 3, 1923; *Linton Daily Citizen*, July 3, 1923; *Bridgeport Telegram*, July 3, 1923; *Knoxville News*, May 30, 1922; *Searchlight*, June 3, 1922, June 9, 1923; *Dawn*, November 11, 1922; Jacobs, "Catholic Response," 282; Greene, "Guardians against Change," 31; Crownover, "Klan in Lancaster County," 66.

51. *Searchlight*, May 27, 1922, November 11, 1922; *Fiery Cross*, December 8, 1922, December 29, 1922, January 5, 1923, January 19, 1923; Shotwell, "Public Hatred," 103; Jacobs, "Catholic Response," 282.

52. *New York Times*, June 22, 1923; *Call of the North*, August 3, 1923, *Fellowship Forum*, January 5, 1924.

53. *Outlook*, November 7, 1923, November 14, 1923, November 21, 1923, November 28, 1923, December 12, 1923, December 19, 1923, December 26, 1923; *New Republic*, November 21, 1923; *Los Angeles Times*, December 26, 1922; *Call of the North*, December 5, 1923; *Imperial Night-Hawk*, December 5, 1923, January 23, 1924; *North American Review*, March-May 1926, June-August 1926; *The Forum*, September 1925, December 1925; *Current History*, July 1927; *New York Times*, March 8, 1926; *Berkeley Daily Gazette*, March 9, 1926; *Kourier Magazine*, July 1927; *Searchlight*, December 15, 1923, December 26, 1923; *The World Tomorrow*, March 1924; *Broad Ax*, March 8, 1924; *McClure's*, May 1924; *Literary Digest*, January 20, 1923; *Fiery Cross*, February 23, 1923, March 2, 1923; *Daily Oklahoman*, March 26, 1922; *Washington Post*, December 3, 1922; *Dawn*, March 10, 1923, December 15, 1923; January 12, 1924; *Time*, June 23, 1924; Jacobs, "Catholic Response," 136-37.

54. *Call of the North*, August 31, 1923, January 16, 1924; *Badger American*, August 1923; *Imperial Night-Hawk*, January 16, 1924; *Searchlight*, August 16, 1924; *National Kourier*, March 6, 1925; Shotwell, "Public Hatred," 76, 78-80; Weaver, "Klan in Wisconsin," 156; Safianow, "Klan Comes to Tipton," 209.

55. Mugleston, "Julian Harris," 289-90; Scharlott, "Hoosier Journalist," 124.

Chapter Three

1. *The Messenger*, January 1923; *Brownsville Herald*, September 7, 1920, July 17, 1922; *Burleson County Ledger and News-Chronicle*, October 21, 1921; *Daily Northwestern*, September 9, 1920; *Galveston Daily News*, July 24, 1922, April 27, 1923; *San Antonio Express*, August 28, 1922; *Kerrville Mountain Sun*, September 1, 1922; Alexander, *Klan in the Southwest*, 193; Greene, "Guardians against Change," 25-26; Susman, *Culture as History*, 111; Miller, *Supreme City*, 338, 340-41, 351.

2. The newspaper's masthead also declared it to be "Not a Moulder But A Chronicler of Public Opinion."

3. *Searchlight*, September 10, 1921; United States Congress, House of Representatives, *Hearings on the Klan*, 11, 76; Fry, *Modern Klan*, 119; Jones, *Story of the Klan*, 93; Jackson, *Klan in the City*, 32-33; Shotwell, "Public Hatred," 113-14, 117; Booth, *Mad Mullah*, 48; Akin, "Klan in Georgia," 194, 237, 507; Alexander, "Kleagles and Cash," 355; *Indianapolis Star*, August 17, 1923; Davis, "Klan in Indiana," 43; Tucker, *Dragon and Cross*, 97; Jackson, *Klan in the City*, 147; "Fiery Cross," in *Encyclopedia of Indianapolis*, 566.

4. *Fellowship Forum*, June 24, 1921, July 1, 1921, July 15, 1921, September 9, 1921, March 24, 1922, April 21, 1922, May 19, 1922, July 14, 1922, October 20, 1922, November 25, 1922, January 20, 1923, March 24, 1923, June 16, 1923, September 22, 1923; Davis, "Klan in Indiana," 43; Shotwell, "Public Hatred," 128; Chalmers, *Hooded Americanism*, 234.

5. *Dawn*, October 21, 1922, November 4, 1922, April 7, 1923, April 13, 1923, June 16, 1923, June 30, 1923, July 7, 1923, August 25, 1923, September 29, 1923; *New York Times*, April 7, 1923; *Chicago Tribune*, April 8, 1923; *Fellowship Forum*, April 14, 1923, August 25, 1923, November 17, 1923; *Searchlight*, April 7, 1923, April 14, 1923; *Buckeye American*, September 11, 1923; *Imperial Night-Hawk*, April 18, 1923, July 4, 1923; *Waterloo Evening Courier and Reporter*, March 28, 1923; *Cedar Rapids Republican*, May 6, 1923; Snell, "Masked Men," 211; *Birmingham Age-Herald*, July 1, 1923; Allerfeldt and Black, *Immigration in the Pacific Northwest*, 68; Jackson, *Klan in the City*, 82, 101, 112–13, 194; Craine, "Klan Moves North," 16, 18; Hallberg, "Klan in Pekin," 83–84, 87; Smith, "Hooded Crusaders," 17.

6. *Chicago Defender*, October 21, 1922; *New York Times*, December 21, 1922, December 23, 1922, January 25, 1923, September 12, 1924; *Ogden Standard-Examiner*, December 21, 1922.

7. *Badger American*, April 1923, May 1923, June 1923, July 1923, September 1923, May 1924, July 1924, September 1924; Jackson, *Klan in the City*, 162; Shotwell, "Public Hatred," 132; *Fiery Cross*, April 13, 1923, April 27, 1923, May 25, 1923, June 1, 1923; *Searchlight*, December 1, 1923, March 1, 1924; *Fellowship Forum*, April 12, 1923, November 3, 1923; *Dawn*, September 1, 1923, September 8, 1923, November 3, 1923; Booth, *Mad Mullah*, 44, 47–48, 50, 64, 76–77; Jackson, *Klan in the City*, 41; Alexander, "Kleagles and Cash," 355.

8. Denning, *Cultural Front*, 232; Seldes, *Lively Arts*, 243–47; Rodgers, *Mencken*, 66; *Badger American*, August 1923, May 1924, July 1924, September 1924.

9. The son of tenant farmers and recipient of a night school law degree, Wood proudly regarded himself as a self-made man. As such, he viewed himself as one of the few Atlanta editors who did not instinctively side with the wealthy citizens of the city. *Galveston Daily News*, September 16, 1921; Akin, "Georgia Klan," 237–39, 243; United States Congress, House of Representatives, *Hearings on the Klan*, 7; *Searchlight*, November 26, 1921, December 24, 1921, January 28, 1922, April 1, 1922, December 15, 1923, May 3, 1924, June 7, 1924, July 5, 1924, August 2, 1924; Jackson, *Klan in the City*, 171; Shotwell, "Public Hatred," 114, 117; Long, " Klan in Western Pennsylvania," 14; Peterson, *Magazines*, 311.

10. The newspaper's politically powerful advisory council included Stephenson; Ed Jackson, soon to be elected governor of Indiana; John Duvall, later mayor of Indianapolis; and George V. Coffin, who became Republican county chairman of Indiana's Marion County.

11. Lutholtz, *Grand Dragon*, 58; Booth, *Mad Mullah*, 25, 50; *Fiery Cross*, December 8, 1922, December 29, 1922, January 19, 1923, February 16, 1923, March 16, 1923.

12. *Dawn*, October 21, 1922, November 4, 1922, April 7, 1923, April 13, 1923, June 16, 1923, June 30, 1923, July 7, 1923; *Call of the North*, July 27, 1923, September 28, 1923, October 31, 1923; Hatle and Vaillancourt, "Minnesota's Klan," 364.

13. *Searchlight*, November 26, 1921, December 24, 1921, January 28, 1922, April 1, 1922, December 15, 1923, May 3, 1924, June 7, 1924, July 5, 1924, August 2, 1924; *Fiery Cross*, December 8, 1922, January 19, 1923; *Birmingham Age-Herald*, July 1, 1923; *Imperial Night-Hawk*, July 4, 1923; Snell, "Masked Men," 211.

14. Although invariably referred to as "newsboys," this is a misleading characterization. Vendors of Klan newspapers included teen boys, but also included women of all ages and were predominantly men in their midtwenties and older. Among the most celebrated news vendors, for example, were teen sisters Viola and Frances Price of Freeport, Illinois—authorized distributors of *Dawn* (*Dawn*, October 20, 1923).

15. *Searchlight*, November 26, 1921, December 24, 1921, January 28, 1922, April 1, 1922, December 15, 1923, May 3, 1924, June 7, 1924, July 5, 1924, August 2, 1924; *Fiery Cross*, January 19,

1923, February 16, 1923, March 16, 1923; *Dawn*, October 21, 1922, November 4, 1922, April 7, 1923, April 13, 1923, June 16, 1923, June 30, 1923, July 7, 1923; *New York Times*, April 7, 1923; *Chicago Tribune*, April 8, 1923; *Fellowship Forum*, April 14, 1923, December 8, 1923, December 15, 1923, January 26, 1924; Jackson, *Klan in the City*, 101, 112–13, 171; Craine, "Klan Moves North," 16, 18; Shotwell, "Public Hatred," 114, 117; Long, "Klan in Western Pennsylvania," 14.

16. *Baltimore Afro-American*, March 17, 1922; *Chicago Defender*, March 25, 1922; Abbey, "Klan in Arizona," 17, 25; *Jayhawker American*, April 5, 1923; *Iola Daily Register*, November 22, 1923; Goldberg, *Hooded Empire*, 181; *Protestant Herald*, July 2, 1926; Untitled newspaper clipping, n.d., Senter Family Papers, WH988, Box 36, Folder 2, Western History Collection, Denver Public Library, Denver, CO; *Woodland Daily Democrat*, January 29, 1923; *Indianapolis Star*, January 4, 1923; *Dawn*, March 10, 1923, March 17, 1923, May 5, 1923; Chalmers, *Hooded Americanism*, 223; *Portsmouth Daily Times*, September 18, 1923; *Arizona Republican*, October 13, 1930; *Fiery Cross*, December 8, 1922; *Call of the North*, January 2, 1924; *Minnesota Fiery Cross*, February 22, 1924, March 14, 1924, April 18, 1924; *Fellowship Forum*, February 27, 1926; Lutholtz, *Grand Dragon*, 58.

17. *Fiery Cross*, February 9, 1923, June 29, 1923; *LaPorte Herald*, February 3, 1923; *Galveston Daily News*, September 16, 1921.

18. *Fiery Cross*, March 23, 1923, June 29, 1923, July 13, 1923; *Fellowship Forum*, March 24, 1923.

19. In June 1923, Lowe was questioned by his abductors about the Klan, robbed, and thrown from a moving car after refusing to cooperate. In December of the same year, he was "beaten almost into unconsciousness" with a blackjack. Most galling, however, was in September 1924, when he was "forced into an automobile, driven to an isolated part of the city, stripped of his clothing and wooden leg, and thrown into a ditch." It is unclear whether Lowe continued with his sales. *Fiery Cross*, January 5, 1923, March 23, 1923, April 27, 1923, June 1, 1923, February 16, 1924; *Fellowship Forum*, December 29, 1923, July 5, 1924, November 15, 1924; *Dawn*, January 5, 1924, February 9, 1924; *Call of the North*, January 16, 1924; *Minnesota Fiery Cross*, March 21, 1924, April 4, 1924; *Massillon Evening Independent*, September 11, 1924; *Searchlight*, April 5, 1924; *Sandusky Register*, December 4, 1923; *Detroit News*, September 14, 1923; Jacobs, "Catholic Response," xiv, 274–76.

20. *Imperial Night-Hawk*, March 28, 1923, July 11, 1923, July 25, 1923; Davis, "Klan in Indiana," 44; Baker, *Gospel*, 21; Jackson, *Klan in the City*, 36, 40.

21. *Fiery Cross*, April 13, 1923, April 27, 1923, May 25, 1923, June 1, 1923; *Searchlight*, December 1, 1923, March 1, 1924; *Imperial Night-Hawk*, August 29, 1923; *Dawn*, September 1, 1923, September 8, 1923, November 3, 1923; *Fellowship Forum*, April 12, 1923, September 15, 1923, November 3, 1923; *Edwardsville Intelligencer*, January 25, 1927; Booth, *Mad Mullah*, 44, 47–48, 50, 64, 76–77; Jackson, *Klan in the City*, 41; Alexander, "Kleagles and Cash," 355.

22. Mayfield of *Mayfield's Weekly*, for example, refused to endorse Felix Robertson, the official Klan candidate for governor of Texas in 1924, and instead promoted his own pick of V. A. Collins. Although Mayfield never had a chance of swaying the state leadership, he did force the *Texas 100 Per Cent American* to enter into a running debate on the question and created sufficient fuss to push Texas Grand Dragon Z. E. Marvin to tour the state, shoring up support among the largest Klans (*American Forum*, January 24, 1924; *San Antonio Light*, October 19, 1924, December 4, 1924; *San Antonio Express*, June 6, 1923, October 25, 1924, December 4, 1924, December 5, 1924; *St. Petersburg Independent*, June 6, 1923; *Reno Evening Gazette*, June 5, 1923; Alexander, "Kleagles and Cash," 362; *Huntingdon Daily News*, July 1, 1924; *Clearfield Progress*, February 2, 1925; *Simpsons' Daily Leader-Times*, September 15, 1925; *Dawn*, October 20, 1923; *New York Times*, April 7, 1923; *Joplin News Herald*, October 11, 1923; *Waterloo Evening Courier*,

March 12, 1926; Alexander, *Crusade for Conformity*, 57–58; *Lubbock Daily Avalanche*, September 23, 1923; *Belton Journal*, February 1, 1924; *Brookshire Times*, January 9, 1925; Frost, *Challenge of the Klan*, 149; Knights of the Klan, *Meeting of Grand Dragons*, 97–98).

23. Elrod had begun the 1920s as the president of a water-softening device manufacturer and author of a "Radio Review" column for the *Fort Wayne News-Sentinel* (*Fort Wayne News-Sentinel*, April 4, 1922).

24. The new Imperial Wizard had dismissed the services of the increasingly troublesome Southern Publicity Association and its directors, Edward Young Clarke and Elizabeth Tyler, shortly after taking control of the Klan from Simmons, and replaced them with an ally from Texas, Philip E. Fox. Fox resigned his position as managing editor of the *Dallas Times Herald* to become both the Klan's national public relations director and editor of the newly founded *Night-Hawk*, but his tenure in Atlanta ended when he went to the office of William S. Coburn, an attorney for Simmons, and shot Coburn four times, killing him instantly. The prosecution built a compelling case that Fox had been engaged in an affair with a woman from Cleveland and Coburn had threatened to expose him. *The Messenger* lamented that "the only thing we are really sorry about is that Coburn did not have his gun out and fire at the same time and with equally deadly accuracy." Other editorials were not much more sympathetic. Eager to avoid the taint of scandal, Evans moved quickly in the wake of the killing and appointed Milton Elrod the new head of the Klan's publicity department. *New York Times*, November 6, 1923, December 16, 1923; *Washington Post*, December 15, 1923; *Lawrence Daily Journal-World*, November 12, 1923; *Joplin News Herald*, November 12, 1923; Payne, *Big D*, 77; Morris, "Saving Society," 192; *The Messenger*, December 1923; Booth, *Mad Mullah*, 123; Fuller, *Visible of the Invisible Empire*, 35.

25. *Imperial Night-Hawk*, December 19, 1923; *Call of the North*, January 9, 1924; *Minnesota Fiery Cross*, February 22, 1924; Davis, "Klan in Indiana," 79.

26. *Fiery Cross*, April 6, 1923; Vinyard, *Michigan's Grassroots*, 46.

27. *Imperial Night-Hawk*, March 28, 1923, December 19, 1923; *Tipton Tribune*, November 9, 1923; Frost, *Challenge of the Klan*, 149; Booth, *Mad Mullah*, 227–33.

28. *Imperial Night-Hawk*, September 5, 1923, December 19, 1923; *Fiery Cross*, May 25, 1923.

29. *Imperial Night-Hawk*, December 19, 1923.

30. *Call of the North*, February 15, 1924; *Minnesota Fiery Cross*, February 22, 1924.

31. *Badger American*, July 1924, September 1924, October 1924; Shotwell, "Public Hatred," 134.

32. Booth, *Mad Mullah*, 232; Knights of the Klan, *Second Imperial Klonvokation*, 64, 78, 188.

33. *Searchlight*, November 15, 1924; Knights of the Klan, *Second Imperial Klonvokation*, 78.

34. *The Kluxer*, August 7, 1923, October 20, 1923, October 27, 1923, November 24, 1923; *Kokomo Daily Tribune*, July 10, 1924; *Gettysburg Times*, July 11, 1924; *San Antonio Express*, July 11, 1924; *Massillon Evening Independent*, July 11, 1924; *Charleston Gazette*, July 11, 1924; *Indianapolis Star*, July 11, 1924.

35. *Searchlight*, November 15, 1924.

36. *New York Times*, March 6, 2013.

37. The *Kourier* was subdivided into both regional and state editions: South Atlantic, North Atlantic, New England, West Virginia, Illinois, Iowa, Kansas, Kentucky, Michigan, Mississippi, Missouri, Nebraska, Ohio, Tennessee, Texas, and Wisconsin. *Wisconsin Kourier*, December 26, 1924, January 16, 1925; *Edwardsville Intelligencer*, May 3, 1924; *LeMars Globe-Post*, June 26, 1924; *Spencer Reporter*, July 16, 1924; *Clearfield Progress*, September 17, 1924; Shotwell, "Public Hatred," 135.

38. Charles G. Palmer to Seward Bristow, January 22, 1925, Ku Klux Klan Carlock Unit No. 71

(Carlock, Ill.) Records, Manuscript Collection No. 903, Box 1, Folder 1, Manuscript, Archives and Rare Book Library, Emory University, Atlanta, GA.

39. *Edwardsville Intelligencer*, May 3, 1924; *Clearfield Progress*, September 17, 1924; *Wisconsin Kourier*, November 14, 1924.

40. Marquis, *Annotated Archy*, xiii–xxx; Anthony, *Marquis*, 640–45.

41. Marquis, *Annotated Archy*, 256, 258–61.

42. *Wisconsin Kourier*, November 14, 1924, November 21, 1924, December 26, 1924, January 16, 1925; *Searchlight*, November 15, 1924; Shotwell, "Public Hatred," 135–36.

43. *Wisconsin Kourier*, November 14, 1924, December 26, 1924, January 16, 1925; Miller, *Supreme City*, 563–64.

44. *Imperial Night-Hawk*, November 12, 1924, November 19, 1924; *Kourier Magazine*, December 1924, February 1925, May 1925, July 1925; *Fellowship Forum*, December 13, 1924.

45. According to Munn & Co., the Klan's patent and trademark attorneys, these were Alabama, California, Connecticut, Delaware, Florida, Idaho, Louisiana, Maine, Maryland, Massachusetts, Minnesota, Montana, Nevada, New Hampshire, New Jersey, New York, North Carolina, North Dakota, Oklahoma, Oregon, Pennsylvania, Rhode Island, South Carolina, South Dakota, Utah, Vermont, Washington, West Virginia, and Wyoming (*New York Times*, August 31, 1925; *Bridgeport Telegram*, September 1, 1925).

46. *Wisconsin Kourier*, February 27, 1925; *National Kourier, North Central Edition*, March 6, 1925; *National Kourier, Eastern and Middle West Edition*, May 16, 1925; *Kourier Magazine*, March 1925; *Stilwell Standard-Sentinel*, May 28, 1926.

47. *Kourier Magazine*, April 1929.

48. *Wisconsin Kourier*, February 20, 1925; *National Kourier*, March 13, 1925; *Kourier Magazine*, March 1925, August 1926, December 1926, January 1927.

49. *Kourier Magazine*, May 1928, July 1928, September 1928, January 1929, March 1929, August 1929, May 1930.

50. *Edwardsville Intelligencer*, May 3, 1924; *Washington Post*, July 20, 1926, April 9, 1927, April 21, 1927; *Davenport Democrat and Leader*, October 25, 1925; *Washington Evening Star*, October 22, 1926; Booth, *Mad Mullah*, 232.

51. Fowler regularly asserted that Jesuits were "trained adepts in the art of hypnotism" who used "mental manipulation" to control prominent Protestants. Notably, Fowler claimed that these "telepathic principles" had been used to kill both Woodrow Wilson's first wife and Warren G. Harding, who had been "poisoned mentally." Jewish Americans, meanwhile, were alleged to be using the newspaper comic strips to undermine the English language with vernacular humor, thus corrupting the nation's youth. Although Fowler did not mention specifics, he made it clear that he considered Albert Einstein and his morally dubious theory of relativity an equally important part of this Yiddish plot (*American Standard*, April 15, 1924, June 1, 1924, July 15, 1924, September 15, 1924, December 1, 1924, October 1, 1925; *Woodland Daily Democrat*, November 6, 1924; *Fellowship Forum*, July 19, 1924, July 26, 1924; *New York Times*, June 26, 1924, June 27, 1924; *Lethbridge Daily Herald*, May 29, 1926, August 13, 1926; *Logansport Pharos Tribune*, May 26, 1925; *Tipton Daily Tribune*, July 2, 1925; *New York Times*, July 12, 1925; *Washington Post*, July 23, 1925; *New American Patriot*, November 6, 1925; *Washington Evening Star*, April 16, 1926, May 22, 1926; Booth, *Mad Mullah*, 69, 121; Akin, "Klan in Georgia," 176; Jackson, *Klan in the City*, 176; Shotwell, "Public Hatred," 129, 131; Winks, *Blacks in Canada*, 321; Alexander, "Klan in Arkansas," 321; Shults, "Klan in Downey," 145).

52. *Stilwell Standard-Sentinel*, May 28, 1925.

53. Fuller, *Visible of the Invisible Empire*, 35; Booth, *Mad Mullah*, 167–8; *Fellowship Forum*, April 19, 1924, May 24, 1924; *Imperial Night-Hawk*, April 23, 1924; *Searchlight*, May 10, 1924; Imperial Commander Robbie Gill Comer to All Klanswomen, May 28, 1929, Women of the Ku Klux Klan, Klan 14 (Chippewa Falls, Wis.) Records, 1926–31, WIHV96-A393, Box 1, Folder 3, Eau Claire Research Center, Wisconsin Historical Society Archives, Eau Claire.

54. Booth, *Mad Mullah*, 232-a.

55. *Fellowship Forum*, June 21, 1924.

56. *Fellowship Forum*, March 22, 1924, June 21, 1924, January 3, 1925, May 15, 1926, September 10, 1927.

57. *Fellowship Forum*, May 24, 1924, September 6, 1924; Minutes, July 24, 1924, Knights of the Ku Klux Klan, Klan No. 51, Mt. Rainier, Maryland Archives, 89–180, Box 1, Folder 2, Special Collections, Hornbake Library, University of Maryland Libraries, College Park.

58. *Fellowship Forum*, March 22, 1924, October 4, 1924, April 25, 1925, August 8, 1925, August 15, 1925, September 19, 1925, December 19, 1925.

59. *Orange County Times Press*, March 3, 1927; *Washington Post*, June 25, 1925, August 7, 1927; *Chicago Defender*, October 6, 1928.

60. *Pittsburgh Courier*, October 27, 1928.

61. *Woodland Daily Democrat*, October 24, 1928; *Washington Post*, November 1, 1928; *Baltimore Afro-American*, August 11, 1928, September 8, 1928; Shotwell, "Public Hatred," 128; Chalmers, *Hooded Americanism*, 234.

62. Many of these attacks focused on a photograph, notorious among white supremacists, showing Ferdinand W. Morton, an African American member of the Civil Service Commission in New York, dictating letters to a white stenographer (*Baltimore Afro-American*, October 20, 1928, November 3, 1928).

63. *New York Times*, September 19, 1928, September 22, 1928, September 24, 1928, October 21, 1928; *Chicago Tribune*, September 24, 1928; *Washington Post*, October 10, 1928; *Baltimore Afro-American*, September 22, 1928, October 13, 1928, October 20, 1928, November 3, 1928; *Pittsburgh Courier*, October 27, 1928; *Fellowship Forum*, June 16, 1928, September 25, 1928; Lichtman, *Prejudice and Old Politics*, 59, 70.

64. *Washington Post*, September 21, 1928; *New York Times*, September 22, 1928; *Baltimore Afro-American*, November 3, 1928.

Chapter Four

1. Miller, *New World*, 199–201; Mencken, *My Life*, 395–97; Stearns, *Civilization*, iii; Schlesinger, "Civilization," 167.

2. Parrish, *Anxious Decades*, 191; Stearns, *Civilization*, vii, 286.

3. Schlesinger, "Civilization," 170; Miller, *New World*, 201; Mencken, *My Life*, 396; Nash, *Nervous Generation*, 102, 137; Rodgers, *Mencken* 114; McParland, *Beyond Gatsby*, ix–x; Greif, *Crisis of Man*, 116–19.

4. Smith, *What Would Jesus Read*, 3; Rodgers, *Mencken*, 114.

5. Lynd and Lynd, *Middletown*, 229; Sullivan, *Our Times*, 382; Boyer, *Purity in Print*, 71–72; Currell, *Culture in the 1920s*, 69; Kyvig, *Daily Life*, 197, 199; Hart, *Popular Book*, 184, 229.

6. Smith, *What Would Jesus Read?* 53–54, 75, 87; Peterson, *Magazines*, 46–47; Kyvig, *Daily Life*, 199.

7. Miller, *Supreme City*, 543–50.

8. Smith, *What Would Jesus Read*, 75–76; Miller, *Supreme City*, 549.

9. *Searchlight*, April 15, 1922, May 17, 1924; *Mayfield's Weekly*, November 21, 1921, December 3, 1921, January 7, 1922; *Minnesota Fiery Cross*, May 23, 1924; *American Standard*, October 15, 1924.

10. It is no coincidence that the U.S. city with perhaps the decade's most strident literary censorship was Boston, by no measure a Klan stronghold.

11. *American Standard*, October 15, 1924; *Zion's Herald*, November 1, 1922; Miller, *Supreme City*, 552; Randel, *Century of Infamy*, 169; Hoffman, *The Twenties*, 74, 362; Sullivan, *Our Times*, 400; Hutner, *What America Read*, 85; Boyer, *Purity in Print*, 70–71, 82–83, 92, 99–100, 104; Boyer, "Boston Book Censorship," 11.

12. Susman, *Culture as History*, 114; Hart, *Popular Book*, 229; Rubin, *Middlebrow Culture*, 41.

13. Lynd and Lynd, *Middletown*, 308, 364–65, 478–84; *The Bookman*, September 1930; *New York Times*, October 19, 1924, March 29, 1925; *Washington Post*, March 30, 1924; Gibbs, *Ten Years After*, 239–40; Slosson, *Great Crusade*, 307–8.

14. Stokes, *Birth*, 191; Lowery, "Reconstructing the Reign of Terror," 9, 155–56, 171–72, 219–20; DuBois, *Black Reconstruction*, 717, 723; John David Smith, introduction to Smith and Lowery, *Dunning School*, 3–4, 18–21; Shepherd W. McKinley, "John W. Burgess," in Smith and Lowery, *Dunning School*, 59–64; James S. Humphreys, "William A. Dunning," in Smith and Lowery, *Dunning School*, 77, 81, 85, 95–97; Michael W. Fitzgerald, "Steel Frame of Fleming," in Smith and Lowery, *Dunning School*, 166–69.

15. Other issues addressed in the series that year included the cancellation of Allied debt, shipping subsidies, and labor issues in Kansas. Sullivan, *Our Times*, 382; Johnsen, *Reference Shelf No. 10*, preface, 2.

16. Clason, *Catholic, Jew, Ku Klux Klan*, 56, 64; "E. Haldeman-Julius," *American National Biography Online*; Haldeman-Julius, *Kreed of the Klansman*, 3; Haldeman-Julius, *Constructive or Destructive?* 8–9, 45; Rodgers, *Mencken*, 90.

17. Jefferson, *Five Present-Day Controversies*, 159, 164, 166–67; Jefferson, *Catholicism and the Klan*, iii.

18. Confirming the importance of the Klan's literary appearances in shaping public appraisals of the organization, Ferguson relied on evidence drawn from earlier work, including William Simmons's *America's Menace*, Leroy Curry's *Klan under the Searchlight*, Henry Fry's *Modern Klan*, E. F. Stanton's *Christ and Other Klansmen*, and Alma White's books (Ferguson, *New Books of Revelations*, preface, 12, 179, 266, 278, 365, 393, 427; *Lubbock Morning Avalanche*, November 13, 1928).

19. *New York Times*, November 25, 1928; *The Bookman*, April 1928, December 1928.

20. Kallen, *Culture and Democracy*, 61; Schmidt, *Kallen*, 31; "Horace Kallen," *American National Biography Online*; Greene, *Jewish Origins of Cultural Pluralism*, 1–11.

21. Kallen, *Culture and Democracy*, 43.

22. Kallen, *Culture and Democracy*, 43; Murphy, *New Era*, 121, 123; Schmidt, *Kallen*, 37; *New York Times*, April 20, 1924.

23. *Imperial Night-Hawk*, July 4, 1923; *New York Times*, November 3, 1924; Mecklin, *Ku Klux Klan*, 13, 15, 30, 95–6, 157.

24. Mecklin, *Ku Klux Klan*, 103–4, 106–7, 109, 233–34.

25. *New York Times*, February 24, 1924, March 16, 1924; *The Bookman*, March 1924; *Janesville Daily Gazette*, May 29, 1924; *Ogden Standard-Examiner*, October 26, 1924; *Washington Post*, September 19, 1937. For more on Mecklin's influence, see chapter 1.

26. Frost, *Challenge of the Klan*, 41, 77, 251–53; Jackson, *Klan in the City*, 235.

27. The series had been widely reprinted in both mainstream publications and Klannish newspapers, including the *Searchlight*, the *Fiery Cross*, and the *Fellowship Forum* (Frost, *Challenge of the Klan*, vii–viii; *Searchlight*, December 29, 1923, January 5, 1924; *Minnesota Fiery Cross*, February 22, 1924, April 25, 1924).

28. Frost, *Challenge of the Klan*, 78, 80, 105, 171.

29. As historians have pulled away from Mecklin's thinking, Frost's argument has played an increasingly important role, echoed in the "civic activist" school of thought pioneered by Leonard Moore and Shawn Lay (Frost, *Challenge of the Klan*, 115; *Minnesota Fiery Cross*, April 25, 1924; *Oakland Tribune*, May 11, 1924; *Washington Post*, May 18, 1924; *Fellowship Forum*, March 21, 1925).

30. Jones was actually the son of the superintendent of the Anti-Saloon League of Georgia, while his brother (soon to become assistant Prohibition director of Georgia) was described as a "constant attendant" of Imperial Wizard Simmons during the congressional hearings into the Klan. It is unclear whether Jones was an official member of the Klan at the time of writing his book, but he was certainly an admirer and ally. By the time of the abridged reissue of his book in 1941, he was sharing an apartment with "Colonel" E. N. Sanctuary, an "arch Klansman" who ran a small Klan publishing firm (Randel, *Century of Infamy*, 170, 179; Jones, *Story of the Klan*, 9; *New York Times*, April 19, 1925; *Jewish Telegraphic Agency Daily News Bulletin*, February 12, 1942).

31. Jones, *Story of the Klan*, 34, 40, 94, 105.

32. Fowler, *Ku Klux Klan*, 3; Dyer, "Klan on Campus," 454, 459, 462, 468–69; *Fellowship Forum*, May 17, 1923; *San Antonio Express*, September 10, 1923; *Dawn*, March 10, 1923, April 7, 1923; Brown, *Facts Concerning Klan*, preface; Sawyer, *Truth about the Invisible Empire*, 5–6.

33. *Badger American*, August 1923.

34. Simmons, *Klan Unmasked*, 13, 105.

35. The ex-Imperial Wizard's book did not even receive particular attention in the Klan press. Simmons ignored the fact that his book was an incoherent shambles and instead blamed Evans for its failure, later claiming that his rival had tried to prevent *The Klan Unmasked* from even being published (Simmons, *America's Menace*, 143).

36. It was not until 1930, far past the peak of the Klan's power, that Evans did eventually write a book, *The Rising Storm*. An analysis of the growing menace of Catholic influence in politics, *The Rising Storm* did not mention the Ku Klux Klan at all.

37. Fleming, *What Is Ku Kluxism?* 2.

38. Mast, *K.K.K., Friend or Foe?* 6, 17, 22, 28, 40, 48, 73.

39. *Fellowship Forum*, April 26, 1924; Lougher, *Klan in Kentucky*, 17; Winter, *What Price Tolerance*, v, 19, 81.

40. Both *Roman Katholic Kingdom* and *Old Cedar School* were by Oregon Klan propagandist George Estes, although they are usually credited to their publisher, Luther Ivan Powell, King Kleagle of the Pacific Northwest.

41. Wright, *Religious and Patriotic Ideals*, 1; White, *Klan in Prophecy*, 14, 26. See also White, *Klansmen: Guardians of Liberty* (1926) and *Heroes of the Fiery Cross* (1928).

42. Stanton, *Christ and Other Klansmen*, 34, 39; Curry, *Klan under the Searchlight*, 32, 41.

43. Fry, *Modern Klan*, vi–vii, 17, 24, 94, 105, 124, 185–91; *The Messenger*, May 1923.

44. *Chicago Defender*, January 14, 1922; *New York Times*, January 15, 1922; *Syracuse Herald*, March 5, 1922; *Oakland Tribune*, February 19, 1923.

45. Dever, *Confessions*; Monteval, *Klan Inside Out*; Likins, *Patriotism Capitalized*; Likins, *Trail of the Serpent*; Sletterdahl, *Nightshirt in Politics*; Simmons, *America's Menace*, 81.

46. Fry, *Modern Klan*, vi; Dever, *Confessions*, 4, 6, 29; *Dawn*, May 12, 1923; *Bakersfield Cali-*

fornian, May 2, 1923; Monteval, *Klan Inside Out*, 11, 29; Likins, *Patriotism Capitalized*, 63; Likins, *Trail of the Serpent*, 5–6, 67; Simmons, *America's Menace*, 81, 230; Booth, *Mad Mullah*, ix, 3–4.

47. Ball, *Faults and Virtues*, 23; Gordon, *Unmasked!* preface; Randel, *Century of Infamy*, 187.

48. Dalrymple, *Liberty Dethroned*, 27, 35; Blake, *Ku Klux Kraze*, 2; *New York Times*, September 8, 1923, October 3, 1923, October 11, 1923, October 22, 1924.

49. *Minnesota Fiery Cross*, May 23, 1924; *Fiery Cross*, February 2, 1923.

50. *Dawn*, December 2, 1922; *Fellowship Forum*, October 27, 1923; *Kourier Magazine*, December 1924, May 1925. For the best analysis of the Ku Klux Klan and public education, see the chapter "Learning Americanism" in Pegram, *One Hundred Percent*; and Laats, *Other School Reformers*.

51. *Fiery Cross*, December 8, 1922; *New York Times*, March 21, 1923; *Searchlight*, April 7, 1923, November 8, 1924; *Imperial Night-Hawk*, May 9, 1923; *Wisconsin Kourier*, January 9, 1925.

52. Pegram, *One Hundred Percent*, 106; Zimmerman, "History Wars," 92–93; Zimmerman, *Whose America?* 16–20, 24–26; Slosson, *Great Crusade*, 316.

53. Condemning the charges as "inherently and obviously absurd," the American Historical Association adopted the resolution, "Genuine and intelligent patriotism, no less than the requirement of honesty and sound scholarship, demand that text-book writers and teachers should strive to present a truthful picture of past and present. . . . Criticism of history text-books should therefore be based not upon grounds of patriotism, but only upon grounds of faithfulness to fact." (Slosson, *Great Crusade*, 316–17).

54. Zimmerman, *Whose America?* 18–19; *Dawn*, September 1, 1923; *Call of the North*, September 7, 1923.

55. Zimmerman, *Whose America?* 18, 21, 24–25; Zimmerman, "History Wars," 92–93, 96, 105; *Chicago Tribune*, October 28, 1927, November 19, 1927; Slosson, *Great Crusade*, 316.

56. By all accounts, the contents of *Convent Cruelties* paled in comparison to Jackson's lectures, often held at the behest of local Klansmen. Sections of the book with sexual undertones were made overt at these live events, at which Jackson described the "sexual horrors" of the convent, where nuns were raped by priests and then forced to have abortions (or have their newborn children murdered) to eliminate any evidence. Catholics across the country (mainly the Midwest) took out newspaper advertisements in which they denounced Jackson's stories and attempted to provide the true details of her life, although they seem to have had little impact on Jackson's popularity (Blee, *Women of the Klan*, 89; *Massillon Evening Independent*, December 7, 1923; *Sheboygan Press*, May 3, 1924; *Logansport Pharos-Tribune*, November 3, 1924).

57. In 1922, *Hearst's Magazine* printed a letter that purported to be from F. S. Webster, a Wisconsin Kleagle, to J. O. Wood, editor of the *Searchlight*, in which Webster encouraged Wood to print an article on the book, which "every Klansman should read," but "do not mention the fact that Stoddard is a Klansman" (MacLean, *Behind the Mask*, 270; "Lothrop Stoddard," *American National Biography Online*; *Capital Times*, December 29, 1922; *Chicago Defender*, January 20, 1923, January 27, 1923).

58. *Kourier Magazine*, September 1926; Jackson, *Convent Cruelties*, 7; Baker, *Gospel*, 149; Blee, *Women of the Klan*, 89; *Searchlight*, September 2, 1922, April 12, 1924; *Fiery Cross*, December 8, 1922, April 13, 1923; *Dawn*, June 2, 1923, February 9, 1924; *Fellowship Forum*, May 17, 1923, January 31, 1925; *Badger American*, June 1923; *Call of the North*, August 24, 1923; Stoddard, *Rising Tide*, 5.

59. It can only be assumed that the Klansman who recommended Cable's fiction had never encountered his nonfiction, or even his earlier fiction, in which he advocated for racial equality and expressed his abhorrence toward Southern racial attitudes.

60. *Fiery Cross*, April 27, 1923, June 29, 1923, July 20, 1923, October 5, 1923; *Fellowship Forum*, August 23, 1924; *Kourier Magazine*, December 1927; Knights of the Klan, *Meeting of Grand Dragons*, 85.

61. Smith, *What Would Jesus Read?* 107–11; *Kourier Magazine*, September 1926, February 1927, November 1927.

62. *Fiery Cross*, May 11, 1923.

63. *Fiery Cross*, February 2, 1923; *Kourier Magazine*, May 1925, February 1927.

64. *Fiery Cross*, July 20, 1923; *Kourier Magazine*, December 1927; *Wisconsin Kourier*, December 5, 1924.

65. Rubin, *Middlebrow Culture*, 149, 159–60, 174–79.

Chapter Five

1. Fitzgerald, *Gatsby*, 9, 86.

2. Michaels, *Our America*, 23–27, 136; Fitzgerald, *Gatsby*, 13, 23, 86.

3. Mordden, *That Jazz!* 228–29.

4. Hart, *Popular Book*, 207, 215, 235, 241, 244; Denning, *Cultural Front*, 197; Miller, *New World*, 215; Smith, *What Would Jesus Read?* 55; Greif, *Crisis of Man*, 109, 112, 116–19.

5. Nash, *Nervous Generation*, 99, 102, 137–40; Nye, *Unembarrassed Muse*, 38–40; Skinner, *Reagan*, 6.

6. Klannish readers may have been particularly fond of the novel because of its anti-Catholic undertones, including blaming the outbreak of the Civil War on a European conspiracy centered on a secret Treaty of Verona (Babcock, *Soul of Abe Lincoln*, 52, 72; *New York Times*, June 10, 1923; *Dawn*, June 30, 1923; *Badger American*, February 1924; Nash, *Nervous Generation*, 140).

7. For a recent example of literary histories of the 1920s that ignore Wright and other mass-market writers, see McParland, *Beyond Gatsby* (Smith, *What Would Jesus Read?* 3, 48, 51–55; Mencken, *Prejudices: Second Series*, 38).

8. Rodgers, *Mencken*, 148–50.

9. Nolan, *Black Mask Boys*, 19–20, 22; Hagemann, "Black Mask," 35; Smith, *Hard-Boiled*, 18; Nye, *Unembarrassed Muse*, 255.

10. Smith, *Hard-Boiled*, 27; McCann, *Gumshoe America*, 40; Mertz, "Carroll John Daly," 21.

11. Moore, *Hard-Boiled Detective*, 4, 39; Nolan, *Black Mask*, 35–36.

12. *Black Mask*, June 1, 1923, 44–46.

13. *Black Mask*, June 1, 1923, 46.

14. *Black Mask*, May 15, 1923, 48.

15. *Black Mask*, June 1, 1923, 32.

16. George W. Sutton to Herman Petersen, February 17, 1923, Herman Petersen Papers, Collection 1339, Box 1, Folder 18b, Department of Special Collections, Manuscripts Division, Charles E. Young Research Library, UCLA, Los Angeles, California; Herman Petersen to George W. Sutton, February 19, 1923, Herman Petersen Papers, Collection 1339, Box 1, Folder 18b, Department of Special Collections, UCLA.

17. Petersen originally set the story in West Virginia "because the Klan is fairly strong there," but changed the locale to the Blue Ridge Mountains of Virginia, where he had lived for several years, on the advice of Sutton (George W. Sutton, Jr., Memo to Herman Petersen, n.d., Herman Petersen Papers, Collection 1339, Box 1, Folder 18b, Department of Special Collections, UCLA; Herman Petersen to George W. Sutton, Jr., March 16, 1923, Herman Petersen Papers, Collection 1339, Box 1, Folder 18b, Department of Special Collections, UCLA).

18. In Petersen's first draft, the Klan was summoned through the ringing of church bells, but Sutton told him to change it because the Klan was "a private organization." Petersen resisted the alteration, arguing that in many localities—including the one in which the story was set—the Klan was certainly popular enough to make use of the local church bells as an alarm. Nonetheless, he eventually acceded to Sutton's request (George W. Sutton, Jr., Memo to Herman Petersen, n.d., Herman Petersen Papers, Collection 1339, Box 1, Folder 18a, Department of Special Collections, UCLA; Herman Petersen to George W. Sutton, Jr., March 16, 1923, Herman Petersen Papers, Collection 1339, Box 1, Folder 18b, Department of Special Collections, UCLA).

19. *Black Mask*, June 1, 1923, 18, 26, 31.

20. Herman Petersen to George W. Sutton, March 2, 1923, Herman Petersen Papers, Collection 1339, Box 1, Folder 18b, Department of Special Collections, UCLA.

21. *Black Mask*, June 1, 1923, 59–60, 78, 90.

22. Correspondents included a Canadian and his wife living in Michigan, who expressed their sadness that they were not eligible to join the Klan, and Robert E. Lee Klan Number One of Birmingham, Alabama (*Black Mask*, August 1, 1923, 118–22; August 15, 1923, 117–21).

23. *Black Mask*, June 15, 1923, 50, 66.

24. Hagemann, "Black Mask," 36; Nolan, *Black Mask*, 28; *Imperial Night-Hawk*, May 2, 1923.

25. Smith, *Hard-Boiled*, 31, 44; McCann, *Gumshoe*, 40–41.

26. Prince, *Stories*, 91–93, 99, 137, 209, 215, 232; Stokes, *Birth*, 42; Lowery, "Reconstructing the Reign of Terror," 3, 68.

27. Harris was also, ironically, father of newspaper editor Julian Harris, a leading crusader against the Invisible Empire in the 1920s.

28. Randel, *Century of Infamy*, 141–43, 151, 157–59; Hart, *Popular Book*, 204; Lowery, "Reconstructing the Reign of Terror," 46, 68. For more on *The Clansman* and *The Birth of a Nation*, see chapter 6.

29. Dixon, *Clansman*, 341–42; *Atlanta Journal*, April 20, 1902; *The Bookman*, February 1905; Stokes, *Birth*, 41–42.

30. Randel, *Century of Infamy*, 143; Michaels, *Our America*, 10; Scott Romine, "Thomas Dixon and the Literary Production of Whiteness," in Gillespie and Hall, *Thomas Dixon Jr.*, 124; Williamson, *Crucible of Race*, 141.

31. Randel, *Century of Infamy*, 143; Rogers, *Ku Klux Spirit*, 36.

32. Jackson, *Klan in the City*, 131, 176; Slide, *American Racist*, 16; *New York Times*, January 23, 1923, February 5, 1923; *Syracuse Herald*, January 23, 1923; *Appleton Post-Crescent*, January 23, 1923.

33. In Dixon's understanding of the Reconstruction Klan, President Grant's investigation into the South and the passage of the Ku Klux Act had no bearing on the demise of the organization—it simply decided to disband without prompting once it understood that it had fulfilled its mission.

34. Dixon, *Traitor*, 58.

35. Dixon, *Sins of the Father*, 19.

36. Dixon, *Black Hood*, 60, 84, 168.

37. *New York Times*, June 22, 1924, August 5, 1924; *New York World*, June 15, 1924; Slide, *American Racist*, 173; Jackson, *Klan in the City*, 176; Chalmers, *Hooded Americanism*, 93.

38. Janken, *White*, 89, 95–96, 110; *Baltimore Afro-American*, October 17, 1924.

39. White, *Fire*, 123, 126. The plot of White's novel was overtly indebted to Ida B. Wells's investigation of allegations of rape as a cover for lynchings motivated by the threat of black economic progress. For more, see Ida Wells, *Southern Horrors: Lynch Law in All Its Phases* (New York: New York Age, 1892).

40. Although this did not deter the mob in the novel from dragging Bob's body through the streets and burning it.

41. White, *Fire*, 230–37, 242, 300.

42. As the NAACP's field secretary, White traveled to Elaine, Arkansas, after the 1919 massacre of African American sharecroppers who had attempted to unionize. The results of his interviews with members of both the black and the white communities were widely republished and represented a major advance in his career (White, *Man Called White*, 47–50; Janken, *White*, 50–53).

43. Janken, *White*, 107–8.

44. Janken, *White*, 108–11; *New York Times*, September 14, 1924; *The Messenger*, October 1924, December 1924; *Baltimore Afro-American*, October 17, 1924; *The Independent*, September 27, 1924.

45. Janken, *White*, 111; *Chicago Defender*, September 13, 1924; *Baltimore Afro-American*, December 6, 1924.

46. *Chicago Defender*, November 1, 1924; *Baltimore Afro-American*, December 6, 1924.

47. *New York Times*, February 7, 1926.

48. Shands, *White and Black*, 136.

49. Shands, *White and Black*, 193, 232; *The Messenger*, December 1922; *The Bookman*, June 1922; *New York Tribune*, April 23, 1922.

50. Rubin, *Tar and Feathers*, 16, 190–92.

51. *Daily Northwestern*, October 6, 1923; *The Bookman*, November 1923; Scott, *Moffett*, 356.

52. The novel gave the author's name as Egbert Ethelred Brown. This may have been an alias, mocking the black Unitarian minister of the same (uncommon) name.

53. Brown, *Final Awakening*, 4, 155, 157.

54. *Fellowship Forum*, September 15, 1923.

55. Brown, *Harold*, 5; Wade, *Fiery Cross*, 182.

56. *Dawn*, December 29, 1923, February 9, 1924; *Badger American*, February 1924; *Fellowship Forum*, December 10, 1927.

57. Saxon, *Knight Vale of the K.K.K.*, 65–6, 111.

58. King, *100%*, 319–23; Gaffney, *Son of a Klansman*, 5–6; *Fellowship Forum*, June 9, 1928.

59. *American Mercury*, January 1928, March 1928, August 1928; Hoopes, *Cain*, 178–79.

60. Stevens, *Mattock*, 8, 236, 317; Maguire, *James Stevens*, 5, 27, 33; *New York Times*, April 24, 1927, May 15, 1927; *The Independent*, May 14, 1927; *The Bookman*, July 1927; *American Mercury*, April 1924.

61. *New York Times*, September 14, 1924.

62. Henle, *Sound and Fury*, 261; *Galveston Daily News*, November 2, 1924; *New York Times*, November 16, 1924; *Danville Bee*, September 9, 1924; *The Bookman*, November 1924; *Boston Transcript*, "Sound and Fury," in Knight and James, *Book Review Digest: Reviews of 1924 Books*, 278.

63. The Klan also made a brief appearance in Lewis's 1922 novel, *Babbitt*, as the "Good Citizens League." This league was organized for the "great work" of controlling the "Undesirable Element." As Virgil Gunch enthuses in the novel, it would "send a little delegation around to inform folks that get too flip that they got to conform to decent standards and quit shooting off their mouths so free" (Lewis, *Elmer Gantry*, 393–94; Lewis, *Babbitt*, 795).

64. Widely recognized as a thinly disguised depiction of his hometown of Fayetteville, Arkansas.

65. Sheehan, *Half-Gods*, 430, 435–39, 449.

66. Sheehan, *Half-Gods*, 436, 439, 441, 457; *New York Times*, May 21, 1961.

67. *New York Times*, April 17, 1927; *Oakland Tribune*, May 1, 1927; *Charleston Gazette*, June 12, 1927; *Los Angeles Times*, September 25, 1927.

68. *Saturday Evening Post*, September 23, 1922.

69. Gordon, *Ku Klux Ball*, 117, 170; *New York Times*, September 5, 1926, November 7, 1926.

70. McNeile, *Black Gang*, 279; Treadwell, *Drummond Encyclopedia*, 1; *McClure's*, June 1923.

71. *New York Times*, December 16, 1923; *International Book Review*, "The Black Gang," in Knight and James, *Book Review Digest: Reviews of 1923 Books*, 331.

72. Cullum, *Saint*, 171; *New York Times*, June 22, 1924; *New York Herald Tribune*, August 3, 1924; *Bookman*, July 1924.

73. *Fiery Cross*, January 5, 1923; Hart, *Popular Book*, 215; Nye, *Unembarrassed Muse*, 38; Mencken, *Prejudices: Third Series*, 416.

74. Beach, *Mating Call*, 91.

75. At the novel's climax, the local Klansmen do set out to whip a philandering husband, who is a Klansman himself, but the husband has already been shot by the father of his suicidal mistress, who is also a Klansman and the local judge (Beach, *Mating Call*, 280).

76. *Waterloo Evening Courier*, September 13, 1927; *New York Times*, July 10, 1927; *New York Herald Tribune*, July 24, 1927.

Chapter Six

1. *Variety*, June 23, 1922.

2. O'Neill, *All God's Chillun Got Wings*; Rodgers, *Mencken*, 264; Bradley, *Culture*, 151.

3. *Searchlight*, March 15, 1924, March 22, 1924; *Minnesota Fiery Cross*, March 28, 1924; *Imperial Night-Hawk*, April 2, 1924; *New York Times*, May 16, 1924, February 17, 1975; *American Standard*, October 15, 1924; Frank, "Tempest," 79; Boyle and Bunie, *Paul Robeson*, 121; Black, *Eugene O'Neill*, 301; Gelbs, *O'Neill*, 552.

4. *Pittsburgh Courier*, March 29, 1924; *American Mercury*, May 1924; *Wisconsin State Journal*, May 25, 1924; *The Crisis*, August 1924; Giordano, *Dance Hall*, 111; Frank, "Tempest," 75; Gelbs, *O'Neill*, 551–52.

5. *The Sign*, June 1928; Houchin, *Censorship*, 102–6, 109, 111–13; Savran, *Highbrow/Lowdown*, 158; Boyer, *Purity in Print*, 161–63; Lichtman, *White Protestant Nation*, 12; Frank, "Tempest," 80–81; Sutton, *American Apocalypse*, 114.

6. *New York Times*, September 29, 1921; *Movie Weekly*, July 14, 1923.

7. *Movie Weekly*, July 14, 1923; *Searchlight*, December 1, 1923, March 22, 1924, April 26, 1924, May 31, 1924, June 7, 1924, August 9, 1924; *American Standard*, July 1, 1924, August 1, 1924; *Dawn*, October 13, 1923, December 29, 1923; *El Paso Herald*, November 17, 1921; *El Paso Times*, November 17, 1921; *Minnesota Fiery Cross*, March 28, 1924, May 2, 1924; *Imperial Night-Hawk*, October 1, 1924; *Call of the North*, August 10, 1923; Rice, "Life after Birth," 93, 97, 259; Lay, *War, Revolution*, 77; White, *Klan in Prophecy*, 53; White, *Heroes of the Fiery Cross*, 10.

8. *Fellowship Forum*, April 7, 1923, May 5, 1923, August 18, 1924; *Fiery Cross*, April 13, 1923, May 11, 1923; *Searchlight*, April 14, 1923, May 5, 1923, May 19, 1923; *Imperial Night-Hawk*, May 9, 1923, June 6, 1923, June 23, 1923; *Dawn*, February 2, 1924; *Sandusky Register*, May 2, 1925; Safianow, "Klan Comes to Tipton," 217; Rice, "Life after Birth," 64; Pegram, *One Hundred Percent*, 29–30; *The Pilgrim*, directed by Charlie Chaplin, 1923, in *The Chaplin Review* (Warner Home Video, 2004, DVD).

9. *Photoplay*, April 1927; *Life*, September 21, 1922; Bradley, *Culture*, 136; Nash, *Nervous Generation*, 100; Seldes, *Lively Arts*, 147; Koritz, *Makers*, 42–43, 45, 56; Rodgers, *Mencken*, 319.

10. Londre and Watermeier, *North American Theater*, 261–62, 265–66; Currell, *American Culture*, 47, 52; Mates, *Musical Stage*, 34–35; Canning, *Most American*, 201–3; Nye, *Unembarrassed Muse*, 160, 170, 195–97; Miller, *Supreme City*, 289.

11. *Fortune*, October 1930; Sklar, *Movie-Made America*, 86, 149, 153; Cousins, *Story of Film*, 62–63; Currell, *Culture*, 103, 105–7; Fischer, *Cinema of the 1920s*, 15; Kyvig, *Daily Life*, 71; Hart, *Popular Book*, 228; Nye, *Unembarrassed Muse*, 377; Miller, *Supreme City*, 270–71; Fuller, *Picture Show*, 2, 19, 76, 90.

12. *The Birth of a Nation*, directed by D. W. Griffith, 1915 (Kino on Video, 2002, DVD).

13. Rice, "Life after *Birth*," 20, 35, 38, 40; Fox, *Everyday Klansfolk*, 33; Slide, *American Racist*, 83–85, 87; Ramsaye, *Million and One Nights*, 638–39, 641–42; Wade, *Fiery Cross*, 132–33; Jackson, *Klan in the City*, 3–4; Louis Menand, "Do Movies Have Rights," in Gillespie and Hall, *Thomas Dixon Jr.*, 201.

14. The best work on this includes Simcovitch, "Impact of *Birth of a Nation*"; Dessommes, "Hollywood in Hoods"; Inscoe, "Clansman on Stage and Screen"; Rice, "Life after *Birth*"; and Rice, *White Robes, Silver Screens*.

15. Lowery, "Reconstructing the Reign of Terror," 179; Prince, *Stories*, 247–48; Stokes, *Birth*, 172, 177, 206.

16. Rice, "Life after *Birth*," 1, 5, 11–12; Lehr, *Birth of a Nation*, 151, 187, 189, 227; Baldwin, "Our Newcomers," in Brundage, *Beyond Blackface*, 166–67; Wood, *Lynching*, 149, 151–52, 167; Stokes, *Birth*, 108, 125, 205.

17. Stokes, *Birth*, 88, 92, 131, 202–7; Cripps, *Black*, 96; Prince, *Stories*, 167, 177; Kibler, *Ridicule*, 21–22.

18. *Variety*, August 6, 1924; Fox, *Everyday Klansfolk*, 22; Rice, "Life after *Birth*," 216.

19. *Elyria Chronicle-Telegram*, February 5, 1932; *Fiery Cross*, August 10, 1923, November 2, 1923, August 23, 1924; *Searchlight*, January 14, 1922, February 16, 1924; *Altoona Mirror*, July 2, 1924; *Fellowship Forum*, April 3, 1923, December 27, 1924, February 11, 1925, June 27, 1925, November 14, 1925, January 9, 1926, January 30, 1926, May 15, 1926, July 25, 1926, September 18, 1926, February 19, 1927, March 17, 1928; *Wisconsin Kourier*, December 26, 1924, January 2, 1925; *National Kourier*, March 20, 1925; Boone, "A Kleagle and His Klan," 46–47; Fox, *Everyday Klansfolk*, 145–46; Jackson, *Klan in the City*, 76; Blee, *Women of the Klan*, 164–65; Minutes, March 13, 1924, Knights of the Ku Klux Klan, Klan No. 51, Mt. Rainier, Maryland Archives, 89–180, Box 1, Folder 2, University of Maryland Libraries; Minutes of the Women's Klan, February 1, 1927, March 1, 1927, March 8, 1927, May 24, 1927, Senter Family Papers, WH988, Box 36, Folder 10, Western History Collection, Denver Public Library; *Kolorado Klan Kourier*, undated clipping, Senter Family Papers, WH988, Box 36, Folder 18, Western History Collection, Denver Public Library; Minutes, September 7, 1927, September 21, 1927, July 31, 1929, August 14, 1929, July 31, 1929, Women of the Ku Klux Klan, Klan 14 (Chippewa Falls, Wis.) Records, 1926–31, WIHV96-A393, Box 1, Folder 1, Eau Claire Research Center, Wisconsin Historical Society Archives.

20. *Moving Picture World*, December 11, 1920, December 25, 1920; *Entertainment Trade Review*, November 27, 1920; Rice, "Life after *Birth*," 25.

21. *New York World*, September 21, 1921, September 22, 1921; *Denver Post*, July 2, 1921, July 8, 1921; *Eugene Morning Register*, January 10, 1922; House of Representatives, *Hearings on the Klan*, 36; Fry, *Modern Klan*, 22; Goldberg, *Hooded Empire*, 14; Jackson, *Klan in the City*, 10, 194, 198; Sawyer, *Truth about the Invisible Empire*, 7, 10.

22. Ramsaye, *Million and One Nights*, 642; Wade, *Fiery Cross*, 81; *Searchlight*, February 18, 1922, February 16, 1924, October 18, 1924, October 25, 1924, November 8, 1924; *New York Times*,

December 3, 1922; *Colorado Springs Gazette*, July 3, 1923, July 6, 1923; *Kokomo Daily Tribune*, September 5, 1923; Safianow, "Klan Comes to Tipton," 209; Rice, "Life after *Birth*," 30; Goldberg, *Hooded Empire*, 52, 152–53; Slide, *American Racist*, 195; Fox, *Everyday Klansfolk*, 33, 35; Jackson, *Klan in the City*, 118, 200; Wade, *Fiery Cross*, 70; Shotwell, "Public Hatred," 107–8; Newton, *Klan in Mississippi*, 83; Gerlach, *Blazing Crosses*, 117.

23. *Imperial Night-Hawk*, August 6, 1924; *Pierce County Herald*, August 19, 1926; *Fellowship Forum*, August 14, 1926, February 12, 1927; *Youngstown Citizen*, February 26, 1925; *Steubenville Herald-Star*, July 26, 1924; *Portsmouth Daily Times*, July 26, 1924; *Toledo Blade*, June 15, 1994; *Uniontown Morning Herald*, November 13, 1925; *Gettysburg Times*, July 20, 1926, July 28, 1926; Slide, *American Racist*, 62; Cook, *Fire from the Flint*, 102; Minutes, December 11, 1924, December 23, 1924, Knights of the Ku Klux Klan, Klan No. 51, Mt. Rainier, Maryland Archives, 89–180, Box 1, Folder 2, University of Maryland Libraries.

24. *Searchlight*, May 19, 1923, March 22, 1924; *Imperial Night-Hawk*, July 4, 1923; *Indiana Fiery Cross*, November 9, 1923; *Fellowship Forum*, November 17, 1923, March 29, 1924, October 17, 1925; *Lawrence Daily Journal-World*, February 14, 1925; *Beatrice Daily Sun*, September 20, 1925; *Joplin Globe*, February 21, 1943; *Variety*, February 25, 1925.

25. *New York Times*, September 16, 1922; *Chicago Tribune*, December 8, 1922, December 24, 1922, January 1, 1923; *Chicago Daily Journal*, January 2, 1923; *Dawn*, December 9, 1922; Fox, *Everyday Klansfolk*, 42; Jackson, *Klan in the City*, 118.

26. *Chicago Defender*, October 28, 1922; *Dawn*, December 9, 1922, December 16, 1922, December 23, 1922, December 30, 1922, January 6, 1923, January 13, 1923; *Chicago Tribune*, December 28, 1922.

27. *Chicago Daily Journal*, January 2, 1923; *Chicago Tribune*, December 31, 1922, January 1, 1923; *Dawn*, January 6, 1923.

28. *Chicago Tribune*, January 1, 1923; *Dawn*, January 6, 1923, January 20, 1923, January 27, 1923.

29. *New York World*, September 25, 1921; *Oakland Tribune*, December 29, 1927; Rice, "Life after *Birth*," 190–91.

30. *Imperial Night-Hawk*, August 22, 1923; *Daily Northwestern*, July 17, 1924; *Fellowship Forum*, March 5, 1927, March 12, 1927, March 26, 1927; Rice, "Life after *Birth*," 240; *Variety*, June 24, 1925.

31. *Variety*, June 23, 1922; *National Kourier*, May 1, 1925; *Fellowship Forum*, July 4, 1925; *Davenport Democrat and Leader*, September 14, 1925; *Abilene Reporter*, October 12, 1924; *Hutchinson News*, March 5, 1925, March 7, 1925; *Xenia Evening Gazette*, April 13, 1925; Rice, "Life after *Birth*," 145; Munden, *AFI Catalog*, 236.

32. *The Toll of Justice*, directed by Corey G. Cook, 1923 (University of North Carolina, Media Resources Center, 65-V7409, 1992, VHS); *Fellowship Forum*, October 20, 1923; *Call of the North*, January 25, 1924; Rice, "Life after *Birth*," 197–98; Pegram, *One Hundred Percent*, 30–31.

33. *Exhibitor's Herald*, May 27, 1922; *Sandusky Register*, October 4, 1923; *Coshocton Tribune*, October 4, 1923; *Movie Weekly*, October 6, 1923; *Pittsburgh Courier*, October 13, 1923; *Fellowship Forum*, October 20, 1923; *Indiana Fiery Cross*, December 14, 1923; *Call of the North*, December 19, 1923, January 25, 1924; *Ashland Times Gazette*, February 19, 1924, February 20, 1924; *Cambridge City Tribune*, May 1, 1924, May 8, 1924; *New Market Herald*, July 24, 1924; *Charleston Gazette*, September 21, 1924, September 22 1924; *Elyria Chronicle-Telegram*, March 3, 1925, March 23, 1925; *Variety*, August 30, 1923, November 8, 1923.

34. Fuller, *Picture Show*, 28, 30, 40.

35. *Coshocton Tribune*, October 4, 1923; Fuller, *Picture Show*, 76, 88, 90–94.

36. Munden, *AFI Catalog*, 9, 410; Rice, "Life after *Birth*," 192, 241; Slide, *American Racist*, 174; *New York Times*, February 12, 1922; *Davenport Democrat and Leader*, March 9, 1923; *Variety*, February 1, 1923.

37. *Moving Picture World*, January 22, 1921; *New York Age*, December 25, 1920, January 1, 1921; Rice, "Life after *Birth*," 117; Stewart, *Migrating to the Movies*, 223; *The Symbol of the Unconquered*, directed by Oscar Micheaux, 1920 (youtube.com).

38. Lisa E. Rivo, "Micheaux," in Gates and Higginbotham, *Harlem Renaissance Lives*, 347; Robert Jackson, "Secret Life of Oscar Micheaux," in Brundage, *Beyond Blackface*, 225–29; *Chicago Star*, October 1, 1921; Stewart, *Migrating*, 223–24; *Chicago Defender*, January 29, 1921; *Baltimore Afro-American*, July 17, 1926.

39. It was also sometimes used to mean "Made In America For Americans."

40. *Moving Picture World*, December 1, 1923; *Newark Advocate*, December 17, 1923; Rice, "Life after *Birth*," 198.

41. *New York World*, April 14, 1923; *New York Times*, April 19, 1923; *Fellowship Forum*, April 21, 1923; *Jasonville Leader*, June 13, 1923; *Indianapolis News*, July 16, 1923; *Kokomo Daily Tribune*, July 26, 1923; *Connersville News-Examiner*, November 13, 1923; Rice, "Life after *Birth*," 199, 201; Lutholtz, *Grand Dragon*, 289.

42. *Fellowship Forum*, March 22, 1924; *Searchlight*, June 21, 1924; *Call of the North*, February 1, 1924; *New York World*, April 14, 1923; Rice, "Life after *Birth*," 201, 206, 220.

43. *Call of the North*, February 1, 1924; *Logansport Pharos-Tribune*, May 2, 1924; *Logansport Morning Press*, May 2, 1924; *Imperial Night-Hawk*, June 4, 1924; *Searchlight*, June 21, 1924; *Fellowship Forum*, June 21, 1924; *Daily Northwestern*, July 17, 1924; *Sheboygan Press-Telegram*, July 17, 1924; *Badger American*, August 1924; *Decatur Review*, August 8, 1924; *Wisconsin Kourier*, February 27, 1925; *Tipton Tribune*, May 9, 1925; *Perry Daily Journal*, May 22, 1925; *Corsicana Sun*, June 30, 1925.

44. *Lawrence Daily Journal-World*, February 14, 1925; *National Kourier*, May 1, 1925; *Movie Weekly*, October 6, 1923; *Perry Journal*, May 20, 1925; *Corsicana Sun*, June 27, 1925; *Chicago Tribune*, December 24, 1922; United States Congress, House of Representatives, *Hearings on the Klan*, 147; *Chicago Tribune*, December 11, 1921, January 8, 1922; *Syracuse Herald*, December 17, 1921, December 25, 1921, December 26, 1921, December 28, 1921; *Variety*, January 6, 1922; *Billboard*, January 7, 1922, February 4, 1922; *New York Tribune*, August 16, 1922; *New York Times*, August 20, 1922, December 10, 1922; *Imperial Night-Hawk*, April 4, 1923; Shotwell, "Public Hatred," 151.

45. *Exhibitor's Herald*, September 10, 1921, November 12, 1921; *Motion Picture News*, January 13, 1923; *Exhibitor's Trade Review*, December 1, 1923, January 5, 1924.

46. *Variety*, September 30, 1921, June 28, 1923, February 28, 1924.

47. Lawson, *Processional*, v; Fisher and Londre, *Modernism*, 384; Horne, *Final Victim*, 28, 30, 32; *The Bookman*, March 1925.

48. Chambers, *New Technique*, 51–53; Lawson, *Processional*.

49. The King Kleagle also announced that "the entire Congress of the United States joined the Ku Klux Klan last night" (Lawson, *Processional*, 183).

50. Lawson, *Processional*, 182–83, 186; *New York Times*, February 1, 1925.

51. Lawson, *Processional*, 212–16.

52. *New York Graphic*, January 13, 1925; *New York Sun*, January 13, 1925; *New York Times*, January 13, 1925, January 18, 1925; *Life*, February 5, 1925; Chambers, *Messiah*, 64–66; Horne, *Blacklist*, 33.

53. *The Dial*, April 1925; *Chicago Tribune*, January 18, 1925; *New York Times*, January 13, 1925, February 1, 1925; *The Bookman*, March 1925; *Los Angeles Times*, December 23, 1926; *Theatre Arts Monthly*, March 1925.

54. *The Bookman*, March 1925; *New York Sun*, January 19, 1925; *New York World*, February 15, 1925; *Vanity Fair*, May 1925; Chambers, *Messiah*, 66–68; Horne, *Blacklist*, 32–33; Beverle Bloch, "Searching for 'The Big American Play': The Theatre Guild Produces John Howard Lawson's *Processional*," in Gerwitz and Kolb, *Theatre of the 1920s*, 9.

55. *New York Sun*, February 26, 1925; *St. Paul Minnesota Pioneer Press*, February 12, 1925; Bloch, "Searching," 7–8; Chambers, *Messiah*, 68; Savran, *Highbrow/Lowdown*, 16–18.

56. *Los Angeles Times*, September 27, 1922, January 10, 1926; *Chicago Tribune*, March 29, 1924; *Harrisonburg Daily News Record*, December 10, 1926.

57. Rice, "Life after *Birth*," 118, 155; *Camera*, November 5, 1921; *Exhibitor's Herald*, November 19, 1921; *Exhibitor's Trade Review*, October 15, 1921; *Young Sherlocks*, directed by Robert F. McGowan and Tom McNamara, 1922 (archive.org); *Lodge Night*, directed by Robert F. McGowan, 1923 (archive.org).

58. *Exhibitor's Herald*, January 29, 1921, December 31, 1921, July 8, 1922, August 12, 1922, October 7, 1922, January 13, 1923, March 22, 1924; *The Film Daily*, February 2, 1921, January 1, 1922, April 30, 1922, August 17, 1922; Rice, "Life after *Birth*," 112, 129, 133, 140, 169–70; *Chicago Tribune*, May 19, 1922, June 17, 1922; *An Eastern Westerner*, directed by Hal Roach, 1920, in *The Harold Lloyd Comedy Collection Vol. 1* (New Line Home Video, 2005, DVD); *Big Stakes*, directed by Clifford S. Elfelt, 1922 (youtube.com).

59. *Variety*, October 10, 1928; *Los Angeles Times*, September 23, 1928; *Life*, November 2, 1928; *New York Times*, October 8, 1928; *Photoplay*, October 1928.

60. Munden, *AFI Catalog*, 567–68; Slide, *American Racist*, 174; Rice, "Life after *Birth*," 140; *Chicago Tribune*, May 16, 1922; *Film Daily*, June 25, 1922; Eyman, *Lion of Hollywood*, 41–42; Greene, *One Clear Call*.

61. *Variety*, June 23, 1922; *New York Times*, June 19, 1922; Rice, "Life after *Birth*," 162–63; *Los Angeles Times*, July 24, 1922; *New Castle News*, November 7, 1922; *Baltimore Afro-American*, November 24, 1922; *Wisconsin Rapids Daily Tribune*, January 17, 1923; *Scandia Journal*, July 26, 1923; *Checotah Times*, March 30, 1923; *New Market Herald*, July 24, 1924.

62. *Port Arthur News*, June 17, 1924, June 22, 1924; *Charleston Gazette*, June 29, 1927; *Port Neches Peoples Press*, July 12, 1929; *The Awakening* playbill, Shubert Belasco Theatre, February 1927, Pamphlet Collection, P3697, Kiplinger Library, Historical Society of Washington, DC; Bradley, *Culture*, 24–25.

63. One of the show's most popular numbers was the recent hit, *Daddy Swiped Our Last Clean Sheet and Joined the Ku Klux Klan*. For more on *Daddy Swiped*, see chapter 7. *Port Arthur News*, May 12, 1924, June 4, 1924, June 8, 1924, June 10, 1924, June 11, 1924, June 16, 1924, June 22, 1924, June 23, 1924, June 26, 1924, June 29, 1924, June 30, 1924.

64. *Norfolk Pilot*, May 3, 1926, May 11, 1926, May 16, 1926; *Roanoke Times*, December 2, 2001; Leidholdt, *Editor for Justice*, 181–82.

65. The D.C. production's official association with the Klan was further enhanced by a playbill that featured photographs of Imperial Wizard Hiram Evans and Imperial Commander Robbie Gill Comer of the Women's Klan (*The Awakening* playbill, Shubert Belasco Theatre, February 1927, Historical Society of Washington).

66. *Washington Post*, February 13, 1927, February 28, 1927, March 20, 1927, March 21, 1927, April 6, 1927; *Fellowship Forum*, March 12, 1927; *Washington Herald*, February 28, 1927; *Charles-*

ton Gazette, June 28, 1927; *The Awakening* playbill, Shubert Belasco Theatre, February 1927, Historical Society of Washington.

67. *Charleston Gazette*, June 18–June 26, 1927, June 28, 1927, June 29, 1927, June 30, 1927, July 2, 1927; *Charleston Daily Mail*, June 30, 1927; Erenberg, *Steppin' Out*, 212, 219–20.

68. *Port Neches Peoples Press*, July 12, 1929.

Chapter Seven

1. *Baltimore Afro-American*, July 25, 1925; *Asbury Park Press*, July 20, 1925.

2. Shaw, *Jazz Age*, vii, 13, 104, 122–23, 134; Tawa, *Serenading*, 1; Mooney, "Music since the 1920s," 68; Mooney, "Songs, Singers, and Society," 225; Doerksen, *American Babel*, 76; Nash, *Nervous Generation*, 94; Nye, *Unembarrassed Muse*, 322–23; Eberly, *Music in the Air*, 4–5; Spaeth, *Popular Music*, xiii; Seldes, *Lively Arts*, 57. See also Fitzgerald, *Tales Of The Jazz Age*.

3. Ogren, *Jazz Revolution*, 3, 7, 139–40, 154; Miller, *Supreme City*, 517.

4. *Smart Set*, December 1919; Mencken, *Prejudices: Fifth Series*, 293.

5. *New York Times*, January 30, 1922, October 8, 1924; Levine, "Jazz and American Culture," 11–12; Abrams, *Selling the Old-Time Religion*, 100; Moore, *Yankee Blues*, 108; Lichtman, *White Protestant Nation*, 20; Ogren, *Jazz Revolution*, 139–40, 153, 157; Fass, *Damned and Beautiful*, 22; Erenberg, *Steppin' Out*, 74; *Ladies' Home Journal*, August 1921, December 1921; Hilmes, *Radio Voices*, 49.

6. *Searchlight*, June 30, 1923; *Fiery Cross*, December 8, 1922; *American Standard*, May 1, 1924, October 15, 1924, November 15, 1924, December 1, 1924; *Sandusky Register*, May 2, 1925; Dickstein, *Dancing in the Dark*, 367.

7. *American Standard*, July 1, 1924, October 15, 1924; *Fiery Cross*, December 8, 1922; *Chicago Tribune*, December 7, 1924; *Time*, November 24, 1924.

8. *Fiery Cross*, February 23, 1923, March 30, 1923; *Fellowship Forum*, March 29, 1924; *New York Times*, October 12, 1924, January 24, 1925; Chalmers, *Hooded Americanism*, 271; Safianow, "Klan Comes to Tipton," 218; Blee, *Women of the Klan*, 85; Minutes, July 25 1928, Women of the Ku Klux Klan, Klan 14 (Chippewa Falls, Wis.) Records, 1926–31, WIHV96-A393, Box 1, Folder 1, Eau Claire Research Center, Wisconsin Historical Society Archives.

9. Spaeth, *Popular Music*, 425; Blom, *Fracture*, 107; Seldes, *Lively Arts*, 96.

10. Eberly, *Music in the Air*, 5–6, 22, 42.

11. McMullen, *Big Top*, 46.

12. A "Kloxology," or religiously tinged song, was usually sung by Klansmen to mark the end of a meeting. A number of these pseudo hymns could be found in the Klan's official handbook, the *Kloran*. United States Congress, House of Representatives, *Hearings on the Klan*, 115; Shotwell, "Public Hatred," 54; Alexander, *Klan in the Southwest*, xxiv, 85; Horowitz, *Inside the Klavern*, 67, 109; Klode Card, Knights of the Ku Klux Klan, Klan No. 51, Mt. Rainier, Maryland Archives, 89–180, Box 1, Folder 3, University of Maryland Libraries; Minutes of the Women's Klan, June 30, 1925, June 22, 1926, June 29, 1926, December 7, 1926, March 15, 1927, August 9, 1927, April 17, 1928, February 12, 1929, Senter Family Papers, WH988, Box 36, Folder 10, Western History Collection, Denver Public Library; *Fiery Cross*, May 25, 1923; *Badger American*, August 1924; *Wisconsin Kourier*, December 19, 1924; *National Kourier*, March 6, 1925; Minutes, April 25 1928, Women of the Ku Klux Klan, Klan 14 (Chippewa Falls, Wis.) Records, 1926–31, WIHV96-A393, Box 1, Folder 1, Eau Claire Research Center, Wisconsin Historical Society Archives.

13. *New York World*, September 22, 1921; *Kokomo Daily Tribune*, September 14, 1923; *Imperial*

Night-Hawk, June 18, 1924; Robert Coughlan, "Konklave in Kokomo," in Leighton, *Aspirin Age*, 109; Jackson, *Klan in the City*, 57; Spaeth, *Popular Music*, 432.

14. *Fiery Cross*, May 25, 1923; *Mexia Daily News*, September 17, 1923; *Call of the North*, September 28, 1923; *The Kluxer*, October 20, 1923; *New York Times*, June 24, 1923, November 11, 1923; *Searchlight*, February 16, 1924; *Fellowship Forum*, August 9, 1924; *Daily Northwestern*, July 17, 1924; *Hutchinson News*, February 23, 1924; *Logansport Pharos Tribune*, July 3, 1924; *Washington Post*, October 8, 1924; *Estherville Enterprise*, August 18, 1926; J. R. Hallitt to Seward Bristow, June 30, 1924, Ku Klux Klan Carlock Unit No. 71 (Carlock, Ill.) Records, Manuscript Collection No. 903, Box 1, Folder 1, Emory University.

15. *Searchlight*, March 22, 1924.

16. Chauncy Oglethorp to Mrs. H. L. Leathers, March 15, 1932, Knights of the Ku Klux Klan, Klan No. 51, Mt. Rainier, Maryland Archives, 89–180, Series 2, Box 1, Folder 1, University of Maryland Libraries; Women's Klan Minutes, March 1, 1927, March 15, 1927, April 19, 1927, November 1, 1927, Senter Family Papers, WH988, Box 36, Folder 10, Western History Collection, Denver Public Library; *Searchlight*, February 24, 1923, August 23, 1924; *Fellowship Forum*, August 9, 1924, September 5, 1925; *Wisconsin Kourier*, December 26, 1924, January 2, 1925, January 9, 1925; *Daily Northwestern*, July 3, 1925; Long, "Western Pennsylvania," 20; Fox, *Everyday Klansfolk*, 104; Horowitz, *Klavern*, 108; Jackson, *Klan in the City*, 100, 121.

17. *Evansville Courier*, June 10, 1922; *Los Angeles Times*, October 7, 1924; *Galveston Daily News*, June 21, 1926; *Baltimore Afro-American*, November 10, 1922, July 11, 1924, August 1, 1925, August 8, 1925, August 14, 1926; *Washington Post*, July 5, 1924; *Pittsburgh Courier*, July 12, 1924; Shults, "Klan in Downey," 165; Tucker, *Dragon and Cross*, 27; Field, *Heavy Breathers*, 160.

18. *Searchlight*, March 29, 1924, June 14, 1924, August 23, 1924; *National Kourier*, March 13, 1925; *Fellowship Forum*, May 17, 1924, July 5, 1924, August 30, 1924, September 20, 1924, March 14, 1925, July 11, 1925, September 18, 1926, December 17, 1927; *Washington Post*, August 9, 1925; *Imperial Night-Hawk*, January 16, 1924, February 27, 1924, May 21, 1924, September 10, 1924; *Dawn*, December 22, 1923, January 12, 1924, January 26, 1924; *Fiery Cross*, December 8, 1922, January 5, 1923, February 16, 1923; *Minnesota Fiery Cross*, May 9, 1924; *Roanoke Times*, December 2, 2001; *Wisconsin Kourier*, February 20, 1925; Fry, *Modern Klan*, 56; Eberly, *Music in the Air*, 25.

19. *Imperial Night-Hawk*, January 16, 1924, July 9, 1924; *Searchlight*, July 5, 1924, July 19, 1924; *Fellowship Forum*, January 20, 1925; *Daily Northwestern*, April 15, 1925, May 13, 1925; *Dawn*, October 6, 1923; *Call of the North*, October 15, 1923; *Manitowoc Herald-News*, July 26, 1924; Jackson, *Klan in the City*, 124; Fox, *Everyday Klansfolk*, 184.

20. *Imperial Night-Hawk*, March 12, 1924, June 11, 1924; *Searchlight*, March 22, 1924; Minutes, July 25, 1928, Women of the Ku Klux Klan, Klan 14 (Chippewa Falls, Wis.) Records, 1926–31, WIHV96-A393, Box 1, Folder 1, Eau Claire Research Center, Wisconsin Historical Society Archives.

21. *Denver Post*, April 15, 1925, April 26, 1925; *Rocky Mountain News*, June 27, 1925; *Dawn*, December 29, 1923, January 19, 1924; *Imperial Night-Hawk*, July 9, 1924; *Decatur Review*, September 8, 1925; Jackson, *Klan in the City*, 219; Goldberg, *Hooded Empire*, 27.

22. *Shreveport Journal*, September 15, 1923; *Call of the North*, September 7, 1923, October 15, 1923; *Imperial Night-Hawk*, July 11, 1923; Coughlan, "Konklave," 110; Wade, *Fiery Cross*, 224; Women of the Ku Klux Klan, *Musiklan*; Truzzi, "Songbag," 34.

23. *Washington Post*, February 23, 1927; Truzzi, "Songbag," 34; Jacobs, "Christian Chorales," 370; Chalmers, *Hooded Americanism*, 96; Shotwell, "Public Hatred," 46; Knights of the Klan, *Second Imperial Klonvokation*, 136; Wight, *American Hymns*, 8, 14.

24. The song also found time to criticize "the greedy Jew" for his "wicked dealings."

25. Shaw, *Jazz Age*, 123; Klamkin, *Old Sheet Music*, 100; Crew, *Klan Sheet Music*, 69, 71, 152, 206; Jacobs, "Co-opting," 370, 372; Wight, "Then I'll Take Off My Mask," 3; Rhinehart, *Red Hot Songs*, 4; Grimes, *Selections*, 20, 22.

26. Crew, *Sheet Music*, 145, 208; Rhinehart, *Red Hot Songs*, 7; Goodwin, *Song Book*, 22; Sullivan, *Our Times*, 455, 457; Klamkin, *Sheet Music*, 106; Shaw, *Jazz Age*, 133–34; Spaeth, *Popular Music*, 436–37.

27. *Badger American*, May 1924; Rhinehart, *Red Hot Songs*, 6; *Parodies by the Queen Quartet*, 12; Crew, *Sheet Music*, 130, 142; Goodwin, *Song Book*, 15.

28. Zterb, "Klansman's Kall"; Metz and Jay, "Ladies of the Ku Klux Klan"; Roy, "American Means the Klan"; Crew, *Sheet Music*, 81, 95, 187, 219.

29. Roy, "They Blame It on the Klan"; Smith, "Fiery Cross on High"; Patterson, "KKK (If Your Heart's True, It Calls to You)"; Crew, *Sheet Music*, 40, 84.

30. Some of the most prolific Klan music publishers included the Fox Music Company of Aurora, Illinois; Akron Music Sales Company of Akron, Ohio; and the Thompson Music Company of Streator, Illinois, which specialized in religiously tinged numbers written by the eponymous owner. Harry F. Windle of Kansas City, Missouri, built a thriving concern on the back of "Mystic City," perhaps the most popular and most widely circulated original Klan number of the decade. Cowritten by John M. Nelson and Noah Tillery, "Mystic City" depicted the "grand and noble" Imperial Wizard as a savior knight and was widely advertised as "the Ku Klux Klan's most beautiful song." While its aesthetic values are debatable, the song was apparently lucrative enough to support widespread sale throughout the 1920s. *Dawn*, April 14, 1923, June 2, 1923, July 14, 1923, September 29, 1923; *Fiery Cross*, March 9, 1923, April 27, 1923, May 11, 1923; Nelson and Tillery, "Mystic City" ; McMahon et al., "We Are All Loyal Klansmen"; Thompson, "Call of a Klansman"; Thompson, "Coming of the Klan"; Crew, *Sheet Music*, 57–61.

31. *Fiery Cross*, December 8, 1922, May 25, 1923; *Williamsport Pioneer*, August 5, 1921; *Franklin Evening Star*, August 22, 1923; *Fellowship Forum*, October 6, 1923, December 15, 1923, July 12, 1924, September 27, 1924; *Minnesota Fiery Cross*, May 9, 1924; *Danville Bee*, July 31, 1924; *Joplin Globe*, August 17, 1924; *Kokomo Daily Tribune*, April 30, 1925; *Dawn*, March 31, 1924; *Badger American*, January 1924, October 1923; Jackson, *Klan in the City*, 148, 164; Blee, *Women of the Klan*; Akin, "Klan in Georgia," 131; Undated Note, Senter Family Papers, WH988, Box 36, Folder 12, Western History Collection, Denver Public Library; Douglas, *Listening In*, 91.

32. *Fellowship Forum*, December 6, 1924, March 21, 1925; *Connellsville Daily Courier*, July 5, 1924, September 2, 1924, October 30, 1924; *McKean County Democrat*, May 26, 1938; *Sandusky Star-Journal*, January 18, 1924; *National Kourier*, May 16, 1925; Wight, *American Hymns*; Lutz, *Catalogue*.

33. Shaw, *Jazz Age*, 12–13, 108–9; Klamkin, *Sheet Music*, 85, 114–15; Sanjeks, *Popular Music Business*, 7, 12, 16; Nye, *Unembarrassed Muse*, 322–23.

34. Jackson, *Klan in the City*, 139; Weaver, "Klan in Wisconsin," 274; *Daily Northwestern*, July 17, 1924; *Wisconsin Kourier*, February 6, 1925; *Fellowship Forum*, June 18, 1927; *Detroit News*, January 25, 1930.

35. Kennedy, *Jelly Roll*, xxi–xxii, 21–23, 28, 35–36; Sutton, *American Record*, 326; Collier, *Louis Armstrong*, 104; Kennedy and McNutt, *Little Labels*, 2–18.

36. As Kennedy notes, Sears executives were aware before signing with Gennett that the record label was used by Klansmen, but that fact does not appear to have dissuaded the company (Kennedy, *Jelly Roll*, 166–67).

37. Kennedy, *Jelly Roll*, 38–41, 166–67; Sutton, *Record Labels*, 327–28; Oliver, *Yonder Come the Blues*, 158.

38. Kennedy, *Jelly Roll*, 40; *Frederick Evening Post*, October 30, 1912; Rhinehart, *Red Hot Songs*, 5; Crew, *Sheet Music*.

39. The song exhorted listeners to join the Klan's "army for the right and all against the wrong" (Seale and Pace, "Wake Up America!").

40. Lena, *Banding Together*, 201; Tosches, *Country*, 215; Sutton, *Record Labels*, 71, 112, 178–79, 215, 321, 327; Kennedy, *Jelly Roll*, 37–38; *Fellowship Forum*, May 17, 1924; Carroll Van West, "James D. Vaughan," *The Tennessee Encyclopedia of History and Culture*, tennesseeencyclopedia .net, accessed February 28, 2011.

41. *Fiery Cross*, May 25, 1923; *Fellowship Forum*, February 9, 1924; *Indianapolis Star*, December 6, 1924; *Danville Bee*, July 31, 1924; *Joplin Globe*, August 17, 1924; *Kokomo Daily Tribune*, April 30, 1925; Lutz, *Catalogue*; Wight, *American Hymns*.

42. Shaw, *Jazz Age*, 104, 106, 123; Crew, *Sheet Music*, 24; Coslow and Friedman, "Bunch of Klucks"; *Billboard*, December 3, 1921; *Talking Machine World*, October 15, 1921.

43. Coslow and Friedman, "Bunch of Klucks"; Frisch and Grossman, "Ku Ku"; Laird and Rust, *OKeh Records*, 196–97; Bradley, *Culture*, 162.

44. *Fellowship Forum*, March 8, 1924, May 17, 1924, December 20, 1924; *Baltimore Afro-American*, April 18, 1924; *Lawrence Daily Journal-World*, January 29, 1927, January 20, 1964; *Charleston Gazette*, June 29, 1927; *Garden City Telegram*, September 8, 1965; *Port Arthur News*, June 22, 1924; Marcell and Hedges, "Daddy Swiped Our Last Clean Sheet."

45. Bradley, *Culture*, 37; Ely, *Amos 'n' Andy*, 45; Stokes, *Birth*, 140–41; Stephanie Dunson, "Black Misrepresentation in Sheet Music Illustration," in Brundage, *Beyond Blackface*, 45; Susan Curtis, "Black Creativity and Black Stereotype," in Brundage, *Beyond Blackface*, 137.

46. Lewis, "Those Dog-Gone Ku-Klux Blues"; Hopper, "Before Them Klu Klux Pages Me"; Ownby, "De Ku Klux Gwine to Git You"; Newton and Cox, "Ku Klux Klan Blues"; Arthur and Barbay, "Those Good Old Ku Klux Blues"; Crew, *Sheet Music*, 30–31, 35, 39, 47; Taylor and Austen, *Darkest America*, 206.

47. Mars and Krause, "Ku Klux Blues"; *Billboard*, August 27, 1921, September 24, 1921, February 18, 1922; *Thomasville Daily Times-Enterprise*, December 7, 1912.

48. *Sylacauga Advance*, May 10–13, 1925; *Fellowship Forum*, October 29, 1927, November 19, 1927; Greenaway, "Country-Western," 35; Huber, *Linthead Stomp*, 65; Feldman, *Klan in Alabama*, 28.

49. Huber, *Linthead*, 56, 59, 61, 71; James C. Cobb, "Country Music and the 'Southernization' of America," in Lewis, *All That Glitters*, 76.

50. Huber, *Linthead*, 84–86, 92; Wiggins, *Fiddlin' Georgia Crazy*, 112, 114; Cobb, "Country Music," 76.

51. Huber, *Linthead*, 74–77, 82; Shaw, *Jazz Age*, 135–36; Green, "Hillbilly Music," 205, 206, 208–9, 210, 211.

52. Greenaway, "Country-Western," 35; Huber, *Linthead*, 61.

53. Cox, *Bowman*, 38; Bristol (VA-TN) *Herald-Courier*, May 12, 1925.

54. Bristol (VA-TN) *Herald-Courier*, May 12, 1925; Cox, *Bowman*, 38–40; Roland, *Country Music Annual 2001*, 160; Wilson, Liner Notes, *Fiddlers' Convention*.

55. Wilson, Liner Notes, *Fiddlers' Convention*; Cox, *Bowman*, 35, 37, 42, 49, 51, 68; Green, "Hillbilly," 213–14.

Chapter Eight

1. Smith, *Glory*, 41, 63, 74–81; Paper, *Empire*, 26; Miller, *Supreme City*, 310–11.

2. Rudel, *Hello Everybody*, 178–79; Sterling and Kittross, *Stay Tuned*, 65–67, 87, 91; Craig, *Fireside Politics*, xi, 10; Head, *Broadcasting in America*, 107–8; Kyvig, *Daily Life*, 71; Hart, *Popular Book*, 228; Eberly, *Music in the Air*, 34; Roscigno and Danaher, *Voice of Southern Labor*, 26–27; Razlogova, *Listener's Voice*, 15, 22; Douglas, *Listening In*, 77; *New York Times*, May 13, 1928.

3. Kyvig, *Daily Life*, 71, 90; Hilmes, *Radio Voices*, 6–7, 34–35; Douglas, *Listening In*, 25, 29; McLuhan, *Understanding Media*, 263–64.

4. Kyvig, *Daily Life*, 71, 90.

5. Craig, *Fireside Politics*, 5, 9; Sterling, *Stay Tuned*, 66–67, 69.

6. *Ottawa Citizen*, July 11, 1931; Miller, *Supreme City*, 325; Eberly, *Music in the Air*, 13, 17; Razlogova, *Listener's Voice*, 20.

7. *Imperial Night-Hawk*, July 30, 1924; *Fellowship Forum*, August 4, 1923; *Kourier Magazine*, March 1927; *Birmingham News*, September 3, 1926; *Birmingham Age-Herald*, September 3, 1926; *Roanoke Times*, December 2, 2001; *Norfolk Pilot*, March 19, 1926; *Denver Post*, June 25, 1925; *Rocky Mountain News*, June 27, 1925; Feldman, *Klan in Alabama*, 85; Snell, "Masked Men," 220; Goldberg, *Hooded Empire*, 97.

8. *Washington Post*, April 13, 1924, April 15, 1924; *Massillon Evening Independent*, April 15, 1924; *Minnesota Fiery Cross*, March 7, 1924, March 14, 1924; *Searchlight*, March 15, 1924; *Wisconsin Kourier*, February 6, 1925; *Shreveport Journal*, February 26, 1929; *Joplin Globe*, August 14, 1925, October 3, 1926; *Joplin News Herald*, August 15, 1925; *Fellowship Forum*, September 5, 1925, June 5, 1926; *Kourier Magazine*, August 1926; *Imperial Night-Hawk*, June 4, 1924; *Chicago Tribune*, October 26, 1924; Barnouw, *Tower in Babel*, 102.

9. *Fayetteville Daily Democrat*, February 8, 1923; *Imperial Night-Hawk*, May 16, 1923; *New York Times*, December 31, 1923; Shotwell, "Public Hatred," 110; *Radio Digest*, May 26, 1923.

10. Rudel, *Hello Everybody!* 10, 69, 79, 82, 85; Sterling, *Stay Tuned*, 146.

11. *Wisconsin Kourier*, February 27, 1925; *National Kourier*, March 13, 1925.

12. *Emporia Daily Gazette*, March 3, 1925; *National Kourier*, March 13, 1925; *Kourier Magazine*, April 1925; Bensman, *Broadcast Regulation*, 124.

13. *Fellowship Forum*, May 19, 1923, May 15, 1924; *Kourier Magazine*, April 1929, May 1929; *American Standard*, October 1, 1925; *Kolorado Klan Kourier*, undated clipping, Senter Family Papers, WH988, Box 36, Folder 18, Western History Collection, Denver Public Library.

14. *Kourier Magazine*, February 1929, June 1929; *American Standard*, October 1, 1925; March 1930 Realm Bulletin by Great Klaliff of Province 2, Women of the Ku Klux Klan, Klan 14 (Chippewa Falls, Wis.) Records, 1926–31, WIHV96-A393, Box 1, Folder 3, Eau Claire Research Center, Wisconsin Historical Society Archives.

15. *Wisconsin Kourier*, January 16, 1925; *Searchlight*, June 10, 1922, December 8, 1922; Fox, *Everyday Klansfolk*, 144.

16. Stetson also claimed that she was immortal and encouraged followers to prepare for Mary Baker Eddy's resurrection.

17. Jaker et al., *Airwaves of New York*, 79–80; Doerksen, *American Babel*, 57–59; Hilmes, *Radio Voices*, 17.

18. Ford himself would be dismissed from jury service late in 1926 because of his prejudiced views, and his name struck from the state's list of potential jurors. Ford appealed this decision to the Appellate Division of the New York Supreme Court, which reinstated him as a potential juror. The court's unanimous decision argued that individuals "can not be removed from the jury

list merely because of bigotry that runs counter to the fundamentals of religious toleration and freedom" (Jaker et al., *Airwaves of New York*, 80; Craig, *Fireside Politics*, 75; Doerksen, *American Babel*, 60, 62, 64–65, 66; *The Sign*, September 1926; *New York Herald Tribune*, August 26, 1926; *New York Times*, December 16, 1926, April 11, 1927, April 17, 1927; *Ogden Standard-Examiner*, December 16, 1926; *Time*, April 12, 1927).

19. *New York Times*, December 16, 1926, December 27, 1926; *Ogden Standard-Examiner*, December 16, 1926; *Fellowship Forum*, April 16, 1927, May 14, 1927, May 28, 1927, June 11, 1927, July 30, 1927.

20. *New York Times*, July 7, 1927, August 12, 1927; *Fellowship Forum*, August 20, 1927, January 7, 1928; Winter, *What Price Tolerance*, 53, 57–58, 60.

21. *Fellowship Forum*, October 23, 1926; *Kourier Magazine*, February 1929, June 1929.

22. *Fellowship Forum*, December 22, 1923, January 19, 1924, March 8, 1924; Rudel, *Hello Everybody!* 178–79; Sterling, *Stay Tuned*, 138; Hangen, *Redeeming the Dial*, 21–25; Himes, *Radio Voices*, 68, 83.

23. Rudel, *Hello Everybody!* 63–64, 165; Head, *Broadcasting*, 108, 116; Sterling, *Stay Tuned*, 71.

24. *Oakland Tribune*, July 5, 1925; *Washington Evening Star*, July 5, 1925; *Broad Ax*, July 11, 1925; *Baltimore Afro-American*, July 11, 1925.

25. *New York Times*, February 26, 1925, June 20, 1926; *Iowa Broadcaster*, February 24, 1927; Neymeyer, "Full Light of Day," 59.

26. Rudel, *Hello Everybody!* 63–64, 165; Sterling, *Stay Tuned*, 116; Hilmes, *Radio Voices*, 68–69, 83.

27. *Fellowship Forum*, April 10, 1926, April 17, 1926, April 24, 1926.

28. *Fellowship Forum*, May 8, 1926, May 22, 1926; Minutes, September 7, 1927, Women of the Ku Klux Klan, Klan 14 (Chippewa Falls, Wis.) Records, 1926–31, WIHV96-A393, Box 1, Folder 1, Eau Claire Research Center, Wisconsin Historical Society Archives.

29. *Fellowship Forum*, May 15, 1926, July 3, 1926.

30. *Fellowship Forum*, July 31, 1926, August 21, 1926, October 9, 1926, October 23, 1926, October 30, 1926, January 29, 1927, April 30, 1927, May 21, 1927, June 18, 1927; *Washington Post*, January 29, 1927; *Chicago Tribune*, January 29, 1927; *Chicago Defender*, February 5, 1927, February 26, 1927.

31. *Fellowship Forum*, June 18, 1927; *Los Angeles Times*, June 28, 1927; *Chicago Tribune*, June 28, 1927; *Washington Post*, June 28, 1927; Craig, *Fireside Politics*, 56.

32. Hilmes, *Radio Voices*, 7–9; Craig, *Fireside Politics*, 60, 66–67, 71–74; Rudel, *Hello Everybody!* 102–3, 257, 261; Head, *Broadcasting*, 132; Sterling, *Stay Tuned*, 115, 141–44; Roscigno and Danaher, *Southern Labor*, 21, 24.

33. Rudel, *Hello Everybody!* 261; *Los Angeles Times*, June 28, 1927; *New York Times*, June 29, 1927; *Danville Bee*, June 29, 1927; *Southwest Times*, June 29, 1927; Douglas, *Listening In*, 91–92.

34. W. E. Downey to Baltimore Supervisor of Radio, April 21, 1927, WJSV File, Box 457, Radio Division: Correspondence Relating to Applications for Broadcast Station Licenses, 1928–32: WJMS to WJZ, Records of the Federal Communications Commission, Record Group 173, National Archives at College Park, MD; W. D. Terrell to Baltimore Supervisor of Radio, April 28, 1927, WJSV File, Box 457, Radio Division: Applications for Broadcast Station Licenses, 1928–32, RG 173, NACP.

35. G. E. Sterling, Acting Supervisor of Radio, Baltimore, to Department of Commerce, Radio Division, April 19, 1927, WJSV File, Box 457, Radio Division: License Applications, 1928–32, RG 173, NACP.

36. G.E. Sterling, Acting Supervisor of Radio, Baltimore, to Department of Commerce, Radio Division, April 19 1927, WJSV File, Box 457, Radio Division: Applications for Broadcast Station Licenses, 1928-32, RG 173, NACP; G. E. Sterling, Acting Supervisor of Radio, Baltimore, to Department of Commerce, Radio Division, May 4, 1927, WJSV File, Box 457, Radio Division: Applications for Broadcast Station Licenses, 1928-32, RG 173, NACP; Roscigno and Danaher, *Southern Labor*, 24; Razlogova, *Listener's Voice*, 34.

37. *New York Times*, June 29, 1927; *Fellowship Forum*, July 2, 1927; Charles I. Stengle to Federal Radio Commission, July 20, 1927, WJSV File, Box 457, Radio Division: Applications for Broadcast Station Licenses, 1928-32, RG 173, NACP; Richard Weber to Federal Radio Commission, July 21 1927, WJSV File, Box 457, Radio Division: Applications for Broadcast Station Licenses, 1928-32, RG 173, NACP.

38. Application for Radio Station License, July 22, 1927, WJSV File, Box 457, Radio Division: Applications for Broadcast Station Licenses, 1928-32, RG 173, NACP; Application for Radio Station Construction/Removal Permit, July 22, 1927, WJSV File, Box 457, Radio Division: Applications for Broadcast Station Licenses, 1928-32, RG 173, NACP; James S. Vance to R. Y. Cadmus, July 23, 1927, WJSV File, Box 457, Radio Division: Applications for Broadcast Station Licenses, 1928-32, RG 173, NACP.

39. G. E. Sterling to Department of Commerce, Radio Division, July 26 1927, WJSV File, Box 457, Radio Division: Applications for Broadcast Station Licenses, 1928-32, RG 173, NACP; W. D. Terrell to Baltimore Supervisor of Radio, July 27, 1927, WJSV File, Box 457, Radio Division: Applications for Broadcast Station Licenses, 1928-32, RG 173, NACP; *Fellowship Forum*, August 20, 1927; Gonzalez and Torres, *News for All the People*, 204-6; Doerksen, *American Babel*, 126.

40. *Fellowship Forum*, August 6, 1927, August 13, 1927; *New York Times*, July 27, 1927, August 3, 1927; *Southwest Times*, July 29, 1927; *Washington Post*, August 1, 1927, August 3, 1927.

41. Based on analysis of donation lists published in the *Fellowship Forum*, May 1, 1926-June 18, 1927.

42. *Sandusky Star-Journal*, October 1, 1927; *Kokomo Daily Tribune*, October 1, 1927; *Manitowoc Herald-News*, October 3, 1927; *New York Times*, October 9, 1927, October 28, 1927; *Washington Post*, October 9, 1927; *Fellowship Forum*, August 27, 1927, October 8, 1927, October 15, 1927, October 22, 1927; *Chicago Tribune*, October 23, 1927.

43. O. H. Caldwell to Independent Publishing Co., November 22, 1927, WJSV File, Box 457, Radio Division: Applications for Broadcast Station Licenses, 1928-32, RG 173, NACP; *New York Times*, November 23, 1927; *Fellowship Forum*, November 26, 1927, December 3, 1927, December 17, 1927; *Washington Post*, December 19, 1927, January 1, 1928; *Kourier Magazine*, January 1928.

44. The three most powerful stations—KDKA of Pittsburgh, WGY of Schenectady, and WEAF of New York City—operated on 50,000 watts. WJZ, also of New York City, transmitted at 15,000 (*Washington Evening Star*, January 1, 1928; *Fellowship Forum*, January 1, 1928, January 7, 1928, March 24, 1928; *Kourier Magazine*, February 1928; *Washington Post*, September 23, 1928; Hilmes, *Radio Voices*, 7).

45. *Washington Evening Star*, January 1, 1928; Application for Renewal of Radio Broadcasting Station License, January 10 1928, WJSV File, Box 457, Radio Division: Applications for Broadcast Station Licenses, 1928-32, RG 173, NACP.

46. Miller, *Supreme City*, 317; Eberly, *Music in the Air*, 13, 17, 23-24; Razlogova, *Listener's Voice*, 20.

47. It seems that the first politician to take advantage of WTFF's power boost was Congressman Albert Johnson (R-Washington), a Klan favorite and cosponsor of the 1924 Immigration Restriction Act. He was followed in short measure by Congressmen Charles Brand (R-Ohio), Robert A. Green (D-Florida), John McSwain (D-South Carolina), Morgan Sanders (D-Texas), Alfred Bulwinkle (D-North Carolina), James Strong (R-Kansas), and Gale Stalker (R-New York). *Washington Post*, December 21, 1927; *Fellowship Forum*, October 15, 1927, February 4, 1928, March 3, 1928.

48. *Washington Post*, December 19, 1927, March 18, 1928; *Fellowship Forum*, January 14, 1928, March 10, 1928, April 14, 1928, June 9, 1928; *Kourier Magazine*, January 1928, February 1928.

49. Rudel, *Hello Everybody!* 202, 218; Sterling, *Stay Tuned*, 71, 75, 79, 80, 82–83, 86, 128; Craig, *Fireside Politics*, 19, 24.

50. Bradley, *Culture*, 184; Craig, *Fireside Politics*, 29–30.

51. Craig, *Fireside Politics*, 29; Bradley, *Culture*, 184; *Fellowship Forum*, April 14, 1928.

52. James S. Vance to Federal Radio Commission, October 29, 1928, WJSV File, Box 457, Radio Division: Applications for Broadcast Station Licenses, 1928–32, RG 173, NACP; W. D. Terrell to James S. Vance, October 29, 1928, WJSV File, Box 457, Radio Division: Applications for Broadcast Station Licenses, 1928–32, RG 173, NACP; *Washington Post*, November 9, 1928.

53. *Kourier Magazine*, November 1928; *New York Times*, November 18, 1928; Program for Radio Station WJSV, October 11, 1930, WJSV File, Box 457, Radio Division: Applications for Broadcast Station Licenses, 1928–32, RG 173, NACP; James S. Vance to Federal Radio Commission, December 23, 1931, WJSV File, Box 457, Radio Division: Applications for Broadcast Station Licenses, 1928–32, RG 173, NACP.

54. *Washington Post*, April 15, 1929, January 3, 1935, December 24, 1938; Application for Radio Broadcast Station Construction Permit or Modification Thereof, May 10, 1932, WJSV File, Box 457, Radio Division: Applications for Broadcast Station Licenses, 1928–32, RG 173, NACP; Application for Consent to Assignment of License, n.d., Docket No. 1656, WJSV File, Box 457, Radio Division: Applications for Broadcast Station Licenses, 1928–32, RG 173, NACP; Gonzalez, *News*, 207; Doerksen, *American Babel*, 127; Miller, *Supreme City*, 324–26.

55. Miller, *Supreme City*, 325; Eberly, *Music in the Air*, 22; Razlogova, *Listener's Voice*, 75–77; Hilmes, *Radio Voices*, 6, 32, 46, 67, 79–80, 85–86; Ely, *Amos 'n' Andy*, 4, 60; Taylor and Austen, *Darkest America*, 145–46, 150.

Chapter Nine

1. Historian Bruce Evensen estimates that eight hundred newspaper correspondents filed over two million words on the fight (Evensen, *Dempsey*, x).

2. Lang, *Prize-Fighting*, 60–61, 69; Kaye, *Pussycat of Prizefighting*, 51; Evensen, *Dempsey*, ix–xi; Miller, *Supreme City*, 403–4, 419–21.

3. Bohn, *Ballyhoo*, 11; Lang, *Prize-Fighting*, 49, 53–54; Rodriguez, *Regulation of Boxing*, 35; Bodner, *Jewish Sport*, 9.

4. *American Standard*, April 1, 1925; *Washington Post*, September 20, 1923; *Imperial Night-Hawk*, January 30, 1924.

5. Bodner, *Jewish Sport*, 1, 7, 9; Levine, *Ellis Island*, 144–45, 153–54; Steven Riess, "Tough Jews," in Riess, *Sports and the American Jew*, 65–75; *American Standard*, April 1, 1925.

6. Lindsay, *Boxing in Black and White*, 5, 7–8, 11–15.

7. Kaye, *Pussycat of Prizefighting*, 50; *The Crisis*, August 1914; Ward, *Unforgivable Blackness*, 381; Runstedtler, *Jack Johnson*, 110.

8. Lang, *Prize-Fighting*, 52–53; *Fiery Cross*, July 6, 1923.

9. *Searchlight*, September 27, 1924, October 11, 1924, November 8, 1924; *Wisconsin Kourier*, February 13, 1925.

10. The impetus for organizing the event remains unclear, although the fact that the organizer, Dale Deane, was the manager of a local tobacco and candy interest suggests that a financial motive cannot be ruled out.

11. *Denver Post*, January 15–29, 1925; *Rocky Mountain News*, January 14, 1925, June 27, 1925; *Fourteenth Census of the United States*, 1920; Goldberg, *Hooded Empire*, 97; Jackson, *Klan in the City*, 230.

12. *Denver Post*, January 18, 1925, January 23, 1925.

13. For the most detailed history of the Herrin riots, see Angle, *Bloody Williamson*. Lisa McGirr adds valuable context to the incident in *War on Alcohol*.

14. *Denver Post*, January 25, 1925.

15. After a series of serious setbacks in the state, Imperial Wizard Evans demanded the resignation of Grand Dragon John Galen Locke in June 1925. Locke organized a new society, the Minute Men of America, and seceded from the Invisible Empire with a significant proportion of the state's Klansmen, leaving Colorado's Klan in turmoil (*Denver Post*, January 15–29, 1925, January 6, 1926; Chalmers, *Hooded Americanism*, 130; Laugen, *Gospel of Progressivism*, n.p.; Goldberg, *Hooded Empire*, 97, 105–9).

16. Johnson detailed the meeting in a 1927 autobiography. No other sources could be found to corroborate his account (Johnson, *Jack Johnson*, 245).

17. *Literary Digest*, December 2, 1922; Gems et al., *Sports in American History*, 229; Bohn, *Ballyhoo*, 5, 11; Lynd and Lynd, *Middletown*, 284; Price, *Rounding the Bases*, 110, 113; Riess, *Touching Base*, 15; Brazil, "Murder Trials," 165; Gorn and Goldstein, *American Sports*, 188–90; Kyvig, *Daily Life*, 158; Miller, *Supreme City*, 377; Nash, *Nervous Generation*, 128–30; Mencken, *Days Trilogy*, 427, 677–78.

18. Lieb, *Baseball*, 57–58; Jenkinson, *Ultimate Power*, 202–3; Holmes, *Cobb*, 39; Ackmann, *Curveball*, 31; Gay, *Speaker*, 35; Alexander, *Hornsby*, 146–47; *Los Angeles Times*, January 3, 1929; *New York Times*, January 3, 1929; *Searchlight*, October 18, 1924.

19. Levine, *Ellis Island*, 25; Pope, *Patriotic Games*, 17; Alpert, *Left Field*, 6–7.

20. *Lewiston Daily Sun*, January 1, 1925; *Colorado Springs Gazette*, July 19, 1925, July 20, 1925; *Los Angeles Times*, July 19, 1925; "Ralph de Palma," *American National Biography Online*; *The Kluxer*, October 20, 1923; *Lubbock Avalanche*, October 27, 1922; Nash, *Nervous Generation*, 129. For the best account of the Notre Dame riot, see Tucker, *Notre Dame vs. the Klan*.

21. Levine, *Ellis Island*, 27, 38; Hoose, *Hoosiers*, 38, 44; Grundman, *Amateur Basketball*, 1; *Wisconsin Kourier*, December 5, 1924, December 12, 1924; *Fellowship Forum*, February 27, 1926.

22. Moore, *Citizen Klansman*, 101; *Logansport Morning Press*, April 3, 1924, April 9, 1924; *Kokomo Daily Tribune*, March 28, 1924, April 3, 1924.

23. *Logansport Pharos-Tribune*, April 3, 1924, April 7, 1924; *Logansport Morning Press*, April 9, 1924; *Wisconsin Kourier*, December 12, 1924, January 16, 1925, January 30, 1925, February 6, 1925, February 13, 1925, March 20, 1925; *National Kourier*, May 16, 1925.

24. *Logansport Morning Press*, April 9, 1924; *National Kourier*, May 16, 1925; *Kokomo Daily Tribune*, December 29, 1924.

25. *Xenia Evening Gazette*, February 23, 1926, March 1, 1926; *Lima Sunday News*, April 3, 1927.

26. *Xenia Evening Gazette*, February 23, 1926, March 1, 1926, March 10, 1927.

27. Lynd and Lynd, *Middletown*, 485.

28. The Christian Israelites were on a mission to gather the lost tribes of Israel in preparation for the Millennium.

29. Levine, *Ellis Island*, 17; Price, *Rounding*, 46–47, 58, 66–67; Riess, *Touching Base*, 233; Kimball, *Sports in Zion*, 12; Gurock, *Judaism's Encounter*, 17. See also Riess, *Sports and the American Jew*; Mormino, "Playing Fields of St. Louis."

30. *New York Times*, February 7, 1924; *Chicago Tribune*, April 2, 1925; *Chicago Defender*, February 17, 1923; *The Messenger*, October 1923; *Imperial Night-Hawk*, April 4, 1923.

31. Jenkins, *Steel Valley Klan*, 106; *Massillon Evening Independent*, July 12, 1924; *Steubenville Herald-Star*, July 12, 1924.

32. Johnson, a native of Youngstown, was a second baseman in the Negro Leagues, having played for the New York Lincoln Stars and the Cleveland Tate Stars (seamheads.com/NegroLgs).

33. *Chicago Defender*, July 13, 1924; *Charleston Daily Mail*, July 13, 1924; *Milford Mail*, July 17, 1924; *Youngstown Citizen*, July 19, 1924.

34. *Port Arthur News*, March 10, 1925, March 13, 1925; *Lubbock Morning Avalanche*, March 7, 1925; *Mexia Weekly Herald*, March 27, 1925; *Hutchinson News*, March 6, 1925; *Mexia Daily News*, March 5, 1925; *San Antonio Light*, March 23, 1925.

35. *Sterling Daily Gazette*, July 16, 1925, August 3, 1925, August 22, 1925; *Chicago Tribune*, July 16, 1925; *Baltimore Afro-American*, July 25, 1925.

36. Pendleton, "Jim Crow," 93–94; Carroll, "Beating the Klan," 51.

37. *Wichita Beacon*, June 21, 1925, June 23, 1925; Pendleton, "Jim Crow," 94; Carroll, "Beating the Klan," 53–55.

38. Carroll, "Beating the Klan," 55; Pendleton, "Jim Crow," 151; Jenkins, *Steel Valley Klan*, 106.

39. Pendleton, "Jim Crow," 94–95; Carroll, "Beating the Klan," 57.

40. Price, *Rounding*, 110, 113; Morris R. Cohen, "Baseball as National Religion," in Schneider, *Religion, Culture and Society*, 36–38; Riess, *Touching Base*, 15; *Atlanta Constitution*, April 20, 1924.

41. *Fiery Cross*, March 30, 1923; *Imperial Night-Hawk*, April 4, 1923.

42. *Port Arthur News*, April 13, 1924; *Altoona Mirror*, April 15, 1924; *Bakersfield Californian*, April 15, 1924; *Portsmouth Herald*, April 16, 1924; *Wisconsin State Journal*, April 16, 1924; *Steubenville Herald Star*, May 1, 1924; *Grand Prairie Texan*, May 23, 1924; *American Mercury*, June 1925.

43. *Atlanta Constitution*, April 20, 1924, June 15, 1924, June 21, 1924.

44. During Evans's struggle with William Joseph Simmons for control of the Klan a year earlier, McKinnon and the Klan's cashier, N. M. Furney, had absconded with a significant amount of cash and bonds (allegedly more than one hundred thousand dollars) from the Imperial palace to keep them out of Simmons's hands. In late 1923, McKinnon took the lead in orchestrating the successful defense of the Klansmen accused of murder in Mer Rouge, Louisiana (*Bradford Era*, April 6, 1923; *Portsmouth Daily Times*, April 7, 1923; *Helena Daily Independent*, October 31, 1923).

45. *Atlanta Constitution*, April 20, 1924, June 21, 1924, July 10, 1924, July 31, 1924.

46. *Edwardsville Intelligencer*, July 1, 1924.

47. Those memories were apparently not pleasant enough to spur the Atlanta Klan to field a team during the 1925 season. In 1926, a Klan team did compete intermittently, but it was not the same. No longer the powerhouse of the Dixie League, the Klan now found itself vying with the team fielded by local company Coca-Cola to keep from ending in last place (*Atlanta Constitution*, August 10, 1924, October 11, 1924, April 26, 1926; Jackson, *Klan in the City*, 41; *Searchlight*, October 11, 1924, October 18, 1924).

48. *Los Angeles Times*, August 17, 1924, August 18, 1924, September 6, 1924, September 23, 1924.

49. *Los Angeles Times*, November 2, 1924, January 5, 1925.

50. Moore, *Citizen Klansman*, 20–21; Wade, *Fiery Cross*, 178–79; Chalmers, *Hooded Americanism*, 110.

51. *Los Angeles Times*, October 16, 1924, October 19, 1924.

52. Unfortunately, no record can be found of the game's result in the *Los Angeles Times*, the *Los Angeles Examiner*, or in the *B'nai B'rith Magazine* (which did not mention this charity series at all). Both Klan No. 1 and No. 3 continued to field teams until the end of the season in February 1925, but the weakened Los Angeles Klan chose not to field a team the next year (*Los Angeles Times*, October 16, 1924, October 19, 1924).

53. It remains unclear why a Klan member was attending historically Catholic Georgetown University, as well as whether Georgetown was aware of Hines's affiliations.

54. *Washington Evening Star*, May 9, 1926.

55. *Washington Post*, June 22, 1926, July 4, 1926, September 21, 1926, September 27, 1926, May 29, 1927, July 3, 1927, September 17, 1927; *Washington Evening Star*, July 13, 1926, October 1, 1926, May 17, 1927, June 5, 1927, June 27, 1927, August 16, 1927, September 16, 1927, October 4, 1927; October 9, 1927; *Fourteenth Census of the United States*, 1920; *Fifteenth Census of the United States*, 1930; Jackson, *Klan in the City*, 179–80; Chalmers, *Hooded Americanism*, 285–90; Wade, *Fiery Cross*, 249–50.

56. McMullen, *Big Top*, 135.

57. Membership in the Capital Klan peaked in early 1925, and began a rapid decline in late 1926. By 1930, there were estimated to be only 124 Klansmen left in the District of Columbia. In something of an upset, the Mechanics also beat the heavily tipped Klan team in 1927, five to three. *Washington Post*, May 2, 1926, July 21, 1926, July 28, 1926, August 1, 1926, August 18, 1927, August 21, 1927, November 2, 1930; *Washington Evening Star*, August 1, 1926, August 21, 1927; 1927 Klan Charity Benefit Baseball Game Booklet, Knights of the Ku Klux Klan, Klan No. 51, Mt. Rainier, Maryland Archives, 89–180, Series 3, Box 1, Folder 1, University of Maryland Libraries; Jackson, *Klan in the City*, 239; Chalmers, *Hooded Americanism*, 240.

58. The Klan's originally scheduled opponents, the Rialtos (another all-Jewish team that had recently won the D.C. Jewish Championship), had canceled, unable to muster the requisite number of players over the Labor Day weekend. Dreyfus, who played for the Rialtos in the Capital City League and the Hebrews in the independent unlimited championship, had called upon his All-Star teammates to step in as last-minute replacements.

59. Although this was the Klan's only game against either the Rialtos or the Hebrew All-Stars, it faced several of the same Jewish players in other matches: Dreyfus also played for, and later managed, the Dreadnaughts; the Sauber brothers rotated around a number of different teams; and Sam Simon pitched against the Klan again for the Alexandria Busmen (*Washington Post*, July 15, 1926; September 1, 1926, September 7, 1926, June 5, 1927; *Washington Evening Star*, September 7, 1926).

60. *Washington Evening Star*, September 15, 1926; September 16, 1926; *Washington Post*, June 5, 1927, June 6, 1927, July 14, 1927.

61. 1927 Klan Charity Benefit Baseball Game Booklet, Knights of the Ku Klux Klan, Klan No. 51, Mt. Rainier, Maryland Archives, 89–180, Series 3, Box 1, Folder 1, University of Maryland Libraries; *Washington Star*, August 1, 1926; Mecklin, *Ku Klux Klan*, 239; Lay, *Hooded Knights*, 56.

62. Mecklin, *Ku Klux Klan*, 82, 109, 233–34.

63. *Washington Post*, October 4, 1926, September 11, 1927; *Washington Evening Star*, July 4, 1926, June 16, 1927; "Texon Oilers," *Handbook of Texas Online*, tshaonline.org, accessed February 3, 2012; Flanigan, *History of Gwinnett County*, 172–74; *Searchlight*, October 18, 1924; *Marion Daily Star*, April 5, 1923; Knights of the Klan, *Second Imperial Klonvokation*, 211–13.

Epilogue

1. *Garden City Telegram*, September 8, 1965; *New York Times*, May 1, 1957; *Port Arthur News*, June 8, 1947.

2. Bowers, *Superman*, 134–37; "Clan of the Fiery Cross," *The Adventures of Superman*, Mutual Network, June 10–July 1, 1946.

3. Bowers, *Superman*, 141.

4. Levitt and Dubner, *Freakonomics*, 58–60, 63–65; "Atlanta," *Drunk History*, Comedy Central, July 23, 2013.

5. *New York Times*, January 8, 2006; Bowers, *Superman*, 146–47, 153–54.

6. "Atlanta," *Drunk History*, Comedy Central, July 23, 2013.

7. Nathan, *Autobiography*, 175–76.

Glossary

Alien: someone who is not a member of the Ku Klux Klan
Citizen: an initiated member of the Ku Klux Klan
Domain: an administrative unit consisting of several combined states
Exalted Cyclops: chief officer of the local Klan or Klavern
Grand Dragon: the Klan leader of the Realm, appointed by the Imperial Wizard
Grand Goblin: administrative officer in charge of a Domain
Imperial Commander: national head of the Women of the Ku Klux Klan
Imperial Kleagle: the commander of the Klan's propagation department
Imperial Palace: Ku Klux Klan headquarters
Imperial Wizard: national leader of the Ku Klux Klan
Invisible Empire: alternative name applied to the Ku Klux Klan
King Kleagle: the chief recruiter of a Realm, responsible for supervising Kleagles
Klankraft: general term for the collective beliefs and rituals of the Klan
Klansman: an individual member of the Klan; also known as a Knight
Klanton: a subdivision of a Province, under the control of a single local Klan
Klavern: Klan's indoor meeting hall; also used to signify local Klan chapter
Kleagle: recruiter or organizer, normally working on commission
Klecktoken: ten-dollar initiation fee
Klokard: Klan lecturer
Klonklave: regular meeting of local Klan
Klonvokation: national annual convention of Klans
Kloran: official guide/rules of the Ku Klux Klan, written by William J. Simmons
Kluxing: Kleagle recruiting or organizing activities
Naturalization: formal rite initiating new member into full "citizenship"
Nighthawk: official messengers of the Klan
Province: administrative unit, generally equivalent to a congressional district
Realm: a subdivision of the Invisible Empire equivalent to a state

Bibliography

Manuscript Collections

Ball State University, Muncie, IN.
   Archives and Special Collections—Periodical Division. Bracken Library.
Cook County Superior Court, Chicago, IL.
   Harry Junker v. American Unity Publishing, S-388057.
Denver Public Library, Denver, CO.
   Senter Family Papers, WH988. Western History Collection.
Eastern Washington State Historical Society/Northwest Museum of Arts & Culture, Spokane, WA.
   Knights of the Ku Klux Klan, Butte, Montana Records, 1916–31, MS131. Joel E. Ferris Research Library and Archives.
Emory University, Atlanta, GA.
   Ku Klux Klan Carlock Unit No. 71 (Carlock, Ill.) Records. Manuscript Collection No. 903. Manuscript, Archives and Rare Book Library.
Historical Society of Washington, DC.
   Pamphlet Collection. Kiplinger Library.
Library of Congress, Washington, DC.
   Ku Klux Klan, Anaheim, Records, 1924–25.
   Ku Klux Klan, Campaign Songs. Performing Arts Division.
   Ku Klux Klan Pamphlets, 1912–46.
National Archives at College Park, MD.
   Records of the Federal Communication Commission, Record Group 173.
University of California, Los Angeles.
   Herman Petersen Papers, Collection 1339. Department of Special Collections, Manuscripts Division. Charles E. Young Research Library.
University of Maryland Libraries, College Park.
   Knights of the Ku Klux Klan, Klan No. 51, Mt. Rainier, Maryland Archives, 89–180. Special Collections. Hornbake Library.
University of North Carolina, Chapel Hill.
   John Edwards Memorial Foundation Collection (20001). Southern Folklife Collection at the Louis Round Wilson Special Collections Library.

Wisconsin Historical Society Archives, Eau Claire.
  Women of the Ku Klux Klan, Klan 14 (Chippewa Falls, Wis.) Records, 1926–31, WIHV96-
  A393. Eau Claire Research Center.

Books, Articles, Theses, Dissertations

Abbey, Sue Wilson. "The Ku Klux Klan in Arizona, 1921–1925." *Journal of Arizona History* 14:1
  (Spring 1973): 10–30.
Abrams, Douglas Carl. *Selling the Old-Time Religion: American Fundamentalists and Mass Cul-
  ture, 1920–1940.* Athens: University of Georgia Press, 2001.
Abrams, Paula. *Cross Purposes: Pierce v. Society of Sisters and the Struggle over Compulsory Public
  Education.* Ann Arbor: University of Michigan Press, 2009.
Ackmann, Martha. *Curveball: The Remarkable Story of Toni Stone.* Chicago: Lawrence Hill
  Books, 2010.
Akin, Edward P. "The Ku Klux Klan in Georgia: Social Change and Conflict, 1915–1930." PhD
  diss., University of California, 1994.
Alexander, Charles C. *Crusade for Conformity: The Ku Klux Klan in Texas, 1920–1930.* Houston:
  Texas Gulf Coast Historical Association, 1962.
———. "Defeat, Decline, Disintegration: The Ku Klux Klan in Arkansas, 1924 and After." *Arkan-
  sas Historical Quarterly* 22:4 (Winter 1963): 311–31.
———. "Kleagles and Cash: The Ku Klux Klan as a Business Organization, 1919–1930." *Business
  History Review* 39 (Autumn 1965): 348–67.
———. *The Ku Klux Klan in the Southwest.* Norman: University of Oklahoma Press, 1995.
———. *Rogers Hornsby: A Biography.* New York: Henry Holt and Company, 1995.
Allerfeldt, Kristofer, and Jeremy Black. *Race, Radicalism, Religion, and Restriction: Immigration
  in the Pacific Northwest, 1890–1924.* Westport, CT: Praeger Publishers, 2003.
Alpert, Rebecca T. *Out of Left Field: Jews and Black Baseball.* New York: Oxford University Press,
  2011.
Anderson, Benedict. *Imagined Communities: Reflections on the Origin and Spread of National-
  ism.* London: Verso, 1983.
Angle, Paul M. *Bloody Williamson: A Chapter in American Lawlessness.* New York: Knopf, 1952.
Anthony, Edward. *O Rare Don Marquis: A Biography.* New York: Doubleday, 1962.
Babcock, Bernie. *The Soul of Abe Lincoln.* New York: Grosset & Dunlap, 1919.
Baker, Kelly J. *Gospel According to the Klan: The KKK's Appeal to Protestant America, 1915–1930.*
  Lawrence: University Press of Kansas, 2011.
Baldasty, Gerald J. *E. W. Scripps and the Business of Newspapers.* Urbana: University of Illinois
  Press, 1999.
Baldwin, Davarian L., and Minkah Makalani, eds. *Escape from New York: The New Negro Renais-
  sance beyond Harlem.* Minneapolis: University of Minnesota Press, 2013.
Ball, Frank P. *Faults and Virtues of the Ku Klux Klan.* Brooklyn: Frank Ball, 1927.
Barnouw, Erik. *A Tower in Babel: A History of Broadcasting in the United States to 1933.* New
  York: Oxford University Press, 1966.
Beach, Rex. *The Mating Call.* New York: Harper & Brothers, 1927.
Bent, Silas. *Newspaper Crusaders: A Neglected Story.* Westport, CT: Greenwood Press, 1939.
Black, Stephen A. *Eugene O'Neill: Beyond Mourning and Tragedy.* New Haven, CT: Yale Univer-
  sity Press, 1999.

Blake, Aldrich. *The Ku Klux Kraze: A Lecture*. Huntington, IN: Our Sunday Visitor Press, 1924.

Blee, Kathleen. *Women of the Klan: Racism and Gender in the 1920s*. Berkeley: University of California Press, 1991.

Blom, Philipp. *Fracture: Life and Culture in the West, 1918–1938*. New York: Basic Books, 2015.

Bodenhamer, David J., ed. *The Encyclopedia of Indianapolis*. Bloomington: Indiana University Press, 1994.

Bodner, Allen. *When Boxing Was a Jewish Sport*. Albany: State University of New York Press, 2011.

Bohn, Michael K. *Heroes & Ballyhoo: How the Golden Age of the 1920s Transformed American Sports*. Washington, DC: Potomac Books, 2009.

Boone, Robert H. "A Kleagle and His Klan: F. Eugene Farnsworth and the Ku Klux Klan in Maine." Honors thesis, Wesleyan University, 1965.

Booth, Edgar Allen. *The Mad Mullah of America*. Columbus, OH: Boyd Ellison, 1927.

Bowers, Rick. *Superman versus the Ku Klux Klan: The True Story of How the Iconic Superhero Battled the Men of Hate*. Washington, DC: National Geographic, 2012.

Boyer, Paul S. "Boston Book Censorship in the Twenties." *American Quarterly* 15:1 (Spring 1963): 3–24.

———. *Purity in Print: Book Censorship in America from the Gilded Age to the Computer Age*. Madison: University of Wisconsin Press, 2002.

Boylan, James R. *The World and the 20s: The Golden Years of New York's Legendary Newspaper*. New York: Dial, 1973.

Boyle, Sheila Tully, and Andrew Bunie. *Paul Robeson: The Years of Promise and Achievement*. Amherst: University of Massachusetts Press, 2001.

Bradley, Patricia. *Making American Culture: A Social History, 1900–1920*. New York: Palgrave Macmillan, 2009.

Braeman, John, Robert H. Bremner, and David Brody, eds. *Change and Continuity in Twentieth-Century America: The 1920s*. Columbus: Ohio State University Press, 1968.

Brazil, John R. "Murder Trials, Murder, and Twenties America." *American Quarterly* 33:2 (Summer 1981): 163–84.

Brown, Egbert Ethelred. *The Final Awakening*. Brunswick, GA: Overstreet & Co., 1923.

Brown, George Alfred. *Harold the Klansman*. Kansas City, MO: Western Baptist Publishing Company, 1923.

Brown, Lester A. *Facts Concerning Knights of the Ku Klux Klan*. Atlanta: Lester A. Brown, 1923.

Brundage, W. Fitzhugh, ed. *Beyond Blackface: African Americans and the Creation of American Popular Culture*. Chapel Hill: University of North Carolina Press, 2011.

Burnham, John C. *Bad Habits: Drinking, Smoking, Taking Drugs, Gambling, Sexual Misbehavior, and Swearing in American History*. New York: New York University Press, 1993.

Canning, Charlotte M. *The Most American Thing in America: Circuit Chautauqua as Performance*. Iowa City: University of Iowa Press, 2005.

Carroll, Brian. "Beating the Klan: Baseball Coverage in Wichita before Integration, 1920–1930." *Baseball Research Journal* 37 (Winter 2008–9): 51–61.

Carter, Paul A. *Another Part of the Twenties*. New York: Columbia University Press, 1977.

Cash, Wilbur J. *The Mind of the South*. New York: Vintage Books, 1991.

Cather, Willa. *Not under Forty*. New York: Alfred A. Knopf, 1936.

Chalmers, David. *Hooded Americanism: The History of the Ku Klux Klan*. New York: Franklin Watts, 1981.

Chambers, Jonathan L. *Messiah of the New Technique: John Howard Lawson, Communism, and American Theatre, 1923–1937.* Carbondale: Southern Illinois University Press, 2006.

Chapman, Erin D. *Prove It on Me: New Negroes, Sex, and Popular Culture in the 1920s.* New York: Oxford University Press, 2012.

Clark, Norman H. *Deliver Us from Evil: An Interpretation of American Prohibition.* New York: W.W. Norton, 1976.

Clason, George S., ed. *Catholic, Jew, Ku Klux Klan: What They Believe, Where They Conflict.* Chicago: Nutshell Publishing, 1924.

Coben, Stanley. *Rebellion against Victorianism: The Impetus for Cultural Change in 1920s America.* New York: Oxford University Press, 1991.

Cocoltchos, Christopher N. "The Invisible Government and the Viable Community: The Ku Klux Klan in Orange County, California, during the 1920s." PhD diss., University of California, Los Angeles, 1979.

Collier, James Lincoln. *Louis Armstrong: An American Genius.* New York: Oxford University Press, 1983.

Cook, Ezra. *Ku Klux Klan: The Strange Society of Blood and Death! Exposed!* Racine, WI: Johnson Smith, ca. 1923.

Cook, Raymond Allen. *Fire from the Flint: The Amazing Careers of Thomas Dixon.* Winston-Salem, NC: John F. Blair, 1968.

Cousins, Mark. *The Story of Film.* New York: Thunder's Mouth Press, 2004.

Cox, Bob L. *Fiddlin' Charlie Bowman: An East Tennessee Old-Time Music Pioneer and His Musical Family.* Knoxville: University of Tennessee Press, 2007.

Craig, Douglas B. *Fireside Politics: Radio and Political Culture in the United States, 1920–1940.* Baltimore: Johns Hopkins University Press, 2000.

Craine, David. "The Klan Moves North." *Chicago History* 34:3 (Fall 2006): 4–25.

Crew, Danny O. *Ku Klux Klan Sheet Music: An Illustrated Catalogue of Published Music, 1867–2002.* Jefferson, NC: McFarland & Co., 2003.

Cripps, Thomas. *Slow Fade to Black: The Negro in American Film, 1900–1942.* New York: Oxford University Press, 1993.

Crownover, Donald A. "The Ku Klux Klan in Lancaster County: 1923–1924." *Journal of the Lancaster County History Society* 68:2 (Easter 1964): 63–84.

Cullum, Ridgwell. *The Saint of the Speedway.* New York: George H. Doran, 1924.

Currell, Susan. *American Culture in the 1920s.* Edinburgh: Edinburgh University Press, 2009.

Curry, Leroy Amos. *The Ku Klux Klan under the Searchlight: An Authoritative, Dignified, and Enlightened Discussion of the American Klan.* Kansas City, MO: Western Baptist Publishing Company, 1924.

Dalrymple, A. V. *Liberty Dethroned: An Indictment of the Ku Klux Klan Based Solely upon Its Own Pronouncements, Philosophy, and Acts of Mob Violence.* Philadelphia: Times Publishing, 1923.

Davis, John A. "The Ku Klux Klan in Indiana, 1920–1930." PhD diss., Northwestern University, 1960.

Denning, Michael. *The Cultural Front: The Laboring of American Culture in the Twentieth Century.* London: Verso, 1996.

Dessommes, Nancy Bishop. "Hollywood in Hoods: The Portrayal of the Ku Klux Klan in Popular Film." *Journal of Popular Culture* 32:4 (Spring 1999): 13–22.

Dever, Lem A. *Confessions of an Imperial Klansman.* Portland: Dever, 1924.

Dickstein, Morris. *Dancing in the Dark: A Cultural History of the Great Depression*. New York: W.W. Norton, 2009.

Diner, Hasia R. *In the Almost Promised Land: American Jews and Blacks, 1915–1935*. Baltimore: Johns Hopkins University Press, 1995.

Dixon, Thomas. *The Black Hood*. New York: D. Appleton & Co., 1924.

———. *The Clansman: A Historical Romance of the Ku Klux Klan*. New York: Grosset & Dunlap, 1905.

———. *The Leopard's Spots: A Romance of the White Man's Burden*. New York: Doubleday, Page & Co., 1902.

———. *The Sins of the Father*. New York: D. Appleton & Co., 1912.

———. *The Traitor: A Story of the Fall of the Invisible Empire*. New York: Grosset & Dunlap, 1907.

Doerksen, Clifford J. *American Babel: Rogue Radio Broadcasters of the Jazz Age*. Philadelphia: University of Pennsylvania Press, 2005.

Douglas, Ann. *Terrible Honesty: Mongrel Manhattan in the 1920s*. New York: Farrar, Straus and Giroux, 1995.

Douglas, George H. *The Golden Age of the Newspaper*. Westport, CT: Greenwood Press, 1999.

Douglas, Susan J. *Listening In: Radio and the American Imagination*. Minneapolis: University of Minnesota Press, 2004.

Dreifort, John, ed. *Baseball History from Outside the Lines: A Reader*. Lincoln: University of Nebraska Press, 2001.

Drowne, Kathleen, and Patrick Huber. *American Popular Culture through History: The 1920s*. Westport, CT: Greenwood Press, 2004.

Dumenil, Lynn. *The Modern Temper: American Culture and Society in the 1920s*. New York: Hill and Wang, 1995.

Dyer, Thomas G. "The Klan on Campus: C. Lewis Fowler and Lanier University." *South Atlantic Quarterly* 77 (1978): 453–69.

Eberly, Philip K. *Music in the Air: America's Changing Tastes in Popular Music, 1920–1980*. New York: Hastings House, 1982.

Ely, Melvin Patrick. *The Adventures of Amos 'n' Andy: A Social History of an American Phenomenon*. Charlottesville: University of Virginia Press, 2001.

Erenberg, Lewis A. *Steppin' Out: New York Nightlife and the Transformation of American Culture, 1890–1930*. Westport, CT: Greenwood Press, 1981.

Erickson, Christine K. "Kluxer Blues: The Klan Confronts Catholics in Butte, Montana, 1923–1929." *Montana: The Magazine of Western History* 53 (Spring 2003): 44–57.

Estes, George. *The Old Cedar School*. Portland, OR: Luther Ivan Powell, 1922.

———. *The Roman Katholic Kingdom and the Ku Klux Klan*. Portland, OR: Empire Publishing Company, 1923.

Evans, Hiram W. *The Rising Storm: An Analysis of the Growing Conflict over the Political Dilemma of Roman Catholics in America*. Atlanta: Buckhead Publishing, 1930.

Evensen, Bruce J. *When Dempsey Fought Tunney: Heroes, Hokum, and Storytelling in the Jazz Age*. Knoxville: University of Tennessee Press, 1996.

Eyerman, Ron, and Andrew Jamison. *Music and Social Movements: Mobilizing Traditions in the Twentieth Century*. Cambridge: Cambridge University Press, 1998.

Eyman, Scott. *Lion of Hollywood: The Life and Legend of Louis B. Mayer*. New York: Simon & Schuster, 2005.

Fantasia, Rick. *Cultures of Solidarity: Consciousness, Action, and Contemporary American Workers*. Berkeley: University of California Press, 1988.

Fass, Paula S. *The Damned and the Beautiful: American Youth in the 1920s*. New York: Oxford University Press, 1977.

Feldman, Glenn. *Politics, Society, and the Klan in Alabama, 1915–1949*. Tuscaloosa: University of Alabama Press, 1999.

Feldstein, Stanley. *The Land That I Show You: Three Centuries of Jewish Life in America*. New York: Doubleday, 1979.

Ferguson, Charles Wright. *The New Books of Revelations: The Inside Story of America's Astounding Religious Cults*. New York: Doubleday, 1929.

Field, Kim. *Harmonicas, Harps, and Heavy Breathers: The Evolution of the People's Instrument*. New York: Cooper Square Press, 2000.

Fischer, Lucy, ed. *American Cinema of the 1920s: Themes and Variations*. New Brunswick, NJ: Rutgers University Press, 2009.

Fisher, James T. *Communion of Immigrants: A History of Catholics in America*. New York: Oxford University Press, 2008.

Fisher, James, and Felicia Hardison Londre. *Historical Dictionary of American Theater: Modernism*. Lanham, MD: Scarecrow Press, 2008.

Fitzgerald, F. Scott. *The Great Gatsby*. New York: Scribner's, 1925.

———. *Tales of the Jazz Age*. New York: Scribner's, 1922.

Flanigan, James C. *A History of Gwinnett County, Georgia*. Vol. 2. Lawrenceville, GA: Tyler & Co., 1984.

Fleming, John Stephen. *What Is Ku Kluxism? Let Americans Answer—Aliens Only Muddy the Waters*. Birmingham, AL: Masonic Weekly Recorder, 1923.

Fowler, C. Lewis. *The Ku Klux Klan: Its Origin, Meaning, and Scope of Operation*. Atlanta: C. Lewis Fowler, 1922.

Fox, Craig. *Everyday Klansfolk: White Protestant Life and the KKK in 1920s Michigan*. East Lansing: Michigan State University Press, 2011.

Frank, Glenda. "Tempest in Black and White: The 1924 Premiere of Eugene O'Neill's *All God's Chillun Got Wings*." *Resources for American Literary Study* 26:1 (2000): 75–89.

Frost, Stanley. *The Challenge of the Klan*. Indianapolis: Bobbs-Merrill Company, 1924.

Fry, Henry P. *The Modern Ku Klux Klan*. Boston: Small, Maynard, 1922.

Fryer, Roland G., Jr., and Steven D. Levitt. "Hatred and Profits: Under the Hood of the Ku Klux Klan." *Quarterly Journal of Economics* 127:4 (2012): 1883–1925.

Fuller, Edgar I. *The Visible of the Invisible Empire*. Denver: Maelstrom, 1925.

Fuller, Kathryn H. *At the Picture Show: Small-Town Audiences and the Creation of Movie Fan Culture*. Washington, DC: Smithsonian Institution Press, 1996.

Gaffney, Albert Sydney. *The Son of a Klansman*. Kansas City, MO: Franklin Hudson, 1926.

Gates, Henry Louis, Jr., and Evelyn Brooks Higginbotham, eds. *Harlem Renaissance Lives*. New York: Oxford University Press, 2009.

Gay, Timothy M. *Tris Speaker: The Rough-and-Tumble Life of a Baseball Legend*. Guilford, CT: Lyons Press, 2007.

Gelb, Arthur, and Barbara Gelb. *O'Neill: Life with Monte Cristo*. New York: Applause Books, 2000.

Gems, Gerald, Linda Borish, and Gertrud Pfister. *Sports in American History: From Colonization to Globalization*. Champaign, IL: Human Kinetics, 2008.

Gerlach, Larry R. *Blazing Crosses in Zion: The Ku Klux Klan in Utah*. Logan: Utah State University Press, 1982.

Gerwitz, Arthur, and James J. Kolb, eds. *Experimenters, Rebels, and Disparate Voices: The Theatre of the 1920s Celebrates American Diversity*. Westport, CT: Praeger, 2003.

Gibbs, Philip. *Ten Years After: A Reminder.* New York: George H. Doran, 1925.

Gillespie, Michele K., and Randal L. Hall, eds. *Thomas Dixon Jr. and the Birth of Modern America.* Baton Rouge: Louisiana State University Press, 2006.

Giordano, Ralph G. *Satan in the Dance Hall: Rev. John Roach Straton, Social Dancing, and Morality in 1920s New York City.* Lanham, MD: Scarecrow Press, 2008.

Gist, Noel P. *Secret Societies: A Cultural Study of Fraternalism in the United States.* Columbia: University of Missouri Press, 1940.

Goldberg, David J. "Unmasking the Ku Klux Klan: The Northern Movement against the KKK, 1920–1925," *Journal of American Ethnic History* 15:4 (Summer 1996): 32–48.

Goldberg, Robert A. *Hooded Empire: The Ku Klux Klan in Colorado.* Urbana: University of Illinois Press, 1981.

———. "The Ku Klux Klan in Madison, 1922–1927." *Wisconsin Magazine of History* 58:1 (1974–75): 31–44.

Gonzalez, Juan, and Joseph Torres. *News for All the People: The Epic Story of Race and the American Media.* New York: Verso, 2011.

Gordon, Glenn. *The Ku Klux Ball: A Satire on the Younger Set.* Macon, GA: J.W. Burke & Co., 1926.

Gordon, John J. *Unmasked!* Brooklyn: J.J. Gordon, 1924.

Gorn, Elliott J., and Warren Goldstein. *A Brief History of American Sports.* Urbana: University of Illinois Press, 1993.

Green, Archie. "Hillbilly Music: Source and Symbol." *Journal of American Folklore* 78:309 (July–September 1965): 204–28.

Greenaway, John. "Country-Western: The Music of America." *The American West* 5:6 (November 1968): 32–41.

Greene, Casey. "Guardians against Change: The Ku Klux Klan in Houston and Harris County, 1920–1925." *Houston Review* 10 (Fall 1988): 3–18.

Greene, Daniel. *The Jewish Origins of Cultural Pluralism: The Menorah Association and American Diversity.* Bloomington: Indiana University Press, 2011.

Greene, Frances Nimmo. *One Clear Call.* New York: Scribner's, 1914.

Greif, Mark. *The Age of the Crisis of Man: Thought and Fiction in America, 1933–1973.* Princeton, NJ: Princeton University Press, 2015.

Grundman, Adolph. *The Golden Age of Amateur Basketball.* Lincoln: University of Nebraska Press, 2004.

Gurock, Jeffrey S. *Judaism's Encounter with American Sports.* Bloomington: Indiana University Press, 2005.

Hagemann, E. R. "The Black Mask: The Magazine Dedicated to Readers of Mystery, Suspense, Thrillers, and Adventure." *Mystery* 2:1 (January 1981): 30–41.

Haldeman-Julius, E. *Is the Ku Klux Klan Constructive or Destructive? A Debate between Imperial Wizard Evans, Israel Zangwill, and Others.* Girard, KS: Haldeman-Julius Little Blue Book, 1924.

———. ed. *KKK: The Kreed of the Klansmen.* Girard, KS: Haldeman-Julius Little Blue Book, 1924.

Hallberg, Carl V. "For God, Country, and Home: The Ku Klux Klan in Pekin, 1923–1925." *Journal of the Illinois State Historical Society* 77:2 (Summer 1984): 82–93.

Hangen, Tona J. *Redeeming the Dial: Radio, Religion, and Popular Culture in America.* Chapel Hill: University of North Carolina Press, 2002.

Harrell, Kenneth. "The Ku Klux Klan in Louisiana." PhD diss., Louisiana State University, 1966.

Hart, James D. *The Popular Book: A History of America's Literary Taste*. Westport, CT: Greenwood Press, 1950.

Hatle, Elizabeth Dorsey, and Nancy M. Vaillancourt. "One Flag, One School, One Language: Minnesota's Ku Klux Klan in the 1920s." *Minnesota History* 61:8 (Winter 2009): 360–71.

Head, Sydney W. *Broadcasting in America: A Survey of Electronic Media*. Boston: Houghton Mifflin, 1998.

Henle, James. *Sound and Fury*. New York: Knopf, 1924.

Higham, John. *Strangers in the Land: Patterns of American Nativism, 1860–1925*. New Brunswick, NJ: Rutgers University Press, 1955.

Hilmes, Michele. *Radio Voices: American Broadcasting, 1922–1952*. Minneapolis: University of Minnesota Press, 1997.

Hoffman, Frederick. *The Twenties: American Writing in the Postwar Decade*. New York: Viking Press, 1955.

Hofstadter, Richard. *The Age of Reform*. New York: Knopf, 1955.

Hohenberg, John. *The Pulitzer Prize Story*. New York: Columbia University Press, 1971.

Holmes, Dan. *Ty Cobb: A Biography*. Westport, CT: Greenwood Press, 2004.

Hoopes, Roy. *Cain*. New York: Holt, Rinehart, and Winston, 1982.

Hoose, Phillip M. *Hoosiers: The Fabulous Basketball Life of Indiana*. Indianapolis: Guild Press of Indiana, Inc., 1995.

Horn, Maurice. *The World Encyclopedia of Cartoons*. New York: Chelsea House Publications, 1998.

Horne, Gerald. *The Final Victim of the Blacklist: John Howard Lawson, Dean of the Hollywood Ten*. Berkeley: University of California Press, 2006.

Houchin, John H. *Censorship of the American Theatre in the Twentieth Century*. New York: Cambridge University Press, 2003.

Huber, Patrick. *Linthead Stomp: The Creation of Country Music in the Piedmont South*. Chapel Hill: University of North Carolina Press, 2008.

Hutner, Gordon. *What America Read: Taste, Class, and the Novel, 1920–1960*. Chapel Hill: University of North Carolina Press, 2009.

Inscoe, John. "The Clansman on Stage and Screen: North Carolina Reacts." *North Carolina Historical Review* 64:2 (April 1987): 139–61.

Jackson, Helen. *Convent Cruelties, or My Life in the Convent: Awful Revelations*. Toledo, OH: Helen Jackson, 1919.

Jackson, Kenneth T. *The Ku Klux Klan in the City, 1915–1930*. New York: Oxford University Press, 1967.

Jacobs, Michael D. "Catholic Response to the Ku Klux Klan in the Midwest, 1921–1928." PhD diss., Marquette University, 2001.

———. "Co-opting Christian Chorales: Songs of the Ku Klux Klan." *American Music* 28:3 (Fall 2010): 368–77.

Jaker, Bill, Frank Sulek, and Peter Kanze. *The Airwaves of New York: Illustrated Histories of 156 AM Stations in the Metropolitan Area, 1921–1996*. Jefferson, NC: McFarland, 1998.

Janken, Kenneth. *White: The Biography of Walter White, Mr. NAACP*. New York: The New Press, 2003.

Jefferson, Charles E. *Five Present-Day Controversies*. New York: Fleming H. Revell, 1924.

———. *Roman Catholicism and the Ku Klux Klan*. New York: Fleming H. Revell, 1925.

Jenkins, William D. *Steel Valley Klan: The Ku Klux Klan in Ohio's Mahoning Valley*. Kent, OH: Kent State University Press, 1990.

Jenkinson, Bill. *Baseball's Ultimate Power: Ranking the All-Time Greatest Distance Home Run Hitters*. Guilford, CT: Lyons Press, 2010.

Johnsen, Julia E., ed. *Reference Shelf No. 10: Ku Klux Klan*. New York: H.W. Wilson, 1923.

Johnson, Jack. *Jack Johnson in the Ring and Out*. Chicago: National Sports Publishing Company, 1927.

Johnson, Walter. *William Allen White's America*. New York: Henry Holt, 1942.

Jones, Winfield. *Story of the Ku Klux Klan*. Washington, DC: American Newspaper Syndicate, 1921.

Kallen, Horace M. *Culture and Democracy in the United States: Studies in the Group Psychology of the American Peoples*. New York: Boni and Liveright, 1924.

Kaye, Andrew M. *The Pussycat of Prizefighting: Tiger Flowers and the Politics of Black Celebrity*. Athens: University of Georgia Press, 2004.

Kennedy, Rick. *Jelly Roll, Bix, and Hoagy: Gennett Records and the Rise of America's Musical Grassroots*. Bloomington: Indiana University Press, 2013.

Kennedy, Rick, and Randy McNutt. *Little Labels—Big Sound: Small Record Companies and the Rise of American Music*. Bloomington: Indiana University Press, 1999.

Kibler, M. Alison. *Censoring Racial Ridicule: Irish, Jewish, and African American Struggles over Race and Representation, 1890–1930*. Chapel Hill: University of North Carolina Press, 2015.

Kimball, Richard Ian. *Sports in Zion: Mormon Recreation, 1890–1940*. Urbana: University of Illinois Press, 2003.

King, Kenneth Kenelm [Albert Edwin Wentz]. *100%*. Washington, DC: The American Sentinel, 1925.

Klamkin, Marian. *Old Sheet Music: A Pictorial History*. New York: Hawthorn Books, 1975.

Knight, Marion, and Mertice James, eds. *The Book Review Digest: Reviews of 1923 Books*. New York: H.W. Wilson, 1924.

———. *The Book Review Digest: Reviews of 1924 Books*. New York: H.W. Wilson, 1925.

Knights of the Ku Klux Klan. *Kloran*. Atlanta: Knights of the Ku Klux Klan, 1928.

———. *Papers Read at the Meeting of Grand Dragons, Knights of the Ku Klux Klan at Their First Annual Meeting Held at Asheville, North Carolina, July 1923; Together With Other Articles of Interest to Klansmen*. Atlanta: Knights of the Ku Klux Klan, 1923.

———. *Proceedings of the Second Imperial Klonvokation: Held in Kansas City, Missouri, September 23, 24, 25, and 26, 1924*. Atlanta: Knights of the Ku Klux Klan, 1924.

Kolb, Felix. *Protest and Opportunities: The Political Outcomes of Social Movements*. Chicago: University of Chicago Press, 2007.

Koritz, Amy. *Culture Makers: Urban Performance and Literature in the 1920s*. Urbana: University of Illinois Press, 2009.

Kyvig, David E. *Daily Life in the United States, 1920–1940: How Americans Lived through the Roaring Twenties and the Great Depression*. Chicago: Ivan R. Dee, 2004.

Laats, Adam. *Fundamentalism and Education in the Scopes Era: God, Darwin, and the Roots of America's Culture Wars*. New York: Palgrave Macmillan, 2010.

———. *The Other School Reformers: Conservative Activism in American Education*. Cambridge, MA: Harvard University Press, 2015.

Ladd, Tony, and James A. Mathisen. *Muscular Christianity: Evangelical Protestantism and the Development of American Sport*. Grand Rapids, MI: Baker Books, 1999.

Laird, Ross, and Brian Rust. *Discography of OKeh Records, 1918–1934*. Westport, CT: Praeger, 2004.

Lalande, Jeff. "Beneath the Hooded Robe: Newspapermen, Local Politics, and the Ku Klux Klan in Jackson County, Oregon, 1921–1923." *Pacific Northwest Quarterly* 83:2 (April 1992): 42–52.

Lang, Arne K. *Prize-Fighting: An American History*. Jefferson, NC: McFarland, 2008.

Laugen, R. Todd. *The Gospel of Progressivism: Moral Reform and Labor War in Colorado, 1900–1930*. Boulder: University Press of Colorado, 2010.

Lawson, John Howard. *Processional: A Jazz Symphony of American Life in Four Acts*. New York: Thomas Seltzer, 1925.

Lay, Shawn. *Hooded Knights on the Niagara*. New York: New York University Press, 1995.

———. ed. *The Invisible Empire in the West: Toward a New Historical Appraisal of the Ku Klux Klan in the 1920s*. Urbana: University of Illinois Press, 1992.

———. *War, Revolution, and the Ku Klux Klan: A Study of Intolerance in a Border City*. El Paso: Texas Western Press, 1985.

Leach, William. *Land of Desire: Merchants, Power, and the Rise of a New American Culture*. New York: Pantheon Books, 1993.

Lears, T. J. Jackson. *Fables of Abundance: A Cultural History of Advertising in America*. New York: BasicBooks, 1994.

———. *No Place of Grace: Antimodernism and the Transformation of American Culture, 1880–1920*. New York: Pantheon Books, 1981.

Lehr, Dick. *The Birth of a Nation: How a Legendary Filmmaker and a Crusading Editor Reignited America's Civil War*. New York: PublicAffairs, 2014.

Leidholdt, Alexander. *Editor for Justice: The Life of Louis Jaffe*. Baton Rouge: Louisiana State University Press, 2002.

Leighton, Isabel, ed. *The Aspirin Age: 1919–1941*. New York: Simon & Schuster, 1949.

Lena, Jennifer C. *Banding Together: How Communities Create Genres in Popular Music*. Princeton, NJ: Princeton University Press, 2012.

Levine, Lawrence W. *Highbrow/Lowbrow: The Emergence of Cultural Hierarchy in America*. Cambridge, MA: Harvard University Press, 1988.

———. "Jazz and American Culture." *Journal of American Folklore* 102:403 (January–March 1989): 6–22.

———. *The Unpredictable Past: Explorations in American Cultural History*. New York: Oxford University Press, 1993.

Levine, Peter. *Ellis Island to Ebbets Field: Sport and the American Jewish Experience*. New York: Oxford University Press, 1992.

Levitt, Steven D., and Stephen J. Dubner. *Freakonomics: A Rogue Economist Explores the Hidden Side of Everything*. New York: William Morrow, 2005.

Lewis, George H., ed. *All That Glitters: Country Music in America*. Bowling Green, OH: Bowling Green State University Popular Press, 1993.

Lewis, Sinclair. *Babbitt*. New York: Library of America, 1992.

———. *Elmer Gantry*. New York: Signet Classics, 2007.

Lichtman, Allan J. *Prejudice and the Old Politics: The Presidential Election of 1928*. Chapel Hill: University of North Carolina Press, 1979.

———. *White Protestant Nation: The Rise of the American Conservative Movement*. New York: Atlantic Monthly Press, 2008.

Lieb, Fred. *Baseball As I Have Known It*. Lincoln: University of Nebraska Press, 1996.

Lienesch, Michael. *In the Beginning: Fundamentalism, the Scopes Trial, and the Making of the Antievolution Movement*. Chapel Hill: University of North Carolina Press, 2007.

Likins, William M. *Patriotism Capitalized, or, Religion Turned into Gold.* Uniontown, PA: Watchman Publishing, 1925.

———. *The Trail of the Serpent.* Uniontown, PA: Watchman Publishing, 1928.

Lindsay, Andrew. *Boxing in Black and White: A Statistical Study of Race in the Ring, 1949–1983.* Jefferson, NC: McFarland, 2004.

Lisby, Gregory. "Julian Harris and the *Columbus Enquirer-Sun*: The Consequences of Winning the Pulitzer Prize." *Journalism Monographs* 105 (April 1988): 1–30.

Lisby, Gregory C., and William F. Mugleston. *Someone Had to Be Hated: Julian LaRose Harris, A Biography.* Durham, NC: Carolina Academic Press, 2002.

Londre, Felicia Hardison, and Daniel J. Watermeier. *The History of North American Theater: The United States, Canada, and Mexico, from Pre-Columbian Times to the Present.* New York: Continuum International, 2000.

Long, David. "The Rise and Fall of the Ku Klux Klan in Western Pennsylvania in the 1920s." MA thesis, Duquesne University, 2009.

Lougher, E. H. *The Kall of the Klan in Kentucky.* Greenfield, IN: W. Mitchell Printing, 1924.

Lowery, James Vincent. "Reconstructing the Reign of Terror: Popular Memories of the Ku Klux Klan, 1877–1921." PhD diss., University of Mississippi, 2008.

Lutholtz, M. William. *Grand Dragon: D. C. Stephenson and the Ku Klux Klan in Indiana.* Lafayette, IN: Purdue University Press, 1991.

Lynd, Robert S., and Helen M. Lynd. *Middletown: A Study in American Culture.* New York: Harcourt, Brace and World, 1929.

MacLean, Nancy. *Behind the Mask of Chivalry: The Making of the Second Ku Klux Klan.* New York: Oxford University Press, 1994.

Maguire, James H. *James Stevens.* Boise State University Western Writers Series 165. Boise, ID: Boise State University, 2005.

Mann, William J. *Tinseltown: Murder, Morphine, and Madness at the Dawn of Hollywood.* New York: Harper, 2014.

Marchand, Roland. *Advertising the American Dream: Making Way for Modernity, 1920–1940.* Berkeley: University of California Press, 1985.

Marquis, Don. *The Annotated Archy and Mehitabel.* New York: Penguin Classics, 2006.

Marsden, George M. *Fundamentalism and American Culture: The Shaping of Twentieth-Century Evangelicalism, 1870–1925.* New York: Oxford University Press, 1980.

Mast, Blaine. *K.K.K., Friend or Foe: Which?* Kittaning, PA: Blaine Mast, 1924.

Mates, Julian. *America's Musical Stage: Two Hundred Years of Musical Theatre.* Westport, CT: Greenwood Press, 1987.

McCann, Sean. *Gumshoe America: Hard-Boiled Crime Fiction and the Rise and Fall of New Deal Liberalism.* Durham, NC: Duke University Press, 2001.

McGirr, Lisa. *The War on Alcohol: Prohibition and the Rise of the American State.* New York: W.W. Norton, 2016.

McKeever, William A. *Training the Boy.* New York: The Macmillan Company, 1913.

McLuhan, Marshall. *Understanding Media: The Extensions of Man.* New York: New American Library, 1964.

McMullen, Josh. *Under the Big Top: Big Tent Revivalism and American Culture, 1885–1925.* New York: Oxford University Press, 2015.

McNeile, Cyril "Sapper." *The Black Gang.* New York: George H. Doran, 1923.

McParland, Robert. *Beyond Gatsby: How Fitzgerald, Hemingway, and Writers of the 1920s Shaped American Culture.* Lanham, MD: Rowman and Littlefield, 2015.

McPherson, Tara. *Reconstructing Dixie: Race, Gender, and Nostalgia in the Imagined South*. Durham, NC: Duke University Press, 2003.

McVeigh, Rory. *The Rise of the Ku Klux Klan*. Minneapolis: University of Minnesota Press, 2009.

Mecklin, John Moffat. *The Ku Klux Klan: A Study of the American Mind*. New York: Harcourt, Brace and Company, 1924.

Melching, Richard. "The Activities of the Ku Klux Klan in Anaheim, California, 1923–1925." *Southern California Quarterly* 56 (Summer 1974): 175–96.

Menand, Louis. "Do Movies Have Rights." In *Thomas Dixon Jr. and the Birth of Modern America*, ed. Michele K. Gillespie and Randal L. Hall, 183–202. Baton Rouge: Louisiana State University Press, 2006.

Mencken, Henry Louis. *Damn! A Book of Calumny*. New York: Philip Goodman Company, 1918.

——. *The Days Trilogy: Expanded Edition* Ed. Marion Rodgers. New York: Library of America, 2014.

——. ed. *Menckeniana: A Schimpflexikon*. New York: Alfred A. Knopf, 1928.

——. *My Life as Author and Editor*. New York: Alfred A. Knopf, 1992.

——. *Prejudices: First Series*. New York: Alfred A. Knopf, 1919.

——. *Prejudices: Second Series*. New York: Alfred A. Knopf, 1920.

——. *Prejudices: Third Series*. New York: Alfred A. Knopf, 1922.

——. *Prejudices: Fourth Series*. New York: Alfred A. Knopf, 1924.

——. *Prejudices: Fifth Series*. New York: Alfred A. Knopf, 1926.

——. *Prejudices: Sixth Series*. New York: Alfred A. Knopf, 1927.

Mertz, Stephen. "In Defense of Carroll John Daly." *Mystery Fancier* 2:3 (May 1978): 19–22.

Michaels, Walter Benn. *Our America: Nativism, Modernism, and Pluralism*. Durham, NC: Duke University Press, 1995.

Miller, Donald L. *Supreme City: How Jazz Age Manhattan Gave Birth to Modern America*. New York: Simon & Schuster, 2014.

Miller, Nathan. *New World Coming: The 1920s and the Making of Modern America*. New York: Scribner, 2003.

Monteval, Marion [Edgar Fuller]. *The Klan Inside Out*. Claremore, OK: Monarch Publishing, 1924.

Mooney, H. F. "Popular Music since the 1920s: The Significance of Shifting Taste." *American Quarterly* 20:1 (Spring 1968): 67–85.

——. "Songs, Singers, and Society, 1890–1954." *American Quarterly* 6:3 (Autumn 1954): 221–32.

Moore, Leonard. *Citizen Klansman: The Ku Klux Klan in Indiana, 1921–1928*. Chapel Hill: University of North Carolina Press, 1991.

Moore, Lewis D. *Cracking the Hard-Boiled Detective: A Critical History from the 1920s to the Present*. Jefferson, NC: McFarland & Company, 2006.

Moore, Macdonald Smith. *Yankee Blues: Musical Culture and American Identity*. Bloomington: Indiana University Press, 1985.

Mordden, Ethan. *That Jazz! An Idiosyncratic Social History of the American Twenties*. New York: G.P. Putnam's Sons, 1978.

Morley, David, and Kuan-Hsing Chen, eds. *Stuart Hall: Critical Dialogues in Cultural Studies*. New York: Routledge, 1996.

Mormino, Gary Ross. "The Playing Fields of St. Louis: Italian Immigrants and Sport, 1925–1941." *Journal of Sport History* 9 (Summer 1982): 5–16.

Morris, Mark. "Saving Society through Politics: The Ku Klux Klan in Dallas, Texas, in the 1920s." PhD diss., University of North Texas, 1997.

Moseley, Clement C. "Invisible Empire: The History of the Ku Klux Klan in Twentieth-Century Georgia." PhD diss., University of Georgia, 1968.

Mugleston, William F. "Julian Harris, the Georgia Press, and the Ku Klux Klan," *Georgia Historical Quarterly* 59:3 (Fall 1975): 284–95.

Munden, Kenneth White, ed. *American Film Institute Catalog: Feature Films, 1921–1930.* Berkeley: University of California Press, 1971.

Murphy, Paul V. *The New Era: American Thought and Culture in the 1920s.* Lanham, MD: Rowman & Littlefield, 2012.

Nash, Roderick. *The Nervous Generation: American Thought, 1917–1930.* Chicago: Ivan R. Dee, 1990.

Nathan, George Jean. *The Autobiography of an Attitude.* New York: Knopf, 1926.

Neill, Maudean. *Fiery Crosses in the Green Mountains: The Story of the Ku Klux Klan in Vermont.* Randolph Center, VT: Greenhills Books, 1989.

Newton, Michael. *The Ku Klux Klan: History, Organization, Language, Influence, and Activities of America's Most Notorious Secret Society.* Jefferson, NC: McFarland & Company, 2007.

———. *The Ku Klux Klan in Mississippi: A History.* Jefferson, NC: McFarland & Company, 2010.

Neymeyer, Robert J. "In the Full Light of Day: The Ku Klux Klan in 1920s Iowa." *The Palimpsest* 76:2 (Summer 1995): 56–63.

Nolan, William F. *The Black Mask Boys: Masters in the Hard-Boiled School of Detective Fiction.* New York: William Morrow, 1985.

Nye, Russel. *The Unembarrassed Muse: The Popular Arts in America.* New York: Dial Press, 1970.

Ogren, Kathy J. *The Jazz Revolution: Twenties America and the Meaning of Jazz.* New York: Oxford University Press, 1989.

Oliver, Paul, Tony Russell, Robert M. W. Dixon, et al. *Yonder Come the Blues: The Evolution of a Genre.* New York: Cambridge University Press, 2001.

O'Neill, Eugene. *All God's Chillun Got Wings & Welded.* New York: Boni and Liveright, 1924.

Paper, Lewis J. *Empire: William S. Paley and the Making of CBS.* New York: St. Martin's Press, 1987.

Parrish, Michael E. *Anxious Decades: America in Prosperity and Depression, 1920–1941.* New York: W.W. Norton, 1994.

Payne, Darwin. *Big D: Triumphs and Troubles of an American Supercity in the 20th Century.* Dallas, TX: Three Forks Press, 1994.

Pegram, Thomas R. *One Hundred Percent: The Rebirth and Decline of the Ku Klux Klan in the 1920s.* Chicago: Ivan R. Dee, 2011.

Pendleton, Jason. "Jim Crow Strikes Out: Interracial Baseball in Wichita, Kansas, 1920–1935." *Kansas History* 20 (Summer 1997): 86–101.

Peterson, Theodore. *Magazines in the Twentieth Century.* Urbana: University of Illinois Press, 1956.

Pitsula, James M. *Keeping Canada British: The Ku Klux Klan in 1920s Saskatchewan.* Vancouver: University of British Columbia Press, 2014.

Pope, Stephen W. *Patriotic Games: Sporting Traditions in the American Imagination, 1876–1926.* New York: Oxford University Press, 1997.

Pound, Ezra. *Guide to Kulchur.* New York: New Directions Books, 1970.

Price, Joseph L. *Rounding the Bases: Baseball and Religion in America.* Macon, GA: Mercer University Press, 2006.

Prince, K. Stephen. *Stories of the South: Race and the Reconstruction of Southern Identity, 1865–1915.* Chapel Hill: University of North Carolina Press, 2014.

Prothero, Stephen. *Why Liberals Win the Culture Wars (Even When They Lose Elections)*. New York: HarperOne, 2016.

Putney, Clifford. *Muscular Christianity: Manhood and Sports in Protestant America, 1880–1920*. Cambridge, MA: Harvard University Press, 2001.

Ramsaye, Terry. *A Million and One Nights: A History of the Motion Picture*. New York: Simon & Schuster, 1964.

Randel, William P. *The Ku Klux Klan: A Century of Infamy*. London: Hamish Hamilton, 1965.

Razlogova, Elena. *The Listener's Voice: Early Radio and the American Public*. Philadelphia: University of Pennsylvania Press, 2011.

Regester, Charlene. "The Cinematic Representation of Race in *The Birth of a Nation*: A Black Horror Film." In *Thomas Dixon Jr. and the Birth of Modern America*, ed. Michele K. Gillespie and Randal L. Hall, 164–82. Baton Rouge: Louisiana State University Press, 2006.

Rice, Arnold S. *The Ku Klux Klan in American Politics*. Washington DC: Public Affairs Press, 1962.

Rice, Tom. "Life after *Birth*: The Klan and Cinema, 1915–1928." PhD diss., University College London, 2006.

———. *White Robes, Silver Screens: Movies and the Making of the Ku Klux Klan*. Bloomington: Indiana University Press, 2015.

Riess, Steven, ed. *Sports and the American Jew*. New York: Syracuse University Press, 1998.

———. *Touching Base: Professional Baseball and American Culture in the Progressive Era*. Westport, CT: Greenwood Press, 1980.

Robinson, Cedric J. *Forgeries of Memory and Meaning: Blacks and the Regimes of Race in American Theater and Film before World War II*. Chapel Hill: University of North Carolina Press, 2007.

Rodgers, Marion Elizabeth. *Mencken: The American Iconoclast*. New York: Oxford University Press, 2005.

Rodriguez, Robert G. *Regulation of Boxing: A History and Comparative Analysis of Policies among American States*. Jefferson, NC: McFarland & Company, 2009.

Rogers, J. A. *The Ku Klux Spirit*. New York: The Messenger Publishing, 1923.

Roland, Charles Pierce. *Country Music Annual 2001*. Lexington: University Press of Kentucky, 2001.

Roscigno, Vincent J., and William F. Danaher. *The Voice of Southern Labor: Radio, Music, and Textile Strikes, 1929–1934*. Minneapolis: University of Minnesota Press, 2004.

Rubin, Joan Shelley. *The Making of Middlebrow Culture*. Chapel Hill: University of North Carolina Press, 1992.

Rubin, Victor. *Tar and Feathers*. Philadelphia: Dorrance & Co., 1923.

Rudel, Anthony. *Hello Everybody! The Dawn of American Radio*. Orlando, FL: Harcourt, 2008.

Runstedtler, Theresa. *Jack Johnson, Rebel Sojourner: Boxing in the Shadow of the Global Color Line*. Berkeley: University of California Press, 2012.

Safianow, Allen. "The Klan Comes to Tipton." *Indiana Magazine of History* 95 (1999): 202–31.

———. "'Konklave in Kokomo' Revisited." *The Historian* 50 (May 1988): 329–47.

Sanjek, Russell, and David Sanjek. *American Popular Music Business in the 20th Century*. New York: Oxford University Press, 1991.

Savran, David. *Highbrow/Lowdown: Theater, Jazz, and the Making of the New Middle Class*. Ann Arbor: University of Michigan Press, 2009.

Sawyer, Reuben Herbert. *The Truth about the Invisible Empire, Knights of the Ku Klux Klan*. Portland: Pacific Northwest Domain No. 5, 1922.

Saxon, William Andrew. *Knight Vale of the K.K.K.* Columbus, OH: Patriot Publishing, 1924.

Scharlott, Bradford W. "The Hoosier Journalist and the Hooded Order: Indiana Press Reaction to the Ku Klux Klan in the 1920s." *Journalism History* 15:4 (Winter 1988): 122–31.

Schlesinger, Arthur M. "Biography of a Nation of Joiners." *American Historical Review* 50:1 (October 1944): 1–25.

———. "Review: *Civilization in the United States* by Harold E. Stearns." *Mississippi Valley Historical Review* 9:2 (September 1922): 167–70.

Schmidt, Sarah. *Horace M. Kallen: Prophet of American Zionism.* New York: Carlson Publishing, 1995.

Schneider, Louis, ed. *Religion, Culture, and Society: A Reader in the Sociology of Religion.* New York: John Wiley & Sons, 1964.

Schuyler, Michael W. "The Ku Klux Klan in Nebraska, 1920–1930." *Nebraska History* 66 (1985): 234–56.

Schwieder, Dorothy. "A Farmer and the Ku Klux Klan in Northwest Iowa." *Annals of Iowa* 61 (2002): 286–320.

Scott, Ellen Corrigan. *That Fool Moffett.* St. Louis, MO: B. Herder Books, 1925.

Seldes, Gilbert. *The 7 Lively Arts.* New York: Sagamore Press, 1957

Shands, Hubert Anthony. *White and Black.* New York: Harcourt Brace, 1922.

Shaw, Arnold. *The Jazz Age: Popular Music in the 1920s.* New York: Oxford University Press, 1987.

Sheehan, Murray. *Half-Gods.* New York: E.P. Dutton & Co., 1927.

Shotwell, John M. "Crystallizing Public Hatred: Ku Klux Klan Public Relations in the Early 1920s." PhD diss., University of Wisconsin-Madison, 1974.

Showalter, James L. "Payne County and the Hooded Klan, 1921–1924." PhD diss., Oklahoma State University, 2000.

Shults, Jane. "The Ku Klux Klan in Downey during the 1920s." PhD diss., California State University, Long Beach, 1991.

Simcovitch, Maxim. "The Impact of Griffith's *Birth of a Nation* on the Modern Ku Klux Klan." *Journal of Popular Film* 1:1 (Winter 1972): 45–54.

Simmons, William Joseph. *America's Menace, or the Enemy Within.* Atlanta: Bureau of Patriotic Books, 1926.

———. *The Klan Unmasked.* Atlanta: William E. Thompson, 1923.

Skinner, Kiron K., Annelise Anderson, and Martin Anderson, eds. *Reagan: A Life in Letters.* New York: Free Press, 2004.

Sklar, Robert. *Movie-Made America: A Cultural History of American Movies.* New York: Vintage Books, 1994.

Sletterdahl, Peter J. *The Nightshirt in Politics.* Minneapolis: Ajax Publishing, 1926.

Slide, Anthony. *American Racist: The Life and Films of Thomas Dixon.* Lexington: University Press of Kentucky, 2004.

Slosson, Preston W. *The Great Crusade and After, 1914–1928.* New York: Macmillan, 1930.

Smith, Erin A. *Hard-Boiled: Working-Class Readers and Pulp Magazines.* Philadelphia: Temple University Press, 2000.

———. *What Would Jesus Read? Popular Religious Books and Everyday Life in Twentieth-Century America.* Chapel Hill: University of North Carolina Press, 2015.

Smith, John David, and J. Vincent Lowery, eds. *The Dunning School: Historians, Race, and the Meaning of Reconstruction.* Lexington: University Press of Kentucky, 2013.

Smith, Mika. "Hooded Crusaders: The Ku Klux Klan in the Panhandle and South Plains, 1921–1925." MA thesis, Texas Tech University, 2008.

Smith, Sally Bedell. *In All His Glory: The Life of William S. Paley*. New York: Simon & Schuster, 1990.

Snell, William R. "Masked Men in the Magic City: The Activities of the Revived Klan in Birmingham, Alabama, 1915–1940." *Alabama Historical Quarterly* 34 (Fall–Winter 1972): 206–27.

Spaeth, Sigmund. *A History of Popular Music in America*. New York: Random House, 1948.

Stanton, E. F. *Christ and Other Klansmen, or Lives of Love: The Cream of the Bible Spread upon Klanism*. Kansas City, MO: Stanton & Harper, 1924.

Stearns, Harold E., ed. *Civilization in the United States: An Inquiry by Thirty Americans*. New York: Harcourt, Brace and Company, 1922.

Sterling, Christopher H., and John M. Kittross. *Stay Tuned: A History of American Broadcasting*. Mahwah, NJ: Lawrence Erlbaum Associates, 2002.

Stevens, James. *Mattock*. New York: Knopf, 1927.

Stewart, Jacqueline Najuma. *Migrating to the Movies: Cinema and Black Urban Mordernity*. Berkeley: University of California Press, 2005.

Stoddard, Lothrop. *The Rising Tide of Color against White World-Supremacy*. New York: Scribner's, 1921.

Stokes, Melvyn. *D. W. Griffith's "The Birth of a Nation": A History of "The Most Controversial Motion Picture of All Time."* New York: Oxford University Press, 2007.

Streitmatter, Rodger. *Mightier Than the Sword: How the News Media Have Shaped American History*. Boulder, CO: Westview Press, 2008.

Sullivan, Dean, ed. *Middle Innings: A Documentary History of Baseball, 1900–1948*. Lincoln: University of Nebraska Press, 1998.

Sullivan, Mark. *Our Times: 1900–1925*. New York: Scribner's, 1972.

Sumner, David E. *The Magazine Century: American Magazines since 1900*. New York: Peter Lang, 2010.

Susman, Warren I. *Culture as History: The Transformation of American Society in the Twentieth Century*. New York: Pantheon Books, 1984.

Sutton, Allan. *American Record Labels and Companies: An Encyclopedia, 1891–1943*. Denver: Mainspring Press, 2000.

Sutton, Matthew Avery. *Aimee Semple McPherson and the Resurrection of Christian America*. Cambridge, MA: Harvard University Press, 2007.

———. *American Apocalypse: A History of Modern Evangelicalism*. Cambridge, MA: Harvard University Press, 2014.

Tarde, Gabriel. *The Public and the Crowd* (1901). In *Gabriel Tarde On Communication and Social Influence: Selected Papers*, ed. Terry N. Clark, 277–96. Chicago: University of Chicago Press, 2010.

Tarrow, Sidney G. *Power in Movement: Social Movements and Contentious Politics*. New York: Cambridge University Press, 2011.

Tawa, Nicholas. *Serenading the Reluctant Eagle: American Musical Life, 1925–1945*. New York: Schirmer Books, 1984.

Taylor, Yuval, and Jake Austen. *Darkest America: Black Minstrelsy from Slavery to Hip-Hop*. New York: W.W. Norton, 2012.

Tosches, Nick. *Country: The Twisted Roots of Rock 'n' Roll*. New York: Da Capo Press, 1996.

Trachtenberg, Alan. *The Incorporation of America: Culture and Society in the Gilded Age*. New York: Hill and Wang, 1982.

Treadwell, Lawrence P., Jr. *The Bulldog Drummond Encyclopedia*. Jefferson, NC: McFarland & Company, 2001.

Truzzi, Marcello. "The 100% American Songbag: Conservative Folksongs in America." *Western Folklore* 28:1 (January 1969): 27–40.

Tucker, Richard. *The Dragon and the Cross*. Hamden, CT: Archon Books, 1991.

Tucker, Todd. *Notre Dame vs. the Klan: How the Fighting Irish Defeated the Ku Klux Klan*. Chicago: Loyola Press, 2004.

United States Congress, House of Representatives, Committee on Rules. *Hearings on the Ku Klux Klan*. 67th Cong., 1st sess. Washington, DC, 1921.

Vinyard, JoEllen McNergney. *Right in Michigan's Grassroots: From the KKK to the Michigan Militia*. Ann Arbor: University of Michigan Press, 2011.

Wade, Wyn Craig. *The Fiery Cross: The Ku Klux Klan in America*. New York: Simon & Schuster, 1987.

Ward, Geoffrey C. *Unforgivable Blackness: The Rise and Fall of Jack Johnson*. New York: Vintage Books, 2006.

Weaver, Norman F. "The Knights of the Ku Klux Klan in Wisconsin, Indiana, Ohio, and Michigan." PhD diss., University of Wisconsin, 1955.

White, Alma. *Heroes of the Fiery Cross*. Zarephath, NJ: Pillar of Fire, 1928.

———. *Klansmen: Guardians of Liberty*. Zarephath, NJ: Pillar of Fire, 1926.

———. *The Ku Klux Klan in Prophecy*. Zarephath, NJ: The Good Citizen, 1925.

White, Walter F. *The Fire in the Flint*. New York: Alfred A. Knopf, 1924.

———. *A Man Called White: The Autobiography of Walter White*. Athens: University of Georgia Press, 1995.

White, William Allen. *The Autobiography of William Allen White*. Lawrence: University Press of Kansas, 1990.

Wiggins, Gene. *Fiddlin' Georgia Crazy: Fiddlin' John Carson, His Real World, and the World of His Songs*. Urbana: University of Illinois Press, 1987.

Williamson, Joel. *The Crucible of Race: Black-White Relations in the American South since Emancipation*. New York: Oxford University Press, 1984.

Wilson, Joe. *A Fiddlers' Convention in Mountain City, Tennessee: 1924–1930 Recordings*. Liner Notes. Floyd, VA: County Records 525, 1972.

Winks, Robin. *The Blacks in Canada: A History*. Montreal: McGill-Queen's University Press, 1997.

Winter, Paul M. *What Price Tolerance*. Hewlett, NY: All-American Book, Lecture and Research Bureau, 1928.

Women of the Ku Klux Klan. *Musiklan*. Little Rock, AR: Women of the Ku Klux Klan, 1925.

Wood, Amy Louise. *Lynching and Spectacle: Witnessing Racial Violence in America, 1890–1940*. Chapel Hill: University of North Carolina Press, 2009.

Wright, Walter C. *Religious and Patriotic Ideals of the Ku Klux Klan*. Waco, TX: Walter C. Wright, 1926.

Zimmerman, Jonathan. "Each 'Race' Could Have Its Heroes Sung: Ethnicity and the History Wars in the 1920s." *Journal of American History* 87:1 (June 2000): 92–111.

———. *Whose America? Culture Wars in the Public Schools*. Cambridge, MA: Harvard University Press, 2002.

Films

Big Stakes. Directed by Clifford S. Elfelt. 1922. youtube.com.

The Birth of a Nation. Directed by D. W. Griffith. 1915. Kino on Video, 2002. DVD.

An Eastern Westerner. Directed by Hal Roach. 1920. In *The Harold Lloyd Comedy Collection Vol. 1*. New Line Home Video, 2005. DVD.

Lodge Night. Directed by Robert F. McGowan. 1923. archive.org.

The Pilgrim. Directed by Charlie Chaplin. 1923. In *The Chaplin Review*. Warner Home Video, 2004. DVD.

The Symbol of the Unconquered. Directed by Oscar Micheaux. 1920. youtube.com.

The Toll of Justice. Directed by Corey G. Cook. 1923. University of North Carolina, Media Resources Center, 65-V7409, 1992. VHS.

Young Sherlocks. Directed by Robert F. McGowan and Tom McNamara. 1922. archive.org.

Sheet Music

Arthur, Charles A., and Vernon Barbay. "Those Good Old Ku Klux Blues." Alexandria, LA: V.L.B. Music Company, 1922.

Coslow, Sam, and Leon Friedman. "There's a Bunch of Klucks in the Ku Klux Klan!" New York: Robert Norton, 1921.

Frisch, Billy, and Bernie Grossman. "Ku Ku: The Klucking of the Ku Klux Klan." New York: Hitland Music, 1922.

Goodwin, Mary I. *Song Book for Women of the Ku Klux Klan*. Pittsburgh: Women of the Klan, ca. 1924.

Grimes, E. G. *A Few 100% Selections to the Good Old Tunes We All Know*. Vincennes, IN: E.G. Grimes, ca. 1924.

Hopper, Charles Meek. "Before Them Klu Klux Pages Me." Clovis, NM: Southern Publishing Company, 1923.

Lewis, John Douglas. "Those Dog-Gone Ku-Klux Blues." N.p.: John Douglas Lewis, 1922.

Lutz, H. A. *Lutz Music Printing Co. Catalogue*. York, PA: Lutz Music Printing, ca. 1924.

Marcell, Helen, and Peggy Hedges. "Daddy Swiped Our Last Clean Sheet and Joined the Ku Klux Klan." Ottawa, KS: R.C. Marcell, 1924.

Mars, Al, and Clarence Krause. "The Ku Klux Blues." Dallas: Krause & Mars, 1921.

McMahon, E. M., William Davis, William M. Hart, and Charles E. Downey. "We Are All Loyal Klansmen." Wyano, PA: Charles E. Downey, 1923.

Metz, Roy, and Harry Jay. "We Are the Ladies of the Ku Klux Klan." Muncie, IN: Metz & Lewis, 1928.

Nelson, John M., and Noah F. Tillery. "Mystic City." Kansas City, MO: Harry F. Windle, 1922.

Newton, William, and Wayne Cox. "Ku Klux Klan Blues." Joplin, MO: William Newton, 1923.

Ownby, Warren D. "De Ku Klux Gwine to Git You Ef You Don't Watch Out." Broken Arrow, OK: Warren D. Ownby, 1923.

Parodies by the Queen Quartet of Alice of Old Vincennes. Vincennes, IN: Women's Klan, ca. 1924.

Patterson, Kenneth A. "KKK (If Your Heart's True, It Calls to You)." Avon by the Sea, NJ: E.S. Taborn, 1924.

Rhinehart, Wilbur. *100% Red Hot Songs*. Muncie, IN: Rhinehart Bros., ca. 1925.

Roy, Francis. "They Blame It on the Ku Klux Klan." Pittsburgh: Fulton Music Publishers, 1924.

Roy, Hugh. "American Means the Klan (When We A-Marching Go)." Schenectady: American Music House, 1925.

Seale, Walter, and Adger M. Pace. "Wake Up America! And Kluck, Kluck, Kluck." Lawrenceburg, TN: James D. Vaughan, 1921.

Smith, J. Owen. "The Fiery Cross on High." Indianapolis: Central States Distributing, 1923.

Thompson, William L. "The Call of a Klansman." Streator, IL: Thompson Music Company, 1924.

——. "The Coming of the Klan." Streator, IL: Thompson Music Company, 1924.

Wight, Paul. *American Hymns.* Buffalo: International Music Company, 1925.

——. "Then I'll Take Off My Mask." Scottdale, PA: Paul S. Wight, 1924.

Zterb, George. "The Klansman's Kall." Warren, OH: H.M. Ketler, 1924.

Newspapers and Periodicals

Abilene Reporter

Albert Lea Evening Tribune

Altoona Mirror

American Ecclesiastical Review

American Forum

American Israelite

American Mercury

American Standard

The Appeal

Appleton Post-Crescent

Arizona Republican

Asbury Park Press

Ashland Times Gazette

Atlanta Constitution

Atlantic News-Telegraph

Badger American

Bakersfield Californian

Baltimore Afro-American

Baltimore Sun

Beatrice Daily Sun

Belton Journal

Berkeley Daily Gazette

Billboard

Birmingham Age-Herald

Birmingham News

Birmingham Post

Black Mask

Bluefield Daily Telegraph

The Bookman

Bradford Era

Bridgeport Telegram

Bristol (VA-TN) Herald-Courier

Broad Ax

Brookshire Times

Brownsville Herald

Buckeye American

Buffalo Commercial

Buffalo Express

Burleson County Ledger and News-Chronicle

Burlington Hawk-Eye

Call of the North

Cambridge City Tribune

Camera

Capital Times

Cedar Rapids Republican

Charleston Daily Mail

Charleston Gazette

Checotah Times

Chicago Daily Journal

Chicago Defender

Chicago Tribune

Christian Century

Clearfield Progress

Cleveland Gazette

Cleveland Plain Dealer

Colorado Springs Gazette

Connellsville Daily Courier

Connersville News-Examiner

Corsicana Sun

Coshocton Tribune

The Crisis

Daily Jewish Courier

Daily Northwestern

Danville Bee

Davenport Democrat and Leader

Dawn

Decatur Review

Denver Post

Detroit News

The Dial

Edwardsville Intelligencer

El Paso Herald

Elyria Chronicle-Telegram

Entertainment Trade Review

Estherville Enterprise

Eugene Morning Register

Exhibitor's Herald

Exhibitor's Trade Review

Fayetteville Daily Democrat

Fellowship Forum

Fiery Cross

Film Daily

Fortune Magazine

Fort Wayne News-Sentinel

The Forum

Franklin Evening Star

Galveston Daily News

Garden City Telegram

Gettysburg Times

Grand Prairie Texan

Harrisburg Daily Reporter

Harrisonburg Daily News Record

Helena Daily Independent

Huntingdon Daily News

Hutchinson Blade

Hutchinson News

Imperial Night-Hawk

The Independent

Indianapolis News

Indianapolis Star

Iola Daily Register

Iowa Broadcaster

Janesville Daily Gazette

Jasonville Leader

Jayhawker American

Jewish Press (Omaha)

Jewish Telegraphic Agency Daily News Bulletin

Joplin Globe

Joplin News-Herald

Kerrville Mountain Sun

The Kluxer

Knoxville News

Kokomo Daily Tribune

Kolorado Klan Kourier

Kourier Magazine

Ladies Home Journal

Lancaster Examiner-New Era

LaPorte Herald

Lawrence Daily Journal-World

LeMars Globe-Post

Leslie's Weekly

Lethbridge Daily Herald

Lewiston Daily Sun

Life

Lima Sunday News

Linton Daily Citizen

Literary Digest

Lockhart Register

Logansport Morning Press

Logansport Pharos-Tribune

Los Angeles Times

Lowell Sun

Lubbock Avalanche

Manitowoc Herald-News

Mansfield News

Marion Daily Star

Massillon Evening Independent

McClure's

McKean County Democrat

The Messenger

Mexia Daily News

Mexia Evening News

Mexia Weekly Herald

Milford Mail

Minnesota Fiery Cross

Montgomery Advertiser

Movie Weekly

Moving Picture World

National Kourier

New American Patriot

Newark Advocate

New Castle News

New Market Herald

New Orleans Times-Picayune

New Republic

New York Age

New York Evening Post

New York Graphic

New York Sun

New York Times

New York Tribune

New York World

Norfolk Pilot

North American Review

Oakland Tribune

Ogden Standard-Examiner

Opportunity

Orange County Times Press

Our Sunday Visitor

Outlook

Oxnard Daily Courier

The Patriot

Perry Daily Journal

Photoplay

Pierce County Herald

Pittsburgh Courier

Port Arthur News

Port Neches Peoples Press

Portsmouth Daily Times

Portsmouth Herald

Prattsville Progress

The Protestant

Protestant Herald

Racine Journal News

The Railsplitter

Reno Evening Gazette

Roanoke Times

Rocky Mountain News

St. Paul Minnesota Pioneer Press

St. Petersburg Independent

San Antonio Express

San Antonio Light

Sandusky Register

Sandusky Star-Journal

Savannah Tribune

Scandia Journal

The Searchlight

Sheboygan Press-Telegram

Shreveport Journal

The Sign

Simpsons' Daily Leader-Times

Smart Set

South Bend Tribune

Southwest Times

The Spectator

Spencer Reporter

Sterling Daily Gazette

Steubenville Herald-Star

Stilwell Standard-Sentinel

Sylacauga Advance

Syracuse Herald

The Tablet

Theatre Arts Monthly

Thomasville Daily Times-Enterprise

Time

Tipton Daily Tribune

Toledo Blade

Topeka Plain Dealer

True Voice

Tulsa Daily World

Uniontown Morning Herald

Vanity Fair

Variety

Washington Bee

Washington Evening Star

Washington Post

Waterloo Evening Courier and Reporter

Wichita Beacon

Williamsport Pioneer

Winnfield News-American

Wisconsin Kourier

Wisconsin Rapids Daily Tribune

Wisconsin State Journal

Wisconsin Superior Telegram

Woodland Daily Democrat

World's Work

The World Tomorrow

Xenia Evening Gazette

Youngstown Citizen

Zion's Herald

Index